Arch

Fuzzy Sets and Fuzzy Systems

Fuzzy Sets and Fuzzy Systems

Guest Editors

Dipak Kumar Jana
Petr Dostál

MDPI

Basel • Beijing • Wuhan • Barcelona • Belgrade • Novi Sad • Cluj • Manchester

Guest Editors
Dipak Kumar Jana
Gangarampur College
Gangarampur, West Bengal
India

Petr Dostál
Faculty of Business and
Management
Brno University of
Technology
Brno
Czech

Editorial Office
MDPI AG
Grosspeteranlage 5
4052 Basel, Switzerland

This is a reprint of the Special Issue, published open access by the journal *Mathematics* (ISSN 2227-7390), freely accessible at: https://www.mdpi.com/si/mathematics/Fuzzy_Set_Syst.

For citation purposes, cite each article independently as indicated on the article page online and as indicated below:

Lastname, A.A.; Lastname, B.B. Article Title. *Journal Name* **Year**, *Volume Number*, Page Range.

ISBN 978-3-7258-4831-7 (Hbk)
ISBN 978-3-7258-4832-4 (PDF)
https://doi.org/10.3390/books978-3-7258-4832-4

Contents

About the Editors

Dipak Kumar Jana

Dipak Kumar Jana obtained his Ph.D. from the Indian Institute of Engineering Science and Technology (IIEST), Shibpur, his post-graduation (M.Sc.) in Applied Mathematics with specialization in Operations Research from Vidyasagar University, and his B.Sc in Math(H) from Tamralipta Mahavidyalaya, Tamluk, West Bengal. He has qualified in the National Eligibility Test (NETCSIR) for Junior Research Fellow (JRF) and GATE. He has been teaching Mathematics both at an undergraduate and postgraduate level. At present, he is working as the Principal of Gangarampur College (Govt. Aided), West Bengal, India, Former HOD, School of Applied Science, Haldia Institute of Technology. Dr. Jana is a member of the Operational Research Society of India, Indian Science Congress Association, Calcutta Mathematical Society. Dr. Jana has published 14 patents and more than 140 papers in esteemed International Journals like *Information Science, Journal of Cleaner Production, Applied Soft Computing, Computers & Industrial Engineering, Journal of Separation and Purification*, etc. To his credit, Dr. Jana has written 14 books, including the following: *A Text Book of Engineering Operations Research, GATE MATHEMATICS-Vol-1, GATE MATHEMATICS-Vol-2, Advanced Engineering Mathematics, Advanced Numerical Methods*, and *Basic Engineering Mathematics*. He has also reviewed several textbooks and reference books of Mathematics and is an Editorial Member of five international journals. Seven Ph.D students have been awarded and, recently, eight students are pursuing their Ph.D under the guidance of Dr. Jana. Dr. Jana is an organizing chair of ICEMC 2019 to ICEMC 2025.

Petr Dostal

Petr Dostal is a Professor of Economy and Management. Mr. Dostal's pedagogical practice exceeds 25 years of his work at the Brno University of Technology, Faculty of Business and Management, Institute of Informatics and Institute of Forensic Engineering. He taught at Masaryk University in Brno, Faculty of Law and University of Tomas Bata in Zlín. His area of interest is the use of soft computing methods and artificial intelligence, such as fuzzy logic, neural networks, evolutionary algorithms and chaos theory in entrepreneurship, public services and information management. He lectures subjects such as Advanced Decision Making in Business and Operational and System Analysis. He taught Financial Risk Management, Risk Management, Operational Research, Optimization and Decision Making and Advanced Methods of Decision Making in Law. He worked as an economic and organizational consultant in private companies and institutions. He was the chairman and board member in several companies. He is a member of multiple international institutions, program committees, scientific and advisory committees and councils, including the following: the editor of *Soft Computing Journal*, a member of the Advisory Board of *Egyptian Computer Science Journal*, editor of *Global Journal of Technology and Optimization* and a member of *Berkeley Initiative in Soft Computing*, Society of Computational Economics. He was a member and advisor of the International Institution of Forecasters and Association for Computing Machinery. He has lectured at various universities at home and abroad—in Europe, USA, Africa and Asia (SUA in Nitra, Nottingham Trent University, Ain Shams University of Cairo, Dominican University of Chicago, University of Chicago, University of Kathmandu, Ariel University, NCCU University, Haldia Institute of Technology, University of Applied Science in Leiden, Netherlands and University of Györ, among others.). He has published numerous books and articles in international journals.

mathematics

MDPI

Article

A Sustainable Green Supply Chain Model with Carbon Emissions for Defective Items under Learning in a Fuzzy Environment

Basim S. O. Alsaedi [1,*], Osama Abdulaziz Alamri [1], Mahesh Kumar Jayaswal [2,*] and Mandeep Mittal [3]

1 Department of Statistics, University of Tabuk, Tabuk 71491, Saudi Arabia
2 Department of Mathematics and Statistics, Banasthali Vidyapith (Banasthali University), Banasthali 304022, India
3 Department of Mathematics, Amity Institute of Applied Sciences, Amity University Uttar Pradesh, Noida 201301, India
* Correspondence: balsaedi@ut.edu.sa (B.S.O.A.); maheshjayaswal17@gmail.com (M.K.J.)

Abstract: Assuming the significance of sustainability, it is considered necessary to ensure the conservation of our natural resources, in addition to minimizing waste. To promote significant sustainable effects, factors including production, transportation, energy usage, product control management, etc., act as the chief supports of any modern supply chain model. The buyer performs the firsthand inspection and returns any defective items received from the customer to the vendor in a process that is known as first-level inspection. The vendor uses the policy of recovery product management to obtain greater profit. A concluding inspection is accomplished at the vendor's end in order to distinguish the returned item as belonging to one of four specific categories, namely re-workable, reusable, recyclable, and disposable, a process that is known as second-level inspection. Then, it is observed that some defective items are suitable for a secondary market, while some are reusable, and some can be disassembled to shape new derived products, and leftovers can be scrapped at the disposal cost. This ensures that we can meet our target to promote a cleaner drive with a lower percentage of carbon emissions, reducing the adverse effects of landfills. The activity of both players in this model is presented briefly in the flowchart shown in the abstract. Thus, our aim of product restoration is to promote best practices while maintaining economic value, with the ultimate goal of removing the surrounding waste with minimum financial costs. In this regard, it is assumed that the demand rate is precise in nature. The learning effect and fuzzy environment are also considered in the present model. The proposed model studies the impacts of learning and carbon emissions on an integrated green supply chain model for defective items in fuzzy environment and shortage conditions. We optimized the integrated total fuzzy profit with respect to the order quantity and shortages. We described the vendor's strategy and buyer's strategy through flowcharts for the proposed integrated supply chain model, and here, in the flowchart, R-R-R stands for re-workable, reusable, and recyclable. The demand rate was treated as a triangular fuzzy number. In this paper, a numerical example, sensitivity analysis, limitations, future scope, and conclusion are presented for the validation of the proposed model.

Keywords: optimization; learning effect; fuzzy environment; singed distance method; carbon emissions; supply chain approach; sustainability

MSC: 90-XX

1. Introduction

In today's ubiquitous environment, sustainability has become a necessity for the creation of clean and green business. Considering the importance of sustainability, it is necessary to ensure the conservation of our natural resources, in addition to reducing waste. In order to promote a significant sustainable impact, factors including production, transportation, energy use, product control management, etc., serve as the main supports of any modern integrated green supply chain model. By observing their roles in the immediate landscape, we can connect them with sustainable policies for both vendors and buyers. In this model, the vendor manages the production of the items and provides the demanded lot to the buyer, according to the single setup and many more delivery strategies. In order to eliminate defective items, a screening process is completed at the vendor and buyer's ends, respectively. These defective items are kept in seclusion, and furthermore, permanent progress is made by asking the customer to return their used products and gain a rebate on their successive purchases. The buyer receives the used products from the customer, and the buyer returns these defective products to the vendor. The vendor inspects the defective-quality products received from the buyer and separates the defective-quality products on the basis of the quality of defective products. After that, it is determined that some imperfect-quality items are suitable for another business sectors, while some are reusable, some can be deconstructed to form new derivative products, and leftovers can be scrapped at the disposal cost. The supply chain system works well when the demand rate is deterministic and all the inventory parameters are controlled by the vendor and the buyer. However, in general, this is not really true, because some inventory parameters depend on the market demand. This ensures our goal of promoting a cleaner drive with a lower percentage of carbon emissions and minimizing the adverse impacts of landfills. The production of defective items in any industry is inescapable, regardless of the implementation of widely recognized techniques. Within the process of manufacturing the goods, there is still potential for a crash, which leads to the production of defective items along with perfect-quality items.

It is impractical for any manufacturing unit to adopt the responsibility of manufacturing items of a 100% perfect quality. There are many factors, including system machinery failure, poor workmanship, etc., that increase the chance of producing imperfect-quality items. Learning theory is beneficial where any work is in the repetition form. The learning effect and fuzzy environment are also assumed in the present model. In our study, an EOQ model with carbon emissions in a supply chain system, as well as shortages and product recovery management, was derived along with a numerical analysis, where the demand rate was treated as a triangular fuzzy number, and the holding and ordering costs were the function of shipment. We defuzzified the joint total fuzzy profit through the singed distance method. The whole paper divided into sections and subsections as follows: Section 1 offers an introduction and literature review; Section 2 explains the notation assumptions; Section 3 presents the basic definitions; Section 4 presents the description of the problems and mathematical formulation; and Section 5 presents the methodology of the optimization of the decision variable and contains subsections describing the solution method, a numerical example, sensitivity analysis, and the managerial insight and observations, which provide the results of the proposed model. Section 6 explains the conclusions of the model. Section 7 discusses the limitations and future scope of the present model. Section 8 presents the applications of the proposed study.

This segment provides an overview of a series of articles which are associated with the present study. Subsequently, to establish the place of the present study within the existing research knowledge, the available gaps are spot-lighted.

Salameh and Jaber [1] contributed their remarkable work in this aspect by considering the impacts that these defective items have using the inventory model and introduced the importance of screenings. Various prevailing studies have made fairly impractical presumptions about supply chain management, stating that shortages are not permitted. Indeed, shortages will occur with unanticipated demand or an irregular production capacity, and these occurrences will periodically influence the decisions of suppliers and retailers. Wee et al. [2] extended the model of Salameh and Jaber [1], where shortfalls were additionally applied in each cycle. The research of Salameh and Jaber [1] was extended by Eroglu and Ozdemir [3] for the consideration of defective-quality items under the condition of shortages. An inventory model was developed by Roy et al. [4] and Sarkar and Iqbal [5] for decaying items of a defective quality under inspection in a process where the defective items were treated as a random variable. An EOQ mathematical model was improved by Jaggi and Mittal [6] for decaying items of a defective quality under inspection in a process where the screening rate is faster than the demand rate. They further concluded that all the defective items are suitable for the secondary market and can be sold in that market at a price lower than the original market price.

This inevitable presence of imperfect-quality items in the inventory was researched further using possible realistic approaches. This research incorporated the proposal of many models which considered planned backorders, along with effective screening tests at the vendor's end, faulty production techniques, etc. The model of Salameh and Jaber [1] was resolved by Maddah and Jaber [7] for the expected whole worth per unit time using the very renowned theorem of Ross [8].

Relative increments in the levels of carbon emissions mainly occur because of the modes of transport through which they are produced. In order to maintain the standard emission norms, the index of carbon emissions must be checked by the organization so as to sustain their due quality standards and, thus, promote their brand value. Hua et al. [9] presented an inventory model based on a carbon footprint. In this vein, Howitt et al. [10] contributed to research through their work based on the CO2 emissions of the global space freight. Guereca et al. [11] discussed cleaner research for the institutes of Mexico based on a carbon footprint. Gurtu et al. [12] proposed an inventory model with the effect of the fuel cost in regard to carbon emissions. Sarkar et al. [13] studied the impacts of variable transportation and carbon emissions on the three-echelon supply chain model. Tiwari et al. [14] presented a sustainable inventory model for deteriorating defective items under carbon emissions. Sarkar et al. [15] explained the best approach by considering the carbon emissions of the supply chain. Thomas and Mishra [16] considered a sustainable supply chain model with waste reduction under carbon emissions for 3D printing and carbon minimization in some plastic industries.

Supply chain model management is helpful in identifying the best methods to apply in numerous industries. Each participant in a supply chain has the objective of fulfilling their tasks and obtaining the best outcomes of their processes. Various theories have previously been stated and proved. Sarkar et al. [17] proposed an SCM with inflation and a credit period for perishable items. Jaber and Goyal [18] explained a three-level supply chain model based on multiple players. Furthermore, Jaber et al. [19] extended a supply chain model, through learning, into a three-level supply chain model. Bazan et al. [20] described an SCM with greenhouse carbon emissions under energy utilization and applied a different approach. Aljazzar et al. [21] proposed a two-level SCM with credit financing for the purpose of strong coordination between the vendor and buyer.

In a recent scenario, Gautam and Khanna [22] derived an integrated SCM for the seller, as well as the buyer, which was sustainable, since it assumed the production of defective-quality items and carbon emissions. Later on, some researchers, such as Gautam et al. [23], Mashud et al. [24], and Rout et al. [25], proposed works with different strategies.

Alamari et al. [26] proposed an EOQ model with inflation and carbon emissions under the effect of learning for deteriorating items. This study was continued using the learning coefficient, as calculated in Khan et al. [27], reporting on the effects of learning and screening errors on the economic production model under supply chain and stochastic lead time demands.

Marchi et al. [28] presented an economic production model with the effects of the energy efficiency, production, reliability, and quality.

Afshari et al. [29] reported the impacts of learning and forgetting on the feasibility of adopting additive manufacturing in a supply chain model. Jaber and Peltokorpi [30] showed the impact of learning on the order quantity problem in regard to the production and group size. Masanta and Giri [31] proposed a closed-loop SCM with the effect of learning in an inspection process where the demand rate is a function of the price.

Jaggi et al. [32] presented an inventory model with a trade credit period and shortages based on a fuzzy concept and inspection of deteriorating items. In order to improve on previous research, Jaggi et al. [33] proposed a mathematical model with a fuzzy environment for deteriorating items under shortage, where the demand rate depends on time. Jaggi et al. [34] improved an EOQ model with a fuzzy environment and trade credit under the condition of shortages. Rout et al. [35] generalized an EOQ model with a fuzz-2 environment under the policy of a refill system. Patro et al. [36] explained an EOQ model with the influence of learning for imperfect-quality items in a fuzzy system. Bhavani et al. [37] presented a green EOQ model with shortages in a fuzzy environment. Jayaswal et al. [38] presented an EOQ with the effects of learning and a credit financing policy in a cloudy fuzzy environment.

In this light, we discussed the research gaps and studied a great deal of literature, described in the review provided above. Jayaswal et al.'s [38] study did not involve the formation of an integrated joint profit model. Considering this fact, the present study was framed by considering the need to develop an integrated model that used the approaches of learning and the fuzzy effect. Jayaswal et al. [39], described a fuzzy based inventory model with learning effect and credit policy under human learning and backorders. Wright [40] gave learning theory which is beneficial for ordering policy. Jayaswal and Mittal [41] presented an imperfect based inventory model with credit policy and inflationary condition under fuzzy environment.

Mittal and Sarkar [42] proposed a supply chain model with a credit policy for imperfect-quality items at a random energy price, where the global minimum cost was calculated for the supply chain model. In this vein, Wang et al. [43] worked on a closed-loop supply chain and also described competitive dual collecting in regard to consumer behavior. Using their model, Wang et al. [43] proposed a hybrid closed-loop supply chain model with competition concerning the reform of imperfect items and different types of product markets. Wang et al. [44] presented a supply chain model for Hybrid closed-loop with competition in recycling and product markets. The process of inspection for the separation of defective items through different approaches was briefly explained by the inventory model of Khanna et al. [45]. We selected some recent literature published between 2000 and 2022, as shown in Table 1. The idea of this proposed model is that it can fulfill the research gaps through a new approach. The present study discussed in this paper is shown at the bottom of Table 1. Our paper studies the impacts of leaning and carbon emissions on an integrated green supply chain model for defective items in a fuzzy environment. The present paper considers case studies of the seller–buyer supply chain model and reviews the available literature on joint inventory models, which were explained in order to manage the data. Consequently, to validate the proposed supply chain model, we constructed a dataset, following Hsu and Hsu [46] and Gautam et al. [23]. The introductory research in the area of defective goods was carried out by Rosenblatt and Lee [47], whose findings were later highlighted by many other scholars. Their research was based on the effects that are observed during the optimal production cycle time due to the production of imperfect products. Furthermore, Cardenas-Barron [48] made efforts to correct the possible mathematical modeling errors identified in the model of Salameh and Jaber [1]. The proposed study reviews the notion of managing the defective items using the best-known approaches, which, in turn, can be applied in an attempt to create cleaner, greener, and more sustainable surroundings. There are numerous industries that are working to make the best use of all the defective items, as well as the used items. This not only in the interest of the retailers but, instead, benefits the overall supply chain.

Table 1. Selected contributions.

Authors	Imperfect Items	SCM	Fuzzy Environment	Carbon Emissions	Learning
Salameh and Jaber [1]	√				
Tiwari et al. [14]	√			√	
Marchi et al. [28]	√			√	
Gautam et al. [23]	√	√			
Masanta and Giri [31]	√	√			√
Jayaswal et al. [38]	√		√		√
Our paper	√	√	√	√	√

2. Assumptions and Notations Used in the Model

Following are the assumptions and notations.

2.1. Notations

The notations and decision variables are shown in Appendix A.

2.2. Assumptions

We made some assumptions in regard to our proposed mathematical model, which are given below:

- ➢ It is considered that the buyer, customer, and vendor are involved in this supply chain model, where one type of item is used.
- ➢ No lead time is considered in this proposed model.
- ➢ The demand rate for the produced items is imprecise in nature.
- ➢ The demand function is taken as the triangular fuzzy number.
- ➢ The upper and lower fuzzy deviations of the demand rate follow the effect of learning.
- ➢ The buyer's holding cost is a decreasing function of the shipment, $H_1(n) = h_{0+}\frac{h_1}{n^{\mu}}$ and $H_2(n) = h_0 + \frac{h_2}{n^{\mu}}$, where h_0, h_1, and h_1 are the fixed holding cost, n is the shipment, and μ is the supporting parameter.
- ➢ The buyer's ordering cost is a decreasing function of the shipment, $A_c(n) = A_o + \frac{A_1}{n^{\mu}}$, where A_0, A_1 are the fixed ordering cost, n is the shipment, and μ is the supp-orting parameter.
- ➢ The process of manufacturing is controlled at the vendor's end, and the manufactured items are delivered at the buyer's end via multiple replacements without a first screening test. This leads to the delivery of a certain number of defective items, which follow a uniform distribution.
- ➢ This model assumes that the rate of demand is less than the rate of production.
- ➢ The buyer performs the first round of the inspection of the lot received from the vendor.
- ➢ The buyer provides the customers with perfect-quality items only. This implies that the rate of inspection is greater than the demand rate.
- ➢ To avert any incoming shortages while the inspection is taking place, the buyer limits α to follow $\alpha < \left(1 - \frac{D}{w}\right)$.
- ➢ All defective items segregated after the first round of inspection at the buyer's end are maintained up to the time of their upcoming procurement, and the cost involved in carrying these defective items is regarded as less than that involved in carrying perfect items.
- ➢ The last consumers return their used goods at the buyer's end in order to conduct a permanent operation, and these returned items collectively follow a uniform distribu-

tion. These items are returned by the vendor, along with the collection of imperfect-quality items.

➢ The communal effort implemented by the vendor and the buyer is proposed to be a modern policy and a cleaner and sustainable action, thus ensuring that no movement of empty vehicles occurs. From this point of view, the lot containing the imperfect-quality items and used goods, on behalf of the buyer, is sent back to the seller upon the delivery of the successive lot by the same vehicle. This means that the buyer is not responsible for paying any transportation costs and carbon emission costs when returning imperfect-quality and used items.
➢ It is considered that the carbon emissions are produced due to the multiple shipments and transportation. Here, we applied some carbon emission costs.
➢ The vendor applies the cost of the warranty for the imperfect-quality items returned by the buyer.
➢ It is assumed that the vendor uses the strategy of product recovery management, and its activities are in the flowchart abstract.
➢ Shortages are entirely backlogged at the buyer's end.
➢ The proposed model is solved using the concept of an integrated approach combining the cost components at the vendor's and buyer's ends.

2.3. Description of the Proposed Mathematical Model through a Flowchart

In this section, we describe all methodology and steps of the calculation of the proposed integrated supply chain model for the joint total fuzzy profit, as given in the Figures 1 and 2.

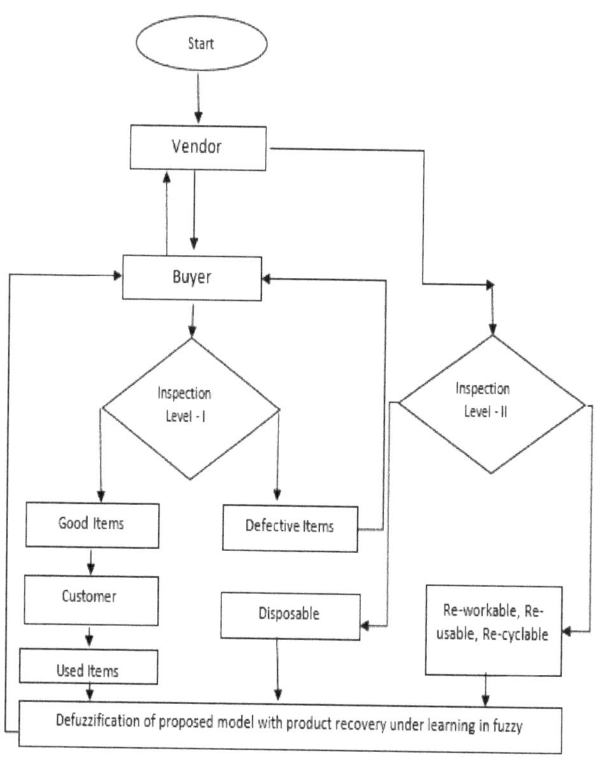

Figure 1. The activity of the vendor and buyer in a flowchart.

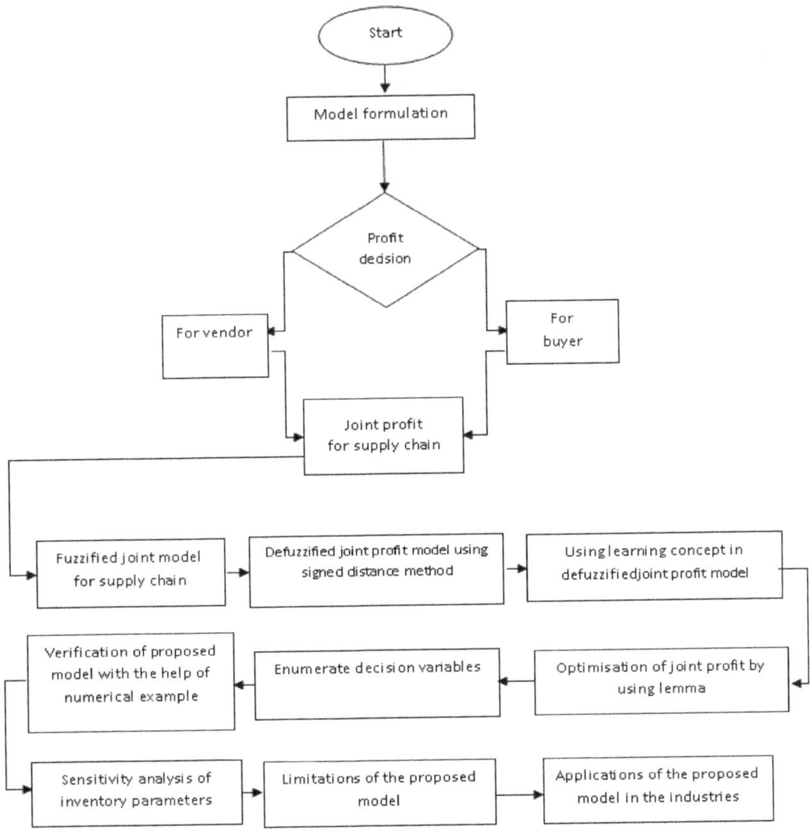

Figure 2. Presentation of the proposed model through a flow chart.

3. Some Basic Definition

There are some basic definitions which are highly important for the enlargement of the present study, and these are explained in Section 3.1.

3.1. Regarding the Fuzzy Concept

In this section, we provide some definitions that are very useful for the development of this model, which are given below:

Definition 1. *If R is a universal set and W is any set on R, then the fuzzy set of W on R is represented by* $\tilde{W}$*, which, mathematically, can be written as* $\tilde{W} = \left\{\left(r, \lambda_{\tilde{W}}\left(\tilde{r}\right)\right) : r \in R\right\}$*, where* $\lambda_{\tilde{W}}$ *represents a membership function, such that* $\lambda_{\tilde{W}} : R \to [0,1]$. *The triplet* (d_1, d_2, d_3) *is used as the triangular fuzzy number, and this number should be associated with the condition* $d_1 < d_2 < d_3$. *The continuous membership function is defined below:*

$$\lambda_{\tilde{W}} = \begin{cases} \dfrac{d - d_1}{d_2 - d_1} d_1 \le d \le d_2 \\ \dfrac{d_3 - d}{d_3 - d_2} d_2 \le d \le d_3 \\ 0 \text{ Otherwise} \end{cases}$$

Definition 2. *If c is any number and $0 \in R$, then the signed distance from c to 0 will be $d(c,0) = c$, and if $c < 0$, then the signed distance from c to 0 will be $d(-c,0) = -c$. Let it be assumed that Ω is the family of fuzzy sets $\tilde{C}$ defined on R. Then, $\alpha - cut, C(\alpha) = [C_L(\alpha), C_U(\alpha)]$ is $\forall \alpha \epsilon [0,1]$, and $C_L(\alpha)$ and $C_U(\alpha)$ will be the continuous function of α. Then, we can write the value of $C(\alpha)$, which is shown below and shown in* Figure 3.

$$C(\alpha) = \bigcup_{0 \ll \alpha \ll 1} [C_L(\alpha)_\alpha, C_U(\alpha)_\alpha]$$

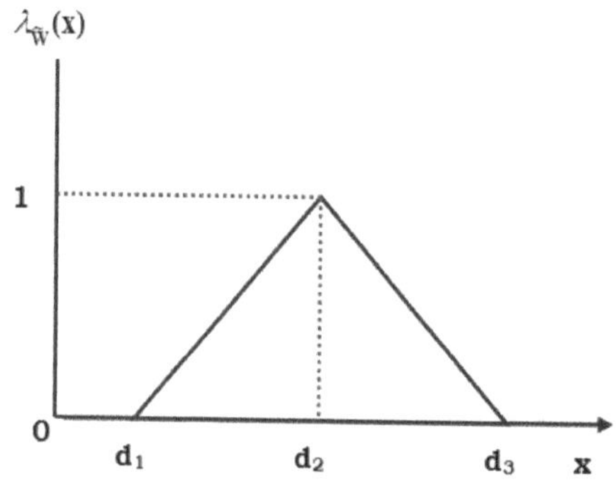

Figure 3. Membership function of a triangular fuzzy number.

Definition 3. *If $\tilde{C}$ is the member of Ω, then the signed distance from $\tilde{C}$ to $\tilde{0}_1$ is as given below:*

(i)

$$d(c,0) = \frac{1}{2}\int_0^1 [C_L(\alpha) + C_U(\alpha)]d\alpha$$

Definition 4 *If $\tilde{C} = (c_1, c_2, c_3)$ is a triangular fuzzy number, then the $\alpha - cut$ of $\tilde{C}$ is $C(\alpha) = [C_L(\alpha), C_U(\alpha)]$, where $C_L(\alpha) = c_1 + (c_2 - c_1)\alpha$ and $C_U(\alpha) = c_3 - (c_3 - c_2)\alpha$ for $\alpha \epsilon [0,1]$. The signed distance from $\tilde{C}$ to $\tilde{0}_1$ is:*

(ii)

$$d(\tilde{C},0) = \frac{(c_1 + 2c_2 + c_3)}{2}$$

3.2. Learning Curve

The learning (learning curve) demonstration is a statistical (geometric) development that expresses the falling cost necessary to achieve any cyclic process (operation). This concept expresses the notion that as the sum amount of the units produced doubles, the price per unit declines by a certain regular percentage. Wright [40] suggested that the learning concept (learning curve) is a power function formulation and is represented by $T_y = T_1 y^{-b}$, where T_y represents the time required to produce the $y_{n\ th}$ units, T_1 represents the time to produce the opening unit y, and b represents the learning slope and shown in the Figure 4.

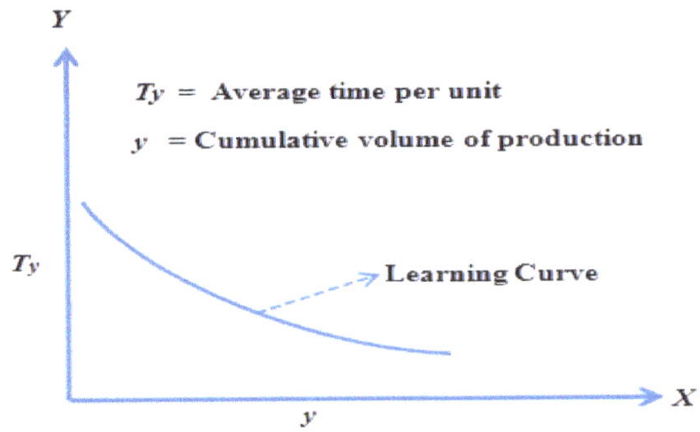

Figure 4. Wright's curve.

4. Mathematical Formulation

4.1. Theoretical Description

This section begins with the hypothetical explanation and meaning of the problem, following an individual and joint view of both the vendor and buyer, respectively. The problem is described in regard to the buyer, customer, and vendor for one kind of item in the supply chain model. The goods involved are proposed to take a fuzzy demand shape. The vendor is responsible for the production of the items, the sale operations are managed at the vendor's end, and the consumer then purchases the item, uses it, and returns it to the buyer. The activities of the vendor and buyer are in the flowchart contained in the abstract. The process starts when the buyer places the order, where the demand rate is imprecise in nature, and the lower and upper deviation of the demand follow the effect of learning, while the holding and ordering costs of the buyer are the function of the shipment. The vendor manufactures the quantity ordered by the buyer and, subsequently, delivers it to the purchaser through several deliveries. Carbon emissions are produced during the construction process and transportation. The delivered lot essentially contains defective items, which are identified and segregated by the buyer through a first round of inspection. A sustainable and clean campaign is inaugurated by supply chain researchers in an effort to achieve better product recovery. This drive encourages consumers to return all used items to the buyer in order to receive a rebate on their sequential purchases. The buyer is responsible for keeping the imperfect-quality products and used goods until the last of the shipment cycle and returns them, collectively, to the seller upon the reception of the successive lots. Defect formation can be found with various possibilities in the lots containing defective and used goods. Thus, to promote the full recovery of these products, another round of screening is encouraged on the vendor's side. Based on the circumstances of the goods, during the second round of inspection carried out by the vendor, the products are classified as re-workable items, reusable items, recyclable items, and disposable items, respectively. A re-workable product is of a good quality in nature and is sold in the secondary market. Reusable goods are not sufficient for trading in another business and are used to produce the derived goods. Those items that do not fit into one of these categories are labeled as recyclable. In the final step, those items that amount to scrap are classified as disposable.

4.2. Problem Description

Keeping in mind today's demand pattern, which does not ensure a compromise between the quality and quantity requirements for a particular type of item, the proposed models based on a single buyer, customer, and vendor for a single item were considered. It is initially assumed that the buyer considers a fuzzy annual rate of demand in D units. The required supply is expressed as nY units, which have to be managed by the vendor, and is delivered in n number of shipments, which are equal to Y units. In view of the inevitable defects in the manufactured lot, the demanded shipments may contain some defective items, which will lead to the development of warranty costs on the part of the vender. As soon as the shipment order is complete, an inspection of the lot is carried out at the buyer's end, and after the inspection, all the imperfect-quality items are isolated from the perfect-quality items. Let us assume that the defective percentage of a lot is α. By the end of the cycle, the total count of imperfect-quality items will be αnY. In addition, the buyer encourages all their consumers to return the items that they used. Since the quantity of items that are of a good quality items is β, the consumers will return βnY to the buyer by the end of the cycle, through which the buyer obtains a cost termed as the discount cost, which is nothing compared to the claim that was initially applied to the consumers to ensure a constant drive by returning their used items. The returned items tend to follow a uniform distribution. In the case of the returned defective items, the buyer uses them as a substitute to obtain an incentive cost from the vendor in order to supply the consumers with a rebate for each item that they returned after using it. The buyer tends to keep all these defective items, along with the used items, for one complete cycle, until the very end of the cycle and afterwards, when they return these isolated items to the vendor via the same transport vehicle that arrives to deliver the next shipment. This allows the vendor to include a warranty cost and an incentive cost on returned lots of items that contain defective and used items. At the vendor's end, a second inspection test of the lot of products returned by the buyer is carried out. The flowchart in the abstract explains the activities of the vendor and buyer in the supply chain. The fraction of re-worked items in the lot is $\eta_1\gamma nY$. The fraction of reused items in the lot is $\eta_2\gamma nY$. The fraction of recycled items in the lot is $\eta_3\gamma nY$. The fraction of disposable products in the lot is $\eta_4\gamma nY$. The present mathematical model was divided into two parts in the form of the vendor' strategy and the buyer's strategy, which are provided in the following sections.

4.2.1. Vendor's Strategy Model

In this section, the vendor's inventory incorporates two time phases. The former is the production phase (production time), and the other is the non-production phase (non-production time). The inventory at the vendor's end is illustrated in Figure 5 and the calculation of the holding cost has shown in the Figure 6.

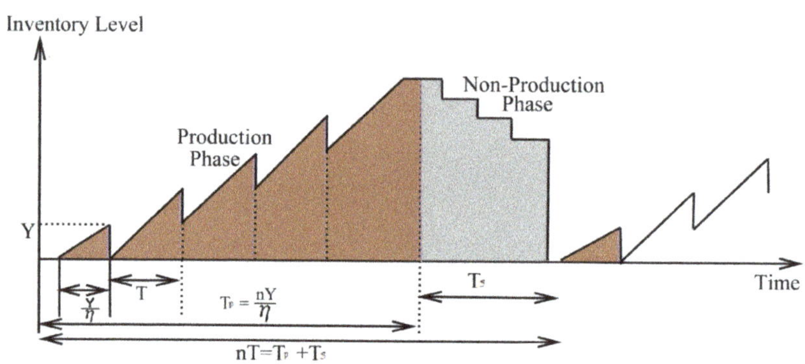

Figure 5. Representation of production and non-production systems in a supply chain model T.

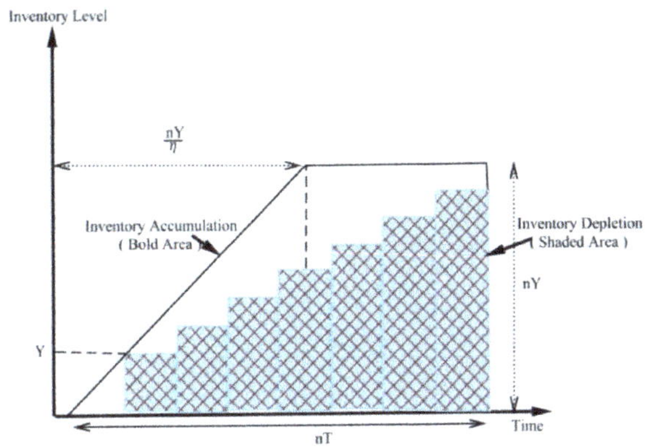

Figure 6. Explanation of the vendor's holding cost.

In reality, without any cost, no one can undertake production; therefore, some cost is required for production. The vendor incorporates the remaining costs during the production phase, defining such costs as the ordering cost (O_v), material and labor cost (ML_v), energy cost (EC_v), fixed transportation cost (FTC_v), variable transportation cost (VTC_v), holding cost (IHC_v), warranty cost (WC_v), incentive cost (IC_v), re-working cost (RC_v), reusing cost (REC_v), recycling cost (RECC_v), screening cost (SC_v), disposal cost (DC_v), carbon emission cost during the production phase (CEPC_v), carbon emission cost during transportation (CETC_v), and carbon emission cost during the disposal process (CEDC_v).

The total cost for vendor during the production process can be defined as shown in Equation (1).

Now, the vendor's total cost, (TC_v), is:

$$TC_v = O_v + ML_v + EC_v + FTC_v + VTC_v + IHC_v + WC_v + IC_v + \mathrm{SC}_v + \mathrm{RC}_v + \mathrm{REC}_v + \mathrm{RECC}_v + \mathrm{DC}_v + \mathrm{CEPC}_v + \mathrm{CETC}_v + \mathrm{CEDC}_v \tag{1}$$

Each cost component of the vendor's total cost (TC_v) is calculated, and these are given by Equations (2)–(16):

$$\text{Ordering cost}(O_v) = O_v \tag{2}$$

$$\text{Material and labor costs}(ML_v) = c_m \eta T_p \tag{3}$$

$$\text{Fixed transportation cost}(\mathrm{FTC}_v) = nF_t \tag{4}$$

$$\text{variable transportation cost}(\mathrm{VTC}_v) = nYV_t(1+\gamma) \tag{5}$$

$$\text{Holding cost}(\mathrm{IHC}_v) = H_c\left[\frac{nY^2}{\eta} - \frac{n^2Y^2}{\eta} + \frac{n(n-1)(1-\alpha)Y^2}{2D}\right] \tag{6}$$

$$\text{Warranty cost}(\mathrm{WC}_v) = w_c \alpha nY \tag{7}$$

$$\text{Incentive cost}(\mathrm{IC}_v) = i_c \beta nY \tag{8}$$

$$\text{Screening cost}(\mathrm{SC}_v) = I_2 \gamma nY \tag{9}$$

$$\text{Reworking cost }(\mathrm{RC}_v) = r_w \eta_1 \gamma nY \tag{10}$$

$$\text{Reusing cost}(\mathrm{REC}_v) = r_u \eta_2 \gamma nY \tag{11}$$

$$\text{Recycling cost}(\mathrm{RECC}_v) = r_c \eta_3 \gamma nY \tag{12}$$

$$\text{Disposal cost}(\mathrm{DC}_v) = d_w \eta_4 \gamma nY \tag{13}$$

$$\text{Carbon emissions during production phase}(\mathrm{CEPC}_v) = c_p nY \tag{14}$$

$$\text{Carbon emissions during transpotation}(\text{CETC}_v) = nc_{t_1} + nYc_{t_1}(1+\gamma) \quad (15)$$

$$\text{Carbon emissions during disposal process}(\text{CEDC}_v) = c_{t_2}\eta_4\gamma nY \quad (16)$$

$$\text{Energycost}(\text{EC}_v) = c_e T_p\left(\frac{\xi + K\eta}{nY}\right) \quad (17)$$

The value of each component cost obtained from Equations (2)–(17) is obtained by adding in Equation (1). Then, we get:

$$\begin{aligned} TC_v(n,Y) = {} & O_v + c_m\eta T_p + nF_t + nYV_t(1+\gamma) + H_c\left[\frac{nY^2}{\eta} - \frac{n^2Y^2}{\eta} + \frac{n(n-1)(1-\alpha)Y^2}{2D}\right] + w_c\alpha nY + i_c\beta nY \\ & + I_2\gamma nY + r_w\eta_1\gamma nY + r_u\eta_2\gamma nY + r_c\eta_3\gamma nY + d_w\eta_4\gamma nY + c_pnY + nc_{t_1} + nYc_{t_1}(1+\gamma) \\ & + c_{t_2}\eta_4\gamma nY + c_eT_p\left(\frac{\xi + K\eta}{nY}\right) \end{aligned} \quad (18)$$

The total revenue of the vender stems from different sources, such as the sale of perfect-quality products ($=c_1(1-\alpha)nY$), the sale of re-worked items which are sold in the secondary market at the reduced price ($= p_1\eta_1\gamma nY$), the sale of reused items which are sold in different markets ($= p_2\eta_2\gamma nY$), and the sale of re-cycled items which are sold in the primary market as raw materials ($= p_3\eta_3\gamma nY$). The total revenue for the vender is the sum of all the revenues from the different sources, which is given below:

$$TR_v(n,Y) = c_1(1-\alpha)nY + p_1\eta_1\gamma nY + p_3\eta_3\gamma nY + p_2\eta_2\gamma nY \quad (19)$$

The total profit for the vender during the production process is:

$$TP_v(n,Y) = TR_v(n,Y) - TC_v(n,Y) \quad (20)$$

The values of $TR_v(n,Y)$ and $TC_v(n,Y)$, adding in Equation (20), are:

$$\begin{aligned} TP_v(n,Y) = {} & [c_1(1-\alpha)nY + p_1\eta_1\gamma nY + p_3\eta_3\gamma nY + p_2\eta_2\gamma nY] \\ & - \Bigg[O_v + c_m\eta T_p + nF_t + nYV_t(1+\gamma) + H_c\left[\frac{nY^2}{\eta} - \frac{n^2Y^2}{\eta} + \frac{n(n-1)(1-\alpha)Y^2}{2D}\right] + w_c\alpha nY \\ & + i_c\beta nY + I_2\gamma nY + r_w\eta_1\gamma nY + r_u\eta_2\gamma nY + r_c\eta_3\gamma nY + d_w\eta_4\gamma nY + c_pnY + nc_{t_1} + nYc_{t_1}(1+\gamma) \\ & + c_{t_2}\eta_4\gamma nY + c_eT_p\left(\frac{\xi + K\eta}{nY}\right)\Bigg] \end{aligned} \quad (21)$$

The total profit for the vender during the production process in a fuzzy environment, as obtained from Equation (21), is given below:

$$\begin{aligned} \widetilde{TP}_v(n,Y) = {} & [c_1(1-\alpha)nY + p_1\eta_1\gamma nY + p_3\eta_3\gamma nY + p_2\eta_2\gamma nY] \\ & - \Bigg[O + c_m\eta T_p + nF_t + nYV_t(1+\gamma) + H_c\left[\frac{nY^2}{\eta} - \frac{n^2Y^2}{\eta} + \frac{n(n-1)(1-\alpha)Y^2}{2\widetilde{D}}\right] + w_c\alpha nY \\ & + i_c\beta nY + I_2\gamma nY + r_w\eta_1\gamma nY + r_u\eta_2\gamma nY + r_c\eta_3\gamma nY + d_w\eta_4\gamma nY + c_pnY + nc_{t_1} + nYc_{t_1}(1+\gamma) \\ & + c_{t_2}\eta_4\gamma nY + c_eT_p\left(\frac{\xi + K\eta}{nY}\right)\Bigg] \end{aligned} \quad (22)$$

The total profit obtained from the Equation (22) for the vender during the production process can be defuzzified using the signed distance method. The signed distance between $\widetilde{TP}_v(n,Y)$ and $\widetilde{0}$ is defined below:

$$
\begin{aligned}
d\left(\widetilde{TP}_v(n,Y),\widetilde{0}\right) = \; & [c_1(1-\alpha)nY + p_1\eta_1\gamma nY + p_3\eta_3\gamma nY + p_2\eta_2\gamma nY] \\
& -\left[O_v + c_m\eta T_p + nF_t + nYV_t(1+\gamma) + H_c\left[\frac{nY^2}{\eta} - \frac{n^2Y^2}{\eta} + \frac{n(n-1)(1-\alpha)Y^2}{2d\left(\widetilde{D}\widetilde{0}\right),}\right] + w_c\alpha nY \right. \\
& +i_c\beta nY + I_2\gamma nY + r_w\eta_1\gamma nY + r_u\eta_2\gamma nY + r_c\eta_3\gamma nY + d_w\eta_4\gamma nY + c_pnY + nc_{t_1} + nYc_{t_1}(1+\gamma) \\
& \left. +c_{t_2}\eta_4\gamma nY + c_eT_p\left(\frac{\xi+K\eta}{nY}\right)\right]
\end{aligned}
\tag{23}
$$

Here, we consider that $d\left(\widetilde{TP}_v(n,Y),\widetilde{0}\right) = \phi_1(n,Y)$ and use the definition of the signed distance concept:

$$
\begin{aligned}
\phi_1(n,Y) = \; & [c_1(1-\alpha)nY + p_1\eta_1\gamma nY + p_3\eta_3\gamma nY + p_2\eta_2\gamma nY] \\
& -\left[O_v + c_m\eta T_p + nF_t + nYV_t(1+\gamma) + H_c\left[\frac{nY^2}{\eta} - \frac{n^2Y^2}{\eta} + \frac{2n(n-1)(1-\alpha)Y^2}{4D+\Delta_h{}^D-\Delta_l{}^D}\right] + w_c\alpha nY \right. \\
& +i_c\beta nY + I_2\gamma nY + r_w\eta_1\gamma nY + r_u\eta_2\gamma nY + r_c\eta_3\gamma nY + d_w\eta_4\gamma nY + c_pnY + nc_{t_1} + nYc_{t_1}(1+\gamma) \\
& \left. +c_{t_2}\eta_4\gamma nY + c_eT_p\left(\frac{\xi+K\eta}{nY}\right)\right]
\end{aligned}
\tag{24}
$$

4.2.2. Buyer's Strategy Model

In this section, we explain the activity of the buyer's policies from the vendor's point of view. As per the agreement contracted between the vendor and buyer, the vendor supplies Y units to the buyer, and the buyer receives Y units. The buyer's inventory includes the sales of defective and non-defective items and the screened Y units in the first round of screening. The buyer supplies the good-quality items to the customers. Moreover, shortages are allowed only under conditions of complete backlogging. A pictorial representation of the inventory at the buyer's end is shown in Figure 7 and for multiple orders have shown in the Figure 8. The buyer presents another strategy, where the customers are permitted to return their used products.

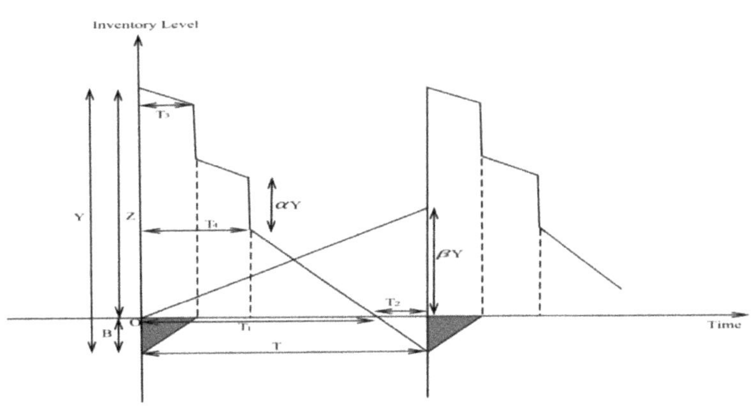

Figure 7. Buyer's inventory representation for time T.

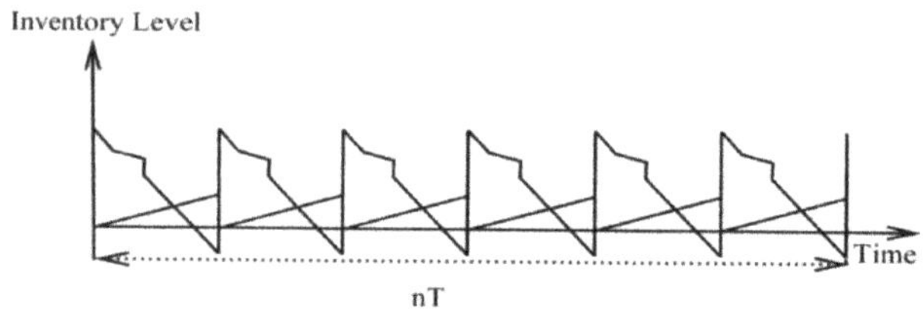

Figure 8. Buyer's inventory representation for nth cycle.

The screening time is given as:

$$T_4 = \frac{Y}{\omega} \tag{25}$$

The inventory level is completed at T_1, and its value is:

$$T_1 = \frac{Y(1-\alpha) - B}{D} \tag{26}$$

The time taken to create shortages after their accumulation, when an inventory is exhausted, is given as:

$$T_2 = \frac{B}{D} \tag{27}$$

The time taken to finish the backorders is given as:

$$T_3 = \frac{B}{w(1-\alpha) - D} \tag{28}$$

The inventory level after removing the backorders, which is equal *to* $Z = Y - B$, can be calculated, i.e., $T_3D + B$ after simplification (the calculation is shown in Appendix A), and we can write:

$$T_3D + B = \frac{BD}{w(1-\alpha) - D} + B = \frac{Bw(1-\alpha)}{w(1-\alpha) - D} \tag{29}$$

$$Z = \frac{Bw(1-\alpha)}{w(1-\alpha) - D} \tag{30}$$

The time taken for one shipment is given as $T = T_1 + T_2$

$$T = \frac{Y(1-\alpha) - B}{D} + \frac{B}{D} \tag{31}$$

The value of the cycle length using the expected approach based on the equation is:

$$E[T] = \frac{Y(1 - E[\alpha])}{D} \tag{32}$$

The total cost for the buyer is the sum of all the costs, including the ordering cost (O_b), screening cost (SC_b), purchase cost (PC), inventory carrying cost for good-quality items ($IHCG_b$), inventory carrying cost for defective items ($IHCD_b$), collection and handling cost of used items (CHC_b), shortage cost (SC_b), and the incentive cost (IC_b).

Now, the total cost for the buyer can be written as given below:

$$TC_b(n, B, Y) = PC + O_b + SC_b + IHCG_b + IHCD_b + CHC_b + SC_b + IC_b \tag{33}$$

From Equation (33), each cost component can be calculated, and they are given below:

$$\text{Ordering cost } (O_b), A_c(n) = A_o + \frac{A_2}{n^{\mu}} \tag{34}$$

$$\text{Screening cost } (\text{SC}_b) = I_1 nY \tag{35}$$

$$\text{Purchase cost (PC)} \;=\; c_1 nY$$

$$\text{Collection and handling cost of used items } (\text{CHC}_b) = c_c \beta nY/2 \tag{36}$$

$$\text{Incentive cost } (\text{IC}_b) = c_i \beta nY \tag{37}$$

➢ inventory carrying cost for good quality items (IHCG_b)

$$\begin{aligned} IHCG_b = h_1(n)\Bigg[n\left\{\frac{2Y(1-\alpha)(w(1-\alpha)-D)-wB(1-\alpha)}{2(w(1-\alpha)-D)}\right\}(T_3) \\ +\frac{n}{2}\left\{\frac{2Y(1-\alpha)(w(1-\alpha)-D)-wB(1-\alpha)}{2(w(1-\alpha)-D)}\right\}(T_1-T_3)\Bigg] \end{aligned} \tag{38}$$

where $h_1(n) = h_o + \dfrac{h_1}{n^{\mu}}$

➢ inventory carrying cost for defective items ($\text{IHC}D_b$)

$$\text{IHC}D_b = h_2(n)\left[\frac{n\alpha Y^2(1-\alpha)}{D}\right] \tag{39}$$

where $h_2(n) = h_o + \frac{h_2}{n^{\mu}}$

$$\text{shortage cost } (SRC_b) = s_c\left[\frac{nB^2}{2D} + \frac{nB^2}{2w\left(1-\alpha-\frac{D}{w}\right)}\right] \tag{40}$$

Calculating the values of all the costs from Equations (34)–(40), adding in Equation (33), we get:

$$\begin{aligned} TC_b(n,B,Y) = \;& c_1 nY + A_o + \tfrac{A_2}{n^{\mu}} + I_1 nY + (h_o \\ & + \frac{h_1}{n^{\mu}})\left[n\left\{\frac{2Y(1-\alpha)(w(1-\alpha)-D)-wB(1-\alpha)}{2(w(1-\alpha)-D)}\right\}(T_3)\right. \\ & \left.+\frac{n}{2}\left\{\frac{2Y(1-\alpha)(w(1-\alpha)-D)-wB(1-\alpha)}{2(w(1-\alpha)-D)}\right\}(T_1-T_3)\right] + (h_o + \frac{h_2}{n^{\mu}})\left[\frac{n\alpha Y^2(1-\alpha)}{D}\right] \\ & + c_c\beta nY/2 + s_c\left[\frac{nB^2}{2D} + \frac{nB^2}{2w\left(1-\alpha-\dfrac{D}{w}\right)}\right] + c_i\beta nY \end{aligned} \tag{41}$$

The total revenue obtained by the buyer from different kinds of sources, such as the sale of good-quality items to the customers ($=c_2(1-\alpha)nY$), the vendor returning all the imperfect-quality items according to the type of warranty cost ($= w_c\alpha nY$), and the vendor returning the used items ($= i_c\beta nY$). The total revenue for the buyer is the sum of all the revenues from the different sources, which is given below:

$$TR_b(n,B,Y) = c_2(1-\alpha)nY + w_c\alpha nY + i_c\beta nY \tag{42}$$

The total profit for the buyer is:

$$TP_b(n,Y,B) = TR_b(n,Y,B) - TC_b(n,Y,B) \tag{43}$$

Calculating the values of $TR_b(n,B,Y)$ and $TC_b(n,B,Y)$ from Equations (42) and (41), replacing in Equation (43), we get:

$$
\begin{aligned}
TP_b(n,Y,B) = {} & [c_2(1-\alpha)nY + w_c\alpha nY + i_c\beta nY] \\
& -\Big[c_1 nY + A_o + \tfrac{A_2}{n^{\mu}} + I_1 nY + (h_o \\
& + \frac{h_1}{n^{\mu}})\Big[n\Big\{\frac{2Y(1-\alpha)(w(1-\alpha)-D) - wB(1-\alpha)}{2(w(1-\alpha)-D)}\Big\}(T_3) \\
& + \frac{n}{2}\Big\{\frac{2Y(1-\alpha)(w(1-\alpha)-D) - wB(1-\alpha)}{2(w(1-\alpha)-D)}\Big\}(T_1 - T_3)\Big] + (h_o + \frac{h_2}{n^{\mu}})\Big[\frac{n\alpha Y^2(1-\alpha)}{D}\Big] \\
& + c_c\beta nY/2 + s_c\left[\frac{nB^2}{2D} + \frac{nB^2}{2w\left(1-\alpha-\frac{D}{w}\right)}\right] + c_i\beta nY\Big]
\end{aligned}
\tag{44}
$$

As per our assumption, the demand rate is imprecise in nature. Thus, the total profit for the buyer in a fuzzy environment, based on Equation (44), is represented by $\widetilde{TP}_b(n,Y,B)$, which is given below:

$$
\begin{aligned}
\widetilde{TP}_b(n,Y,B) = {} & [c_2(1-\alpha)nY + w_c\alpha nY + i_c\beta nY] \\
& -\Big[c_1 nY + A_o + \tfrac{A_2}{n^{\mu}} + I_1 nY + (h_o \\
& + \tfrac{h_1}{n^{\mu}})\left[n\left\{\frac{2Y(1-\alpha)\left(w(1-\alpha)-\widetilde{D}\right) - wB(1-\alpha)}{2\left(w(1-\alpha)-\widetilde{D}\right)}\right\}(T_3)\right. \\
& \left. + \tfrac{n}{2}\left\{\frac{2Y(1-\alpha)\left(w(1-\alpha)-\widetilde{D}\right) - wB(1-\alpha)}{2\left(w(1-\alpha)-\widetilde{D}\right)}\right\}(T_1 - T_3)\right] + \left(h_o + \tfrac{h_2}{n^{\mu}}\right)\left[\frac{n\alpha Y^2(1-\alpha)}{\widetilde{D}}\right] \\
& + c_c\beta nY/2 + s_c\left[\frac{nB^2}{2\widetilde{D}} + \frac{nB^2}{2w\left(1-\alpha-\frac{\widetilde{D}}{w}\right)}\right] + c_i\beta nY\Big]
\end{aligned}
\tag{45}
$$

The total fuzzy profit based on Equation (45) for the buyer can be defuzzified using the signed distance method. The signed distance between $\widetilde{TP}_b(n,Y,B)$ and $\widetilde{0}$ is defined below:

$$
\begin{aligned}
& d\left(\widetilde{TP}_b(n,Y,B), \widetilde{0}\right) \\
& = [c_2(1-\alpha)nY + w_c\alpha nY + i_c\beta nY] \\
& -\Big[c_1 nY + A_o + \tfrac{A_2}{n^{\mu}} + I_1 nY + (h_o \\
& + \tfrac{h_1}{n^{\mu}})\left[n\left\{\frac{2Y(1-\alpha)\left(w(1-\alpha)-d\left(\widetilde{D},\widetilde{0}\right)\right) - wB(1-\alpha)}{2\left(w(1-\alpha)-d\left(\widetilde{D},\widetilde{0}\right)\right)}\right\}(T_3)\right. \\
& \left. + \tfrac{n}{2}\left\{\frac{2Y(1-\alpha)\left(w(1-\alpha)-d\left(\widetilde{D},\widetilde{0}\right)\right) - wB(1-\alpha)}{2\left(w(1-\alpha)-d\left(\widetilde{D},\widetilde{0}\right)\right)}\right\}(T_1 - T_3)\right] + \left(h_o + \tfrac{h_2}{n^{\mu}}\right)\left[\frac{n\alpha Y^2(1-\alpha)}{d\left(\widetilde{D},\widetilde{0}\right)}\right] \\
& + c_c\beta nY/2 + s_c\left[\frac{nB^2}{2d\left(\widetilde{D},\widetilde{0}\right)} + \frac{nB^2}{2w\left(1-\alpha-\frac{d\left(\widetilde{D},\widetilde{0}\right)}{w}\right)}\right] + c_i\beta nY\Big]
\end{aligned}
\tag{46}
$$

Here, we consider that $d\left(\widetilde{TP}_b(n,Y,B),\widetilde{0}\right)=\phi_2(n,Y,B)$ and use the definition of the signed distance concept in Equation (46). Then, we get:

$$\begin{aligned}\phi_2(n,Y,B)= &\ [c_2(1-\alpha)nY+w_c\alpha nY+i_c\beta nY]\\ &-\Big[c_1nY+A_o+\tfrac{A_2}{n^\mu}+I_1nY+(h_o\\ &+\tfrac{h_1}{n^\mu})\Bigg[n\left\{\frac{2Y(1-\alpha)\left(w(1-\alpha)--\frac{4D+\Delta_h{}^D-\Delta_l{}^D}{4}\right)-wB(1-\alpha)}{2\left(w(1-\alpha)-\frac{4D+\Delta_h{}^D-\Delta_l{}^D}{4}\right)}\right\}(T_3)\\ &+\tfrac{n}{2}\left\{\frac{2Y(1-\alpha)\left(w(1-\alpha)--\frac{4D+\Delta_h{}^D-\Delta_l{}^D}{4}\right)-wB(1-\alpha)}{2\left(w(1-\alpha)-\frac{4D+\Delta_h{}^D-\Delta_l{}^D}{4}\right)}\right\}(T_1-T_3)\Bigg]+(h_o\\ &+\tfrac{h_2}{n^\mu})\left[\frac{4n\alpha Y^2(1-\alpha)}{4D+\Delta_h{}^D-\Delta_l{}^D}\right]+c_c\beta nY/2+s_c\left[\frac{2nB^2}{4D+\Delta_h{}^D-\Delta_l{}^D}+\frac{nB^2}{2w\left(1-\alpha--\frac{4D+\Delta_h{}^D-\Delta_l{}^D}{4w}\right)}\right]\\ &+c_i\beta nY\Big]\end{aligned}\tag{47}$$

4.2.3. Integrated Model

In this case, we combined total the defuzzified profit of the vendor and buyer for the supply chain based on Equations (24) and (47), and it is represented by $\phi_3(n,Y,B)$. Then, we get:

$$\phi_3(n,Y,B)=\phi_1(n,Y,B)+\phi_2(n,Y,B)$$

$$\begin{aligned}\phi_3(n,Y,B)= &\ [c_1(1-\alpha)nY+p_1\eta_1\gamma nY+p_3\eta_3\gamma nY+p_2\eta_2\gamma nY]\\ &-\Big[O+c_m\eta T_p+nF_t+nYV_t(1+\gamma)+H_c\left[\frac{nY^2}{\eta}-\frac{n^2Y^2}{\eta}+\frac{2n(n-1)(1-\alpha)Y^2}{4D+\Delta_h{}^D-\Delta_l{}^D}\right]+w_c\alpha nY\\ &+i_c\beta nY+I_2\gamma nY+r_w\eta_1\gamma nY+r_u\eta_2\gamma nY+r_c\eta_3\gamma nY+d_w\eta_4\gamma nY+c_pnY+nc_{t_1}+nYc_{t_1}(1+\gamma)\\ &+c_{t_2}\eta_4\gamma nY+c_eT_p\left(\tfrac{\xi+K\eta}{nY}\right)\Big]+[c_2(1-\alpha)nY+w_c\alpha nY+i_c\beta nY]\\ &-\Big[c_1nY+A_o+\tfrac{A_2}{n^\mu}+I_1nY+(h_o\\ &+\tfrac{h_1}{n^\mu})\Bigg[n\left\{\frac{2Y(1-\alpha)\left(w(1-\alpha)--\frac{4D+\Delta_h{}^D-\Delta_l{}^D}{4}\right)-wB(1-\alpha)}{2\left(w(1-\alpha)-\frac{4D+\Delta_h{}^D-\Delta_l{}^D}{4}\right)}\right\}(T_3)\\ &+\tfrac{n}{2}\left\{\frac{2Y(1-\alpha)\left(w(1-\alpha)--\frac{4D+\Delta_h{}^D-\Delta_l{}^D}{4}\right)-wB(1-\alpha)}{2\left(w(1-\alpha)-\frac{4D+\Delta_h{}^D-\Delta_l{}^D}{4}\right)}\right\}(T_1-T_3)\Bigg]+(h_o\\ &+\tfrac{h_2}{n^\mu})\left[\frac{4n\alpha Y^2(1-\alpha)}{4D+\Delta_h{}^D-\Delta_l{}^D}\right]+c_c\beta nY/2+s_c\left[\frac{2nB^2}{4D+\Delta_h{}^D-\Delta_l{}^D}+\frac{nB^2}{2w\left(1-\alpha--\frac{4D+\Delta_h{}^D-\Delta_l{}^D}{4w}\right)}\right]\\ &+c_i\beta nY\Big]\end{aligned}\tag{48}$$

Thus, the expected integrated defuzzified total fuzzy profit per unit time can be determined, and it is denoted by $\phi_4(n,Y,B)$. Then:

$$\phi_4(n,Y,B)=\frac{1}{E[T]}E[\phi_3(n,Y,B)]\tag{49}$$

The values of $E[\phi_3(n,Y,B)]$ and $E[T]$ are shown in Appendix A.

5. Integrated Model under Learning in a Fuzzy Environment

In this sequence, we move in the direction of learning shaped and governed by Wright [40], which is mathematically shown below:

$$S_n = S_{n1}n^{-l} \tag{50}$$

where S_n is the time for the nth order, S_{n1} is the initial time, and l is the learning factor. Using Equation (50) and the defined learning for the upper and lower triangular fuzzy numbers of the demand rate, we get:

$$\nabla^D_{h.i} = \begin{cases} \nabla^D_{h.1}, i = 1 \\ \nabla^D_{h.i}\left((i-1)\frac{365}{n}\right)^{-l}, i > 1 \end{cases} \tag{51}$$

$$\nabla^D_{l.i} = \begin{cases} \nabla^D_{l.1}, i = 1 \\ \nabla^D_{l.i}\left((i-1)\frac{365}{n}\right)^{-l}, i > 1 \end{cases} \tag{52}$$

Thus, the expected joint defuzzified total profit per unit time under learning in a fuzzy environment can be calculated using (49), (51), and (52), and it is denoted by $\phi_5(n, Y, B)$. Then:

$$\phi_5(n, Y, B) = \frac{1}{E_L[T]}E_L[\phi_3(n, Y, B)] \tag{53}$$

The values of $E_L[\phi_3(n, Y, B)]$ and $E_L[T]$ are shown in the Appendix A.

5.1. Solution Method

We used some useful lemma to identify the optimal values of the order quantity and backorders under learning in a fuzzy environment, and the statement and proof of the lemma are as given below:

Lemma 1. *The joint defuzzified total profit $\phi_5(n, Y, B)$ of the supply chain under learning in a fuzzy environment is concave.*

Proof. The conditions that must initially be satisfied for a specific value of the decision variable n are given as:

$$\frac{\partial \phi_5(n, Y, B)}{\partial Y} = 0 \tag{54}$$

and

$$\frac{\partial \phi_5(n, Y, B)}{\partial B} = 0 \tag{55}$$

Using Equations (53) and (54), we obtain the maximum value of the lot size Y and shortage units B, which, finally, are given below:

$$Y^*(n) = \sqrt{\left(\frac{\begin{array}{c}\frac{\left(A_o+\frac{A_2}{n^\mu}\right)\left(D+\frac{\left((i-1)\frac{365}{n}\right)^{-b}\left(\nabla^D_{h.i}-\nabla^D_{l.i}\right)}{4}\right)}{n(1-E[\alpha])}+\frac{s_cB^2\left(D+\frac{\left((i-1)\frac{365}{n}\right)^{-b}\left(\nabla^D_{h.i}-\nabla^D_{l.i}\right)}{4}\right)}{2(1-E[\alpha])}\left[+\frac{\frac{4}{4D+\left((i-1)\frac{365}{n}\right)^{-b}\left(\nabla^D_{h.i}-\nabla^D_{l.i}\right)}}{w\left(1-E[\alpha]-\frac{\left((i-1)\frac{365}{n}\right)^{-b}\left(\nabla^D_{h.i}-\nabla^D_{l.i}\right)}{w}\right)}\right]- \\ \frac{\left(h_0+\frac{h_1}{n^\mu}\right)B^2\left(4D+\left((i-1)\frac{365}{n}\right)^{-b}\left(\nabla^D_{h.i}-\nabla^D_{l.i}\right)\right)w}{\left[wE\left[(1-\alpha)^2\right]-\frac{\left(4D+\left((i-1)\frac{365}{n}\right)^{-b}\left(\nabla^D_{h.i}-\nabla^D_{l.i}\right)\right)(1-E[\alpha])}{4}\right]}+\frac{O_v\left(4D+\left((i-1)\frac{365}{n}\right)^{-b}\left(\nabla^D_{h.i}-\nabla^D_{l.i}\right)\right)}{4n(1-E[\alpha])}+\frac{F_t\left(4D+\left((i-1)\frac{365}{n}\right)^{-b}\left(\nabla^D_{h.i}-\nabla^D_{l.i}\right)\right)}{4(1-E[\alpha])}+\frac{c_{t_1}\left(4D+\left((i-1)\frac{365}{n}\right)^{-b}\left(\nabla^D_{h.i}-\nabla^D_{l.i}\right)\right)}{4(1-E[\alpha])}\end{array}}{\frac{H_c\left(4D+\left((i-1)\frac{365}{n}\right)^{-b}\left(\nabla^D_{h.i}-\nabla^D_{l.i}\right)\right)}{4(1-E[\alpha])}\left[\frac{1}{\eta}-\frac{n}{2\eta}+\frac{2(n-1)(1-E[\alpha])}{\left(4D+\left((i-1)\frac{365}{n}\right)^{-b}\left(\nabla^D_{h.i}-\nabla^D_{l.i}\right)\right)}\right]+\left(h_0+\frac{h_2}{n^\lambda}\right)\alpha+\left(h_0+\frac{h_1}{n^\lambda}\right)(1-E[\alpha])}\right)} \tag{56}$$

and

$$B^*(n) = \frac{\frac{\left(h_0+\frac{h_1}{n^{\lambda}}\right)\left(4D+\left((i-1)\frac{365}{n}\right)^{-b}\left(\nabla^D_{h.i}-\nabla^D_{l.i}\right)\right)}{4}}{\left[\frac{\left(h_0+\frac{h_1}{n^{\mu}}\right)w\left(4D+\left((i-1)\frac{365}{n}\right)^{-b}\left(\nabla^D_{h.i}-\nabla^D_{l.i}\right)\right)}{4\left[YwE\left[(1-\alpha)^2\right]-\frac{\left(4D+\left((i-1)\frac{365}{n}\right)^{-b}\left(\nabla^D_{h.i}-\nabla^D_{l.i}\right)\right)Y(1-E[\alpha])}{4}\right]}-\frac{\left(h_0+\frac{h_1}{n^{\mu}}\right)w^2}{\left[w^2E\left[(1-\alpha)^2\right]+\frac{\left(4D+\left((i-1)\frac{365}{n}\right)^{-b}\left(\nabla^D_{h.i}-\nabla^D_{l.i}\right)\right)^2}{16}-\frac{w\left(4D+\left((i-1)\frac{365}{n}\right)^{-b}\left(\nabla^D_{h.i}-\nabla^D_{l.i}\right)\right)}{2}(1-E[\alpha])\right]}+\frac{sc\left(4D+\left((i-1)\frac{365}{n}\right)^{-b}\left(\nabla^D_{h.i}-\nabla^D_{l.i}\right)\right)}{8Y(1-E[\alpha])}\left[\frac{4}{\left(4D+\left((i-1)\frac{365}{n}\right)^{-b}\left(\nabla^D_{h.i}-\nabla^D_{l.i}\right)\right)}+\frac{1}{\left(1-E[\alpha]-\frac{\left(4D+\left((i-1)\frac{365}{n}\right)^{-b}\left(\nabla^D_{h.i}-\nabla^D_{l.i}\right)\right)}{4w}\right)}\right]\right]} \tag{57}$$

Additionally, we calculated the maximum value of the shipment, given in relation to and satisfying [24]:

$$\begin{aligned}\phi_5(n+1, Y^*(n+1), B^*(n+1)) &\geq \phi_5(n^*, Y^*(n), B^*(n)) \\ &\leq \phi_5(n-1, Y^*(n-1), B^*(n-1))\end{aligned} \tag{58}$$

The conditions required to satisfy the optimal condition are as follows: $\frac{\partial^2[\phi_5(n,Y,B)]}{\partial Y^2} < 0$, $\frac{\partial^2[\phi_5(n,Y,B)]}{\partial B^2} < 0$ and $\left(\frac{\partial^2[\phi_5(n,Y,B)]}{\partial Y^2}\right)\left(\frac{\partial^2[\phi_5(n,Y,B)]}{\partial B^2}\right) - \left(\frac{\partial^2[\phi_5(n,Y,B)]}{\partial Q \partial S}\right)\left(\frac{\partial^2[\phi_5(n,Y,B)]}{\partial S \partial Q}\right) > 0$. The concavity of the joint defuzzified total profit $\phi_5(n, Y, B)$ of the supply chain under learning in a fuzzy environment was proved with help of the concavity figures given in Figures 9–11. □

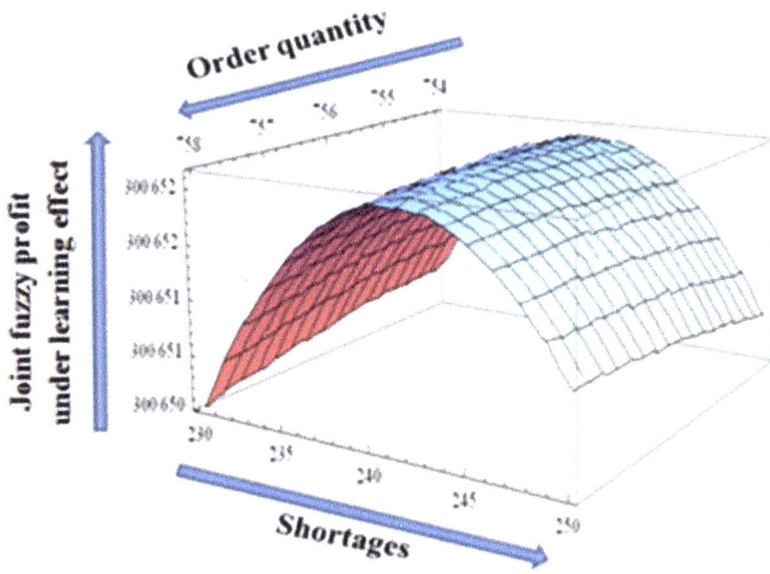

Figure 9. Concavity of the joint fuzzy profit with respect to the order quantity and shortages under learning in a fuzzy environment.

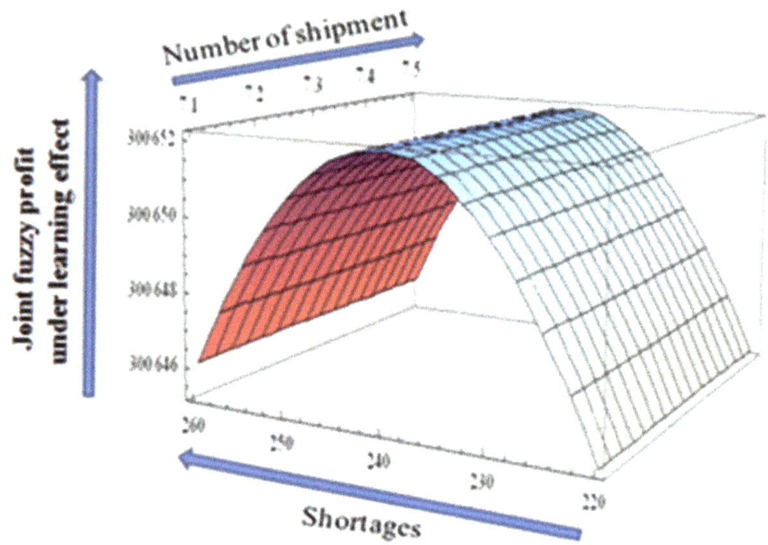

Figure 10. Concavity of the joint fuzzy profit with respect to the number of shipments and shortages under learning in a fuzzy environment.

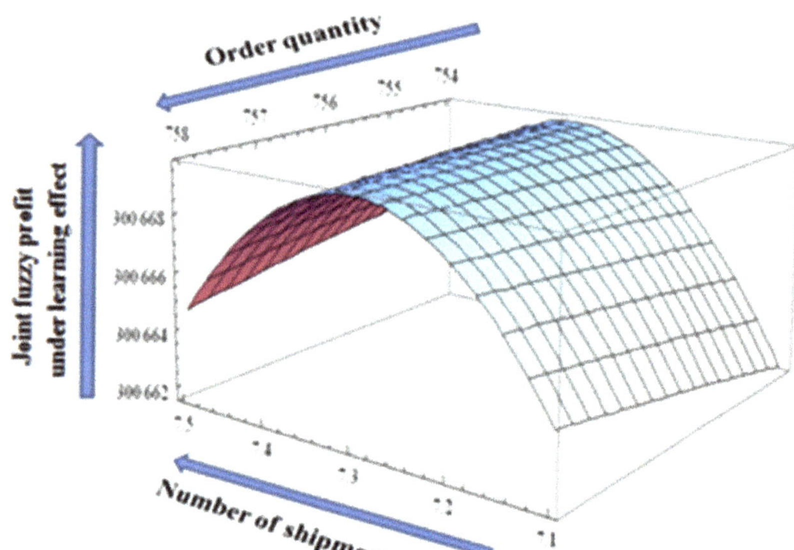

Figure 11. Concavity of the joint fuzzy profit with respect to the number of shipments and order quantity under learning in a fuzzy environment.

5.2. Numerical Analysis

For the justification of the proposed model, we took all the input inventory parameters from the works of some authors, including Salameh and Jaber [1], Gautam and Khanna [22], Jayaswal et al. [39], and Jayaswal et al. [41]. To execute the numerical analysis, all the inventory parameters, with notations, were collected in Table 2. The lot size (Y), shortages (B), and number of shipments are the decision variables, and the carbon dioxide and carbon footprint were not considered as dependent variables. Instead, they were discussed only to enable a better understanding of the carbon emission sources.

Table 2. Input parameter values used in the proposed model.

The Input Parameters for the Proposed Model	The Numerical Values of the Input Parameters	The Input Parameters for the Proposed Model	The Numerical Values of the Input Parameters	The Input Parameters for the Proposed Model	The Numerical Values of the Input Parameters
Production rate (η)	16,000 per units per year	Variable cost due to transportation (V_r)	USD 0.5 per unit	Variable ordering cost for buyer (A_0)	USD 200 per order
Ordering cost for vendor (O_v)	USD 500 per setup	Learning rate (b)	0.153	Purchase cost (c_1)	USD 35 per unit
Material and labor cost (c_m)	USD 30 per cycle	Variable cost due to carbon emissions (c_v)	USD 0.5 per unit	Fixed holding cost for good items (h_1)	USD 6 per unit per year
Energy cost for production (c_e)	USD 0.15 per kWh	Warranty cost (w_c)	USD 36 per defective unit	Fixed holding cost for defective items (h_2)	USD 2 per unit per year
Standard power system (ξ)	100 kW	Incentive unit cost (i_c)	USD 7 per used item	Screening cost for buyer (I_1)	USD 0.4 per unit
Constant (k)	10 kWh per unit	Fixed carbon emission cost due to disposed units (c_{t_2})	USD 5 per unit	Shortage unit cost (s_c)	USD 10 per unit per year
Fixed emission cost for production (c_p)	USD 4 per delivery	Re-worked unit cost (c_2)	USD 40 per unit	Collective cost for buyer (c_c)	USD 1 per unit per year
Holding cost for vendor (H_c)	USD 4 unit per year	Re-worked product price (p_1)	USD 18 per unit	Incentive unit cost (C_i)	USD 4 per used item
Screening cost for vendor (I_2)	USD 0.6 per unit	Derived item price (p_2)	USD 22 per unit	Demand rate (D)	50,000 Units/year
Fraction of re-workable goods (η_1)	0.2	Recycled product price (p_3)	USD 28 per unit	Screening rate (w)	175,200 units/year
Fraction of reusable goods (η_2)	0.3	Re-worked unit cost (r_w)	USD 5 per unit	Expected defective percentage ($E[\alpha]$)	0.04
Fraction of re-cyclable goods (η_3)	0.4	Reused unit cost (r_u)	USD 10 per unit	Product recovery ($E[\beta]$)	0.4

Table 2. *Cont.*

The Input Parameters for the Proposed Model	The Numerical Values of the Input Parameters	The Input Parameters for the Proposed Model	The Numerical Values of the Input Parameters	The Input Parameters for the Proposed Model	The Numerical Values of the Input Parameters
Fraction of waste goods (η_4)	0.1	Recycled unit cost (r_c)	USD 15 per unit	Learning supporting parameter (μ)	0.02
Variable cost for transportation (F_r)	USD 25 per delivery	Disposed unit cost (d_w)	USD 8 per unit	Upper deviation demand rate (Δ_h^D)	1000
Fixed holding cost for buyer (h_0)	USD 2 per unit per year	Fixed ordering cost for buyer (A_2)	USD 20 per order	Lower deviation demand rate $\left(\Delta_l^D\right)$	5000
Fixed emission cost due to disposed unit (c_{t_2})	USD 5 per unit	Fixed emission cost due to transportation (c_{t_1})	USD 1.5 per unit		

Continuing with our consideration that the defective proportion of the lot and the defective proportion of the used products follow the uniform probability distribution (UPD), the values are given below:

$$f(\alpha) = \begin{cases} 1/0.08, 0 \le \alpha \le 0.08 \\ 0, \text{Otherwise} \end{cases} \text{ and } f(\beta) = \begin{cases} 1/0.08, 0 \le \beta \le 0.08 \\ 0, \text{Otherwise} \end{cases}$$

Now, all the input parameters can be inserted into Equations (55) and (56), and using Equation (57), first of all, we obtain the optimal lot size and shortage units using the Mathematica software version(Mathematica 9.0, Wolfram Research, Champaign, IL, USA). The optimized values of the lot size, number of shipments, and shortages are:

$$Y^* = 775 \text{ units}, n^* = 7 \text{ and } B^* = 240 \text{ units}$$

Substituting the values of Y^*, n^*, and B^* in Equation (52), the total expected integrated fuzzy profit per unit time under the learning effect, $\phi_5(n^*, Y^*, B^*)$, for the given model is USD 300,652. In the absence of learning, the optimized values of the lot size, number of shipments, and shortages are $Y^* = 887$ units, $n^* = 10$ and $B^* = 300$ units. Substituting the values of Y^*, n^*, and B^* in Equation (51), the total expected integrated fuzzy profit per unit time, $\phi_4(n^*, Y^*, B^*)$, for the given model is USD 300,300. This model yields more profit (USD 300,652) under learning in a fuzzy environment through the product recovery process as compared with the traditional studies without product recovery (USD 131,920.88) and the study of Gautam and Khanna [22] with product recovery (USD 296,712.55). The learning in fuzzy environment concept gave positive effect in this this model has shown in Table 3.

Table 3. Representation of the comparison with and without the learning effect.

Models	Order Size Y (Units)	Backorder B (Units)	Joint Profit ($)
Present study without learning in a fuzzy environment ($\phi_4(n^*, Y^*, B^*)$)	887	300	300,300
Present study with learning in a fuzzy environment ($\phi_5(n^*, Y^*, B^*)$)	755	240	300,652

5.3. Sensitivity Analysis

In this section, we discuss the effects of the inventory parameters (shown in Table 2) on the decision variable and total integrated profit according to the change in their values. The sensitivity analysis of the present model is presented in Tables 4–22, and managerial insight is also discussed.

Table 4. Impact of the learning rate on the decision variable and joint total fuzzy profit.

Learning Rate (b)	Number of Shipments n	Lot Size Y (Units)	Shortages B (Units)	Joint Fuzzy Profit (USD) ($\phi_5(n^*,Y^*,B^*)$)
0.100	7	776	247	301,706
0.120	7	766	247	301,277
0.140	7	759	247	300,887
0.150	7	756	247	300,705
0.151	7	756	240	300,687
0.152	7	756	240	300,670
0.153	7	755	240	300,652
0.154	7	755	240	300,652
0.155	7	755	240	300,612

Table 5. Impacts of upper and lower fuzzy deviations on the decision variables and joint fuzzy profit.

Upper Deviation Δ_h^D	Lower Deviation Δ_l^D	Number of Shipments n	Lot Size Y (Units)	Shortages B (Units)	Joint Fuzzy Profit (USD) $(\phi_5(n^*,Y^*,B^*))$
6000	3000	6	805	257	299,138
10,000	5000	7	755	240	300,652
20,000	10,000	9	652	203	304,527
30,000	15,000	11	547	172	308,537

Table 6. Impacts of the defective percentage parameters on the decision variables and joint fuzzy profit.

Defective Percentage $E[\alpha]$	Number of Shipments n	Lot Size Y (Units)	Shortages B (Units)	Joint Fuzzy Profit (USD) $(\phi_5(n^*,Y^*,B^*))$
0.01	6	740	260	300,780
0.02	7	745	252	300,698
0.03	7	749	245	300,674
0.04	7	755	240	300,652

Table 7. Impacts of the product recovery parameters on the decision variables and joint fuzzy profit.

Product Recovery E[β]	Number of Shipments n	Lot Size Y (Units)	Shortages B (Units)	Joint Fuzzy Profit (USD) $(\phi_5(n^*,Y^*,B^*))$
0.1	7	783	154	300,528
0.2	7	777	234	300,590
0.3	7	767	237	300,640
0.4	7	755	240	300,652

Table 8. Impact of the vendor's holding cost on the decision variable and joint fuzzy profit.

Holding Cost H_c	Number of Shipments n	Lot Size Y (Units)	Shortages B (Units)	Joint Fuzzy Profit (USD) $(\phi_5(n^*,Y^*,B^*))$
1	17	678	214	307,858
2	11	703	223	304,792
3	8	728	231	302,522
4	7	755	240	300,652

Table 9. Impact of the buyer's holding cost of the good items on the decision variable and joint fuzzy profit.

h_1	n	Y (Units)	B (Units)	Joint Fuzzy Profit (USD)
2	5	1020	214	301,539
3	6	919	223	301,267
4	6	849	230	301,036
5	6	796	236	300,838
6	7	755	240	300,652

Table 10. Impact of the buyer's holding cost of the defective items on the decision variables and joint fuzzy profit.

Buyer's Holding Cost of Defec-tive Items h_2	Number of Shipments n	Lot Size Y (Units)	Shortages B (Units)	Joint Fuzzy Profit (USD) $(\phi_5(n^*,Y^*,B^*))$
0.50	7	765	743	300,696
1.0	7	762	242	300,681
2.56	7	758	241	300,666
2.00	7	755	240	300,652

Table 11. Impact of the shortage cost on the decision variables and joint fuzzy profit.

Shortage Cost S_c	Number of Shipments n	Lot Size Y (Units)	Shortages B (Units)	Joint Fuzzy Profit (USD) $(\phi_5(n^*,Y^*,B^*))$
2	5	976	537	301,433
4	6	876	407	301,130
8	7	784	278	300,779
10	7	755	240	300,652

Transportation Parameters

Table 12. Impact of the fixed cost of transportation on the decision variables and joint fuzzy profit.

Fixed Cost of Transportation F_t	Number of Shipments n	Lot Size Y (Units)	Shortages B (Units)	Joint Fuzzy Profit (USD) $(\phi_5(n^*,Y^*,B^*))$
5	14	383	121	302,519
10	11	496	157	301,919
15	9	593	188	301,435
20	8	678	215	301,020
25	7	755	240	300,652

Table 13. Impact of the variable cost of transportation on the decision variables and joint fuzzy profit.

Variable Cost of Transportation V_t	Number of Shipments n	Lot Size Y (Units)	Shortages B (Units)	Joint Fuzzy Profit (USD) $(\phi_5(n^*,Y^*,B^*))$
0.1	7	743	236	331,024
0.2	7	746	237	323,431
0.3	7	749	238	315,838
0.4	7	752	239	308,245
0.5	7	755	240	300,652

Table 14. Impact of the fixed cost on the joint fuzzy profit.

Fixed Cost C_p	Number of Shipments n	Lot Size Y (Units)	Shortages B (Units)	Joint Fuzzy Profit (USD) $(\phi_5(n^*,Y^*,B^*))$
1	7	731	232	363,927
2	7	739	235	342,835
3	7	747	237	321,743
4	7	755	240	300,652
5	7	765	243	279,561
6	7	722	245	258,471
7	7	781	248	237,382
8	6	789	251	216,293

Carbon Emission

Table 15. Impact of the fixed carbon emission cost due to production on the decision variables and joint fuzzy profit.

Fixed Carbon Emissions Cost C_{t_1}	Number of Shipments n	Lot Size Y (Units)	Shortages B (Units)	Joint Fuzzy Profit (USD) $(\phi_5(n^*,Y^*,B^*))$
1	7	745	237	327,016
1.5	7	755	240	300,652
2	7	766	243	274,289
3	6	787	250	221,565

Table 16. Impact of the fixed carbon emission cost due to disposal on the decision variables and joint fuzzy profit.

C_{t_1}	n	Y (Units)	B (Units)	Joint Fuzzy Profit (USD)
1	7	745	237	327,016
1.5	7	755	240	300,652
2	7	766	243	274,289
3	6	787	250	221,565

Table 17. Impact of the vendor's ordering cost on the decision variables and joint fuzzy profit.

Vendor's Ordering Cost O_v	Number of Shipments n	Lot Size Y (Units)	Shortages B (Units)	Joint Fuzzy Profit (USD) $(\phi_5(n^*,Y^*,B^*))$
500	7	755	240	300,652
600	7	755	240	299,730
700	7	755	240	298,860
800	8	754	239	298,036
900	9	754	239	297,249

Table 18. Impact of the buyer's ordering cost on the decision variables and joint fuzzy profit.

Buyer's Ordering Cost O_b	Number of Shipments n	Lot Size Y (Units)	Shortages B (Units)	Joint Fuzzy Profit (USD) $(\phi_5(n^*,Y^*,B^*))$
200	7	755	240	300,652
300	7	751	239	299,766
400	8	748	237	298,930
500	8	745	236	297,324
600	9	742	235	297,383

Table 19. Impact of the material and labor cost on the decision variables and joint fuzzy profit.

Material and Labor Cost C_m	Number of Shipments n	Lot size Y (Units)	Shortages B (Units)	Joint Fuzzy Profit (USD) $(\phi_5(n^*,Y^*,B^*))$
30	7	755	240	300,652
31	7	776	247	247,927
32	6	798	254	195,204
33	6	820	261	142,485
34	6	842	268	89,769
35	6	865	275	39,057

Table 20. Impact of the energy cost on the decision variables and joint fuzzy profit.

Energy Cost C_e	Number of Shipments n	Lot Size Y (Units)	Shortages B (Units)	Joint Fuzzy Profit (USD) ($\phi_5(n^*,Y^*,B^*)$)
0.15	7	755	240	300,652
0.16	7	775	241	300,645
0.17	7	758	241	300,638
0.18	7	760	241	300,631
0.19	7	761	241	300,624

Table 21. Impact of the buyer's screening cost on the decision variables and joint fuzzy profit.

Buyer's Screening Cost I_1	Number of Shipments n	Lot Size Y (Units)	Shortages B (Units)	Joint Fuzzy Profit (USD) ($\phi_5(n^*,Y^*,B^*)$)
0.4	7	755	240	300,652
0.5	7	757	241	297,324
0.6	7	759	241	290,107
0.7	7	762	242	284,834
0.8	7	764	243	279,541

Table 22. Impact of the vendor's screening cost on the decision variables and joint fuzzy profit.

Vendor's Screening Cost I_2	Number of Shipments n	Lot Size Y (Units)	Shortages B (Units)	Joint Fuzzy Profit (USD) ($\phi_5(n^*,Y^*,B^*)$)
0.6	7	755	240	300,652
0.7	7	756	240	298,332
0.8	7	757	241	296,012
0.9	7	758	241	293,692
1.0	7	769	241	291,372

5.4. Managerial Insights and Observations

From Table 4, we can see that if the rate of learning increases from 0.10 to 0.153, then the order quantity and total fuzzy profit decrease. After that, if the learning rate increases, then the order quantity, backorder quantity, and total fuzzy profit remain constant, while the number of shipments is constant. This means that the order quantity and backorder quantity are in a maturity situation. From Table 5, we can see that when the values of the upper deviation and lower deviation of the demand rate increase, the demand rate increases, and then the number of shipments and profit increase, but the order quantity and shortage unit decrease, while the other input parameters are constant.

The impacts of the defective percentage and defective percentage of the recovery product on the joint total fuzzy profit and decision variables can be described as follows. From Table 6, if the value of the percentage of defective items increases, then the number of shipments and order quantity increase, while the shortage units and total fuzzy profit decrease. In this regard, from the Table 7, we can observe that the defective percentage of the recovery product increases, and then the shortages and total fuzzy profit increase, while the order quantity decreases, but the number of shipments remains constant. From Table 8, we can see that if the vendor's holding cost increases, then the number of shipments and total fuzzy profit decrease, but the order quantity and shortages increase.

From Table 9, we can see that if the buyer's holding cost of the good-quality items increases, then the number of shipments and total fuzzy profit decrease, but the order quantity and shortages increase.

Table 10, we can see that if the buyer's holding cost of the imperfect-quality items increases, the lot size and total fuzzy profit decrease, but the shortage units increase, while the that numbers of shipment is approximately constant. It can easily be seen from Table 11 that when the value of the shortage cost increases, then the lot size, shortage units, and total fuzzy profit decrease, while the number of shipments becomes constant.

It can be analyzed from Table 12 and Figure 12 that when the value of the fixed transportation cost increases, then the lot size and shortage units increase, but the total fuzzy profit and number of shipments decrease. Similarly, as shown in Table 13 and Figure 13, when the value of the variable transportation cost increases, then the lot size and shortage units increase, but the total fuzzy profit increases, while the number of shipments remains unchanged. Table 14, show that when the value of the fixed unit cost increases, the lot size and shortages increase as the number of shipments and total fuzzy profit decrease. From the Figure 14, carbon emission cost due to production increases then total fuzzy profit increases. From the Figure 15, if lower and upper deviation increase then total fuzzy profit increases. Table 15, we can see that if the fixed carbon emission cost due production increases, then the number of shipment remains almost constant, and the total fuzzy profit decreases as the order lot size and shortages increase. From Table 16 and Figure 16, we can see that when the value of the carbon emission cost due to disposal increases, the order quantity increases, and total fuzzy profit decreases, while the number of shipments and shortages remain constant. We analyzed the effects of the vendor's ordering cost on the decision variables and total fuzzy profit, and it can easily be seen from the Table 17 that if the value of the vendor's ordering cost increases, then the number of shipments increases following some values of the vendor's ordering, whereas the shortages, lot size, and total fuzzy profit decrease. Observing the buyer's ordering cost, from Table 18, we can see that if the buyer's ordering cost increases, then the lot size, shortages, and total fuzzy profit decrease, and the number of shipments increases. From Table 19 and Figure 17, it is clear that if the value of the material and labor cost increases, then the order lot size and shortage units increase, but the joint total profit decreases, and the number of shipments remains constant. It can be observed from Table 20 and Figure 18 that when the value of the energy cost increases, then the total joint fuzzy profit increases, but the order quantity and shortages increase, whereas the number of shipments remains constant.

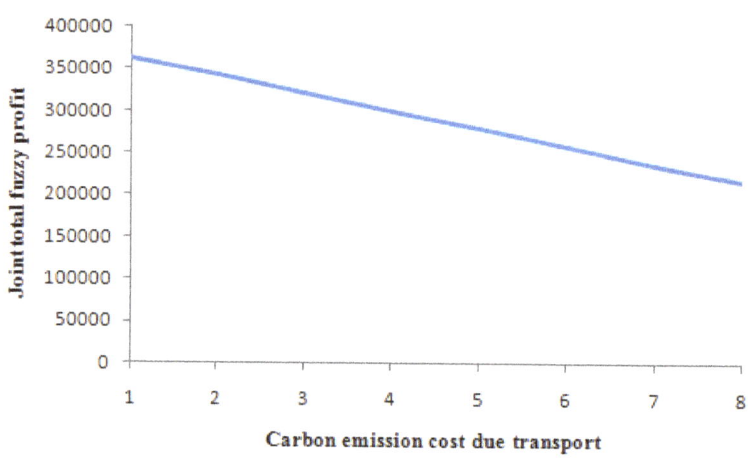

Figure 12. The carbon emission cost due to transportation vs. the total fuzzy profit.

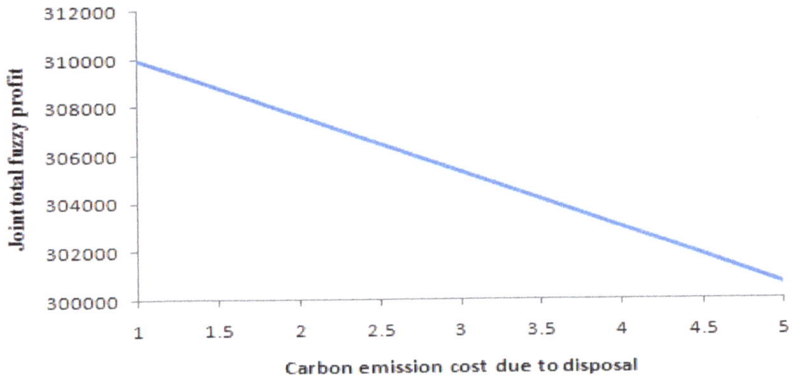

Figure 13. The carbon emission cost due to disposal vs. the total fuzzy profit.

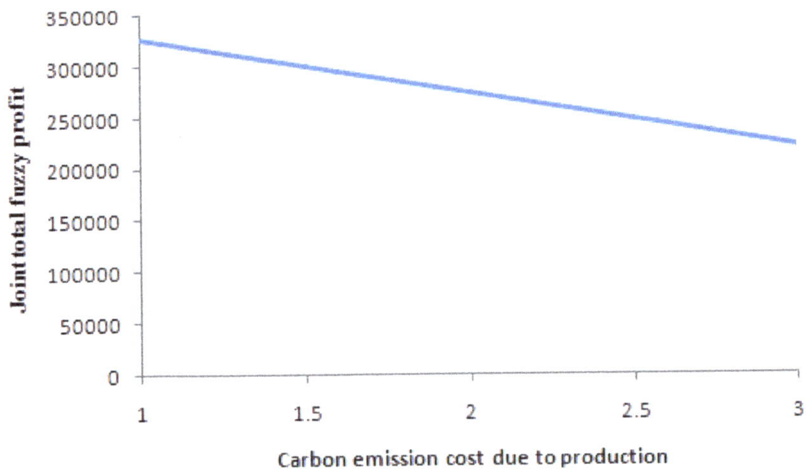

Figure 14. The carbon emission cost due to production vs total fuzzy profit.

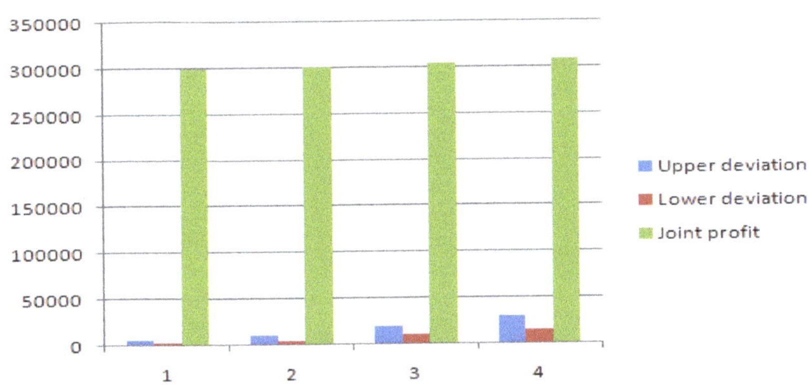

Figure 15. Upper and lower deviation of the demand rate vs. the joint total fuzzy profit.

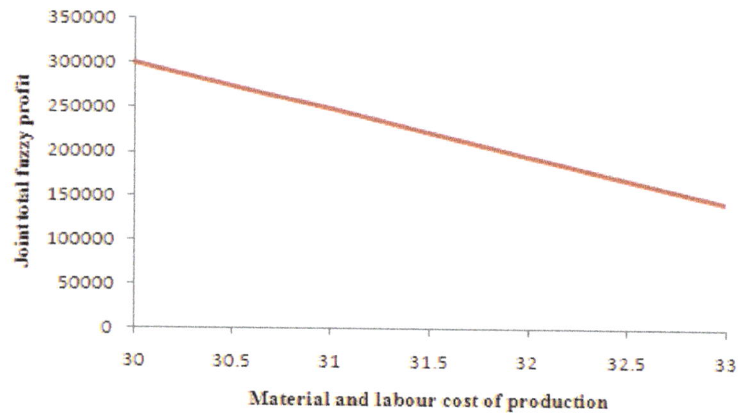

Figure 16. Material and labor cost vs. the joint total fuzzy profit.

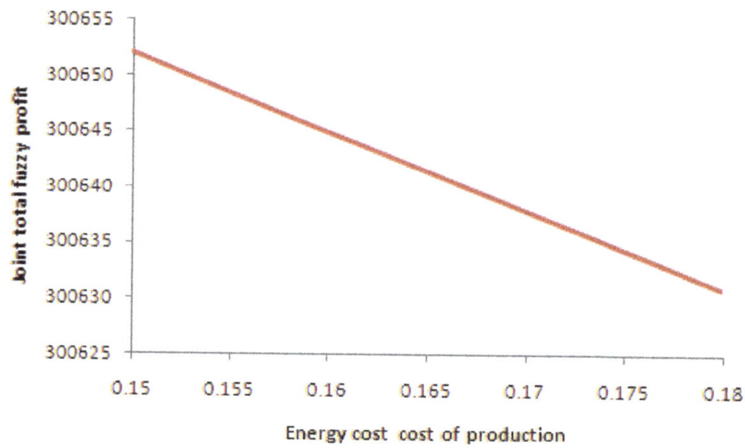

Figure 17. Energy cost of production vs. the joint total fuzzy profit.

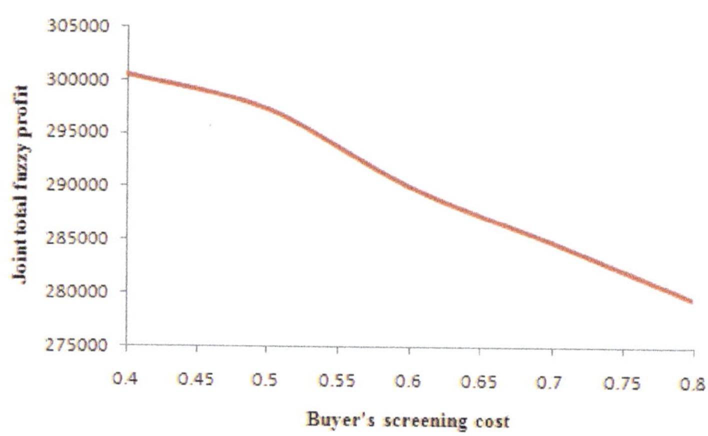

Figure 18. Buyer's screening cost vs. the joint total fuzzy profit.

It can easily be seen from Table 21 and Figure 18 that if the value of the buyer's screening cost increases, then the total joint fuzzy profit increases, but the order quantity and shortages increase, whereas the number of shipments remains constant. It can easily be seen from Table 22 and Figure 19 that if the value of the buyer's screening cost increases, then the total joint fuzzy profit increases, but the order quantity and shortages increase, whereas the number of shipments remains constant.

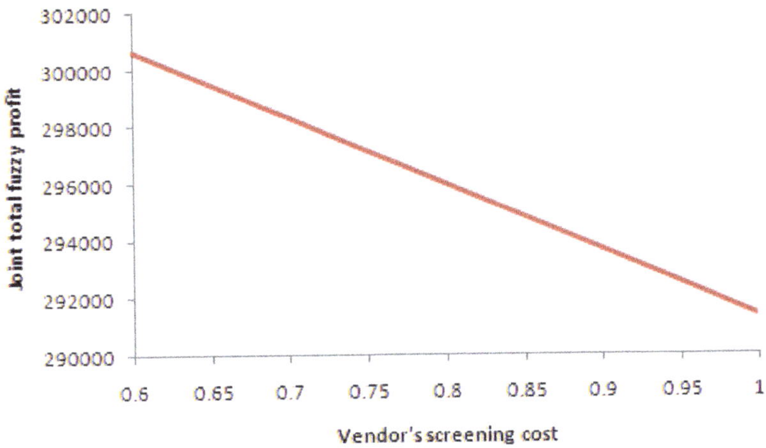

Figure 19. Vendor's screening cost vs. the joint total fuzzy profit.

6. Conclusions

In this paper, we analyzed the impacts of learning and carbon emissions on an integrated green supply chain model for defective items in a fuzzy environment. Our study revealed that several sustainable supply chain models would be helpful for both the vendor and buyer in cases where the demand rate takes the form of a triangular fuzzy number. From the managerial insight and observations, we obtained more information about the inventory parameters in regard to the decision variables and joint total fuzzy profit. This information is more beneficial for the supply chain players. The learning concept is a good decision maker in this model. The buyer wants a lesser order quantity obtained more frequently and to earn more profit. The vendor will yield less production when the demand rate is imprecise in nature, as this may pose a greater risk for sale. A joint model was formulated by taking the vendor's and buyer's strategies into account, respectively. The aim was to optimize the joint total profit $\phi_5(n, Y, B)$ with the effect of learning (b) in a fuzzy environment for the integrated supply chain value by simultaneously optimizing the number of shipments (n), order quantity value (Y), and the shortage amount (B). The formulated model was compared with and without learning in a fuzzy environment and is discussed in the Table 3. The results revealed demand deviation, i.e., when the values of the upper deviation and lower deviation of the demand rate and the demand rate increase, then the number of shipments and profit increase, but the order quantity and shortage units decrease, while the other input parameters are constant. The numerical analysis and sensitivity analysis were used to explore the model's viability. The present study could be developed with the credit financing policy and applied in the textile industry and in many science laboratories, and this study is also useful for omnichannel.

7. Limitations and Future Research Strategy of Our Present Study

The limitations and future scope of the present paper are explained in this section. The present proposed model is optimized for a supply chain where the rate of demand follows the triangular fuzzy number. Furthermore, the researcher can investigate new policies to manage waste and recovered items. The limitation of the model is that the inspection is performed at the vendor's and buyer's ends in the supply chain. The inspection process may have errors or human error, and the carbon emission cost, as well as the carbon emissions, can be considered as a decision variable in the newest version.

8. Applications of Our Present Study

The demand rate of any product is not fixed. In general, it varies according to time. By considering this concept, we studied the supply chain model in cases when the demand rate is imprecise in nature. The present work could be beneficial in the field of omnichannel environments where the demand rate is imprecise in nature and the buyer uses the strategy of product recovery management, performing the firsthand inspection of the lot received from the vendor. Online shopping on Amazon, Flipkart, and Snapdeal, etc., are good examples of the present research work's applications.

Author Contributions: B.S.O.A.: conceptualization, visualization, data curation, funding acquisition, review, methodology, writing—original draft, software; O.A.A.: data curation, methodology, supervision, writing—review and editing, investigation, software; M.K.J.: supervision, writing—review and editing; M.M.: investigation, supervision, writing—review and editing, software. All authors have read and agreed to the published version of the manuscript.

Funding: This research was funded by the Deanship of Scientific Research at the University of Tabuk for funding this work through research no. S-0218-1443.

Data Availability Statement: Not available.

Acknowledgments: The authors extend their appreciation to the Deanship of Scientific Research at the University of Tabuk for funding this work through research no. S-0218-1443.

Conflicts of Interest: The authors declare that there was no conflict of interest.

Appendix A

Appendix A.1 Notations and Assumptions

Notations

Y(Decision variable): Lot size (units)
B(Decision variable): Shortage inventory level of quantity (units)
$Z = Y - B$: Positive inventory level (units)
n(Decisionvariable): Number of shipments
D: Demand rate (units/year)
$\tilde{D}$: Fuzzy demand rate (units/year)
Δ_h^D: Upper deviation of fuzzy demand rate (units/year)
Δ_l^D: Lower deviation of fuzzy demand rate (units/year)
b: Learning slope
μ: Learning supporting parameter
α: The proportion of defective products in a lot which are considered to obey a uniform distribution, with the probability density function (Pdf) $f(\alpha)$.
β: The proportion of defective items among the used products which are considered to obey a uniform distribution, with the probability density function (Pdf) $f(\beta)$.
$\gamma = \alpha + \beta$: The total proportion of defective items (in a lot and among the used products)
w: The rate of screening in the buyer model (units per year)
n: Number of shipments (integer)
$A_c(n)$: Buyer's ordering cost, which is a decreasing function of the shipment (n)
$H_1(n)$: Buyer's holding cost for the good items, which is a decreasing function of the shipment (n) (USD/unit/year)
$H_2(n)$: Buyer's holding cost for the defective items, which is a decreasing function of the shipment (n) (USD/unit/year)
I_1: The cost associated with the inspection of the unit on the buyer side (dollar per unit)
s_c: The cost associated with the shortage of units for the buyer (dollar per unit per year)
C_c: The cost associated with the collection of units for the buyer (dollar per unit per year)
C_i: The cost associated with the incentive unit for the buyer (dollar per unit per year)
T_1: The time associated with the inventory level, where the stock will be zero (years)
T_2: The time associated with the time required for the build-up shortage time (years)
T_3: The time associated with the finished shortage time (years)
T_4: The time associated with the inspection on the buyer side (in years)
η: The rate of production (unit per year)

O_v: The ordering cost associated with the shipment in the production phase for the vendor (dollar per shipment)

c_m : The cost associated with the material sources and labor work in the production phase for the vendor (dollar per cycle)

c_e : The cost associated with the energy in the production phase for the vendor (dollar cycle)

ξ: Standard power system when production starts (kW)

k: Variable component of the power consumption during production (kWh per unit)

c_p : The fixed cost associated with the carbon emissions in the production phase (dollar per disposed unit)

c_{t_1} : The fixed cost associated with the carbon emissions from the transportation (dollar per transport)

c_{t_2} : The fixed cost associated with the carbon emissions from disposed unit (dollar per disposed unit)

c_v: The variable cost associated with the carbon emission unit (dollar per unit) on the vendor side

V_t: The variable cost associated with the transportation (dollar per unit)

F_t: The fixed cost associated with the transportation (dollar per transport)

H_c: The cost associated with the holding unit of the vendor (dollar per unit per year)

I_2: The cost associated with the screened defective items on the vendor side (dollar per imperfect quality item)

r_w: The cost associated with the re-worked units (dollar per unit)

r_u: The cost associated with the reused units (dollar per unit)

r_c: The cost associated with the recycled unit (dollar per unit)

d_w: The cost associated with the disposed units (dollar per unit)

w_c: The cost associated with the warranty unit (dollar per imperfect unit)

i_c : The cost associated with the incentive unit (dollar per used unit)

p_1: The price associated with the re-worked product in the supply chain (dollar per re-worked unit)

p_2: The price associated with the derived items in the supply chain (dollar per derived unit)

p_3: The price associated with the recycled products in the supply chain (dollar per re-cycled unit)

T_p: Total production runtime (years)

T_n: Whole time period for the non-production phase (in years)

T: Time for one shipment (in years)

T_c: Whole cycle time (in years)

η_1: Fraction of re-workable goods with pdf$f(\eta_1)$

η_2: Fraction of reusable goods with pdf$f(\eta_2)$

η_3: Fraction of recyclable goods with pdf$f(\eta_3)$

η_4: Fraction of waste with the probability density function $f(\eta_4)$, where $\eta_1 + \eta_2 + \eta_3 + \eta_4 = 1$, and pdf stands for the probability density function

$E[.]$: Expected value operator

$TC_v(n, Y)$: Total vendor cost (in USD)

$TR_v(n, Y)$: Total vendor revenue (in USD)

$TP_v(n, Y)$: Total vendor revenue (in USD)

$TC_b(n, Y)$: Total vendor cost (in USD)

$TR_b(n, Y)$: Total vendor revenue (in USD)

$TP_b(n, Y)$: Total vendor revenue (in USD)

$\phi_1(n, Y, B)$: Total defuzzified vendor profit (in USD)

$\phi_2(n, Y, B)$: Total defuzzified buyer profit (in USD)

$\phi_3(n, Y, B)$: Total joint defuzzified profit (in USD) for the supply chain

$\phi_4(n, Y, B)$: Total joint defuzzified profit (in USD) per unit time for the supply chain system

$\phi_5(n, Y, B)$: Joint total fuzzy profit per unit time for the supply chain system under learning in a fuzzy environment (in USD)

$\phi_5(n^* Y^*, B^*)$: Optimized joint total fuzzy profit per unit time for the supply chain system under learning in a fuzzy environment (in USD)

Appendix A.2 Mathematical Formulation

Due to the large size of the equation, we assumed some new notations in Section 4.2.3 and Equation (48), which is given below:

$$
\begin{aligned}
E[\phi_3(n,Y,B)] = \; & [c_1(1-E[\alpha])nY + p_1\eta_1 E[\gamma]nY + p_3\eta_3 E[\gamma]nY + p_2\eta_2 E[\gamma]nY] \\
& -\Bigg[O_v + c_m\eta T_p + nF_t + nYV_t(1+\gamma) + H_c\left[\frac{nY^2}{\eta} - \frac{n^2Y^2}{\eta} + \frac{2n(n-1)(1-E[\alpha])Y^2}{4D+\Delta_h{}^D-\Delta_l{}^D}\right] \\
& + w_c E[\alpha]nY + i_c E[\beta]nY + I_2 E[\gamma]nY + r_w\eta_1 E[\gamma]nY + r_u\eta_2 E[\gamma]nY + r_c\eta_3 E[\gamma]nY \\
& + d_w\eta_4 E[\gamma]nY + c_p nY + nc_{t_1} + nYc_{t_1}(1+E[\gamma]) + c_{t_2}\eta_4 E[\gamma]nY + c_e T_p\left(\frac{\xi + K\eta}{nY}\right)\Bigg] \\
& + [c_2(1-E[\alpha])nY + w_c E[\alpha]nY + i_c E[\beta]nY] \\
& - \Bigg[c_1 nY + A_o + \frac{A_2}{n^\mu} + I_1 nY + (h_o \\
& + \frac{h_1}{n^\mu})\left[n\left\{\frac{2Y(1-E[\alpha])\left(w(1-E[\alpha]) - -\frac{4D+\Delta_h{}^D-\Delta_l{}^D}{4}\right) - wB(1-E[\alpha])}{2\left(w(1-E[\alpha]) - \frac{4D+\Delta_h{}^D-\Delta_l{}^D}{4}\right)}\right\}(T_3)\right. \\
& \left. + \frac{n}{2}\left\{\frac{2Y(1-E[\alpha])\left(w(1-E[\alpha]) - -\frac{4D+\Delta_h{}^D-\Delta_l{}^D}{4}\right) - wB(1-E[\alpha])}{2\left(w(1-E[\alpha]) - \frac{4D+\Delta_h{}^D-\Delta_l{}^D}{4}\right)}\right\}(T_1 - T_3)\right] + (h_o \\
& + \frac{h_2}{n^\mu})\left[\frac{4n\alpha Y^2(1-E[\alpha])}{4D+\Delta_h{}^D-\Delta_l{}^D}\right] + c_c E[\beta]nY/2 \\
& + s_c\left[\frac{2nB^2}{4D+\Delta_h{}^D-\Delta_l{}^D} + \frac{nB^2}{2w\left(1-E[\alpha] - -\frac{4D+\Delta_h{}^D-\Delta_l{}^D}{4w}\right)}\right] + c_i E[\beta]nY
\end{aligned}
$$

and $E[T] = \frac{4nY(1-E[\alpha])}{4D+\Delta_h{}^D-\Delta_l{}^D}$.

and in Equation (52):

$$
\begin{aligned}
E_L[\phi_3(n,Y,B)] = \; & [c_1(1-E[\alpha])nY + p_1\eta_1 E[\gamma]nY + p_3\eta_3 E[\gamma]nY + p_2\eta_2 E[\gamma]nY] \\
& -\Bigg[O + c_m\eta T_p + nF_t + nYV_t(1+\gamma) + H_c\left[\frac{nY^2}{\eta} - \frac{n^2Y^2}{\eta} + \frac{2n(n-1)(1-E[\alpha])Y^2}{4D+\left((i-1)\frac{365}{n}\right)^{-b}(\nabla^D_{h.i}-\nabla^D_{l.i})}\right] \\
& + w_c E[\alpha]nY + i_c E[\beta]nY + I_2 E[\gamma]nY + r_w\eta_1 E[\gamma]nY + r_u\eta_2 E[\gamma]nY + r_c\eta_3 E[\gamma]nY \\
& + d_w\eta_4 E[\gamma]nY + c_p nY + nc_{t_1} + nYc_{t_1}(1+E[\gamma]) + c_{t_2}\eta_4 E[\gamma]nY + c_e T_p\left(\frac{\xi + K\eta}{nY}\right)\Bigg] \\
& + [c_2(1-E[\alpha])nY + w_c E[\alpha]nY + i_c E[\beta]nY] \\
& - \Bigg[c_1 nY + A_o + \frac{A_2}{n^\mu} + I_1 nY + (h_o \\
& + \frac{h_1}{n^\mu})\left[n\left\{\frac{2Y(1-E[\alpha])\left(w(1-E[\alpha]) - -\frac{4D+\left((i-1)\frac{365}{n}\right)^{-b}(\nabla^D_{h.i}-\nabla^D_{l.i})}{4}\right) - wB(1-E[\alpha])}{2\left(w(1-E[\alpha]) - \frac{4D+\left((i-1)\frac{365}{n}\right)^{-b}(\nabla^D_{h.i}-\nabla^D_{l.i})}{4}\right)}\right\}(T_3)\right. \\
& \left. + \frac{n}{2}\left\{\frac{2Y(1-E[\alpha])\left(w(1-E[\alpha]) - -\frac{4D+\left((i-1)\frac{365}{n}\right)^{-b}(\nabla^D_{h.i}-\nabla^D_{l.i})}{4}\right) - wB(1-E[\alpha])}{2\left(w(1-E[\alpha]) - \frac{4D+\left((i-1)\frac{365}{n}\right)^{-b}(\nabla^D_{h.i}-\nabla^D_{l.i})}{4}\right)}\right\}(T_1 - T_3)\right] \\
& + (h_o + \frac{h_2}{n^\mu})\left[\frac{4n\alpha Y^2(1-E[\alpha])}{4D+\left((i-1)\frac{365}{n}\right)^{-b}(\nabla^D_{h.i}-\nabla^D_{l.i})}\right] + c_c E[\beta]nY/2 \\
& + s_c\left[\frac{2nB^2}{4D+\left((i-1)\frac{365}{n}\right)^{-b}(\nabla^D_{h.i}-\nabla^D_{l.i})} + \frac{nB^2}{2w\left(1-E[\alpha] - -\frac{4D+\left((i-1)\frac{365}{n}\right)^{-b}(\nabla^D_{h.i}-\nabla^D_{l.i})}{4w}\right)}\right] \\
& + c_i E[\beta]nY]
\end{aligned}
\tag{A1}
$$

and $E_L[T] = \frac{nY(1-E[\alpha])}{D + \frac{\left((i-1)\frac{365}{n}\right)^{-b}(\nabla^D_{h.i}-\nabla^D_{l.i})}{4}}$.

References

1. Salameh, M.; Jaber, M.Y. Economic production quantity model for items with imperfect quality. *Int. J. Prod. Econ.* **2000**, *64*, 59–64. [CrossRef]
2. Wee, H.; Yu, J.; Chen, M. Optimal inventory model for items with imperfect quality and shortage backordering. *Omega* **2007**, *35*, 7–11. [CrossRef]
3. Eroglu, A.; Ozdemir, G. An economic order quantity model with defective items and shortages. *Int. J. Prod. Econ.* **2007**, *106*, 544–549. [CrossRef]
4. Das Roy, M.; Sana, S.S.; Chaudhuri, K. An optimal shipment strategy for imperfect items in a stock-out situation. *Math. Comput. Model.* **2011**, *54*, 2528–2543. [CrossRef]
5. Iqbal, M.W.; Sarkar, B. A Model for Imperfect Production System with Probabilistic Rate of Imperfect Production for Deteriorating Products. *DJ J. Eng. Appl. Math.* **2018**, *4*, 1–12. [CrossRef]
6. Jaggi, C.K.; Goel, S.K.; Mittal, M. Economic order quantity model for deteriorating items with imperfect quality and permissible delay on payment. *Int. J. Ind. Eng. Comput.* **2011**, *2*, 237–248. [CrossRef]
7. Maddah, B.; Jaber, M.Y. Economic order quantity for items with imperfect quality: Revisited. *Int. J. Prod. Econ.* **2008**, *112*, 808–815. [CrossRef]
8. Ross, S.M.; Kelly, J.J.; Sullivan, R.J.; Perry, W.J.; Mercer, D.; Davis, R.M.; Washburn, T.D.; Sager, E.V.; Boyce, J.B.; Bristow, V.L. *Stochastic Processes*; Wiley: New York, NY, USA, 1996; Volume 2.
9. Hua, G.; Cheng, T.; Wang, S. Managing carbon footprints in inventory management. *Int. J. Prod. Econ.* **2011**, *132*, 178–185. [CrossRef]
10. Howitt, O.J.; Revol, V.G.; Smith, I.J.; Rodger, C.J. Carbon emissions from international cruise ship passengers' travel to and from New Zealand. *Energy Policy* **2010**, *38*, 2552–2560. [CrossRef]
11. Güereca, L.P.; Torres, N.; Noyola, A. Carbon Footprint as a basis for a cleaner research institute in Mexico. *J. Clean. Prod.* **2013**, *47*, 396–403. [CrossRef]
12. Gurtu, A.; Jaber, M.Y.; Searcy, C. Impact of fuel price and emissions on inventory policies. *Appl. Math. Model.* **2015**, *39*, 1202–1216. [CrossRef]
13. Sarkar, B.; Ganguly, B.; Sarkar, M.; Pareek, S. Effect of variable transportation and carbon emission in a three-echelon supply chain model. *Transp. Res. Part E Logist. Transp. Rev.* **2016**, *91*, 112–128. [CrossRef]
14. Tiwari, S.; Daryanto, Y.; Wee, H.M. Sustainable inventory management with deteriorating and imperfect quality items considering carbon emission. *J. Clean. Prod.* **2018**, *192*, 281–292. [CrossRef]
15. Sarkar, B.; Sarkar, M.; Ganguly, B.; Cárdenas-Barrón, L.E. Combined effects of carbon emission and production quality improvement for fixed lifetime products in a sustainable supply chain management. *Int. J. Prod. Econ.* **2020**, *231*, 107867. [CrossRef]
16. Thomas, A.; Mishra, U. A sustainable circular economic supply chain system with waste minimization using 3D printing and emissions reduction in plastic reforming industry. *J. Clean. Prod.* **2022**, *345*, 131128. [CrossRef]
17. Sarker, B.R.; Jamal, A.; Wang, S. Supply chain models for perishable products under inflation and permissible delay in payment. *Comput. Oper. Res.* **2000**, *27*, 59–75. [CrossRef]
18. Jaber, M.Y.; Goyal, S. Coordinating a three-level supply chain with multiple suppliers, a vendor and multiple buyers. *Int. J. Prod. Econ.* **2008**, *116*, 95–103. [CrossRef]
19. Jaber, M.Y.; Bonney, M.; Guiffrida, A.L. Coordinating a three-level supply chain with learning-based continuous improvement. *Int. J. Prod. Econ.* **2010**, *127*, 27–38. [CrossRef]
20. Bazan, E.; Jaber, M.Y.; Zanoni, S. Supply chain models with greenhouse gases emissions, energy usage and different coordination decisions. *Appl. Math. Model.* **2015**, *39*, 5131–5151. [CrossRef]
21. Aljazzar, S.M.; Jaber, M.Y.; Moussawi-Haidar, L. Coordination of a three-level supply chain (supplier–manufacturer–retailer) with permissible delay in payments and price discounts. *Appl. Math. Model.* **2017**, *48*, 289–302. [CrossRef]
22. Gautam, P.; Khanna, A. An imperfect production inventory model with setup cost reduction and carbon emission for an integrated supply chain. *Uncertain Supply Chain Manag.* **2018**, *6*, 271–286. [CrossRef]
23. Gautam, P.; Kishore, A.; Khanna, A.; Jaggi, C.K. Strategic defect management for a sustainable green supply chain. *J. Clean. Prod.* **2019**, *233*, 226–241. [CrossRef]
24. Mashud, A.H.; Pervin, M.; Mishra, U.; Daryanto, Y.; Tseng, M.-L.; Lim, M.K. A sustainable inventory model with controllable carbon emissions in green-warehouse farms. *J. Clean. Prod.* **2021**, *298*, 126777. [CrossRef]
25. Rout, C.; Paul, A.; Kumar, R.S.; Chakraborty, D.; Goswami, A. Integrated optimization of inventory, replenishment and vehicle routing for a sustainable supply chain under carbon emission regulations. *J. Clean. Prod.* **2021**, *316*, 128256. [CrossRef]
26. Alamri, O.A.; Jayaswal, M.K.; Khan, F.A.; Mittal, M. An EOQ Model with Carbon Emissions and Inflation for Deteriorating Imperfect Quality Items under Learning Effect. *Sustainability* **2022**, *14*, 1365. [CrossRef]
27. Khan, M.; Hussain, M.; Cárdenas-Barrón, L.E. Learning and screening errors in an EPQ inventory model for supply chains with stochastic lead time demands. *Int. J. Prod. Res.* **2016**, *55*, 4816–4832. [CrossRef]
28. Marchi, B.; Zanoni, S.; Zavanella, L.; Jaber, M. Supply chain models with greenhouse gases emissions, energy usage, imperfect process under different coordination decisions. *Int. J. Prod. Econ.* **2019**, *211*, 145–153. [CrossRef]
29. Afshari, H.; Jaber, M.Y.; Searcy, C. Investigating the effects of learning and forgetting on the feasibility of adopting additive manufacturing in supply chains. *Comput. Ind. Eng.* **2019**, *128*, 576–590. [CrossRef]

30. Jaber, M.Y.; Peltokorpi, J. The effects of learning in production and group size on the lot-sizing problem. *Appl. Math. Model.* **2020**, *81*, 419–427. [CrossRef]
31. Masanta, M.; Giri, B.C. A closed-loop supply chain model with learning effect, random return and imperfect inspection underprice-and quality-dependent demand. *Opsearch* **2022**, *59*, 1094–1115. [CrossRef]
32. Jaggi, C.K.; Sharma, A.; Mittal, M. A fuzzy inventory model for deteriorating items with initial inspection and allowable shortage under the condition of permissible delay in payment. *Int. J. Invent. Control Manag.* **2012**, *2*, 167–200.
33. Jaggi, C.K.; Pareek, S.; Sharma, A. A Fuzzy Inventory Model for Weibull Deteriorating Items with Price-Dependent Demand and Shortages under Permissible Delay in Payment. *Int. J. Appl. Ind. Eng.* **2012**, *1*, 53–79. [CrossRef]
34. Jaggi, C.K.; Sharma, A.; Jain, R. EOQ model with permissible delay in payments under fuzzy environment. In *Analytical Approaches to Strategic Decision-Making: Interdisciplinary Considerations*; IGI Global: Hershey, PA, USA, 2014; pp. 281–296.
35. Rout, C.; Kumar, R.S.; Paul, A.; Chakraborty, D.; Goswami, A. Designing a single-vendor and multiple-buyers' integrated production inventory model for interval type-2 fuzzy demand and fuzzy rule based deterioration. *RAIRO-Oper. Res.* **2021**, *55*, 3715–3742. [CrossRef]
36. Patro, R.; Acharya, M.; Nayak, M.M.; Patnaik, S. A fuzzy EOQ model for deteriorating items with imperfect quality using proportionate discount under learning effects. *Int. J. Manag. Decis. Mak.* **2018**, *17*, 171–198. [CrossRef]
37. Bhavani, G.D.; Meidute-Kavaliauskiene, I.; Mahapatra, G.S.; Činčikaitė, R. A Sustainable Green Inventory System with Novel Eco-Friendly Demand Incorporating Partial Backlogging under Fuzziness. *Sustainability* **2022**, *14*, 9155. [CrossRef]
38. Jayaswal, M.K.; Mittal, M.; Alamri, O.A.; Khan, F.A. Learning EOQ Model with Trade-Credit Financing Policy for Imperfect Quality Items under Cloudy Fuzzy Environment. *Mathematics* **2022**, *10*, 246. [CrossRef]
39. Jayaswal, M.K.; Mittal, M.; Sangal, I.; Tripathi, J. Fuzzy-Based EOQ Model With Credit Financing and Backorders Under Human Learning. *Int. J. Fuzzy Syst. Appl.* **2021**, *10*, 14–36. [CrossRef]
40. Wright, T.P. Factors affecting the cost of airplanes. *J. Aeronaut. Sci.* **1936**, *3*, 122–128. [CrossRef]
41. Jayaswal, M.K.; Mittal, M. Impact of Learning on the Inventory Model of Deteriorating Imperfect Quality Items with Inflation and Credit Financing Under Fuzzy Environment. *Int. J. Fuzzy Syst. Appl.* **2022**, *11*, 1–36. [CrossRef]
42. Mittal, M.; Sarkar, B. Stochastic behavior of exchange rate on an international supply chain under random energy price. *Math. Comput. Simul.* **2023**, *205*, 232–250. [CrossRef]
43. Wang, N.; Song, Y.; He, Q.; Jia, T. Competitive dual-collecting regarding consumer behavior and coordination in closed-loop supply chain. *Comput. Ind. Eng.* **2020**, *144*, 106481. [CrossRef]
44. Wang, N.; He, Q.; Jiang, B. Hybrid closed-loop supply chains with competition in recycling and product markets. *Int. J. Prod. Econ.* **2019**, *217*, 246–258. [CrossRef]
45. Khanna, A.; Kishore, A.; Sarkar, B.; Jaggi, C.K. Inventory and pricing decisions for imperfect quality items with inspection errors, sales returns, and partial backorders under inflation. *RAIRO-Oper. Res.* **2020**, *54*, 287–306. [CrossRef]
46. Hsu, J.-T.; Hsu, L.-F. An integrated vendor–buyer cooperative inventory model in an imperfect production process with shortage backordering. *Int. J. Adv. Manuf. Technol.* **2012**, *65*, 493–505. [CrossRef]
47. Rosenblatt, M.J.; Lee, H.L. Economic Production Cycles with Imperfect Production Processes. *IIE Trans.* **1986**, *18*, 48–55. [CrossRef]
48. Cárdenas-Barrón, L.E. Observation on: Economic production quantity model for items with imperfect quality. *Int. J. Prod. Econ.* **2000**, *67*, 201. [CrossRef]

mathematics

MDPI

Article

A Cloud-Based Software Defect Prediction System Using Data and Decision-Level Machine Learning Fusion

Shabib Aftab [1,2], Sagheer Abbas [1], Taher M. Ghazal [3,4], Munir Ahmad [1], Hussam Al Hamadi [5], Chan Yeob Yeun [6,*] and Muhammad Adnan Khan [7,*]

1 School of Computer Science, National College of Business Administration and Economics, Lahore 54000, Pakistan
2 Department of Computer Science, Virtual University of Pakistan, Lahore 54000, Pakistan
3 Center for Cyber Security, Faculty of Information Science and Technology, Universiti Kebangsaan Malaysia (UKM), Bangi 43600, Selangor, Malaysia
4 College of Computer and Information Technology, American University in the Emirates, Dubai Academic City, Dubai 503000, United Arab Emirates
5 College of Engineering and IT, University of Dubai, Dubai 14143, United Arab Emirates
6 Center for Cyber Physical Systems, EECS Dept, Khalifa University, Abu Dhabi 127788, United Arab Emirates
7 Department of Software, Faculty of Artificial Intelligence and Software, Gachon University, Seongnam 13120, Republic of Korea
* Correspondence: chan.yeun@ku.ac.ae (C.Y.Y.); adnan@gachon.ac.kr (M.A.K.)

Abstract: This research contributes an intelligent cloud-based software defect prediction system using data and decision-level machine learning fusion techniques. The proposed system detects the defective modules using a two-step prediction method. In the first step, the prediction is performed using three supervised machine learning techniques, including naïve Bayes, artificial neural network, and decision tree. These classification techniques are iteratively tuned until the maximum accuracy is achieved. In the second step, the final prediction is performed by fusing the accuracy of the used classifiers with a fuzzy logic-based system. The proposed fuzzy logic technique integrates the predictive accuracy of the used classifiers using eight if–then fuzzy rules in order to achieve a higher performance. In the study, to implement the proposed fusion-based defect prediction system, five datasets were fused, which were collected from the NASA repository, including CM1, MW1, PC1, PC3, and PC4. It was observed that the proposed intelligent system achieved a 91.05% accuracy for the fused dataset and outperformed other defect prediction techniques, including base classifiers and state-of-the-art ensemble techniques.

Keywords: machine learning; software defect prediction; data fusion; machine learning fusion; fuzzy system

MSC: 68N30

1. Introduction

An exponent increase in the use of smart computing devices has been observed during the last few years due to the availability of high-speed internet at a lower cost. Nowadays, the demand for automated online software systems is increasing steadily, which has triggered the need for high-quality software applications at a lower cost. Testing is the most expensive activity in the software development process, and plays a key role in the quality assurance process by ensuring that the end product is bug-free [1].

Many researchers in the software engineering community are working to reduce the cost of development by focusing on cost-effective testing methods [2–4]. The cost of testing can be significantly decreased if the faulty software modules (defective modules) are identified before the testing stage [1–3,5]. A software module is considered as defective when it produces an error during execution, or does not produce the expected results. Software defect prediction (SDP) is the process used to predict the defective modules; it can also reduce the testing cost. Such a prediction can guide the quality assurance team, enabling them to focus on defective modules during testing, through which the costs of testing for non-defective modules can be saved [1,5–7]. In the modern era, all of our day-to-day activities directly or indirectly include interactions with software systems, especially since the recent COVID-19 pandemic, which has urged us to transition towards online systems. Therefore, an effective and efficient software defect prediction system must form part of the modern software development paradigm in order to achieve high-quality software with lower costs [8–10].

This research contributes an intelligent cloud-based system for SDP using data and decision-level machine learning fusion techniques. The proposed fusion-based software defect prediction system (FSDPS) incorporates two fusion modules: data fusion and decision-level machine learning fusion. The data fusion approach renders the proposed SDP system more robust, enabling it to work effectively with the diverse datasets extracted from multiple sources. This approach can also resolve the issue of training with limited datasets. Decision-level machine learning fusion involves the integration of the predictive accuracy of three supervised classifiers, including naïve Bayes (NB), artificial neural network (ANN), and decision tree (DT). In this approach, the prediction is performed using classification techniques, in which iterative tuning is performed until the maximum accuracy is achieved for each classifier. The accuracies of the optimized classification models are then integrated using a fuzzy logic-based technique for an effective performance. The proposed fuzzy logic-based fusion method integrates the predictions of the used classifiers by following eight if–then fuzzy rules. These rules were developed by analyzing the prediction accuracy of each of the used classification techniques. The cloud storage was used to store the fused prediction model so that it could be accessed from anywhere. This strategy can also be an aid in the paradigm of global software development. Five datasets from NASA's cleaned repository, including CM1, MW1, PC1, PC3, and PC4, were integrated using instance-level fusion in order to implement the proposed system. The results show that the proposed FSDPS outperforms the other techniques.

This paper is organized as follows. Section 2 provides a summary of the related studies. Section 3 proposes the FSDPS and discusses its stages and activities in detail. Section 4 discusses the detailed results of the proposed system after its implementation. Section 5 presents the threats to the validity of the proposed research. Section 5 concludes this research, together with the directions for future work.

2. Literature Review

Researchers have been working to reduce development costs by identifying faulty software modules before the testing stage. Some related studies are discussed in this section.

The authors of [11] proposed a cloud-based framework for SDP. They explored four training functions in ANN using the back-propagation method. The training functions compared in the proposed framework included Bayesian regularization (BR), scaled conjugate gradient (SCG), Broyden–Fletcher–Goldfarb–Shanno Quasi-Newton (BFGS-QN), and Levenberg–Marquardt (LM). A fuzzy logic-based engine was also incorporated to identify which training function performed better. The cleaned versions of NASA datasets were used by the researchers for the experiments, along with multiple performance measures. It was observed that the BR training function showed a higher accuracy as compared to the other functions. The authors of [12] proposed a framework for SDP using feature selection and ensemble machine learning approaches. In ensemble learning, multiple variants of each classification technique are generated by optimizing various parameters, and then the best-performing variants are integrated using ensemble learning methods. However, the used feature selection method reduced the feature set by removing the metrics not participating in the classification process. NASA defect datasets were used to implement the proposed method, which showed a higher performance as compared to the other techniques.

The authors of [13] presented a classification framework for the detection of faulty software modules before the testing stage. The proposed framework used an ensemble machine learning-based classification model with the multi-layer perceptron (MLP) technique. The proposed framework detected the faulty modules in three dimensions. This was achieved firstly by tuning the MLP until the maximum accuracy was achieved; secondly, the tuned version of MLP was ensembled with the bagging technique; and thirdly, the tuned version was ensembled with the boosting technique. To implement the proposed ensemble machine learning-based classification framework, cleaned versions of NASA's software defect datasets were used. The performance was compared with the techniques known from published research. In [14], the researchers presented a novel feature selection technique for SDP. They proposed a feature selection and ANN-based framework to limit the testing costs in SDLC. They used MLP architecture along with the oversampling method in order to tackle the class imbalance in the dataset. To implement the proposed framework, clean versions of software defect datasets from the NASA repository were used, and various statistical measures are used to assess the performance. The results indicated that the proposed technique performed well, especially with the oversampling technique.

In [15], the researchers used a hybrid classification technique for SDP, which integrated NB and ANN. For its implementation, five benchmark datasets were used, including KC1, KC2, CM1, JM1, and PC1. The proposed technique performed better when compared with NB, ANN, and SVM. The authors of [16] predicted software defects using various supervised machine learning techniques. The SMOTE technique was used by the researchers to resample the data, along with the feature selection method for dimensionality reduction. The experiments were performed on two widely used datasets from the PROMISE repository, KC1 and JM1. The results indicated that RF performed better when compared to the other techniques, with the best results obtained when boosting with RF and bagging with DT. The authors of [17] proposed an enhanced wrapper-based feature selection method which selects the features in an iterative manner. For the prediction, DT and NB were used after tuning, and the experiments were performed on 25 benchmark datasets for a detailed analysis. The performance of the proposed feature selection technique with the used classification methods was analyzed using three measures, including the AUC, F-measure, and accuracy. The results showed that the proposed enhanced feature selection technique performed better than the other methods and selected fewer features with a lower computational cost and high accuracy. In [18], the effectiveness of an ensemble of classification techniques for SDP was discussed. The researchers developed two approaches in this research. In the first approach, the classification is performed using base classifiers, including the k-nearest neighbor (k-NN), DT, and NB. In the second approach, ensembles are used for classification, and the results indicated that the ensemble approach has a tendency to perform better than the other classification techniques. The experiments were performed on 21 benchmark software defect datasets. The authors of [19] presented an integrated technique to predict the workload for the next time slot in distributed clouds. The proposed technique integrates the Savitzky–Golay filter and wavelet decomposition with stochastic configuration networks. The researchers highlighted the significance of the effective and efficient services that could be provided by distributed cloud data centers after the implementation of the proposed technique.

Table 1 presents a summary of the literature review. It shows the proposed techniques for SDP, the dataset repository from which the datasets were extracted for experiments, the names of the used datasets, and the performance measures which were used for the performance analysis.

Table 1. Literature review summary.

Reference	Prediction Technique	Dataset Repository	Datasets	Performance Measures
Daoud, M. S. et al. [11]	Four training functions of back propagation in ANN are used for SDP. The fuzzy logic-based technique is proposed for the identification of the best training function.	NASA	CM1, JM1, KC1, KC3, MC1, MC2, MW1, PC1, PC2, PC3, PC4, PC5	Specificity, precision, F-measure, recall, accuracy, AUC, R2, MSE
Ali, U. et al. [12]	A metric selection-based variant ensemble machine learning technique is proposed for software defect prediction.	NASA	JM1, KC1, PC4, PC5	F-measure, accuracy, MCC
Iqbal, A. et al. [13]	An ANN-based ensemble machine learning technique is proposed for SDP.	NASA	KC1, MW1, PC4, PC5	F-measure, accuracy, AUC, MCC
Iqbal, A. et al. [14]	A multi-filter feature selection technique is used with ANN for SDP.	NASA	CM1, JM1, KC1, KC3, MC1, MC2, MW1, PC1, PC2, PC3, PC4, PC5	F-measure, accuracy, AUC, MCC
Arasteh, B. et al. [15]	Proposes a technique by integrating the ANN and NB for SDP.	PROMISE	KC1, KC2, CM1, PC1, JM1	Accuracy, precision
Alsaeedi, A. et al. [16]	Various supervised classification techniques are used for SDP, including: SVM, DT, RF, bagging, and boosting. The SMOTE technique is used to tackle the issue of class imbalance.	NASA	PC1, PC2, PC3, PC4, PC5, MC1, MC2, JM1, MW1, KC3	Accuracy, precision, F-measure, recall, true-positive rate, false-positive rate, probability of false alarm, specificity, G-measure
Balogun, A. O. et al. [17]	An enhanced wrapper feature selection technique is proposed. The proposed technique is used with NB and DT.	PROMISE, NASA, AEEEM,	EQ, JDT, ML PDE, CM1, KC1, KC2, KC3, MW1, PC1, PC3, PC4, PC5, ANT, CAMEL, JEDIT, REDKITOR, TOMCAT, VELOCITY, XALAN, SAFE, ZXING, APACHE, ECLIPSE, SWT	Accuracy, F-measure, AUC
Alsawalqah, H. et al. [18]	Heterogeneous ensemble classifiers are used for SDP.	PROMISE, NASA,	PC1, PC2, PC3, PC4, PC5, KC1, KC3, CM1, JM1, MC1, MW1, ant-1.7, camel-1.6, ivy-2.0, jedit-4.3, log4j-1.2, ucene-2.4, poi-3.0, tomcat-6, xalan-2.6, xerces-1.4	Precision, recall, G-mean

To the body of previously published work, this research contributes an intelligent system using data and decision-level machine learning fusion to detect defect-prone software modules. The major contributions of the proposed framework are discussed below.

1. Data fusion was performed, through which the developed classification models were rendered more robust and effective for the test datasets. The proposed system was implemented on a fused dataset, which was generated by fusing publicly available defect prediction datasets from NASA's repository, including CM1, MW1, PC1, PC3, and PC4.
2. The prediction accuracy of three classifiers, including NB, ANN, and DT, was integrated using a fuzzy logic technique. The proposed framework used eight fuzzy logic-based if–then rules for decision-level accuracy fusion.

3. The performance of the proposed fusion-based intelligent system was compared with that of other state-of-the-art defect prediction systems, and it was observed that the proposed system outperformed the other methods and achieved a 91.05% accuracy for the fused dataset.

3. Materials and Methods

This research presents an intelligent SDP system using data and decision-level machine learning fusion techniques (Figure 1). There are two layers in the proposed FSDPS: training and testing. Each of the two layers further consist of several stages. The training layer consists of four stages: (1) data fusion, (2) data pre-processing, (3) classification, and (4) fusion. This layer involves the development of the fused classification model by integrating the predictive accuracy of NB, ANN, and DT. The test layer consists of one stage, namely prediction. This stage involves the classification of the software module as defective or non-defective using the fused model.

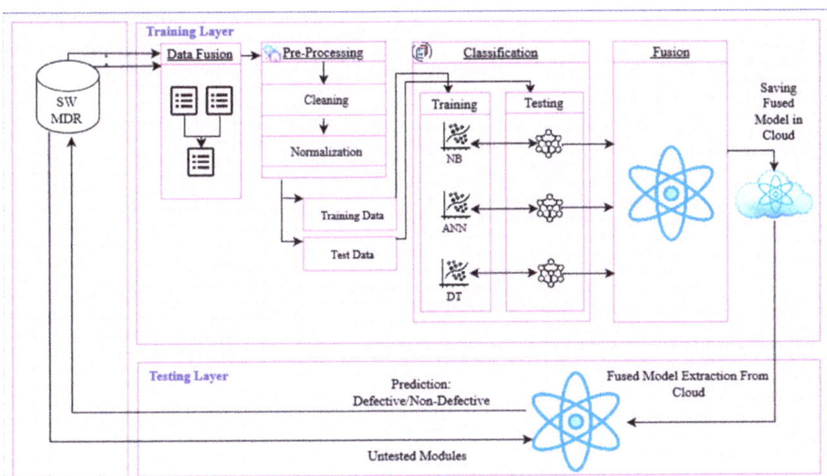

Figure 1. Proposed FSDPS architecture.

The workflow of the training layer begins with the data fusion stage, in which multiple datasets are extracted from the software metric dataset repository (SWMDR) and then integrated using instance-level fusion. The prediction model, which is trained on the fused dataset, is more effective and robust for the test datasets, which are extracted from multiple resources. In this research, five widely used, cleaned datasets from the NASA repository were selected for fusion [20], including CM1, MW1, PC1, PC3, and PC4. These datasets are available in [21]. There are, in total, 38 attributes and 3579 instances in the fused dataset. Each of the selected datasets represents one software component, and the instances in the dataset reflect the software modules. The features represent the software quality metrics, which are recorded during development. One of these 38 features of the fused dataset is the output class to be predicted, whereas the other 37 features are used for the prediction. The output class reflects whether the particular module is defective or not.

The second stage of the training layer is data pre-processing, which is responsible for performing three activities using the fused dataset: (1) cleaning, (2) normalization, and (3) splitting. The data cleaning activity in the pre-processing stage handles the missing values using the mean imputation method. Missing and null values in the attributes can lead to false results. Normalization is the second activity in the pre-processing stage; it involves the transformation of the attribute values into a specific range. The activities of cleaning and normalization both simplify the data so as to help the classification framework to work effectively and efficiently. The data splitting activity involves the division of the data into training and test sets, following the class split rule, with a 70:30 ratio.

Classification is the third stage of the training layer; it is responsible for classifying the modules as defective or non-defective. The input of this stage is the pre-processed training and testing datasets. For the classification, three techniques in the family of supervised machine learning are used, including NB, ANN, and DT. During the development of the classification model, the classifiers are optimized repeatedly until the maximum accuracy is achieved. First, the classification model is developed using the training data, and the optimization is iteratively performed until the maximum accuracy is achieved using the test data. For NB, the default parameters are used, as their optimization decreases the performance. In ANN, two hidden layers are used, with 33 neurons in each layer. In this study, the initial learning rate value was 0.01; however, the highest performance was achieved with 0.02. DT was tuned by setting the value of the confidence factor to 0.3. However, during this stage, the default values of the remaining parameters are used. This stage finishes by producing the classification models of NB, ANN, and DT.

The decision-level fusion is the fourth and last stage of the training layer. This stage involves the fusion of the optimized classification models using fuzzy logic. Fuzzy rules are used to generate the membership functions through which the prediction accuracies of the used machine learning techniques are integrated for a higher performance. These rules are developed by carefully analyzing the performance of each of the classifiers used on the test dataset. The fusion stage finishes by storing the fused model in the cloud for later use. As compared to server storage, cloud storage was selected here due to its many advantages, including its easy access and security. Moreover, the strategy of cloud storage can be helpful in global software development, as in this case, the fused model will be easily accessible from anywhere.

The if–then conditions based on fuzzy rules are listed below:

IF (naïve Bayes predicts defective, neural network predicts defective and decision tree predicts defective) THEN (the module is defective).

IF (naïve Bayes predicts defective, neural network predicts defective and decision tree predicts non-defective) THEN (module is defective).

IF (naïve Bayes predicts defective, neural network predicts non-defective and decision tree predicts defective) THEN (module is defective).

IF (naïve Bayes predicts non-defective, neural network predicts defective and decision tree predicts defective) THEN (module is defective).

IF (naïve Bayes predicts non-defective, neural network predicts non-defective and decision tree also predicts non-defective) THEN (module is not defective).

IF (naïve Bayes predicts defective, neural network predicts non-defective and decision tree predicts non-defective) THEN (module is not defective).

IF (naïve Bayes predicts non-defective, neural network predicts non-defective and decision tree predicts defective) THEN (module is not defective).

IF (naïve Bayes predicts non-defective, neural network predicts defective and decision tree predicts non-defective) THEN (module is not defective).

The membership functions developed by following the if–then fuzzy rules are shown in Table 2. These membership functions are used to integrate the accuracy of NB, ANN, and DT. These if–then rules, which work as the base of membership functions, were developed after various experiments on the fusion of the predictive accuracy of the used classifiers.

Table 2. Membership functions of the proposed fuzzy logic-based fusion technique.

Membership Functions	Graphical Representation
$\gamma_{\mathcal{NBY}}(nb)=\left\{\max\left(\min\left(1,\frac{0.5-nb}{0.05}\right),0\right)\right\}$	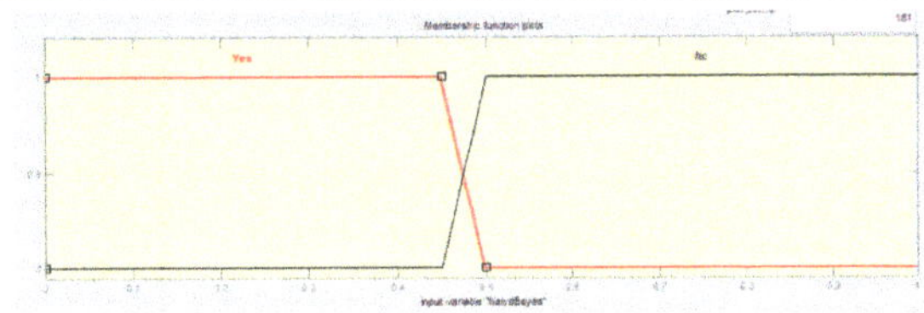
$\gamma_{\mathcal{NBN}}(nb)=\left\{\max\left(\min\left(\frac{nb-0.45}{0.05},1\right),0\right)\right\}$	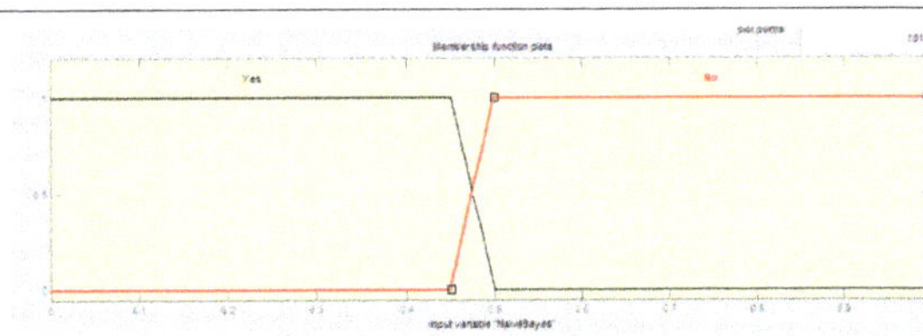
$\gamma_{\mathcal{NNY}}(nn)=\left\{\max\left(\min\left(1,\frac{0.5-nn}{0.05}\right),0\right)\right\}$	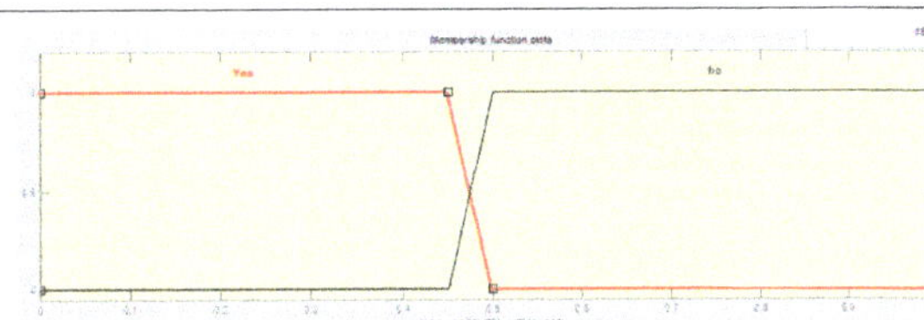
$\gamma_{\mathcal{NNN}}(nn)=\left\{\max\left(\min\left(\frac{nn-0.45}{0.05},1\right),0\right)\right\}$	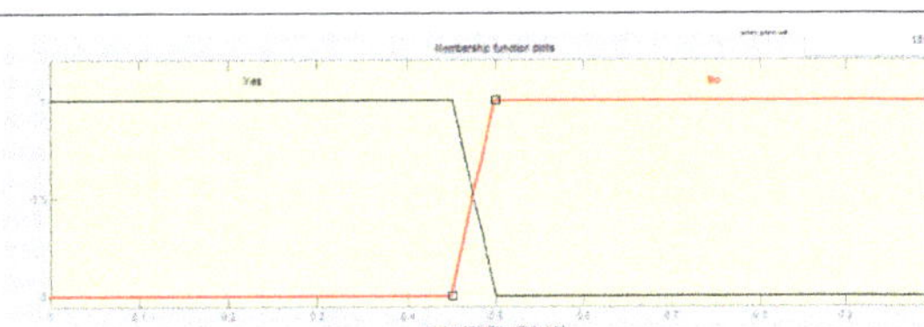
$\gamma_{\mathcal{DTY}}(dt)=\left\{\max\left(\min\left(1,\frac{0.5-dt}{0.05}\right),0\right)\right\}$	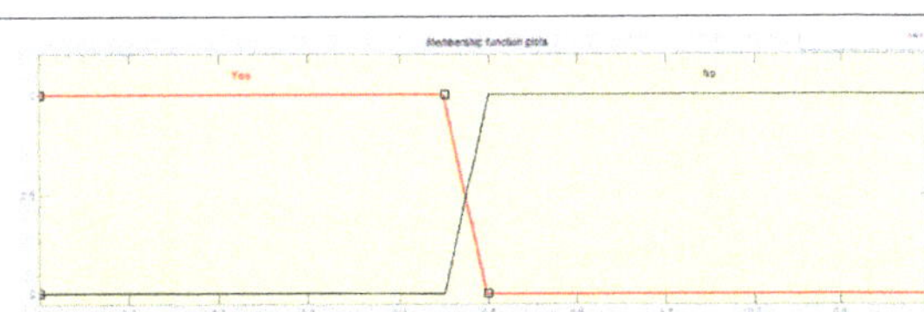
$\gamma_{\mathcal{DTN}}(dt)=\left\{\max\left(\min\left(\frac{dt-0.45}{0.05},1\right),0\right)\right\}$	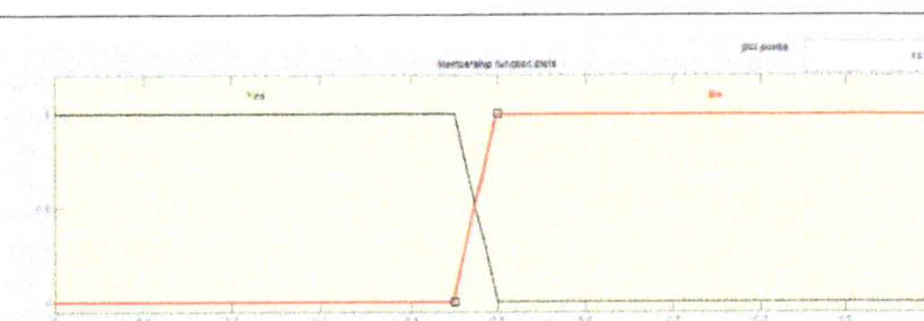

Table 2. *Cont.*

Membership Functions	Graphical Representation
$\gamma_{\mathcal{DY}}(\text{đ}) = \left\{\max\left(\min\left(1, \frac{0.5-\text{đ}}{0.05}\right), 0\right)\right\}$	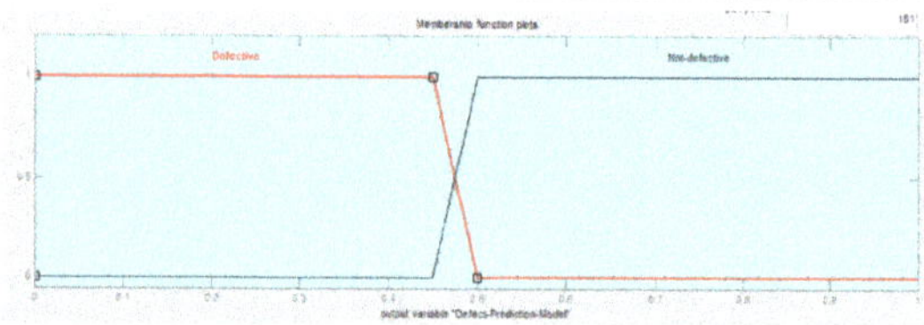
$\gamma_{\mathcal{DN}}(\text{đ}) = \left\{\max\left(\min\left(\frac{\text{đ}-0.45}{0.05}, 1\right), 0\right)\right\}$	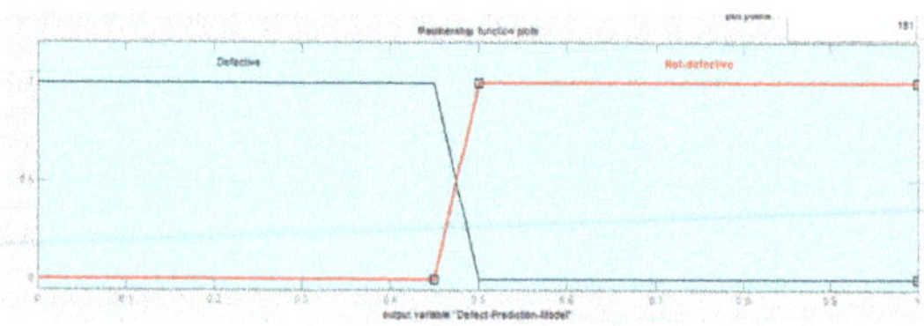

Figure 2 shows the rule surface of the proposed fuzzy logic-based fusion technique for defect prediction with respect to the NB and ANN results. Figure 3 shows the prediction process with the accuracy fusion technique, which predicts that the software module is non-defective. NB predicts that the module is non-defective with a 0.127 confidence factor, and ANN predicts the same with a 0.259 confidence factor; DT predicts that the module is defective with a 0.801 confidence factor. However, as per the defined fuzzy rules, the proposed technique predicts that the module is non-defective with a 0.248 confidence factor.

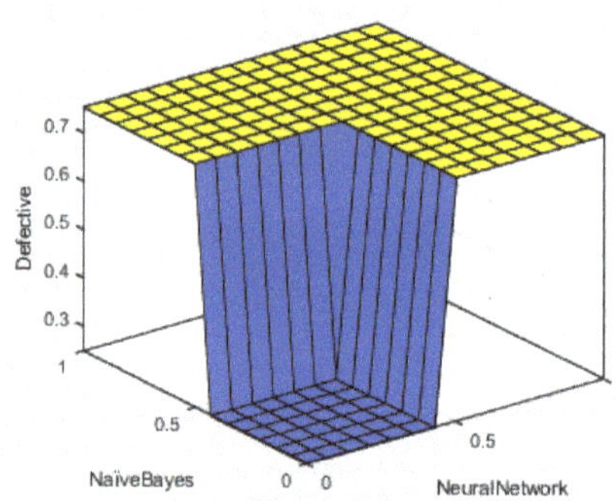

Figure 2. Rule surface of the proposed fuzzy logic-based fusion technique with NB and ANN.

It is demonstrated in Figure 4 that NB predicts that the module is non-defective with a 0.127 confidence factor, whereas ANN and DT both predict that the module is defective with 0.62 and 0.801 confidence factors, respectively; therefore, that the proposed fused model predicts that the module is defective with a 0.752 confidence factor.

The second layer of the proposed system is the testing layer, which performs real-time prediction to identify which software module is defective and requires extensive testing. This layer involves four activities. The first activity is the extraction of the dataset of the untested software module for prediction. The second activity is the extraction of the fused classification model that was saved in the cloud in the last activity of the training layer. The third activity is the prediction, in which the data of the untested software component function is used as the input to the fused model, and the output is extracted; this indicates whether the module is defective or not. The fourth and last activity of this layer is the submission of the prediction to the software defect dataset repository.

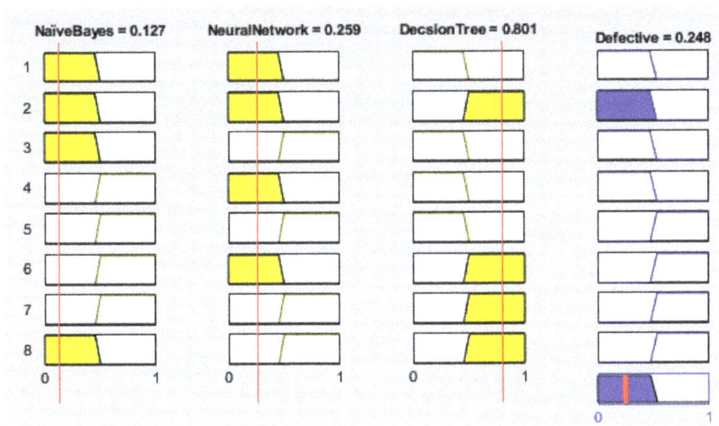

Figure 3. Results of the proposed fuzzy logic based fusion technique for a non-defective module (0).

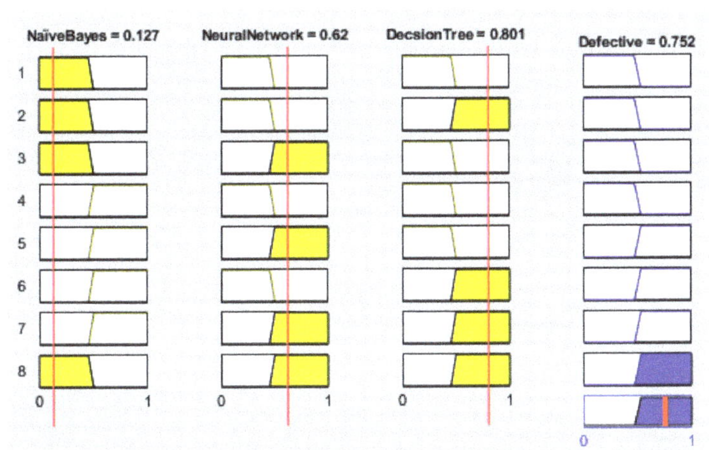

Figure 4. Results of the proposed fuzzy logic-based fusion technique for a defective module (1).

4. Results and Discussion

The proposed FSDPS was implemented using a fused software defect dataset. Matlab 2021a was used in this research to conduct the experiments and simulations. The fused dataset was created by integrating the five datasets from NASA's cleaned repository, named CM1, MW1, PC1, PC3, and PC4. The fused dataset consists of 3579 instances, of which 428 indicate that the modules are defective, whereas 3151 indicate that they are non-defective. In the pre-processing stage, the used dataset underwent cleaning and normalization processes and was then divided into two further subsets, the training set and test set, using a 70:30 ratio. The training dataset consists of 2506 instances, and the test dataset consists of 1073 instances. For the prediction, initially, three supervised machine learning techniques were used, including NB, ANN, and DT. Each classifier was optimized so that we could obtain maximum accuracy. To analyze the performance of the proposed fusion-based software defect prediction system, the following measures were used [22,23].

$$Accuracy = \frac{(\partial OR_0/\epsilon OR_0 + \partial OR_1/\epsilon OR_1)}{\epsilon OR_0 + \epsilon OR_1} \tag{1}$$

$$Positive\ Prediction\ Value = \frac{\partial OR_1/\epsilon OR_1}{(\partial OR_1/\epsilon OR_1 + \partial OR_0/\epsilon OR_1)} \tag{2}$$

$$Negative\ Prediction\ Value = \frac{\partial OR_0/\epsilon OR_0}{(\partial OR_0/\epsilon OR_0 + \partial OR_1/\epsilon OR_0)} \tag{3}$$

$$Specificity = \frac{\partial OR_0/\epsilon OR_0}{(\partial OR_0/\epsilon OR_0 + \partial OR_0/\epsilon OR_1)} \tag{4}$$

$$Sensitivity = \frac{\partial OR_1/EOR_1}{(\partial OR_1/\epsilon OR_0 + \partial OR_1/\epsilon OR_1)} \tag{5}$$

$$False\ Positive\ Ratio = 1 - Specificity \tag{6}$$

$$False\ Negitive\ Ratio = 1 - Senstivity \tag{7}$$

$$Likelihood\ Ratio\ Positive = \frac{Sensitivity}{(1 - Specificity)} \tag{8}$$

$$Likelihood\ Ratio\ Negative = \frac{(1 - \ Sensitivity)}{Specificity} \tag{9}$$

In the formulas shown above, ∂OR_0 reflects the predicted non-defective modules, and ∂OR_1 reflects the predicted defective modules, whereas ϵOR_0 reflects the expected non-defective modules, and ϵOR_1 reflects the expected defective modules.

To train the NB classifier, the reserved training dataset consisting of 2506 instances was used. During the training process, 1948 instances were classified as negative out of 2206 instances, whereas 107 instances were classified as positive out of 300 instances. After analyzing and comparing the output result and expected result in Table 3, we achieved 82% accuracy in the training process with NB. During the process of testing with NB, 872 instances were predicted as negative out of 945, whereas 22 instances were predicted as positive out of 128. The comparison of the expected result and output result in Table 4 reflects that 83.32% accuracy was achieved during testing with NB.

Table 3. NB training.

N = 2506 (No. of Records)		**Predicted Result ∂OR_0, ∂OR_1**	
	Expected output result (ϵOR_0, ϵOR_1)	∂OR_0 (Non-defective -0)	∂OR_1 (Defective -1)
INPUT	ϵOR_0 = 2206 (Non-defective -0)	1948	258
	ϵOR_1 = 300 (Defective -1)	193	107

Table 4. NB Testing.

N = 1073 (No. of Records)		**Predicted Result ∂OR_0, ∂OR_1**	
	Expected output result (ϵOR_0, ϵOR_1)	∂OR_0 (Non-defective -0)	∂OR_1 (Defective -1)
INPUT	ϵOR_0 = 945 (Non-defective -0)	872	73
	ϵOR_1 = 128 (Defective -1)	106	22

During the training of ANN, 2100 instances out of 2206 were classified as negative, and 56 instances out of 300 were classified as positive. The training accuracy achieved with ANN was 86.03 % (Table 5). During the testing process, 905 instances were predicted as negative out of 945, and 16 instances were predicted as positive out of 128. The comparison of the expected output and achieved output in Table 6 reflects an 85.83% accuracy.

Table 5. ANN training.

N = 2506 (No. of Records)		**Predicted Result ∂OR_0, ∂OR_1**	
INPUT	Expected output result (ϵOR_0, ϵOR_1)	∂OR_0 (Non-defective -0)	∂OR_1 (Defective -1)
	$\epsilon OR_0 = 2206$ (Non-defective -0)	2100	106
	$\epsilon OR_1 = 300$ (Defective -1)	244	56

Table 6. ANN Testing.

N = 1073 (No. of Records)		**Predicted Result ∂OR_0, ∂OR_1**	
INPUT	Expected output result (ϵOR_0, ϵOR_1)	∂OR_0 (Non-defective -0)	∂OR_1 (Defective -1)
	$\epsilon OR_0 = 945$ (Non-defective -0)	905	40
	$\epsilon OR_1 = 128$ (Defective -1)	112	16

In the training process with DT, 2073 instances out of 2206 were classified as negative, and 199 instances out of 300 were classified as positive. The output result and expected result are shown in Table 7. After comparing both the results, we achieved 90.66% accuracy. During the testing process, DT classified 887 records out of 945 records as negative, whereas 26 records out of 128 were classified as positive. The comparison of the expected output and achieved output in Table 8 reflects an accuracy of 85.09%.

Table 7. DT training.

N = 2506 (No. of Records)		**Predicted Result ∂OR_0, ∂OR_1**	
INPUT	Expected output result (ϵOR_0, ϵOR_1)	∂OR_0 (Non-defective -0)	∂OR_1 (Defective -1)
	$\epsilon OR_0 = 2206$ (Non-defective -0)	2073	133
	$\epsilon OR_1 = 300$ (Defective -1)	101	199

Table 8. DT testing.

N = 1073 (No. of Records)		**Predicted Result ∂OR_0, ∂OR_1**	
INPUT	Expected output result (ϵOR_0, ϵOR_1)	∂OR_0 (Non-defective -0)	∂OR_1 (Defective -1)
	$\epsilon OR_0 = 945$ (Non-defective -0)	887	58
	$\epsilon OR_1 = 128$ (Defective -1)	102	26

Finally, the test data were subjected to the proposed fuzzy system, along with the three predictions provided by the classifiers. The proposed FSDPS classifies the testing data on the basis of the developed fuzzy rules. The fuzzy rules were developed by keeping in mind the achieved accuracy of the classification models for the test data. The proposed fused system classified 935 out of 945 records as negative, whereas 42 instances out of 128 were classified as positive. The expected results are compared with the achieved results in Table 9, which reflects a 91.05% accuracy.

Table 9. Fused testing.

N = 1073 (No. of Records)		**Predicted Result ∂OR_0, ∂OR_1**	
INPUT	Expected output result (ϵOR_0, ϵOR_1)	∂OR_0 (Non-defective -0)	∂OR_1 (Defective -1)
	$\epsilon OR_0 = 945$ (Non-defective -0)	935	10
	$\epsilon OR_1 = 128$ (Defective -1)	86	42

The detailed results of the used classifiers, along with the result of the proposed fusion-based system, are shown in Table 10. The results of NB, ANN, and DT for the training and test datasets are shown, whereas only the results of the proposed FSDPS for the test dataset are shown. The used classifiers were tuned multiple times until we achieved the maximum accuracy. The proposed fusion-based system outperformed the other used classifiers. The accuracy of NB, ANN and DT for the test datasets was 83.32%, 85.83%, and 85.09%, respectively, whereas the proposed system outperformed all three techniques and achieved a 91.05% accuracy for the test dataset. It can be observed that the proposed fusion-based defect prediction system showed a significantly higher performance, as it integrated the predictive accuracy of all three classifiers using the fuzzy logic technique.

Table 10. ML Algorithm Comparison.

ML Algorithm	**Dataset**	**Accuracy**	**Specificity**	**Sensitivity**	**Positive Prediction Value**	**Negative Prediction Value**	**False Positive Value**	**False Negative Value**	**Likelihood Ratio Positive**	**Likelihood Ratio Negative**
Naïve Bayes	Training	0.8200	0.8830	0.3567	0.2932	0.9099	0.1170	0.6433	3.049	0.8200
	Testing	0.8332	0.9228	0.1719	0.2316	0.8916	0.0772	0.8281	2.225	0.8332
Artificial neural network	Training	0.8603	0.9519	0.1867	0.3456	0.8959	0.0481	0.8133	3.885	0.8603
	Testing	0.8583	0.9577	0.125	0.2857	0.8899	0.0423	0.875	2.953	0.8583
Decision tree	Training	0.9066	0.9397	0.6633	0.5994	0.9535	0.0603	0.3367	11.00	0.9066
	Testing	0.8509	0.9386	0.2031	0.3095	0.8969	0.0614	0.7969	3.310	0.8509
Fused/proposed method	Testing	0.9105	0.9894	0.3281	0.8077	0.9158	0.0106	0.6719	31.01	0.9087

The accuracy of the proposed FSDPS is compared with that of other state-of-the-art software defect prediction techniques in Table 11. It can be observed that the proposed system performed better than the other techniques using the fused dataset, and achieved 91.05% accuracy. Training a classification model on a fused dataset is a complex process, and is considered a challenging task compared to the training of a model on a single-source dataset. It has been observed that the pattern recognition ability of machine learning methods for prediction can be enhanced by using the fuzzy logic technique [24]. The high accuracy achieved by the proposed system for the fused dataset reflects the effectiveness of fuzzy logic-based machine learning fusion techniques.

Table 11. Performance comparison of the proposed ISDPS with the other techniques.

Prediction Technique	Accuracy (%)
Stacked ensemble [9]	89.10
Fused-ANN-BR [11]	85.45
FS-VEML [12]	84.97
Boosting-OPT-MLP [13]	79.08
MLP-FS [14]	85.13
NB [18]	82.65
ANN [25]	89.96
Tree [25]	84.94
Bagging [26]	80.20
Boosting [26]	81.30
Heterogeneous [27]	89.20
ADBBO-RBFNN [28]	88.65
Bagging LWL [29]	90.10
Proposed FSDPS	91.05

5. Threat to Validity

The threat to validity is a crucial aspect of any proposed research. According to [30], it is important to explicitly analyze and mitigate threats to the validity of the proposed solution.

External validity: This type of validity analyzes whether the proposed solution is equally effective for other datasets belonging to the same problem canvas. In this study, five widely used benchmark software defect datasets, including CM1, MW1, PC1, PC3, and PC4, were fused to implement the proposed FSDPS. The datasets were taken from NASA's cleaned software defect repository. All of the five datasets have the same attributes, which is necessary for instance-level fusion. The conclusion of this study cannot be generalized to other defect datasets. However, the comprehensive experimental setup, along with the iterative parameter tuning used in this study, can be adopted by other researchers using other datasets.

Internal validity: This form of validity analyzes whether the selected prediction techniques are good enough for the selected datasets or for other datasets used to address the same problem. According to [31], various factors, including the datasets, prediction techniques, and software tools, can affect the internal validity of a software defect prediction system. In this study, three supervised classification techniques were used in the proposed FSDPS, including NB, ANN, and DT. These techniques were selected on the basis of their heterogeneity and performance. Moreover, a fuzzy logic-based fusion technique was proposed to integrate the predictive accuracy of the used classification techniques. In future studies, researchers could use other classification algorithms with different fuzzy logic techniques.

Construct validity: This form of validity concerns the selection of the performance measures that are used to analyze the performance of the proposed system. In this research, various performance measures were calculated, including the accuracy, specificity, sensitivity, positive prediction value, negative prediction value, false-positive value, false-negative value, likelihood ratio positive, and likelihood ratio negative. However, among all of the calculated performance measures, the accuracy was used to compare the performance of the proposed FSDPS with respect to the other techniques.

6. Conclusions and Future Work

Software defect prediction involves the detection of faulty modules before the testing stage so that only defect-prone modules will be subjected to testing. An effective defect prediction system can decrease software development costs by limiting the effort involved in quality assurance activities in the testing phase. In this research, we proposed a system for software defect prediction using data and decision-level machine learning fusion techniques. The proposed system fused the predictive accuracy of three supervised classifiers: NB, ANN, and DT. The accuracy was fused using fuzzy logic-based if–then rules. To empirically evaluate the proposed system, five cleaned software defect datasets from NASA's repository were integrated using instance-level fusion. The datasets which were fused for the experiments included CM1, MW1, PC1, PC3, and PC4. The experiments reflected the higher accuracy of the proposed fusion-based defect prediction system as compared to the other techniques. The proposed system outperformed the other techniques, which reflects the effectiveness and robustness of the proposed decision-level fusion technique. In future work, a feature selection technique should be incorporated into the system for a cost-effective solution. Ensemble machine learning should also be considered for the decision-level fusion. Moreover, workload prediction for the next time slot should also be performed so as to render cloud data services effective and efficient in software defect prediction.

Author Contributions: S.A. (Shabib Aftaband), S.A. (Sagheer Abbas) and M.A. fused the data, performed the analysis, and conducted the experiments. S.A. (Shabib Aftaband), M.A. and T.M.G. prepared the original draft. H.A.H., M.A.K. and M.A. performed the detailed review and editing. C.Y.Y. and M.A.K. performed the supervision. T.M.G., S.A. (Shabib Aftaband) and T.M.G. drafted the pictures and tables. S.A. (Shabib Aftaband), C.Y.Y., H.A.H. and M.A.K. performed the revision and improved the quality of the draft. All authors have read and agreed to the published version of the manuscript.

Funding: This work was supported by the Center for Cyber-Physical Systems, Khalifa University, under Grant 8474000137-RC1-C2PS-T5.

Institutional Review Board Statement: Not applicable.

Informed Consent Statement: Not applicable.

Data Availability Statement: The simulation files/data used to support the findings of this study are available from the corresponding author upon request.

Conflicts of Interest: The authors declare no conflict of interest.

References

1. Suresh Kumar, P.; Behera, H.S.; Nayak, J.; Naik, B. Bootstrap aggregation ensemble learning-based reliable approach for software defect prediction by using characterized code feature. *Innov. Syst. Softw. Eng.* **2021**, *17*, 355–379. [CrossRef]
2. Balogun, A.O.; Basri, S.; Abdulkadir, S.J.; Hashim, A.S. Performance analysis of feature selection methods in software defect prediction: A search method approach. *Appl. Sci.* **2019**, *9*, 2764. [CrossRef]
3. Balogun, A.O.; Basri, S.; Mahamad, S.; Abdulkadir, S.J.; Capretz, L.F.; Imam, A.A.; Almomani, M.A.; Adeyemo, V.E.; Kumar, G. Empirical analysis of rank aggregation-based multi-filter feature selection methods in software defect prediction. *Electronics* **2021**, *10*, 179. [CrossRef]
4. Huda, S.; Alyahya, S.; Ali, M.M.; Ahmad, S.; Abawajy, J.; Al-Dossari, H.; Yearwood, J. A framework for software defect prediction and metric selection. *IEEE Access* **2017**, *6*, 2844–2858. [CrossRef]
5. Song, Q.; Jia, Z.; Shepperd, M.; Ying, S.; Liu, J. A general software defect-proneness prediction framework. *IEEE Trans. Softw. Eng.* **2010**, *37*, 356–370. [CrossRef]
6. Zhang, Q.; Ren, J. Software-defect prediction within and across projects based on improved self-organizing data mining. *J. Supercomput.* **2021**, *78*, 6147–6173. [CrossRef]
7. Ibrahim, D.R.; Ghnemat, R.; Hudaib, A. Software defect prediction using feature selection and random forest algorithm. In Proceedings of the International Conference on New Trends in Computer Science, Amman, Jordan, 11–13 October 2017; pp. 252–257.

8. Mahajan, R.; Gupta, S.; Bedi, R.K. Design of software fault prediction model using br technique. *Procedia Comput. Sci.* **2015**, *46*, 849–858. [CrossRef]
9. Goyal, S.; Bhatia, P.K. Heterogeneous stacked ensemble classifier for software defect prediction. *Multimed. Tools Appl.* **2021**, *81*, 37033–37055. [CrossRef]
10. Mehta, S.; Patnaik, K.S. Stacking based ensemble learning for improved software defect prediction. In *Proceeding of Fifth International Conference on Microelectronics, Computing and Communication Systems*; Springer: Singapore, 2021; pp. 167–178.
11. Daoud, M.S.; Aftab, S.; Ahmad, M.; Khan, M.A.; Iqbal, A.; Abbas, S.; Ihnaini, B. machine learning empowered software defect prediction system. *Intell. Autom. Soft Comput.* **2022**, *31*, 1287–1300. [CrossRef]
12. Ali, U.; Aftab, S.; Iqbal, A.; Nawaz, Z.; Bashir, M.S.; Saeed, M.A. Software defect prediction using variant based ensemble learning and feature selection techniques. *Int. J. Mod. Educ. Comput. Sci.* **2020**, *12*, 29–40. [CrossRef]
13. Iqbal, A.; Aftab, S. Prediction of defect prone software modules using MLP based ensemble techniques. *Int. J. Inf. Technol. Comput. Sci.* **2020**, *12*, 26–31. [CrossRef]
14. Iqbal, A.; Aftab, S. A classification framework for software defect prediction using multi-filter feature selection technique and MLP. *Int. J. Mod. Educ. Comput. Sci.* **2020**, *12*, 42–55. [CrossRef]
15. Arasteh, B. Software fault-prediction using combination of neural network and Naive Bayes algorithm. *J. Netw. Technol.* **2018**, *9*, 95. [CrossRef]
16. Alsaeedi, A.; Khan, M.Z. Software defect prediction using supervised machine learning and ensemble techniques: A comparative study. *J. Softw. Eng. Appl.* **2019**, *12*, 85–100. [CrossRef]
17. Balogun, A.O.; Basri, S.; Capretz, L.F.; Mahamad, S.; Imam, A.A.; Almomani, M.A.; Kumar, G. software defect prediction using wrapper feature selection based on dynamic re-ranking strategy. *Symmetry* **2021**, *13*, 2166. [CrossRef]
18. Alsawalqah, H.; Hijazi, N.; Eshtay, M.; Faris, H.; Radaideh, A.A.; Aljarah, I.; Alshamaileh, Y. Software defect prediction using heterogeneous ensemble classification based on segmented patterns. *Appl. Sci.* **2020**, *10*, 1745. [CrossRef]
19. Bi, J.; Yuan, H.; Zhou, M. Temporal prediction of multiapplication consolidated workloads in distributed clouds. *IEEE Trans. Autom. Sci. Eng.* **2019**, *16*, 1763–1773. [CrossRef]
20. Shepperd, M.; Song, Q.; Sun, Z.; Mair, C. Data quality: Some comments on the NASA software defect datasets. *IEEE Trans. Softw. Eng.* **2013**, *39*, 1208–1215. [CrossRef]
21. NASA Defect Dataset. Available online: https://github.com/klainfo/NASADefectDataset (accessed on 17 September 2022).
22. Ahmed, U.; Issa, G.F.; Khan, M.A.; Aftab, S.; Khan, M.F.; Said, R.A.; Ghazal, T.M.; Ahmad, M. Prediction of diabetes empowered with fused machine learning. *IEEE Access* **2022**, *10*, 8529–8538. [CrossRef]
23. Rahman, A.U.; Abbas, S.; Gollapalli, M.; Ahmed, R.; Aftab, S.; Ahmad, M.; Khan, M.A.; Mosavi, A. Rainfall prediction system using machine learning fusion for smart cities. *Sensors* **2022**, *22*, 3504. [CrossRef]
24. Naeem, Z.; Farzan, M.; Naeem, F. Predicting the performance of governance factor using fuzzy inference system. *Int. J. Comput. Innov. Sci.* **2022**, *1*, 35–50.
25. Goyal, S.; Bhatia, P.K. Comparison of machine learning techniques for software quality prediction. *Int. J. Knowl. Syst. Sci.* **2020**, *11*, 20–40. [CrossRef]
26. Balogun, A.O.; Lafenwa-Balogun, F.B.; Mojeed, H.A.; Adeyemo, V.E.; Akande, O.N.; Akintola, A.G.; Bajeh, A.O.; Usman-Hamza, F.E. SMOTE-based homogeneous ensemble methods for software defect prediction. In *International Conference on Computational Science and Its Applications*; Springer: Cham, Switzerland, 2020; pp. 615–631.
27. Khuat, T.T.; Le, M.H. Evaluation of sampling-based ensembles of classifiers on imbalanced data for software defect prediction problems. *SN Comput. Sci.* **2020**, *1*, 108. [CrossRef]
28. Kumudha, P.; Venkatesan, R. Cost-sensitive radial basis function neural network classifier for software defect prediction. *Sci. World J.* **2016**, *11*, 126–134. [CrossRef] [PubMed]
29. Abdou, A.S.; Darwish, N.R. Early prediction of software defect using ensemble learning: A comparative study. *Int. J. Comput. Appl.* **2018**, *179*, 29–40.
30. Wohlin, C.; Runeson, P.; Höst, M.; Ohlsson, M.C.; Regnell, B.; Wesslén, A. *Experimentation in Software Engineering*; Springer Science & Business Media: Berlin/Heidelberg, Germany, 2012.
31. Gao, K.; Khoshgoftaar, T.M.; Seliya, N. Predicting high-risk program modules by selecting the right software measurements. *Softw. Qual. J.* **2012**, *20*, 3–42. [CrossRef]

mathematics

MDPI

Article

On Nash Equilibria in a Finite Game for Fuzzy Sets of Strategies

Svajone Bekesiene [1,*] and Serhii Mashchenko [2]

1 Logistics and Defense Technology Management Science Group, General Jonas Zemaitis Military Academy of Lithuania, Silo 5a, LT-10322 Vilnius, Lithuania
2 Department of System Analysis and Decision-Making Theory, Faculty of Computer Science and Cybernetics, Taras Shevchenko National University of Kyiv, 64/13, Volodymyrska Street, 01601 Kyiv, Ukraine
* Correspondence: svajone.bekesiene@lka.lt

Abstract: The present paper investigates a finite game with fuzzy sets of player strategies. It is proven that Nash equilibria constitute a type-2 fuzzy set defined on the universal set of strategy profiles. Furthermore, the corresponding type-2 membership function is provided. This paper demonstrates that the Nash equilibria type-2 fuzzy set of the game can be decomposed based on the secondary membership grades into a finite collection of crisp sets. Each of these crisp sets represents the Nash equilibria set of the corresponding game with crisp sets of player strategies. A characteristic feature of the proposed decomposition approach is its independence from the chosen method for calculating the Nash equilibria in crisp subgames. Some properties of game equilibria T2FSs are studied. These sets correspond to specific partitions or cuts of the original fuzzy sets of player strategies. An illustrative example is also included for clarity.

Keywords: game theory; Nash equilibrium; type-2 fuzzy set

MSC: 91A86

1. Introduction

In classical game theory, it is traditionally assumed that all the data of a game are precisely known. However, in real-world scenarios, a notable feature of games is the inherent uncertainty and inaccuracy of available information. To address this issue, one powerful tool for modeling uncertainty is the theory of fuzzy sets (FSs).

Fuzzy sets allow for the representation of imprecise or vague data within various components of a game model. These components include the sets of players, sets of strategies, payoffs of players, and more. Early pioneers such as Orlovskii [1], Butnariu [2–4], and Billot [5] were among the first to introduce fuzzy sets into the realm of non-cooperative games. Orlovskii, for instance, leveraged the principle of decision-making in a fuzzy environment, as outlined by Zadeh and Bellman [6], to defuzzify game-related concepts. Building on the work of Butnariu [2–4] and Billot [5], other researchers have explored the modeling of each player's beliefs about the actions of other players in a fuzzy set form.

Additionally, Campos [7] made significant contributions by delving into non-cooperative games with fuzzy payoffs. Campos' approach is founded on a ranking method of fuzzy numbers to defuzzify the game. By utilizing Yager's ordering method [8] for fuzzy numbers, Campos transformed the challenge of finding a solution for a fuzzy matrix game into a linear programming problem.

In the context of fuzzy non-cooperative games, the Nash equilibrium, much like in scenarios with crisp information, remains a fundamental principle of optimality. Notably, this article focuses on aspects other than fuzzy matrix games; for those interested in exploring this subject further, a detailed review is available in [9]. Generalizations of the Nash equilibrium concept have primarily been cultivated within the domain of bimatrix games featuring fuzzy payoffs. This inclination can be attributed to the wealth of well-established methods for constructing Nash equilibria in the realm of crisp bimatrix games.

One notable approach, advanced by Vijay et al. [10], leverages the theory of fuzzy duality and employs a ranking function for fuzzy numbers to calculate equilibria in bimatrix games with fuzzy payoffs. This innovative methodology ultimately leads to the formulation of a fuzzy nonlinear programming problem, which is subsequently defuzzified.

When player payoffs are expressed as triangular fuzzy numbers, Maeda [11] introduces a method employing fuzzy number ranking to convert the computation of Nash equilibria into a crisp optimization problem whenever feasible. In the context of games involving n-players, there has been a development that delves into non-cooperative games featuring fuzzy parameters. Notably, in [12], a game is examined wherein payoffs depend on certain parameters expressed as fuzzy numbers. These parameters reflect the influence of nature, and the players possess full information, including knowledge of the membership functions of the fuzzy parameters. The approach to solving such a game draws upon methods designed for addressing multicriteria problems with fuzzy parameters, as originally proposed in [13].

It is essential to acknowledge that the body of research in the domain of games with fuzzy payoffs significantly outweighs the research conducted in games featuring fuzzy sets of strategies. This disparity, in our view, can be attributed to the advancements in fuzzy arithmetic, which have made it relatively straightforward to introduce fuzzification in games with fuzzy payoffs. However, it is important to note that, in both fuzzy optimization problems and games, models with fuzzy parameters cannot entirely supplant models utilizing fuzzy sets of strategies. The exploration of game models involving fuzzy sets of strategies is warranted when such sets more naturally and effectively formalize the strategic choices made by players.

Additionally, there are instances where players are unable to precisely formulate their sets of strategies. The foundations of the approach to studying games with fuzzy strategies and fuzzy sets of strategies were established by Orlovskii [1], Butnariu [2–4], and Billot [5]. In [1], a two-person game with FSs of strategies and players' goals is examined. For each player, crisp numerical assessments of game strategic profiles are provided. The players' goals are expressed in the form of FSs over the set of assessments. The game model is grounded in Bellman and Zade's [6] principle of decision-making in a fuzzy environment. For each player, a decision FS is defined as the intersection of the FSs representing the goal and strategies. In a defuzzified game, the membership functions (MFs) of decision FSs serve as the players' payoff functions. A similar fuzzy game model is also explored in Aristidou and Sarangi [14]. The concept of equilibrium in this context aligns with the Nash equilibrium, with the sole distinction that it is defined within a fuzzy extension of the game. The existence of an equilibrium in a fuzzy game is demonstrated. Garazic and Cruz [15] propose an approach grounded in the development of fuzzy controllers. According to Arfi [16], a linguistic fuzzy game is defined utilizing linguistic fuzzy strategies, linguistic fuzzy preferences, and various forms of reasoning and inference. While it is important to acknowledge that this review is not exhaustive in its coverage of the existing literature, it is evident that models involving FSs of strategies and/or fuzzy strategies incorporate them indirectly by leveraging the Bellman and Zadeh approach or various types of preference relations in tandem with fuzzy goals.

We believe that the adoption of these alternative approaches arises from a lack of mathematical methods that directly facilitate the study of the impact of fuzzy sets of players' strategies on a set of Nash equilibria. This research is motivated by the aspiration to develop the requisite methodology and derive the corresponding outcomes. It is important to note that the research conducted is fundamentally theoretical in nature. Practical applications of these findings warrant a separate investigation and fall beyond the scope of this article. The primary objectives of this article can be summarized as follows:

- To establish a rationale for the assertion that fuzzy sets (FSs) of players' strategies in a finite game give rise to a type-2 fuzzy set (T2FS) of Nash equilibria, characterized by a specific, simplified form that is practical for real-world applications, as opposed to the general form T2FS.

- To conduct an in-depth examination of the properties of this T2FS.
- To develop a decomposition method for the construction of Nash equilibria T2FS.
- The practical significance of this research lies in its capacity to:
- Explore game scenarios in which the adoption of crisp strategies constrains players' abilities to effectively resolve conflicts. Example 1 in Section 5.4 provides insight into such a scenario.
- Enable the modeling of uncertainty inherent in human judgments and the uncertainty associated with determining acceptable strategies. Such FSs of strategies might encompass categories like 'Proven strategies', 'Robust strategies', 'Acceptable strategies', and similar distinctions.

Finally, this article presents a compelling argument for the incorporation of FSs of player strategies in a game, highlighting that they give rise to Nash equilibria in the form of a T2FS defined over the set of strategy profiles. This approach not only enriches the modeling of strategic interactions but also provides a more nuanced perspective on decision-making in situations characterized by imprecision and ambiguity. Through this exploration, we contribute to the growing body of research at the intersection of game theory and fuzzy logic, further enhancing our understanding of strategic behavior in complex, uncertain environments.

2. Materials and Methods

2.1. A Classic Finite Game

A finite non-cooperative game can be formally represented in the normal form $\langle X_i, u_i : i \in N \rangle$, where $N = \{1, \ldots, n\}$ is the finite set of players; $n = |N| \geq 2$ is the cardinality of this set; X_i is the finite set of strategies x_i of the player $i \in N$; $u_i(x)$ is the payoff function of the player $i \in N$, which is defined on the set $X = \prod_{i \in N} X_i$ of the strategies profiles $x = (x_1, \ldots, x_n) = (x_i)_{i \in N}$.

A Nash equilibrium of the game $\langle X_i, u_i : i \in N \rangle$ is the strategies profile $\hat{x} = (\hat{x}_1, \ldots, \hat{x}_n) = (\hat{x}_i)_{i \in N}$ for which the inequalities

$$u_i(\hat{x}) \geq u_i(x_i, \hat{x}_{N \backslash i}) \text{ for all } x_i \in X_i \text{ and } i \in N \tag{1}$$

hold, where $\hat{x}_{N \backslash i} = (\hat{x}_1, \ldots, \hat{x}_{i-1}, \hat{x}_{i+1} \ldots, \hat{x}_n) = (\hat{x}_j)_{j \in N \backslash \{i\}}$ is the collection of strategies of the players $j \in N \backslash \{i\}$. The choice of the strategy $\hat{x}_i$ by each player $i \in N$ seems reasonable. Indeed, it is not profitable to deviate from these strategies for each of them individually. We denote by $NE(X)$ the set of Nash equilibria of the game $\langle X_i, u_i : i \in N \rangle$.

2.2. Type-2 Fuzzy Sets

The T2FS concept was proposed by Zadeh in [17] as an extension of the type-1 fuzzy sets (T1FSs). According to Mizumoto and Tanaka [18], a T2FS, denoted by $\tilde{C}$, on a crisp set X is characterized by the fuzzy membership function $M_{\tilde{C}} : X \to [0,1]^{[0,1]}$. For fixed $x' \in X$, the value of $M_{\tilde{C}}(x')$ is the T1FS $M_{\tilde{C}}(x') = \left\{(u, \mu_{\tilde{M}_{\tilde{C}}(x')}(u)) : u \in U_{x'}\right\}$ on the set $U_{x'} \subseteq [0,1]$ of primary membership degrees u of x' to the T2FS $\tilde{C}$ with corresponding membership function $\mu_{\tilde{M}_{\tilde{C}}(x')}(u)$, $u \in U_{x'}$. In [19], the representation of the T2FS $\tilde{C}$ in the form $\tilde{C} = \{(x, \tilde{M}_{\tilde{C}}(x')) : x \in X\} = \left\{(x, \left\{(u, \mu_{\tilde{M}_{\tilde{C}}(x)}(u)) : u \in U_x\right\}) : x \in X\right\}$ is called the vertical-slice manner.

Another definition, based on the ideas of Karnik and Mendel [20], was given by Mendel and John [21]. A T2FS $\tilde{C}$ on a crisp set $\tilde{X}$ is characterized by the type-2 membership function (T2MF) $\eta_{\tilde{C}}(x, u)$, that is $\tilde{C} = \{((x, u), \eta_{\tilde{C}}(x, u)) : x \in X, u \in [0,1]\}$, where $\eta_{\tilde{C}}(x, u) = \mu_{\tilde{M}_{\tilde{C}}(x)}(u)$ for all $u \in U_x$, and $\eta_{\tilde{C}}(x, u) = 0$ for all $u \notin U_x$. The value $\eta_{\tilde{C}}(x, u)$ is a crisp number from the interval [0, 1], known as a secondary grade of pair (x, u) to $\tilde{C}$.

Remark 1. *The primary membership degree u is usually understood as the degree of manifestation of some property (that defines the given fuzzy set) for $x \in X$. The secondary grade is usually [19] associated with the degree of truth of the corresponding primary degree u of this property for x.*

Following [21], we define embedded T2FSs and T1FSs for a T2FS $\tilde{C} = \{((x,u), \eta_{\tilde{C}}(x,u)) : x \in X, u \in [0,1]\}$. Assume that $u_x = \mu_{C^{e1}}(x) \in [0,1]$ is a unique primary degree of membership for each $x \in X$, where $\mu_{C^{e1}}(x)$, $x \in X$ is the MF of the T1FS $C^{e1} = \{(x, \mu_{C^{e1}}(x)) : x \in X\}$. This T1FS is called embedded in the T2FS $\tilde{C}$. We define the embedded T2FS $\tilde{C}^{e2}$ in $\tilde{C}$ in the form $\tilde{C}^{e2} = \{((x,u_x), \eta_{\tilde{C}^{e2}}(x,u_x)) : x \in X\}$ with $\eta_{\tilde{C}^{e2}}(x,u_x) = \eta_{\tilde{C}}(x, \mu_{C^{e1}}(x))$ for all $x \in X$.

Remark 2. *Each element of the type-2 fuzzy collection $\tilde{C} = \{((x,u), \eta_{\tilde{C}}(x,u)) : x \in X, u \in [0,1]\}$ is interpreted as a subset. Thus, the collection is represented as the classical union of its elements in the sense of T1FSs.*

In [21], Mendel and John stated that each T2FS can be represented as a collection of all possible embedded T2FSs. We shall need one special case of a T2FS to be defined according to [22–25]. Let $A = \{\eta_{\tilde{C}}(x,u) : \eta_{\tilde{C}}(x,u) > 0, x \in X, u \in [0,1]\}$ be the set of all possible positive values of secondary grades for the T2FS $\tilde{C} = \{((x,u), \eta_{\tilde{C}}(x,u)) : x \in X, u \in [0,1]\}$. Assume that the set A is finite.

According to [22], an embedded T2FS $\tilde{C}^{e2}(\alpha) = \left\{((x,u_x), \eta_{\tilde{C}^{e2}(\alpha)}(x,u_x)) : x \in X\right\}$ in the T2FS $\tilde{C}$ has a constant secondary grade $\alpha \in A$ if, for each $x \in X$, the unique primary degree $u_x = \mu_{C^{e1}(\alpha)}(x) \in [0,1]$ exists for which $\eta_{\tilde{C}^{e2}(\alpha)}(x,u_x) \equiv \alpha$, i.e., $\tilde{C}^{e2}(\alpha) = \left\{((x, \mu_{C^{e1}(\alpha)}(x)), \alpha) : x \in X\right\}$. Here, $\mu_{C^{e1}(\alpha)}(x)$, $x \in X$ is the MF of the embedded T1FS $C^{e1}(\alpha) = \left\{(x, \mu_{C^{e1}(\alpha)}(x)) : x \in X\right\}$ in the T2FS $\tilde{C}$.

Remark 3 ([25]). *Obviously, for the T2FS $\tilde{C}$ and each $\alpha \in A$, there is the unique embedded T1FS $C^{e1}(\alpha) = \left\{(x, \mu_{C^{e1}(\alpha)}(x)) : x \in X\right\}$, which is corresponding to the embedded T2FS $\tilde{C}^{e2}$ (α) with the constant secondary grade α. Hence, $\tilde{C}^{e2}(\alpha) = \{(C^{e1}(\alpha), \alpha)\} = \left\{(\left\{(x, \mu_{C^{e1}(\alpha)}(x)) : x \in X\right\}, \alpha)\right\} = \left\{((x, \mu_{C^{e1}(\alpha)}(x)), \alpha) : x \in X\right\}$.*

Further, we consider another special case of a T2FS.

Definition 1. *We say that the T2FS $\tilde{C}$ is decomposable by secondary grades into a collection of embedded T2FSs with constant secondary grades if there are the T2FSs $\tilde{C}^{e2}(\alpha) = \left\{((x, \mu_{C^{e1}(\alpha)}(x)), \alpha) : x \in X\right\} = \{(C^{e1}(\alpha), \alpha)\}$ with constant secondary grades $\alpha \in A$, respectively, which are embedded in the T2FS $\tilde{C}$ satisfying $\tilde{C} = \{\tilde{C}^{e2}(\alpha) : \alpha \in A\}$.*

Remark 4. *In view of Remark 3, if the T2FS $\tilde{C}$ is decomposable by secondary grades $\alpha \in A$ into the collection $\tilde{C} = \{C^{e2}(\alpha) : \alpha \in A\}$ of embedded T2FSs with constant secondary grades, then the T2FS $\tilde{C}$ is represented as a collection $\tilde{C} = \{(C^{e1}(\alpha), \alpha) : \alpha \in A\}$ of embedded T1FSs $C^{e1}(\alpha)$, $\alpha \in A$, each of which is assigned the constant secondary grade $\alpha \in A$, respectively.*

3. Formulation of the Problem

Consider a finite non-cooperative game in the normal form $\langle X_i, u_i : i \in N \rangle$.

Assumption 1. *Assume that the game $\langle X_i, u_i : i \in N \rangle$ has at least one Nash equilibrium in pure strategies, that is $NE(X) \neq \varnothing$.*

Let $\tilde{X}_i = \left\{(x, \mu_{\tilde{X}_i}(x_i)) : x_i \in X_i\right\}$, $i \in N$ be some FSs with the MFs $\mu_{\tilde{X}_i}(x_i)$, $x_i \in X_i$ $i \in N$ on the sets X_i of pure strategies of players $i \in N$, respectively. We shall call $\tilde{X}_i$, $i \in N$ the FSs of strategies. We represent a game with FSs of strategies in the normal form

$\langle \tilde{X}_i, u_i : i \in N \rangle$. A natural question is: 'When is there a need for such game formulation?' To answer this question, we consider the following examples. Suppose that some decision maker (DM) is trying to predict the outcome of a conflict between players, which can be formulated as some classical finite game with crisp sets of player strategies. The issue is that the DM only knows the degrees of membership of the player strategies to some FSs of their strategies. The following question arises: 'What is the set of Nash equilibria in the case when the sets of players' strategies are fuzzy?'

4. Main Idea

First, we generalize inequalities (1) for the case of arbitrary subsets $S_i \subseteq X_i$, $i \in N$ of strategies. They take the form

$$u_i(\hat{x}) \geq u_i(x_i, \hat{x}_{N\setminus i}) \text{ for all } x_i \in S_i \text{ and } i \in N. \tag{2}$$

We denote by $S = \prod_{i \in N} S_i \subseteq X$ the set of the strategy profiles. The subsets $S_i \subseteq X_i$, $i \in N$ of strategies are parameters of inequalities (2) that the sets of constraints depend upon. In addition, for the game $G(S) = \langle S_i, u_i : i \in N \rangle$, we denote by

$$NE(S) = \left\{ (x, \mu_{NE(S)}(x)) : x \in X \right\} \tag{3}$$

the crisp set of Nash equilibria with the MF characteristic function

$$\mu_{NE(S)}(x) = \begin{cases} 1, & u_i(x) \geq u_i(y_i, x_{N\setminus i}) \text{ for all } y_i \in S_i \text{ and } i \in N; \\ 0, & \text{otherwise;} \end{cases} \tag{4}$$

and with the support $\text{supp}(NE(S)) = \left\{ x \in S : \mu_{NE(S)}(x) = 1 \right\}$ of the set $NE(S)$.

Remark 5. *We use the MF (4) representation of a crisp set of Nash equilibria for the convenience of presenting the proposed method.*

For each fixed strategy profile $x \in X = \prod_{i \in N} X_i$ of the initial game $\langle X_i, u_i : i \in N \rangle$, consider the mapping $V^x : 2^S \to [0,1]$ given by

$$V^x(S) = \begin{cases} 1, & x \in \text{supp}(NE(S)); \\ 0, & \text{otherwise;} \end{cases} \tag{5}$$

$S = \prod_{i \in N} S_i$, $S_i \subseteq X_i$, $i \in N$. For any strategic profile $x \in X$, the mapping V^x associates each collection of the subsets $S_i \subseteq X_i$, $i \in N$ of strategies with the value of the MF

$$\mu_{NE(S)}(x) = V^x(S),\ x \in \text{supp}(NE(S)) = \{ x \in X : V^z(S) \neq 0 \} \tag{6}$$

of the crisp set of Nash equilibria $NE(S)$. With Zadeh's extension principle [26] at hand, we extend the domain of the mapping V^x to the collection of FSs $\tilde{X}_i = \left\{ (x, \mu_{\tilde{X}_i}(x_i)) : x_i \in X_i \right\}$, $i \in N$ of strategies that are defined on universal sets X_i, $i \in N$ of strategies, respectively, and generalize formulae (3) and (6) to this case. We denote by $\tilde{E}$ a set of Nash equilibria of the game $\langle \tilde{X}_i, u_i : i \in N \rangle$ for FSs of strategies, and we denote by $M_{\tilde{E}}(x)$, $x \in X$ the corresponding MF. In this case, for each fixed $x = x^*$, the value of the MF $M_{\tilde{E}}(x)$ coincides with the image $V^{x^*}(\tilde{X})$ of the FS $\tilde{X} = \prod_{i \in N} \tilde{X}_i$ of strategies profiles under the mapping V^{x^*}, that is,

$$M_{\tilde{E}}(x^*) = V^{x^*}(\tilde{X}). \tag{7}$$

According to Zadeh's extension principle [26], the image of the FS $\tilde{X}$ of strategies profiles under the mapping $V^{x^*} : 2^X \to [0,1]$ (see (5)) is the FS

$$V^{x^*}(\tilde{X}) = \left\{(u, \mu_{V^{x^*}(\tilde{X})}(u)) : u \in \{0,1\}\right\} \tag{8}$$

with the MF

$$\mu_{V^{x^*}(\tilde{X})}(u) = \max\left\{\min_{i\in N}\{\alpha_i\} : \alpha_i \in [0,1];\ u = V^{x^*}(X(\alpha))\right\} \tag{9}$$

$u \in \mathrm{supp}(V^{x^*}(X(\alpha)))$, where

$$\mathrm{supp}(V^{x^*}(X(\alpha)) = \left\{u \in \{0,1\} :\ u = V^{x^*}(X(\alpha)); \alpha = (\alpha_i),\ \alpha_i \in [0,1],\ i \in N\right\} \tag{10}$$

is the support of the FS $V^{x^*}(X(\alpha))$;

$X(\alpha) = \prod_{i\in N} X_i(\alpha)$ is the set of strategies profiles of the game $G(X(\alpha)) = \langle X_i(\alpha), u_i : i \in N\rangle$;

$X_i(\alpha_i) = \left\{x_i \in X_i : \mu_{\tilde{X}_i}(x_i) \geq \alpha_i\right\}$ is the α_i-cut, $\alpha_i \in [0,1]$ of the FS $\tilde{X}_i = \left\{(x, \mu_{\tilde{X}_i}(x_i)) : x_i \in X_i\right\}$ of strategies of the player $i \in N$;

$\alpha = (\alpha_i)_{i\in N}$ is the vector of α_i-cuts levels, $\alpha_i \in [0,1], i \in N$ of strategies FSs;

$$V^{x^*}(X(\alpha)) = \mu_{NE(X(\alpha))}(x^*) \tag{11}$$

is the image of the collection of cuts $X_i(\alpha_i) = \left\{x_i \in X_i : \mu_{\tilde{X}_i}(x_i) \geq \alpha_i\right\}, \alpha_i \in [0,1], i \in N$ of the FSs $\tilde{X}_i, i \in N$ of strategies under the mapping V^{x^*} (see Equation (6)).

Remark 6. *Let* $\Omega_i = \left\{\mu_{\tilde{X}_i}(x_i) : x_i \in X_i\right\}$, $i \in N$ *be the sets of membership degrees values* $\mu_{\tilde{X}_i}(x_i)$, $x_i \in X_i$, $i \in N$ *of the FSs* $\tilde{X}_i = \left\{(x, \mu_{\tilde{X}_i}(x_i)) : x_i \in X_i\right\}$, $i \in N$ *of strategies, respectively. Note that the cardinalities of the sets* Ω_i, $i \in N$ *are* $|\Omega_i| \leq |X_i|$, $i \in N$, *respectively. It is clear that when obtaining* α_i*-cuts,* $\alpha_i \in [0,1]$, $i \in N$ *of the FS* $\tilde{X}_i$, $i \in N$ *we can assume that* $\alpha_i \in \Omega_i$, $i \in N$ *rather than* $\alpha_i \in \Omega_i$, $i \in N$, *respectively.*

Thus, in view of (7)–(11) and Remark 6, for fixed $x = x^*$, the values of the MF $M_{\tilde{E}}(x^*)$ form the FS $\left\{(u, \mu_{M_{\tilde{E}}(x^*)}(u)) : u \in \{0,1\}\right\}$ on $\{0,1\}$ with the MF $\mu_{M_{\tilde{E}}(x^*)}(u) = \max\left\{\min_{i\in N}\alpha_i :\ \alpha_i \in \Omega_i,\ i \in N,\ u = V^{x^*}(X(\alpha))\right\}, u \in \mathrm{supp}(M_{\tilde{E}}(x^*))$, where $\mathrm{supp}(M_{\tilde{E}}(x^*)) = \left\{u \in \{0,1\} :\ u = V^{x^*}(X(\alpha)),\ \alpha_i \in \Omega_i,\ i \in N\right\}$ is the support of the FS $M_{\tilde{E}}(x^*)$. Then, invoking (10) and (11) yields

$$\begin{aligned} &\mu_{M_{\tilde{E}}(x^*)}(u) = \max\left\{\min_{i\in N}\alpha_i :\ \alpha_i \in \Omega_i,\ i \in N,\ u = \mu_{NE(X(\alpha))}(x^*)\right\}, \\ &u \in \mathrm{supp}(M_{\tilde{E}}(x^*)) = \left\{u \in \{0,1\} : u = \mu_{NE(X(\alpha))}(x^*),\ \alpha_i \in \Omega_i,\ i \in N\right\}. \end{aligned} \tag{12}$$

Therefore, we conclude that the set of Nash equilibria $\tilde{E}$ is an FS on X with the MF whose values form FSs on $\{0,1\}$ for each $x \in X$. Then, according to [17], $\tilde{E}$ is the T2FS on X. In the manner of vertical slices (see Section 2.2), the T2FS $\tilde{E}$ on X has the form $\tilde{E} = \{(x, M_{\tilde{E}}(x)) : x \in X\} = \left\{(x, \left\{(u, \mu_{M_{\tilde{E}}(x)}(u)) :\ u \in U_x\right\}) :\ x \in X\right\}$. In this formula, $\mu_{M_{\tilde{E}}(x)}(u), u \in \{0,1\}$ is the MF of the FS $M_{\tilde{E}}(x) = \left\{\left\{(u, \mu_{M_{\tilde{E}}(x)}(u)) :\ u \in \{0,1\}\right\}\right.$ of values of fuzzy degree of membership of the strategies profile $x \in X$ to the T2FS $\tilde{E}$, and $U_x = \mathrm{supp}(M_{\tilde{E}}(x))$ is the set of primary membership degrees, where $\mathrm{supp}(M_{\tilde{E}}(z))$ is the support of the FS $M_{\tilde{E}}(x)$ for $x \in X$. According to Section 2.2, we can also characterize the T2FS $\tilde{E}$ by means of the T2MF $\eta_{\tilde{E}}(x,u) = 0$ for $u \notin U_x$ and $\eta_{\tilde{E}}(x,u) = \max\left\{\min_{i\in N}\alpha_i : \alpha_i \in \Omega_i,\ i \in N,\ u = \mu_{NE(X(\alpha))}(x)\right\}$ for $u \in U_x$. This conclusion allows us to introduce the following notion.

Definition 2. *By the set of Nash equilibria of the game* $\langle \tilde{X}_i, u_i : i \in N\rangle$ *for the FSs* $\tilde{X}_i = \left\{(x, \mu_{\tilde{X}_i}(x_i)) : x_i \in X_i\right\}$ *of strategies is meant the T2FS*

$$\tilde{E} = \{((x,u), \eta_{\tilde{E}}(x,u)) :\ u \in \{0,1\},\ x \in X\} \tag{13}$$

on X with the T2MF

$$\eta_{\tilde{E}}(x,u) = \begin{cases} \max\left\{\min_{i\in N}\alpha_i :\ \alpha_i \in \Omega_i,\ i \in N,\ u = \mu_{NE(X(\alpha))}(x^*)\right\}, & u \in U_x; \\ 0, & u \notin U_x. \end{cases} \tag{14}$$

In this definition,

$$U_x = \left\{u \in \{0,1\} :\ u = \mu_{NE(X(\alpha))}(x), \alpha_i \in \Omega_i,\ i \in N\right\} \tag{15}$$

is the set of primary membership degrees $u \in \{0,1\}$ with strictly positive secondary grades $\eta_{\tilde{E}}(x,u)$, which coincides with the support $\mathrm{supp}(M_{\tilde{E}}(x))$ (see (12)) of the FS $M_{\tilde{E}}(x)$ of fuzzy membership degrees of the strategy profile $x \in X$;

$$\mu_{NE(X(\alpha))}(x) = \begin{cases} 1, & x \in NE(X(\alpha)); \\ 0, & \text{otherwise} \end{cases} \tag{16}$$

is the MF (characteristic function) of the crisp set

$$NE(X(\alpha)) = \left\{(x, \mu_{X(\alpha)}(x)) : x \in X\right\} \tag{17}$$

of Nash equilibria of the game $G(X(\alpha)) = \langle X_i(\alpha_i), u_i : i \in N\rangle$ for the sets $X_i(\alpha_i), i \in N$ of strategies (see (3),(4) with $S = X(\alpha)$ and $S_i = X_i(\alpha_i), i \in N$);

$$X_i(\alpha_i) = \left\{x_i \in X_i : \mu_{\tilde{X}_i}(x_i) \geq \alpha_i\right\},\ i \in N \tag{18}$$

is the α_i-cuts, $\alpha_i \in \Omega_i$ of the FS $\tilde{X}_i$ of strategies of the player $i \in N$;

$\alpha = (\alpha_i)_{i\in N}$ is the vector of α_i-cuts levels, $\alpha_i \in \Omega_i$, $i \in N$ of the FSs $\tilde{X}_i$, $i \in N$ of strategies;

$\Omega_i = \left\{\mu_{\tilde{X}_i}(x_i) : x_i \in X_i\right\}$, $i \in N$ are the sets of the membership degrees values $\mu_{\tilde{X}_i}(x_i)$, $x_i \in X_i, i \in N$ of the FSs $\tilde{X}_i, i \in N$ of strategies (see Remark 6), respectively;

$X(\alpha) = \prod_{i\in N} X_i(\alpha_i)$ is the set of strategies profiles of the game $G(X(\alpha)) = \langle X_i(\alpha_i), u_i : i \in N\rangle$, $\alpha = (\alpha_i)_{i\in N}$, $\alpha_i \in \Omega_i, i \in N$.

Remark 7. *Since primary membership degrees $u \in \{0,1\}$ of the T2FS $\tilde{E}$ take only two values, 0 or 1, by Remark 2, this yields an interesting interpretation of the T2FS $\tilde{E}$. Similarly to a crisp set, there are only two options for each strategy profile $x \in X$: either x completely belongs to the T2FS $\tilde{E}$ (the primary membership degree is $u = 1$), or it does not belong completely ($u = 0$). Unlike a crisp set, the degrees $\eta_{\tilde{E}}(x,0)$ and $\eta_{\tilde{E}}(x,1)$ of truth of the identification of these two facts can differ from 1 and take values in the closed interval $[0,1]$.*

5. Nash Equilibria T2FS of a Game with Fuzzy Sets of Strategies

5.1. A Decomposition of Nash Equilibria T2FS

Proposition 1 justifies the decomposability (see Definition 1) of Nash equilibria T2FS of a game with FSs of strategies on a collection of embedded T2FSs with constant secondary grades.

Proposition 1. *The Nash equilibria T2FS $\tilde{E}$ of the game $\langle \tilde{X}_i, u_i : i \in N \rangle$ for FSs of strategies is decomposable by secondary grades $\min_{i \in N} \alpha_i$ into the collection*

$$\tilde{E} = \left\{ \tilde{E}^{e2}(X(\alpha)) : \ \alpha = (\alpha_i)_{i \in N}, \ \alpha_i \in \Omega_i, \ i \in N \right\} \tag{19}$$

of the embedded T2FSs

$$\tilde{E}^{e2}(X(\alpha)) = \left\{ (NE(X(\alpha)), \min_{i \in N} \alpha_i) \right\} \tag{20}$$

where $NE(X(\alpha))$ is the embedded T1FS. It is a crisp set (a crisp set is a special case of a T1FS), which is the set of Nash equilibria of the game $G(X(\alpha)) = \langle X_i(\alpha_i), u_i : i \in N \rangle$ with the crisp sets $X_i(\alpha_i)$, $i \in N$of strategies.

Proof of Proposition 1. By (13), the Nash equilibria T2FS is given by $\tilde{E} = \{((x,u), \eta_{\tilde{E}}(x,u)) : \ u \in \{0,1\}, \ x \in X\}$. According to (14), $\tilde{E} = \{((x,u),0) : u \notin U_x\} : x \in X\}$ $\cup \left\{ \left\{ ((x,u), \max\left\{ \min_{i \in N} \alpha_i : \ \alpha_i \in \Omega_i, \ i \in N, \ u = \mu_{NE(X(\alpha))}(x) \right\}) : u \in U_x \right\} \right.$. Since Remark 2 allows us to ignore the pairs (x,u) that have secondary grades equal to 0, we conclude that $\tilde{E} = \left\{ \left\{ ((x,u), \max\left\{ \min_{i \in N} \alpha_i : \ \alpha_i \in \Omega_i, \ i \in N, \ u = \mu_{NE(X(\alpha))}(x) \right\}) : \ u \in U_x, \ x \in X \right\} \right.$, which is equivalent $\tilde{E} = \left\{ (x, \left\{ (\mu_{NE(X(\alpha))}(x), \min_{i \in N} \alpha_i) : \ \alpha_i \in \Omega_i, \ i \in N \right\}), \ x \in X \right\}$ according to (14). Further, regrouping the elements leads to $\tilde{E} = \left\{ (x, (\mu_{NE(X(\alpha))}(x), \min_{i \in N} \alpha_i)) : \ \alpha_i \in \Omega_i, \ i \in N, \ x \in X \right\}$ $= \left\{ \left\{ ((x, (\mu_{NE(X(\alpha))}(x)), \min_{i \in N} \alpha_i) : x \in X \right\} : \ \alpha_i \in \Omega_i, \ i \in N \right\}$. Then, invoking (17) yields $\tilde{E} = \left\{ (NE(X(\alpha)), \min_{i \in N} \alpha_i) : \ \alpha_i \in \Omega_i, \ i \in N \right\}$ whence (19) comes by (20). □

A characteristic feature of the proposed decomposition approach is its independence from the chosen method for calculating the sets $NE(X(\alpha))$ of Nash equilibria of games $G(X(\alpha)) = \langle X_i(\alpha_i), u_i : i \in N \rangle$ for crisp sets $X_i(\alpha_i)$, $i \in N$ of strategies. Denote by

$$\Omega = \left\{ \min_{i \in N} \alpha_i : \ \alpha_i \in \Omega_i, \ i \in N \right\} \tag{21}$$

the set of secondary grades of the Nash equilibria T2FS $\tilde{E}$ of the game $\langle \tilde{X}_i, u_i : i \in N \rangle$. Corollary 1 states that the T2FS $\tilde{E}$ can be directly decomposed by the set Ω of secondary grades.

Corollary 1. *The Nash equilibria T2FS $\tilde{E}$ of the game $\langle \tilde{X}_i, u_i : i \in N \rangle$ for FSs of strategies is decomposable by secondary grades $\gamma \in \Omega$ into the collection*

$$\tilde{E} = \left\{ (E^{e1}_{\gamma}, \gamma) : \ \gamma \in \Omega \right\} \tag{22}$$

of the embedded T2FSs $\tilde{E}^{e2}_{\gamma} = \left\{ (E^{e1}_{\gamma}, \gamma) \right\}$. For each $\gamma \in \Omega$, the embedded T1FS

$$E^{e1}_{\gamma} = \bigcup_{\alpha = (\alpha_i)_{i \in N}, \ \alpha_i \in \Omega_i, \ i \in N: \ \min_{i \in N} \alpha_i = \gamma} NE(X(\alpha)), \gamma \in \Omega \tag{23}$$

is the union of the crisp sets $NE(X(\alpha))$ (a crisp set is a special case of a T1FS). For each $\alpha = (\alpha_i)_{i\in N}$, $\alpha_i \in \Omega_i$, $i \in N$ such that $\min_{i\in N}\alpha_i = \gamma$, the set $NE(X(\alpha))$ is a Nash equilibria set of the game $G(X(\alpha)) = \langle X_i(\alpha_i), u_i : i \in N\rangle$ for the sets $X_i(\alpha_i)$, $i \in N$ of strategies.

Proof of Corollary 1. Formulae (19) and (20) imply that $\tilde{E}^{e2}(X(\alpha)) = \left\{(NE(X(\alpha)), \min_{i\in N}\alpha_i) :\ \alpha = \left(\alpha_i\right)_{i\in N}, \alpha_i \in \Omega_i, i \in N\right\}$. According to Remark 3, each element of this collection can be interpreted as a subset. Thus, the collection is represented as the classical union of its elements in the sense of T1FSs. With this at hand, we conclude that by (21), associated to each $\gamma \in \Omega$ is the subset $\bigcup_{\alpha=(\alpha_i)_{i\in N},\ \alpha_i\in\Omega_i,\ i\in N:\ \min_{i\in N}\alpha_i=\gamma} \{(NE(X(\alpha)), \gamma)\}$ in the collection $\tilde{E}$. Therefore, an appeal to (23) yields (22). □

5.2. Calculation of a Nash equilibria T2FS

First, we construct the sets $\Omega_i = \left\{\mu_{\tilde{X}_i}(x_i) : x_i \in X_i\right\}$, $i \in N$ of membership degrees values of the FSs $\tilde{X}_i = \left\{(x, \mu_{\tilde{X}_i}(x_i)) : x_i \in X_i\right\}$, $i \in N$ of strategies, respectively. For each $\alpha_i \in \Omega_i$, $i \in N$, according to (18), we construct the α_i-cuts $X_i(\alpha_i) = \left\{x_i \in X_i : \mu_{\tilde{X}_i}(x_i) \geq \alpha_i\right\}$, $i \in N$ of the FS $\tilde{X}_i$, $i \in N$, respectively. Next, we construct the Nash equilibria sets $NE(X(\alpha))$ of the games $G(X(\alpha)) = \langle X_i(\alpha_i), u_i : i \in N\rangle$, $\alpha = (\alpha_i)_{i\in N}$ for crisp sets $X_i(\alpha_i)$, $i \in N$, $\alpha_i \in \Omega_i$, $i \in N$. To construct the Nash equilibria sets $NE(X(\alpha))$, one can use any known method. Further, we use the representation of the T2FS $\tilde{E}$ in the form of a collection of embedded T2FSs with constant secondary grades (see Corollary 1). To this end, we need to construct the embedded T1FS $E_\gamma^{e1} = \bigcup_{\alpha=(\alpha_i)_{i\in N},\ \alpha_i\in\Omega_i,\ i\in N:\ \min_{i\in N}\alpha_i=\gamma} NE(X(\alpha))$ for each $\gamma \in \Omega$ according to (23). Once all embedded T1FS E_γ^{e1} with constant secondary grades $\gamma \in \Omega$ have been obtained, the resulting Nash equilibria T2FS has the form $\tilde{E} = \left\{(E_\gamma^{e1}, \gamma) :\ \gamma \in \Omega\right\}$ according to (22) and (23).

By Remark 1, the T2FS $\tilde{E}$ can be interpreted as the collection of unions $E_\gamma^{e1} = \bigcup_{\alpha=(\alpha_i)_{i\in N},\ \alpha_i\in\Omega_i,\ i\in N:\ \min_{i\in N}\alpha_i=\gamma} NE(X(\alpha))$, $\gamma \in \Omega$ of Nash equilibria sets $NE(X(\alpha))$ of the fuzzy games $G(X(\alpha)) = \langle X_i(\alpha_i), u_i : i \in N\rangle$ for the corresponding crisp sets $X_i(\alpha_i)$, $i \in N$ of strategies for $\alpha = (\alpha_i)_{i\in N}$, $\alpha_i \in \Omega_i$, $i \in N$, such that $\min_{i\in N}\alpha_i = \gamma$ with the degree of truth of the set E_γ^{e1} being equal to γ.

5.3. Properties of Constructing of the Nash equilibria T2FS

Propositions 2 and 3 point at some useful properties of the Nash equilibria T2FS of the game with FSs of strategies.

Proposition 2. *If a strategy profile $x \in X$ is (is not) a Nash equilibrium of the game $G(X(\alpha^*)) = \langle X_i(\alpha_i^*), u_i : i \in N\rangle$ for the collection of levels $\alpha_i^* \in \Omega_i$, $i \in N$ of cuts $X_i(\alpha_i^*)$ of FSs $\tilde{X}_i$, $i \in N$ of strategies, then a primary degree of membership $u = 1$ ($u = 0$) of the strategy profile x to the Nash equilibria T2FS has a secondary grade (degree of truth) not smaller than $\gamma^* = \min_{i\in N}\alpha_i^*$, i.e., $\eta_{\tilde{E}}(x, 1) \geq \gamma^*$ ($\eta_{\tilde{E}}(x, 0) \geq \gamma^*$).*

Proof Proposition 2. Let $\alpha_i^* \in \Omega_i$, $i \in N$ and $u = \mu_{NE(X(\alpha^*))}(x) = 1$ ($u = \mu_{NE(X(\alpha^*))}(x) = 0$). Then, by (15), $u \in U_x$. Therefore, in view of (14), $\eta_{\tilde{E}}(x, 1) = \max\left\{\min_{i\in N}\alpha_i :\ \alpha_i \in \Omega_i, i \in N,\right.$ $\left.\mu_{NE(X(\alpha^*))}(x) = 1 = \mu_{NE(X(\alpha))}(x)\right\} \geq \min_{i\in N}\alpha_i^* = \gamma^*$ ($\eta_{\tilde{E}}(x, 0) = \max\left\{\min_{i\in N}\alpha_i :\ \alpha_i \in \Omega_i, i \in N,\right.$ $\left.(\mu_{NE(X(\alpha^*))}(x) = 0 = \mu_{NE(X(\alpha))}(x)\right\} \geq \min_{i\in N}\alpha_i^* = \gamma^*$). □

In other words, according to Proposition 2, the guaranteed value of the degree of truth $\gamma^* \in \Omega$ of the primary degree of membership $u = 1$ ($u = 0$) of the strategy profile $x \in X$ to the Nash equilibria T2FS is determined by the levels $\alpha_i^* \in \Omega_i$, $i \in N$ of cuts of the FSs $\tilde{X}_i$, $i \in N$ of strategies, under which the strategy profile x is (is not) a Nash equilibrium of the game $G(X(\alpha^*)) = \langle X_i(\alpha_i^*), u_i : i \in N \rangle$.

Proposition 3. *The Nash equilibria T2FS $\tilde{E}$ is not empty.*

Proof Proposition 3. We denote by $\alpha^{\min} = (\alpha_i^{\min})_{i \in N}$ the vector of least levels $\alpha_i^{\min} = \min\limits_{\alpha_i \in \Omega_i} \alpha_i$ of α_i-cuts of FSs $\tilde{X}_i$ of players strategies $i \in N$. Assume that $\tilde{E} = \varnothing$. Then, according to formulae (19) and (20), the equality $\tilde{E} = \left\{ (NE(X(\alpha)), \min\limits_{i \in N} \alpha_i) : \alpha = (\alpha_i)_{i \in N}, \ \alpha_i \in \Omega_i, \ i \in N \right\} = \varnothing$ is held. This entails $NE(X(\alpha)) = \varnothing$ for any $\alpha = (\alpha_i)_{i \in N}, \alpha_i \in \Omega_i$, $i \in N$ including for $\alpha^{\min} = (\alpha_i^{\min})_{i \in N}$. Therefore, $NE(X(\alpha^{\min})) = \varnothing$. With the equalities $X_i(\alpha_i^{\min}) = X_i, i \in N$ at hand, we conclude that $NE(X) = \varnothing$ having utilized (18) and Remark 6, a contradiction to Assumption 1. □

5.4. Example of Constructing the Nash Equilibria T2FS

Assume that some DM analyzes a conflict of two players. The model of this conflict is a generalization of the well-known prisoner's dilemma game to the case of fuzzy sets "Predictable Strategies" of players 1 and 2. The DM perceives sets $X_1 = \{P_1, A_1, F_1\}$ and $X_2 = \{P_2, A_2, F_2\}$ of players 1 and 2 strategies in the form of FSs $\tilde{X}_1 = \{(P_1; 1), (A_1; 1), (F_1; 0{,}7)\}$ and $\tilde{X}_2 = \{(P_2; 1), (A_2; 1), (F_2; 0{,}5)\}$, respectively. Here, the strategies P_i, A_i, F_i have a sense of a peaceful, aggressive, and frenzied behavior, respectively, of the player $i = 1, 2$. Table 1 contains the payoffs vectors $(u_1(x_1, x_2), u_2(x_1, x_2))$, $x_1 \in \{P_1, A_1, F_1\}$, $x_2 \in \{P_2, A_2, F_2\}$ of players. The DM intends to predict *Nash equilibria*.

Table 1. Payoffs vectors of players.

Strategy	F_2	A_2	P_2
F_1	(0, 0)	(2, −1)	(4, −2)
A_1	(−1, 2)	(1, 1)	(3, 0)
P_1	(−2, 4)	(0, 3)	(2, 2)

According to Remark 6, the sets of membership degrees of FSs $\tilde{X}_1$ and $\tilde{X}_2$ of strategies are given by $\Omega_1 = \{0{,}7; 1\}$ and $\Omega_2 = \{0{,}5; 1\}$, respectively. For each pair $\alpha_1 = \{0{,}7; 1\}$ and $\alpha_2 = \{0{,}5; 1\}$, we use (18) to construct the corresponding cuts $X_i(\alpha_i) = \left\{ x_i \in X_i : \mu_{\tilde{X}_i}(x_i) \geq \alpha_i \right\}$, $i = 1, 2$ of FSs $\tilde{X}_i$, $i = 1, 2$, respectively. Then, we construct the sets $NE(X(\alpha_1; \alpha_2))$ of *Nash equilibria* of the games $G(X(\alpha_1; \alpha_2)) = \langle X_1(\alpha_1), u_1; X_2(\alpha_2), u_2 \rangle$, $\alpha_1 = \{0{,}7; 1\}$, $\alpha_2 = \{0{,}5; 1\}$ in the form (3)–(4). We get

$$NE(X(0{,}7; 0{,}5)) = \{((F_1, F_2); 1)\} \cup \{((x_1, x_2); 0) : (x_1, x_2) \in \{P_1, A_1, F_1\} \times \{P_2, A_2, F_2\} \backslash \{(F_1, F_2)\}\}, \tag{24}$$

$$NE(X(0{,}7; 1)) = \{((F_1, A_2); 1)\} \cup \{((x_1, x_2); 0) : (x_1, x_2) \in \{P_1, A_1, F_1\} \times \{P_2, A_2, F_2\} \backslash \{(F_1, A_2)\}\}, \tag{25}$$

$$NE(X(1; 0{,}5)) = \{((A_1, F_2); 1)\} \cup \{((x_1, x_2); 0) : (x_1, x_2) \in \{P_1, A_1, F_1\} \times \{P_2, A_2, F_2\} \backslash \{(A_1, F_2)\}\}, \tag{26}$$

$$NE(X(1; 1)) = \{((A_1, A_2); 1)\} \cup \{((x_1, x_2); 0) : (x_1, x_2) \in \{P_1, A_1, F_1\} \times \{P_2, A_2, F_2\} \backslash \{(A_1, A_2)\}\}. \tag{27}$$

According to Remark 2, the Nash equilibria T2FS has the form

$$\begin{gathered} \tilde{E} = \{(NE(X(0{,}7; 0{,}5)) \cup NE(X(1; 0{,}5)); 0{,}5), (NE(X(0{,}7; 1)); 0{,}7), (NE(X(1; 1)); 1)\} = \\ \{(((F_1, F_2); 1); 0{,}5), (((A_1, F_2); 1); 0{,}5), (((F_1, A_2); 1); 0{,}7), (((A_1, A_2); 1); 1)\} \cup \\ \{(((x_1, x_2); 0); 1) : (x_1, x_2) \in \{P_1, A_1, F_1\} \times \{P_2, A_2, F_2\} \backslash \{(A_1, A_2)\}\}. \end{gathered} \tag{28}$$

6. Discussion

In this section, we discuss the Nash equilibria T2FS obtained in Section 5.4 in comparison with solutions for crisp game settings. The DM who is analyzing a two-player conflict in the example might interpret the T2FS $\tilde{\tilde{E}}$ as follows:

- The strategic profile (A_1, A_2) is a Nash equilibrium with the degree of truth being equal to 1;
- The strategic profile (F_1, A_2) is a Nash equilibrium with the degree of truth being equal to 0,7;
- The strategic profiles (F_1, F_2) and (A_1, F_2) are Nash equilibria with degrees of truth being equal to 0,5;
- Any strategic profile other than the above is a Nash equilibrium with the degree of truth being equal to 0.

If this DM perceives sets of players' strategies crisply, then the following Nash equilibria would exist for him:

- (A_1, A_2) in the case of a pessimistic assessment of possible strategies of players in the form of crisp sets $\{P_1, A_1\}$ and $\{P_2, A_2\}$ of player 1 and 2, respectively;
- (F_1, F_2) in the case of a pessimistic assessment of possible strategies of players in the form of crisp sets $\{P_1, A_1, F_1\}$ and $\{P_2, A_2, F_2\}$ of player 1 and 2, respectively.

At the same time, the DM does not know degrees of truth of all Nash equilibria and misses the equilibria (A_1, F_2) and (F_1, A_2). Thus, we conclude that game models with fuzzy sets of strategies are more informative.

7. Conclusions

According to the proposed approach, the set of Nash equilibria for the game with fuzzy sets of strategies can be decomposed into a collection of embedded T2FSs with constant secondary grades. These sets are relatively simple to use in practice, in contrast to general T2FSs. The results we have obtained allow us to break down the Nash equilibria T2FS based on secondary grades into finite collections of sets. These collections represent Nash equilibria sets for games corresponding to different cuts of FSs of players' strategies. Thus, the proposed approach allows us to determine several solutions to the same game depending on the required degree of truth. The properties of the Nash equilibria T2FS are studied.

One possible avenue for future research could involve developing a similar approach for coalition games. Along with other studies of fuzzy games, the authors hope that the proposed approach certainly expands the scope of game theory in social sciences, artificial intelligence, and many other fields.

Author Contributions: Conceptualization, S.M. and S.B.; Methodology, S.M. and S.B.; Resources, S.B.; Writing—original draft, S.B. and S.M.; Writing—review & editing, S.B. and S.M.; Project administration, S.B. All authors have read and agreed to the published version of the manuscript.

Funding: This research was funded by the Lithuania Ministry of National Defence as part of the study project Study Support Projects No VI-18, 2 December 2021 (2021–2024), General Jonas Žemaitis, Military Academy of Lithuania, Vilnius, Lithuania.

Data Availability Statement: Data are contained within the article.

Conflicts of Interest: The authors declare no conflict of interest. Any opinions, findings, conclusions, or recommendations expressed in this material are those of the authors and do not necessarily reflect the view of the funding agency.

References

1. Orlovskii, S.A. Games in fuzzy conditions. *USSR Comput. Math. Math. Phys.* **1976**, *16*, 44–52. [CrossRef]
2. Butnariu, D. Fuzzy games a description of the concept. *Fuzzy Sets Syst.* **1978**, *1*, 181–192. [CrossRef]
3. Butnariu, D. *Solution concept for n-person games, In Advances in Fuzzy Set Theory and Application*; Gupta, M.M., Ragade, R.K., Yager, R.R., Eds.; North-Holland Publishing Company: Amsterdam, The Netherlands, 1979; pp. 339–354.

4. Butnariu, D. An existence theorem for possible solutions of a two-person fuzzy game. *Bull. Math. Soc. Sci. Repub. Social. Roum.* **1979**, *23*, 29–35.
5. Billot, A. *Economic Theory of Fuzzy Equilibria: An Axiomatic Analysis*; Springer: Berlin, Germany, 1992.
6. Bellman, R.E.; Zadeh, L.A. Decision making in a fuzzy environment. *Manag. Sci.* **1970**, *17B*, 209–215. [CrossRef]
7. Campos, L. Fuzzy linear programming models to solve fuzzy matrix games. *Fuzzy Sets Syst.* **1989**, *32*, 275–289. [CrossRef]
8. Yager, R.R. A Procedure for ordering fuzzy numbers in the unit interval. *Inf. Sci.* **1981**, *24*, 143–161. [CrossRef]
9. Larbani, M. Non cooperative fuzzy games in normal form: A survey. *Fuzzy Sets Syst.* **2009**, *160*, 3184–3210. [CrossRef]
10. Vijay, V.; Chandra, S.; Bector, C.R. Bimatrix games with fuzzy payoffs and fuzzy goals. *Fuzzy Optim. Decis. Mak.* **2004**, *3*, 327–344.
11. Maeda, T. On characterization of equilibrium strategy of the bimatrix game with fuzzy payoffs. *J. Math. Anal. Appl.* **2000**, *251*, 885–896. [CrossRef]
12. Kacher, F.; Larbani, M. A concept of solution for a non cooperative game with fuzzy parameters. *Int. Game Theory Rev.* **2006**, *8*, 489–498. [CrossRef]
13. Sakawa, M.; Yano, H. Interactive decision making for multiobjective non linear programming problems with fuzzy parameters. *Fuzzy Sets Syst.* **1989**, *29*, 315–326. [CrossRef]
14. Aristidou, M.; Sarangi, S. Games in fuzzy environments. *South. Econ. J.* **2006**, *72*, 645–659.
15. Garazic, D.; Cruz, J.F. An approach to fuzzy non cooperative Nash games. *J. Optim. Theory Appl.* **2003**, *18*, 475–491. [CrossRef]
16. Arfi, B. Linguistic fuzzy-logic social game of cooperation. *Ration. Soc.* **2006**, *18*, 471–537. [CrossRef]
17. Zadeh, L.A. Quantitative fuzzy semantics. *Inf. Sci.* **1971**, *3*, 159–176. [CrossRef]
18. Mizumoto, M.; Tanaka, K. Some properties of fuzzy sets of type-2. *Inf. Control.* **1976**, *31*, 312–340. [CrossRef]
19. Mendel, J.M. Type-2 fuzzy sets: Some questions and answers. *IEEE Connect. Newsl. IEEE Neural Netw. Soc.* **2003**, *1*, 10–13.
20. Karnik, N.N.; Mendel, J.M. Introduction to type-2 fuzzy logic systems. *IEEE Int. Conf. Fuzzy Syst.* **1998**, 2, 915–920.
21. Mendel, J.M.; John, R.I. Type-2 fuzzy sets made simple. *IEEE Trans. Fuzzy Syst.* **2002**, *10*, 117–127. [CrossRef]
22. Mashchenko, S.O. Sums of fuzzy set of summands. *Fuzzy Sets Syst.* **2021**, *417*, 140–151. [CrossRef]
23. Mashchenko, S.O. Sum of discrete fuzzy numbers with fuzzy set of summands. *Cybern. Syst. Anal.* **2021**, *57*, 374–382. [CrossRef]
24. Mashchenko, S.O. Minimum of fuzzy numbers with a fuzzy set of operands. *Cybern. Syst. Anal.* **2022**, *58*, 210–219. [CrossRef]
25. Mashchenko, S.O.; Kapustian, D.O. Decomposition of intersections with fuzzy sets of operands. In *Contemporary Approaches and Methods in Fundamental Mathematics and Mechanics. Understanding Complex Systems*; Sadovnichiy, V.A., Zgurovsky, M.Z., Eds.; Springer: Cham, Switzerland, 2021; pp. 417–432. [CrossRef]
26. Zadeh, L. The concept of a linguistic variable and its application to approximate reasoning—I. *Inf. Sci.* **1975**, *8*, 199–249. [CrossRef]

mathematics

MDPI

Article

Ideals and Homomorphism Theorems of Fuzzy Associative Algebras

Xiaoman Yang [1] and Xin Zhou [1,2,*]

[1] School of Mathematics and Statistics, Yili Normal University, Yining 835000, China; 19399178030@163.com
[2] Institute of Applied Mathematics, Yili Normal University, Yining 835000, China
* Correspondence: zhoux566@nenu.edu.cn

Abstract: Based on the definitions of fuzzy associative algebras and fuzzy ideals, it is proven that the intersections of fuzzy subalgebras are fuzzy subalgebras, and the intersections of fuzzy ideals are fuzzy ideals. Moreover, we prove that the kernels of fuzzy homomorphisms are fuzzy ideals. Using fuzzy ideals, the quotient structures of fuzzy associative algebras are constructed, their corresponding properties are discussed, and their homomorphism theorems are proven.

Keywords: fuzzy associative algebras; fuzzy ideals; fuzzy homomorphisms; quotient algebras; homomorphism theorems

MSC: 08A72

1. Introduction

Zadeh [1] pioneered the concept of fuzzy sets and laid the foundation for fuzzy mathematics. Following this, Liu [2] introduced the notions of fuzzy invariant subgroups and fuzzy ideals and subsequently discussed several fundamental properties. Ahsan et al. [3–6] conducted extensive research on the structures and properties of fuzzy semirings, integrating fuzzy concepts into semiring structures and catalyzing further research in this area. Liu [7] provided precise definitions of the operations of L-fuzzy ideals in rings. Consequently, numerous researchers have delved into the studies of fuzzy prime ideals in rings. Swamy [8] introduced the concepts of fuzzy ideals and fuzzy prime ideals of rings with truth values in a complete lattice. Furthermore, Malik and Mordeson [9] undertook a thorough examination to characterize all fuzzy prime ideals and confirmed the key properties associated with them. Nanda [10,11] contributed by defining fuzzy fields and subsequently introduced the notions of fuzzy algebras and fuzzy ideals over fuzzy fields. Biswas [12] enhanced the definitions of fuzzy fields and fuzzy linear spaces. Subsequently, Kuraoka and Kuroki [13] introduced fuzzy quotient rings derived from fuzzy ideals and investigated the relationship between fuzzy quotient rings and fuzzy ideals. Gu and Lu [14] raised concerns regarding the validity of Nanda's definition of fuzzy fields, prompting redefinitions of fuzzy fields and fuzzy algebras. Then, they proved that the homomorphic image is a fuzzy algebra. Moreover, researchers have delved into the studies of fuzzy quotient algebras. In subsequent works, scholars primarily focused on exploring fuzzy ideals in semigroups [15–18]. Zhou, Chen, and Chang [19] introduced the concepts of L-fuzzy ideals and L-fuzzy subalgebras. Additionally, Addis, Kausar, and Munir [20] provided the concept of homomorphic kernels on fuzzy rings and proved three homomorphism theorems. Korma, Parimi, and Kifetew [21] conducted a study on the properties of homomorphisms on fuzzy lattices and their quotients. As a result, three isomorphism theorems regarding the quotients of fuzzy lattices were developed by them.

Adak, Nilkamal, and Barman [22] conducted a research on fuzzy semiprime ideals of ordered semigroups. Hamidi and Borumand [23] explored the properties of EQ-algebras. Kumduang and Chinram [24] investigated fuzzy ideals and fuzzy congruences in Menger algebras. Furthermore, various scholars [25–27] have examined alternative approaches to analyzing distinct algebraic structures. Since associative algebra is a very important class of algebraic structures, its theories can be applied to group, ring, and semiring structures. It is an important foundation of modern mathematics. On the other hand, algebraic structures hold a significant position in mathematics with wide-ranging applications in many disciplines such as theoretical physics, computer sciences, information sciences, coding theories, and so on. The study of fuzzy associative algebra is helpful to better understand other fuzzy algebraic structure theories. This serves as ample motivation for us to revisit assorted concepts and findings from the realms of abstract algebras, thereby extending their applications to the broader framework of fuzzy sets.

In this paper, we provide the preliminaries in Section 2. In Section 3, we introduce the concepts of fuzzy subalgebras and fuzzy ideals, and then we discuss their properties. The quotients constructed by fuzzy ideals are presented in Section 4. In Section 5, we provide three isomorphism theorems of fuzzy algebras.

2. Preliminaries

In this section, we provide fundamental theoretical knowledge, serving as the basis for subsequent sections.

Definition 1 ([28])**.** *Let $(L, \leq)$ be a poset. A poset $(L, \leq, \wedge, \vee)$ is a lattice if any two elements a, b have a least upper bound $a \vee b$ and a greatest lower bound $a \wedge b$, which we denote as L for short. A lattice L is called a complete lattice if each of its subsets S has $\vee S$ and $\wedge S$, where $\vee S$ and $\wedge S$ represent the least upper bound and the greatest lower bound of all elements in S, respectively. In particular, $\vee\varnothing$ and $\wedge\varnothing$ represent the smallest element 0 and the largest element 1 of L, respectively.*

Definition 2 ([29])**.** *Let X be a nonempty set and L be a complete lattice. A fuzzy subset of X is a function $\mu : X \to L$, where μ is called the membership function, X is called the carrier of μ, L is called the truth set of μ, and for all x belonging to X, $\mu(x)$ is called the degree of membership of x.*

We use $F_L(X) = \{\mu \mid \mu : X \to L\}$ to represent the set of all membership functions on X.

Definition 3 ([29])**.** *We define operations $\wedge$, $\vee$ on $F_L(X)$ as follows:*

$$\mu(x) \vee \mu'(x) = \max\{\mu(x),\mu'(x)\},$$
$$\mu(x) \wedge \mu'(x) = \min\{\mu(x),\mu'(x)\},$$
$$\bar{\mu}(x) = 1 - \mu(x),$$

for all $x \in X$, μ, $\mu' \in F_L(X)$.

Definition 4 ([30])**.** *Let A be a linear space on a field F, in which the multiplication operation is defined as $(\alpha, \beta) \to \alpha\beta$, and it satisfies the axioms*

(1) $\alpha(\beta + \gamma) = \alpha\beta + \alpha\gamma$,
(2) $(\alpha + \beta)\gamma = \alpha\gamma + \beta\gamma$,
(3) $(k\alpha)\beta = \alpha(k\beta) = k(\alpha\beta)$,
(4) $\alpha(\beta\gamma) = (\alpha\beta)\gamma$,

for all α, β, $\gamma \in A$, $k \in F$; then, A is called an associative algebra over F.

Definition 5. *Let A and B be associative algebras. Then, B is a subalgebra of A if $B \subseteq A$, and every fundamental operation of B is the restriction of the corresponding operation of A.*

3. Fuzzy Subalgebras and Fuzzy Ideals

In this section, we first give the concept of fuzzy associative algebras. Secondly, we define fuzzy subalgebras, fuzzy homomorphisms, and fuzzy ideals in fuzzy associative algebras and prove that the intersections of fuzzy subalgebras are fuzzy subalgebras, the intersections of fuzzy ideals are fuzzy ideals, and both the homomorphic images and preimages of fuzzy ideals are fuzzy ideals.

Definition 6. *Let A be an associative algebra over the number field F and L be a complete lattice.* $\mu_A \in F_L(A)$ *is a fuzzy algebra on A, satisfying*

(1) $\mu_A(a_1)\wedge\mu_A(a_2)\leq\mu_A(a_1+a_2)$,

(2) $\mu_A(a_1)\wedge\mu_A(a_2)\leq\mu_A(a_1\cdot a_2)$,

(3) $\mu_A(a_1)\leq\mu_A(k\cdot a_1)$,

(4) $\mu_A(e)=1$;

for all $a_1, a_2 \in A$, $k \in F$, *e is a constant in A, and we denote it as* (A,μ_A).

Remark 1. *If A is a ring, then it satisfies (1), (2), and (4) of Definition 6; if A is a group, then it satisfies (1), (4) or (2), (4) of Definition 6; if A is a semiring, then it satisfies (1), (2), and (4) of Definition 6, and it is a commutative semigroup under addition; and if A is an associative algebra, then it is a commutative group under addition, and the associative algebra has one more scalar multiplication operation than a semiring.*

Definition 7. *Let A be an associative algebra, B be a subalgebra of A, L be a complete lattice, and* $\mu_{A|_B} \in F_L(A)$*; then,* $(B,\mu_{A|_B})$ *is a fuzzy subalgebra of* (A,μ_A).

Definition 8. *Let* (A,μ_A), (B,μ_B) *be fuzzy algebras and a function* $\alpha : A \to B$ *be a homomorphism from A to B. A mapping* $\alpha : (A,\mu_A) \to (B,\mu_B)$ *is called a fuzzy homomorphism from* (A,μ_A) *to* (B,μ_B) *if*

$$\mu_A(a) \leq \mu_B(\alpha(a)),$$

for all $a \in A$.

Example 1. *The addition, multiplication, and scalar multiplication of polynomial sets over a field F form associative algebras.*

Let $f_1(x) = a_1x^2+b_1x+c_1$ *and* $f_2(x) = a_2x^2+b_2x+c_2$*; then,* $(f_1(x),\mu_1)$ *and* $(f_2(x),\mu_2)$ *are fuzzy algebras. Suppose that* $\alpha : (f_1(x),\mu_1) \to (f_2(x),\mu_2)$ *and* $\mu_2(f_2(x)) = 1.5\big(\mu_1(f_1(x))\big)$*, for any* $ax^2+bx+c \in f_1(x)$ *and* $\mu_2(\alpha(ax^2+bx+c)) = 1.5\mu_1(ax^2+bx+c)$*; thus,* α *is a fuzzy homomorphism.*

Remark 2. *(1) A fuzzy homomorphism* $\alpha : (A,\mu_A) \to (B,\mu_B)$ *is called a fuzzy monomorphism from* (A,μ_A) *to* (B,μ_B) *if* $\alpha : A \to B$ *is an injection;*

(2) A fuzzy homomorphism $\alpha : (A,\mu_A) \to (B,\mu_B)$ *is called a fuzzy epimorphism from* (A,μ_A) *to* (B,μ_B) *if* $\alpha : A \to B$ *is a surjection;*

(3) A fuzzy homomorphism $\alpha : (A,\mu_A) \to (B,\mu_B)$ *is called a fuzzy isomorphism from* (A,μ_A) *to* (B,μ_B) *if* $\alpha : A \to B$ *is a bijection.*

Remark 3. *(1) For all* $a \in A$, $\mu_B(\alpha(a)) = \vee\mu_A\big(\alpha^{-1}(\alpha(a))\big)$ *if a mapping* $\alpha : (A,\mu_A) \to (B,\mu_B)$ *is a fuzzy homomorphism;*

(2) For all $a \in A$, $\mu_B(\alpha(a)) = \mu_A(a)$ *if a mapping* $\alpha : (A,\mu_A) \to (B,\mu_B)$ *is a fuzzy isomorphism.*

Definition 9. *Let A be an associative algebra, R be a subalgebra of A, L be a complete lattice, and a fuzzy set of R be a function* $\mu_R : R \to L$*. Then,*

(1) (R,μ_R) *is a fuzzy left ideal of* (A,μ_A) *if* $\mu_R(a\cdot b) \geq \mu_R(b)$ *for all* $a \in A, b \in R$;

(2) (R,μ_R) *is a fuzzy right ideal of* (A,μ_A) *if* $\mu_R(a\cdot b) \geq \mu_R(a)$ *for all* $a \in R, b \in A$;

(3) (R,μ_R) *is a fuzzy ideal of* (A,μ_A) *if* $\mu_R(a\cdot b) \geq \mu_R(a) \vee \mu_R(b)$ *for all* $a \in R, b \in R$.

Theorem 1. *Let* (A,μ_A) *be a fuzzy algebra and* $\{(B_i,\mu_{B_i})|i \in I\}$ *be a set of fuzzy subalgebras of* (A,μ_A)*. Then,* $\bigwedge\limits_{i\in I}(B_i,\mu_{B_i})$ *is a fuzzy subalgebra of* (A,μ_A).

Proof. It is obvious that $\bigwedge_{i \in I} B_i \subset A$ and $\bigwedge_{i \in I} B_i$ is a subalgebra of A. Then, we have

$$\begin{aligned}\bigwedge_{i \in I} \mu_{B_i}(a_i + b_i) &\geq \bigwedge_{i \in I} (\mu_{B_i}(a_i) \wedge \mu_{B_i}(b_i)) \\ &= \bigwedge_{i \in I} \mu_{B_i}(a_i) \wedge \bigwedge_{i \in I} \mu_{B_i}(b_i),\end{aligned}$$

$$\begin{aligned}\bigwedge_{i \in I} \mu_{B_i}(a_i \cdot b_i) &\geq \bigwedge_{i \in I} (\mu_{B_i}(a_i) \wedge \mu_{B_i}(b_i)) \\ &= \bigwedge_{i \in I} \mu_{B_i}(a_i) \wedge \bigwedge_{i \in I} \mu_{B_i}(b_i),\end{aligned}$$

and

$$\begin{aligned}\bigwedge_{i \in I} \mu_{B_i}(ka_i) &= \mu_{B_1}(ka_1) \wedge \ldots \wedge \mu_{B_n}(ka_n) \\ &\geq \mu_{B_1}(a_1) \wedge \ldots \wedge \mu_{B_n}(a_n) \\ &= \bigwedge_{i \in I} \mu_{B_i}(a_i);\end{aligned}$$

for all $a_i, b_i \in B_i$, $k \in F$, and $\bigwedge_{i \in I} \mu_{B_i}(e) = 1$.

In conclusion, $\bigwedge_{i \in I} (B_i, \mu_{B_i})$ is a fuzzy subalgebra of (A, μ_A). □

Theorem 2. *Let (A, μ_A) be a fuzzy algebra and $\{(R_i, \mu_{R_i}) | i \in I\}$ be a set of fuzzy ideals of (A, μ_A). Then, $\bigwedge_{i \in I} (R_i, \mu_{R_i})$ is a fuzzy ideal of (A, μ_A).*

Proof. It is easy to obtain that $\bigwedge_{i \in I} R_i$ is a subalgebra of A. Then, we have

$$\begin{aligned}\bigwedge_{i \in I} \mu_{R_i}(a_i \cdot b_i) &\geq \bigwedge_{i \in I} (\mu_{R_i}(a_i) \vee \mu_{R_i}(b_i)) \\ &= \bigwedge_{i \in I} \mu_{R_i}(a_i) \vee \bigwedge_{i \in I} \mu_{R_i}(b_i),\end{aligned}$$

for all $a_i, b_i \in R_i$.

In conclusion, $\bigwedge_{i \in I} (R_i, \mu_{R_i})$ is a fuzzy ideal of (A, μ_A). □

Remark 4. *Let (A, μ_A) be a fuzzy algebra and $\{(B_i, \mu_{B_i}) | i \in I\}$ be a set of fuzzy subalgebras of (A, μ_A) [respectively, let $\{(R_i, \mu_{R_i}) | i \in I\}$ be a set of fuzzy ideals of (A, μ_A)]. Then, $\bigvee_{i \in I} (B_i, \mu_{B_i})$ may not be a fuzzy subalgebra of (A, μ_A) [respectively, $\bigvee_{i \in I} (R_i, \mu_{R_i})$ may not be a fuzzy ideal of (A, μ_A)].*

Example 2. *Consider polynomial algebras in Example 1, where addition, multiplication, and scalar multiplication are defined in a conventional manner. Consider that two of these fuzzy subalgebras, $(F1, \mu_1)$ and $(F2, \mu_2)$ are sets of fuzzy polynomial algebras:*

(1) $(F1, \mu_1)$: The fuzzy degree of the fuzzy subsets of all constant polynomials is 1; the fuzzy degree of the other polynomials is 0.

(2) $(F2, \mu_2)$: The fuzzy degree of fuzzy subsets of all linear polynomials is 1; the fuzzy degree of the other polynomials is 0.

Obviously, both $(F1, \mu_1)$ and $(F2, \mu_2)$ are fuzzy subalgebras. However, $(F1, \mu_1) \vee (F2, \mu_2)$ is not a fuzzy subalgebra; for example, the fuzzy degree of quadratic polynomial x^2 is 0 in $(F1, \mu_1) \vee (F2, \mu_2)$; however, x^2 is neither a constant polynomial nor a linear polynomial.

Remark 5. *One can provide an example of fuzzy ideals by following the construction method described in Example 2.*

Theorem 3. *Let (A, μ_A), (B, μ_B) be fuzzy algebras, $f : (A, \mu_A) \to (B, \mu_B)$ be a fuzzy epimorphism, and (R, μ_R) be a fuzzy ideal of (A, μ_A). Then, $(f(R), \mu_{f(R)})$ is a fuzzy ideal of (B, μ_B).*

Proof. It is easy to obtain that $f(R)$ is a subalgebra of B.

Suppose that a, $b \in R$; thus, $f(a), f(b) \in f(R)$. Then,

$$\begin{aligned} \mu_{f(R)}(f(a) \cdot f(b)) &= \bigvee_{f(z)=f(a)\cdot f(b)} \mu_R(z) \\ &= \bigvee_{z=a\cdot b} \mu_R(a \cdot b) \\ &\geq \bigvee_{z=a\cdot b} (\mu_R(a) \vee \mu_R(b)) \\ &= (\bigvee \mu_R(a)) \vee (\bigvee \mu_R(b)) \\ &= \mu_{f(R)}(f(a)) \vee \mu_{f(R)}(f(b)). \end{aligned}$$

In conclusion, $(f(R), \mu_{f(R)})$ is a fuzzy ideal of (B, μ_B). □

Theorem 4. *Let (A, μ_A), (B, μ_B) be fuzzy algebras, $f : (A, \mu_A) \to (B, \mu_B)$ be a fuzzy homomorphism, and (R, μ_R) be a fuzzy ideal of (B, μ_B). Then, $(f^{-1}(R), \mu_{f^{-1}(R)})$ is a fuzzy ideal of (A, μ_A).*

Proof. It is easy to obtain that $f^{-1}(R)$ is a subalgebra of A.

Suppose that a, $b \in f^{-1}(R)$; thus, $f(a), f(b) \in R$. Then, from Remark 3(1), we have

$$\begin{aligned} \bigvee \mu_{f^{-1}(R)}(a \cdot b) &= \mu_R(f(a \cdot b)) \\ &= \mu_R(f(a) \cdot f(b)) \\ &\geq \mu_R(f(a)) \vee \mu_R(f(b)) \\ &= \bigvee \mu_{f^{-1}(R)}(a) \vee \bigvee \mu_{f^{-1}(R)}(b). \end{aligned}$$

In conclusion, $(f^{-1}(R), \mu_{f^{-1}(R)})$ is a fuzzy ideal of (A, μ_A). □

4. Quotients of Fuzzy Algebras

In this section, we define the quotients constructed by fuzzy ideals and establish the existences of fuzzy homomorphisms and fuzzy isomorphisms between these quotient structures.

Definition 10. *Let (A, μ_A) be a fuzzy algebra and (R, μ_R) be a fuzzy ideal of (A, μ_A). We define an addition, a multiplication, and a scalar multiplication operations on A/R as follows:*

(1) $(a \cdot R) + (b \cdot R) = (a + b) \cdot R$,

(2) $(a \cdot R) \cdot (b \cdot R) = (a \cdot b) \cdot R$,

(3) $k(a \cdot R) = (ka) \cdot R$,

for all $a, b \in A, k \in F$.

Theorem 5. *Let (A, μ_A) be a fuzzy algebra, (R, μ_R) be a fuzzy ideal of (A, μ_A). There exists an $a \in A$ such that $\mu_A(a) = 1$, $\mu_{A/R}$ is defined by*

$$\mu_{A/R}(a'/R) = \begin{cases} 1, & a' \in R, \\ \sup\limits_{b \in R} \mu_A(a' \cdot b), & a' \notin R, \end{cases};$$

then, $(A/R, \mu_{A/R})$ is a fuzzy algebra, which is called a fuzzy quotient algebra of (A, μ_A).

Remark 6. *First, we prove that the operations on A/R are well-defined.*

Let $a', a'', b', b'' \in A$, $r \in R$, $a' \cdot r$ and $b' \cdot r$ belong to the same class, $a'' \cdot r$ and $b'' \cdot r$ belong to the same class, thus,

$$\mu_A(a' \cdot r) = \mu_A(b' \cdot r), \mu_A(a'' \cdot r) = \mu_A(b'' \cdot r),$$

$$\sup_{r\in R} \mu_A(a' \cdot r) = \sup_{r\in R} \mu_A(b' \cdot r), \text{ and } \sup_{r\in R} \mu_A(a'' \cdot r) = \sup_{r\in R} \mu_A(b'' \cdot r).$$

(1) If $a', b' \in R$, $a'', b'' \in R$, then

$$\mu_A\big((a' \cdot a'') \cdot r\big) = 1 = \mu_A\big((b' \cdot b'') \cdot r\big).$$

(2) If $a', b' \notin R$, $a'', b'' \notin R$, then

$$\sup_{r\in R} \mu_A\big((a' \cdot a'') \cdot r\big) = \sup_{r\in R} \mu_A\big(a' \cdot (a'' \cdot r)\big) = \sup_{\substack{a''\cdot r = \bar{r},\\ \bar{r}\in R}} \mu_A(a' \cdot \bar{r}),$$

$$\sup_{r\in R} \mu_A\big((b' \cdot b'') \cdot r\big) = \sup_{r\in R} \mu_A\big(b' \cdot (b'' \cdot r)\big) = \sup_{\substack{b''\cdot r = \bar{\bar{r}},\\ \bar{\bar{r}}\in R}} \mu_A(b' \cdot \bar{\bar{r}}),$$

and $a' \cdot \bar{r} \in a' \cdot R$, $b' \cdot \bar{\bar{r}} \in b' \cdot R$, then $\sup_{\substack{a''\cdot r = \bar{r},\\ \bar{r}\in R}} \mu_A(a' \cdot \bar{r}) = \sup_{\substack{b''\cdot r = \bar{\bar{r}},\\ \bar{\bar{r}}\in R}} \mu_A(b' \cdot \bar{\bar{r}})$, thus, $\sup_{r\in R} \mu_A\big((a' \cdot a'') \cdot r\big)$ $= \sup_{r\in R} \mu_A\big((b' \cdot b'') \cdot r\big)$, we can obtain that the multiplication operation is well-defined. In the same way, we can obtain that addition and scalar multiplication operations are well-defined.

Next, we prove Theorem 5.

Proof. Let us prove that the result under multiplication is true.

Suppose that $a_1, a_2 \in A$.

(1) If $a_1, a_2 \in R$, then

$$\mu_{A/R}\big((a_1 \cdot R) \cdot (a_2 \cdot R)\big) = \mu_{A/R}\big((a_1 \cdot a_2) \cdot R\big) = 1;$$

thus, $\mu_{A/R}(a_1 \cdot R) \wedge \mu_{A/R}(a_2 \cdot R) \leq \mu_{A/R}((a_1 \cdot R) \cdot (a_2 \cdot R))$.

(2) If $a_1 \in R$, $a_2 \notin R$, then

$$\begin{aligned} \mu_{A/R}\big((a_1 \cdot R) \cdot (a_2 \cdot R)\big) &= \sup_{b\in R} \mu_A\big((a_1 \cdot a_2) \cdot b\big) \\ &\geq \sup_{a_1\in R, a_2\notin R} \mu_A(a_1 \cdot a_2) \wedge \sup_{b\in R} \mu_A(b) \\ &\geq \sup_{a_1\in R, a_2\notin R} \mu_A(a_1 \cdot a_2) \wedge 1 \\ &= \mu_{A/R}(a_2 \cdot R). \end{aligned}$$

In addition, $\mu_{A/R}(a_1 \cdot R) = 1$; then, $\mu_{A/R}(a_1 \cdot R) \wedge \mu_{A/R}(a_2 \cdot R) = \mu_{A/R}(a_2 \cdot R)$. Thus, $\mu_{A/R}(a_1 \cdot R) \wedge \mu_{A/R}(a_2 \cdot R) \leq \mu_{A/R}\big((a_1 \cdot R) \cdot (a_2 \cdot R)\big)$.

In conclusion, the result under multiplication is true.

Similarly, we can prove that the results under addition and scalar multiplication are true.

Thus, $(A/R, \mu_{A/R})$ is a fuzzy algebra. □

Remark 7. *The definition of $\mu_{A/R}$ in Theorem 5 conforms to the Zadeh extension principle.*

Theorem 6. *Let (A, μ_A) be a fuzzy algebra; there exists an $a \in A$ such that $\mu_A(a) = 1$. Let (R, μ_R) be a fuzzy ideal of (A, μ_A) and $(A/R, \mu_{A/R})$ be a fuzzy quotient algebra of (A, μ_A). $\mu_{A/R}$ is defined by*

$$\mu_{A/R}(a'/R) = \begin{cases} 1, & a' \in R, \\ \sup_{b\in R} \mu_A(a' \cdot b), & a' \notin R, \end{cases}.$$

We define a mapping as follows:

$$v : (A, \mu_A) \to (A/R, \mu_{A/R}), v(a') = a'/R,$$

for all $a' \in A$; then, v is a fuzzy homomorphism.

Proof. First, it is easy to obtain that v is a homomorphism.

Next, we prove that v is a fuzzy homomorphism.

(1) If $a_1, a_2 \in R$, then

$$\mu_{A/R}((a_1 \cdot R) \cdot (a_2 \cdot R)) = \mu_{A/R}((a_1 \cdot a_2) \cdot R) = 1.$$

Thus, $\mu_A(a_1) \wedge \mu_A(a_2) \leq \mu_{A/R}((a_1 \cdot R) \cdot (a_2 \cdot R))$.

(2) If $a_1 \in R, a_2 \notin R$, then

$$\begin{aligned} \mu_{A/R}((a_1 \cdot R) \cdot (a_2 \cdot R)) &= \sup_{b \in R} \mu_A((a_1 \cdot a_2) \cdot b) \\ &\geq \sup_{a_1 \in R} \mu_A(a_1) \wedge \sup_{a_2 \notin R} \mu_A(a_2) \wedge \sup_{b \in R} \mu_A(b) \\ &= \sup_{a_1 \in R} \mu_A(a_1) \wedge \sup_{a_2 \notin R} \mu_A(a_2) \wedge 1 \\ &\geq \mu_A(a_1) \wedge \mu_A(a_2). \end{aligned}$$

Thus, $\mu_A(a_1) \wedge \mu_A(a_2) \leq \mu_{A/R}((a_1 \cdot R) \cdot (a_2 \cdot R))$.

In conclusion, the result under multiplication is true. Similarly, we can prove that the results under addition and scalar multiplication are true.

Hence, v is a fuzzy homomorphism. □

Theorem 7. *Let (A, μ_A), (B, μ_B) be fuzzy algebras, $f' : (A, \mu_A) \to (B, \mu_B)$ be a fuzzy homomorphism, (R, μ_R) and $(R', \mu_{R'})$ be fuzzy ideals of (A, μ_A) and (B, μ_B), respectively, and $(A/R, \mu_{A/R})$ and $(B/R', \mu_{B/R'})$ be fuzzy quotient algebras of (A, μ_A) and (B, μ_B), respectively. A mapping $f : (A/R, \mu_{A/R}) \to (B/R', \mu_{B/R'})$ is defined as follows:*

$$f(a \cdot R) = b \cdot R', f(R) \subseteq R', f(a \cdot R) = f(a) \cdot R,$$

for all $a \cdot R \in A/R$, $b \cdot R' \in B/R'$, $\mu_{B/R'}$ is defined by

$$\mu_{B/R'}(b/R') = \begin{cases} 1, & b \in R', \\ \sup\limits_{f(a/R)=b/R'} \mu_A(a \cdot R), & b \notin R'; \end{cases}$$

then, f is a fuzzy homomorphism.

$$\begin{array}{ccc} (A, \mu_A) & \xrightarrow{f'} & (B, \mu_B) \\ {\scriptstyle\alpha}\downarrow & & \downarrow{\scriptstyle\beta} \\ (A/R, \mu_{A/R}) & \xrightarrow{f} & (B/R', \mu_{B/R'}) \end{array}$$

Proof. First, it is easy to obtain that f is a homomorphism.

Next, we prove that f is a fuzzy homomorphism.

Let us prove that the result under multiplication is true.

(1) If $b \in R'$, then $\mu_{B/R'}(b \cdot R') = 1$; thus, $\mu_{A/R}(a \cdot R) \leq \mu_{B/R'}(b \cdot R')$.

(2) If $b \notin R'$, then

$$\begin{aligned} \mu_{B/R'}(b \cdot R') &= \sup_{f(a \cdot R)=b \cdot R'} \mu_{A/R}(a \cdot R) \\ &= \bigvee_{f(a \cdot R)=b \cdot R'} \mu_{A/R}(a \cdot R) \\ &\geq \mu_{A/R}(a \cdot R). \end{aligned}$$

In conclusion, the result under multiplication is true.

Similarly, we can prove that the results under addition and scalar multiplication are true.

Hence, f is a fuzzy homomorphism. □

Theorem 8. *Let (A, μ_A), (B, μ_B) be fuzzy algebras, $f : (A, \mu_A) \to (B, \mu_B)$ be a fuzzy homomorphism, and (R, μ_R) be a fuzzy ideal of (B, μ_B). Thus, $(f^{-1}(R), \mu_{f^{-1}(R)})$ is a fuzzy ideal of (A, μ_A), and $(A/f^{-1}(R), \mu_1)$ is a fuzzy quotient algebra. We define a mapping as follows:*

$$\alpha : (A/f^{-1}(R), \mu_1) \to (B/R, \mu_2), \alpha(a/f^{-1}(R)) = b/R,$$

for all $a/f^{-1}(R) \in A/f^{-1}(R)$, and μ_2 is defined as follows:

$$\mu_2(b/R) = \begin{cases} 1, & b \in R, \\ \sup\limits_{\alpha(a'/f^{-1}(R))=b'/R, b' \in R} \mu_1((a \cdot a') \cdot f^{-1}(R)), & b \notin R, \cdot \end{cases}$$

If $b \in R$, then $\mu_1(\alpha^{-1}(b/R)) = 1$, and there exists an $a''/f^{-1}(R) \in A/f^{-1}(R)$ such that $\mu_1(a''/f^{-1}(R)) = 1$; then, α is a fuzzy isomorphism.

Proof. First, we prove that α is a homomorphism.

Suppose that $a_1/f^{-1}(R)$, $a_2/f^{-1}(R)$,$(a_1 \cdot a_2)/f^{-1}(R)$,$(a_1 + a_2)/f^{-1}(R) \in A/f^{-1}(R)$, $b_1/R, b_2/R, (b_1+b_2)/R$,$(b_1 \cdot b_2)/R$,$b/R, b^*/R \in B/R$,$\alpha(a_1/f^{-1}(R)) = b_1 \cdot R, \alpha(a_2/f^{-1}(R)) = b_2 \cdot R$,$\alpha((a_1 \cdot a_2)/f^{-1}(R)) = b \cdot R, \alpha((a_1 + a_2)/f^{-1}(R)) = b^* \cdot R, b_1 \cdot b_2 = b, b_1 + b_2 = b^*$; then, we have

$$\begin{aligned} \alpha\Big((a_1/f^{-1}(R)) \cdot (a_2/f^{-1}(R))\Big) &= \alpha((a_1 \cdot a_2)/f^{-1}(R)) \\ &= b \cdot R \\ &= (b_1 \cdot b_2) \cdot R \\ &= (b_1 \cdot R) \cdot (b_2 \cdot R) \\ &= \alpha(a_1/f^{-1}(R)) \cdot \alpha(a_2/f^{-1}(R)), \end{aligned}$$

$$\begin{aligned} \alpha\Big((a_1/f^{-1}(R)) + (a_2/f^{-1}(R))\Big) &= \alpha((a_1 + a_2)/f^{-1}(R)) \\ &= b^* \cdot R \\ &= (b_1 + b_2) \cdot R \\ &= (b_1 \cdot R) + (b_2 \cdot R) \\ &= \alpha(a_1/f^{-1}(R)) + \alpha(a_2/f^{-1}(R)), \end{aligned}$$

and

$$\begin{aligned} \alpha\Big(k(a_1/f^{-1}(R))\Big) &= \alpha\Big(k(a_1/f^{-1}(R))\Big) \\ &= (kb_1) \cdot R \\ &= k\alpha(a_1/f^{-1}(R)). \end{aligned}$$

Thus, α is a homomorphism.

Next, we prove that α is a bijection.

(i) For any $a_1/f^{-1}(R), a_2/f^{-1}(R) \in A/f^{-1}(R)$, if $a_1/f^{-1}(R) \neq a_2/f^{-1}(R)$, then $\alpha(a_1/f^{-1}(R)) \neq \alpha(a_2/f^{-1}(R))$; thus, α is an injection.

(ii) For any $b/R \in B/R$, there exists an $a_1/f^{-1}(R) \in A/f^{-1}(R)$ such that $\alpha(a_1/f^{-1}(R)) = b_1/R$; thus, α is a surjection.

From the above proof, we can obtain that α is an isomorphism.

Finally, we prove that α is a fuzzy isomorphism.

Suppose that $b_1, b_2 \in B$; then,

(1) If $b_1, b_2 \in R$, then

$$\mu_2\big((b_1\cdot R)\cdot(b_2\cdot R)\big)=\mu_2\big((b_1\cdot b_2)\cdot R\big)=1=\mu_1\big((a_1\cdot a_2)\cdot f^{-1}(R)\big).$$

Thus, $\mu_2\big((b_1\cdot R)\cdot(b_2\cdot R)\big)=\mu_1\big((a_1\cdot a_2)\cdot f^{-1}(R)\big)$.

(2) If $b_1 \in R$, $b_2 \notin R$, since $(A/f^{-1}(R),\mu_1)$ is a fuzzy algebra, we have $\mu_1\big((a_1\cdot a_2\cdot a')\cdot f^{-1}(R)\big)\geq \mu_1\big(a_1\cdot f^{-1}(R)\big)\wedge\mu_1\big(a_2\cdot f^{-1}(R)\big)\wedge\mu_1\big(a'\cdot f^{-1}(R)\big)$; thus,

$$\begin{aligned}
\mu_2\big((b_1\cdot R)\cdot(b_2\cdot R)\big) &= \mu_2\big((b_1\cdot b_2)\cdot R\big)\\
&= \sup \mu_1\big((a_1\cdot a_2\cdot a')\cdot f^{-1}(R)\big)\\
&\geq \sup_{\alpha\left(a_1\cdot f^{-1}(R)\right)=b_1\cdot R,} \mu_1\big(a_1\cdot f^{-1}(R)\big)\\
&\wedge \sup_{\alpha\left(a_2\cdot f^{-1}(R)\right)=b_2\cdot R} \mu_1\big(a_2\cdot f^{-1}(R)\big)\\
&\wedge \sup_{\alpha\left(a'\cdot f^{-1}(R)\right)=b'\cdot R, b'\in R} \mu_1\big(a'\cdot f^{-1}(R)\big)\\
&= 1\wedge \sup_{\alpha\left(a_2\cdot f^{-1}(R)\right)=b_2\cdot R} \mu_1\big(a_2\cdot f^{-1}(R)\big)\wedge 1\\
&= \sup_{\alpha\left(a_2\cdot f^{-1}(R)\right)=b_2\cdot R} \mu_1\big(a_2\cdot f^{-1}(R)\big)\\
&\geq \mu_1\big(a_2\cdot f^{-1}(R)\big).
\end{aligned}$$

From the definition of fuzzy algebras, we have $\mu_1\big((a_1\cdot a_2)\cdot f^{-1}(R)\big)\geq\mu_1\big(a_1\cdot f^{-1}(R)\big)\wedge\mu_1\big(a_2\cdot f^{-1}(R)\big)$; thus, $\mu_1\big((a_1\cdot a_2)\cdot f^{-1}(R)\big)\leq\mu_2\big((b_1\cdot R)\cdot(b_2\cdot R)\big)$.

Conversely, whether $b_1\cdot b_2\in R$ or $b_1\cdot b_2\notin R$, there always exists an $(a_1\cdot a_2)\cdot f^{-1}(R)\in A/f^{-1}(R)$ such that $\mu_1\big((a_1\cdot a_2)\cdot f^{-1}(R)\big)\leq\mu_2\big((b_1\cdot R)\cdot(b_2\cdot R)\big)$.

In conclusion, the result under multiplication is true.

Similarly, we can prove that the results under addition and scalar multiplication are true.

In conclusion, α is a fuzzy isomorphism. □

5. Homomorphism Theorems

In this section, we give the concept of homomorphic kernels and prove that they are fuzzy ideals. In addition, three homomorphism theorems are proved.

Definition 11. *Let (A,μ_A),(B,μ_B) be fuzzy algebras, $\alpha:(A,\mu_A)\to(B,\mu_B)$ be a fuzzy homomorphism, and L be a complete lattice. Then, the kernel of α is defined as follows:*

$$Ker\alpha=\{a\in A\mid \alpha(a)=0\},\mu: Ker\alpha\to L,\mu(a)=1,$$

which we denote as $(Ker\alpha,\mu)$ for short.

Example 3. *Let (A,μ_A),(B,μ_B) be fuzzy matrices, $\alpha:(A,\mu_A)\to(B,\mu_B)$, and for all (a,μ_a), $(c,\mu_c)\in(A,\mu_A)$, $\alpha\big((a,\mu_a)\big)=(a,\mu_a)\cdot(c,\mu_c)=(b,\mu_b)$; then, $Ker\alpha=\{(c,\mu_c)\in(A,\mu_A)|(a,\mu_a)\cdot(c,\mu_c)=0\}$, and the 0 here represents the null matrix.*

Theorem 9. *$(Ker\alpha,\mu)$ is a fuzzy ideal of (A,μ_A).*

Proof. Suppose that $a,b\in Ker\alpha$; then,

$$\mu(a\cdot b)\geq\mu(a)\wedge\mu(b)=1\wedge 1=1=\mu(a)\vee\mu(b).$$

Thus, $(Ker\alpha,\mu)$ is a fuzzy ideal of (A,μ_A). □

Theorem 10. *Let (A,μ_A), (B,μ_B) be fuzzy algebras and $\alpha : (A,\mu_A) \to (B,\mu_B)$ be a fuzzy epimorphism. There exists an $a \in A$ such that $\mu_A(a) = 1$, $(A/Ker\alpha, \mu_{A/Ker\alpha})$ is a fuzzy quotient algebra of (A,μ_A), and $\mu_{A/Ker\alpha}$ is defined by*

$$\mu_{A/Ker\alpha}(a'/Ker\alpha) = \begin{cases} 1, & a' \in a/Ker\alpha, \\ \sup\limits_{b\in a/Ker\alpha} \mu_A(a' \cdot b), & a' \notin a/Ker\alpha, \end{cases}$$

If $a' \in a/Ker\alpha$, then, $\mu_B(\alpha(a')) = 1$. $v : (A,\mu_A) \to (A/Ker\alpha, \mu_{A/Ker\alpha})$ is a fuzzy homomorphism, and $v(a') = a'/Ker\alpha$ for all $a' \in A$. We define a mapping as follows:

$$\beta{:}(A/Ker\alpha, \mu_{A/Ker\alpha}) \to (B,\mu_B), \beta(a'/Ker\alpha) = \alpha(a'),$$

for all $a' \in A$; then, β is a fuzzy isomorphism.

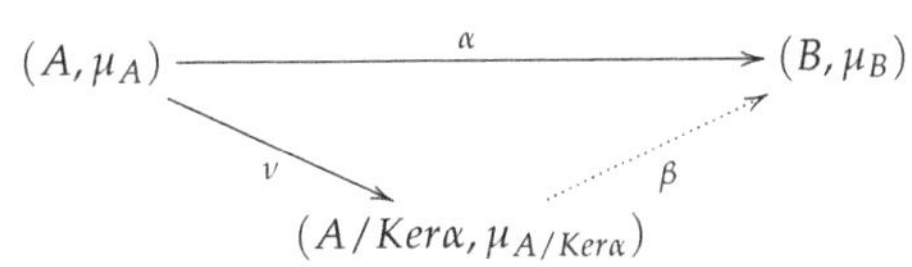

Proof. Suppose that $a_1, a_2 \in A$. We can obtain that β is a homomorphism using Theorem 6. We only need to prove that β is a bijection and $\mu_B\Big(\beta((a_1 \cdot a_2)/Ker\alpha)\Big) = \mu_{A/Ker\alpha}((a_1 \cdot a_2)/Ker\alpha)$.

First, we prove that β is a bijection.

(i) For any $a_1, a_2 \in A$, if $a_1/Ker\alpha \neq a_2/Ker\alpha$, then, $\alpha(a_1) \neq \alpha(a_2)$; thus, β is an injection.

(ii) For any $c \in B$, since α is surjective, there exists an $a' \in A$ such that $\alpha(a') = c$. Since $a'/Ker\alpha \in A/Ker\alpha$, then $\beta(a'/Ker\alpha) = \alpha(a') = c$; thus, β is a surjection.

Next, we prove that $\mu_B\Big(\beta((a_1 \cdot a_2)/Ker\alpha)\Big) = \mu_{A/Ker\alpha}((a_1 \cdot a_2)/Ker\alpha)$.

(1) If $a_1, a_2 \in a/Ker\alpha$, then $\mu_{A/Ker\alpha}((a_1 \cdot Ker\alpha)\cdot(a_2 \cdot Ker\alpha)) = \mu_{A/Ker\alpha}((a_1 \cdot a_2)\cdot Ker\alpha) = 1$. In this case, $\mu_B(\alpha(a_1 \cdot a_2)) = 1$.

Thus, $\mu_{A/Ker\alpha}((a_1 \cdot a_2) \cdot Ker\alpha) = \mu_B\Big(\beta((a_1 \cdot a_2) \cdot Ker\alpha)\Big)$.

(2) If $a_1 \in a/Ker\alpha$, $a_2 \notin a/Ker\alpha$, then

$$\begin{aligned} \mu_{A/Ker\alpha}((a_1 \cdot Ker\alpha) \cdot (a_2 \cdot Ker\alpha)) &= \mu_{A/Ker\alpha}((a_1 \cdot a_2) \cdot Ker\alpha) \\ &= \sup_{b\in a/Ker\alpha} \mu_A((a_1 \cdot a_2) \cdot b) \\ &\geq \sup_{a_1\in a/Ker\alpha} \mu_A(a_1) \wedge \sup_{a_2\notin a/Ker\alpha} \mu_A(a_2) \wedge \sup_{b\in a/Ker\alpha} \mu_A(b) \\ &= \sup_{a_1\in a/Ker\alpha} \mu_A(a_1) \wedge \sup_{a_2\notin a/Ker\alpha} \mu_A(a_2) \wedge 1 \\ &\geq \mu_A(a_1) \wedge \mu_A(a_2). \end{aligned}$$

For any $a_1, a_2 \in A$,

$$\begin{aligned} \mu_B(\alpha(a_1 \cdot a_2)) &= \vee \mu_A\Big(\alpha^{-1}(\alpha(a_1 \cdot a_2))\Big) \\ &\geq \mu_A(a_1) \wedge \mu_A(a_2); \end{aligned}$$

then, $\mu_{A/Ker\alpha}((a_1 \cdot a_2) \cdot Ker\alpha) \leq \mu_B\Big(\beta((a_1 \cdot a_2) \cdot Ker\alpha)\Big)$.

Let $\beta' : (B, \mu_B) \to (A/Ker\alpha, \mu_{A/Ker\alpha})$, and $\beta'(\alpha(a')) = a'/Ker\alpha$ for all $a' \in A$.
(3) If $a_1, a_2 \in a/Ker\alpha$, then the process of the proof is similar to (1).
(4) If $a_1 \in a/Ker\alpha, a_2 \notin a/Ker\alpha$, then

$$\begin{aligned}
\mu_{A/Ker\alpha}((a_1 \cdot Ker\alpha) \cdot (a_2 \cdot Ker\alpha)) &= \mu_{A/Ker\alpha}((a_1 \cdot a_2) \cdot Ker\alpha) \\
&= \sup_{b \in a/Ker\alpha} \mu_A((a_1 \cdot a_2) \cdot b) \\
&\geq \sup_{a_1 \in a/Ker\alpha} \mu_A(a_1) \wedge \sup_{a_2 \notin a/Ker\alpha} \mu_A(a_2) \wedge \sup_{b \in a/Ker\alpha} \mu_A(b) \\
&= 1 \wedge \sup_{a_2 \notin a/Ker\alpha} \mu_A(a_2) \wedge 1 \\
&\geq \mu_A(a_2).
\end{aligned}$$

From the definition of μ_B, $\mu_B(\alpha(a_1 \cdot a_2)) \geq \mu_A(a_1) \wedge \mu_A(a_2)$, we have

$$\mu_B\Big(\beta((a_1 \cdot a_2) \cdot Ker\alpha)\Big) = \mu_B(\alpha(a_1 \cdot a_2)) \leq \mu_{A/Ker\alpha}((a_1 \cdot a_2) \cdot Ker\alpha).$$

Hence, $\mu_B\Big(\beta((a_1 \cdot a_2) \cdot Ker\alpha)\Big) = \mu_{A/Ker\alpha}((a_1 \cdot a_2) \cdot Ker\alpha)$.

In conclusion, the result under multiplication is true. Similarly, we can prove that the results under addition and scalar multiplication are true; thus, β is a fuzzy isomorphism. □

Theorem 11. *Let (A, μ_A) be a fuzzy algebra, (R_1, μ_{R_1}) and (R_2, μ_{R_2}) be fuzzy ideals of (A, μ_A), (R_2, μ_{R_2}) be a fuzzy subalgebra of (R_1, μ_{R_1}), $(A/R_1, \mu_1)$ and $(A/R_2, \mu_2)$ be fuzzy quotient algebras of (A, μ_A), $((A/R_2)/(R_1/R_2), \mu_3)$ be a fuzzy quotient algebra of $(A/R_2, \mu_2)$. There exists an $(a''/R_2)/(R_1/R_2) \in (A/R_2)/(R_1/R_2)$ such that $\mu_3((a''/R_2)/(R_1/R_2)) = 1$, μ_1 is defined as follows:*

$$\mu_1(a/R_1) = \begin{cases} 1, & a \in (a''/R_2)/(R_1/R_2), \\ \sup\limits_{a' \in (a''/R_2)/(R_1/R_2)} \mu_3\Big(((a \cdot a')/R_2)/(R_1/R_2)\Big), & a \notin (a''/R_2)/(R_1/R_2), \end{cases}.$$

We define a mapping as follows:

$$\alpha : ((A/R_2)/(R_1/R_2), \mu_3) \to (A/R_1, \mu_1), \alpha((a/R_2)/(R_1/R_2)) = a/R_1,$$

for all $(a/R_2)/(R_1/R_2) \in (A/R_2)/(R_1/R_2)$; then, α is a fuzzy isomorphism.

Proof. For any $a_1, a_2 \in A$, $a_1/R_1, a_2/R_1 \in A/R_1$,$(a_1/R_2)/(R_1/R_2)$,$(a_2/R_2)/(R_1/R_2) \in (A/R_2)/(R_1/R_2)$, we have $\alpha((a_1/R_2)/(R_1/R_2)) = \alpha((a_2/R_2)/(R_1/R_2)) \Leftrightarrow a_1/R_1 = a_2/R_1$; thus, α is a well-defined bijection.

Similarly, we can obtain that α is a homomorphism using Theorem 6; thus, α is an isomorphism.

Next, we prove that α is a fuzzy isomorphism.

(1) If $a_1, a_2 \in (a''/R_2)/(R_1/R_2)$, then

$$\mu_1((a_1 \cdot R_1) \cdot (a_2 \cdot R_1)) = \mu_1((a_1 \cdot a_2) \cdot R_1) = 1 = \mu_3\Big(((a_1 \cdot a_2)/R_2)/(R_1/R_2)\Big).$$

Thus, $\mu_1((a_1 \cdot R_1) \cdot (a_2 \cdot R_1)) = \mu_3\Big(((a_1 \cdot a_2)/R_2)/(R_1/R_2)\Big)$.

(2) If $a_1 \in (a''/R_2)/(R_1/R_2)$, $a_2 \notin (a''/R_2)/(R_1/R_2)$, since $((A/R_2)/(R_1/R_2), \mu_3)$ is a fuzzy algebra, we have $\mu_3\Big(((a_1 \cdot a_2 \cdot a')/R_2)/(R_1/R_2)\Big) \geq \mu_3((a_1/R_2)/(R_1/R_2)) \wedge$

$\mu_3((a_2/R_2)/(R_1/R_2)) \wedge \mu_3((a'/R_2)/(R_1/R_2))$; thus,

$$\begin{aligned}
\mu_1((a_1 \cdot R_1) \cdot (a_2 \cdot R_1)) &= \mu_1((a_1 \cdot a_2) \cdot R_1) \\
&= \sup_{a' \in (a''/R_2)/(R_1/R_2)} \mu_3\Big(((a_1 \cdot a_2 \cdot a')/R_2)/(R_1/R_2)\Big) \\
&\geq \sup_{a_1 \in (a''/R_2)/(R_1/R_2)} \mu_3((a_1/R_2)/(R_1/R_2)) \\
&\wedge \sup_{a_2 \notin (a''/R_2)/(R_1/R_2)} \mu_3((a_2/R_2)/(R_1/R_2)) \\
&\wedge \sup_{a' \in (a''/R_2)/(R_1/R_2)} \mu_3((a'/R_2)/(R_1/R_2)) \\
&= \sup_{a_1 \in (a''/R_2)/(R_1/R_2)} \mu_3((a_1/R_2)/(R_1/R_2)) \\
&\wedge \sup_{a_2 \notin (a''/R_2)/(R_1/R_2)} \mu_3((a_2/R_2)/(R_1/R_2)) \wedge 1 \\
&= \sup_{a_1 \in (a''/R_2)/(R_1/R_2)} \mu_3((a_1/R_2)/(R_1/R_2)) \\
&\wedge \sup_{a_2 \notin (a''/R_2)/(R_1/R_2)} \mu_3((a_2/R_2)/(R_1/R_2)) \\
&\geq \mu_3((a_1/R_2)/(R_1/R_2)) \wedge \mu_3((a_2/R_2)/(R_1/R_2)).
\end{aligned}$$

Thus, $\mu_3((a_1 \cdot R_2)/(R_1/R_2)) \wedge \mu_3((a_2 \cdot R_2)/(R_1/R_2)) \leq \mu_1((a_1 \cdot a_2)/R_1)$.

Conversely, whether $a_1 \cdot a_2 \in (a''/R_2)/(R_1/R_2)$ or $a_1 \cdot a_2 \notin (a''/R_2)/(R_1/R_2)$, there always exists an $a \in (a''/R_2)/(R_1/R_2)$ such that $\mu_1(a/R_1) = \mu_1((a_1 \cdot a_2)/R_1) = \mu_3\Big(((a_1 \cdot a_2)/R_2)/(R_1/R_2)\Big)$.

In conclusion, the result under multiplication is true. Similarly, we can prove that the results under addition and scalar multiplication are true.

Hence, α is a fuzzy isomorphism. □

Theorem 12. *Let (A, μ_A) be a fuzzy algebra, (H, μ_H) be a fuzzy algebra of (A, μ_A), and (R, μ_R) be a fuzzy ideal of (A, μ_A); then, $(HR/R, \mu_4)$ and $(H/H \cap R, \mu_5)$ are fuzzy quotient algebras. We define a mapping as follows:*

$$\alpha' : (HR/R, \mu_4) \to (H/H \cap R, \mu_5), \alpha(hr/r) = h/h \cap r,$$

for all $hr/r \in HR/R$, there exists an $h''r/r \in HR/R$ such that $\mu_4(h''r/r) = 1$, and $\mu_5(h/h \cap r)$ is defined by

$$\mu_5(h/h \cap r) = \begin{cases} 1, & h \in h''r/r, \\ \sup_{h' \in h''r/r} \mu_4((hr \cdot h'r)/r), & h \notin h''r/r, \end{cases};$$

then, similar to the proof of Theorem 11, we can obtain that α' is a fuzzy isomorphism.

6. Conclusions

In this paper, we discussed the properties of fuzzy ideals and quotients of fuzzy associative algebras. In Section 3, we provided the concepts of fuzzy associative algebras, fuzzy homomorphisms, and fuzzy ideals over a common number field. In Theorems 1 and 2, we proved that the intersections of the subalgebras were fuzzy subalgebras and the intersections of fuzzy ideals were fuzzy ideals. In Theorems 3 and 4, we showed that if $f : (A, \mu_A) \to (B, \mu_B)$ is a fuzzy epimorphism, then the homomorphic images and preimages of fuzzy ideals are fuzzy ideals. In Section 4, we defined an addition, a multiplication, and a scalar multiplication operation on quotient structures constructed by fuzzy ideals. We proved that the quotient structures created by fuzzy ideals were fuzzy algebras and there were fuzzy homomorphisms between fuzzy algebras and its fuzzy quotient algebras. In Theorem 7, we proved that if (R, μ_R) and $(R', \mu_{R'})$ are fuzzy ideals of (A, μ_A) and (B, μ_B), respectively, then $f : (A/R, \mu_{A/R}) \to (B/R', \mu_{B/R'})$ is a fuzzy homomorphism. In Section 5, we defined the concepts of *kernels* in fuzzy homomorphisms, and in Theorem 9, we proved that the *kernels* were fuzzy ideals. In particular, we proved that if $\alpha : (A, \mu_A) \to (B, \mu_B)$ is a fuzzy epimorphism, then $A/Ker\alpha$ is isomorphic to (B, μ_B). Moreover, we proved two other homomorphism theorems.

This work helps us to better understand other specific fuzzy algebra structure theories and provides important theoretical support for the study of other algebraic theories. On this basis, the classification and representation of fuzzy associative algebras can be studied in the future.

Author Contributions: Writing—original draft, X.Y.; writing—review and editing, X.Z. All authors have read and agreed to the published version of the manuscript.

Funding: This research was funded by the University Science Programming of Xin Jiang (grant number: XJEDU2021Y042), the Doctoral Research Foundation of Yili Normal University(grant number: 2021YSBS011), the Science and Technology Plan Project of Yili State (grant number: YZ2022Y010), the Research and Innovation Team Project of Yili Normal University (grant number: CXZK2021014), and the High-level Nurturing Program of Yili Normal University (grant number: YSPY2022011).

Data Availability Statement: Data are contained within the article.

Acknowledgments: The author wishes to thank the reviewers for their excellent suggestions that have been incorporated into this paper.

Conflicts of Interest: The authors declare no conflicts of interest.

References

1. Zadeh, L.A. Fuzzy sets. *Inf. Control* **1965**, *8*, 338–353. [CrossRef]
2. Liu, W. Fuzzy invariant subgroups and fuzzy ideals. *Fuzzy Sets Syst.* **1982**, *8*, 133–139. [CrossRef]
3. Ahsan, J.; Saifullah, K.; Khan, M.F. Fuzzy semirings. *Fuzzy Sets Syst.* **1993**, *60*, 309–320. [CrossRef]
4. Kim, C.B. Isomorphism theorems and fuzzy k-ideals of k-semirings. *Fuzzy Sets Syst.* **2000**, *112*, 333–342. [CrossRef]
5. Mandal, D. Fuzzy ideals and fuzzy interior ideals in ordered semirings. *Fuzzy Inf. Eng.* **2014**, *6*, 101–114. [CrossRef]
6. Muhiuddin, G.; Abughazalah, N.; Mahboob, A.; Al-Kadi, D. A Novel study of fuzzy bi-ideals in ordered semirings. *Axioms* **2023**, *12*, 626. [CrossRef]
7. Liu, W. Operations on fuzzy ideals. *Fuzzy Sets Syst.* **1983**, *11*, 31–39.
8. Swamy, U.M.; Swamy, K.L.N. Fuzzy prime ideals of rings. *J. Math. Anal. Appl.* **1988**, *134*, 94–103. [CrossRef]
9. Malik, A.S.; Mordeson, J.N. Fuzzy prime ideals of a ring. *Fuzzy Sets Syst.* **1990**, *37*, 93–98. [CrossRef]
10. Nanda, S. Fuzzy algebras over fuzzy fields. *Fuzzy Sets Syst.* **1990**, *37*, 99–103. [CrossRef]
11. Nanda, S. Fuzzy linear spaces over valued fields. *Fuzzy Sets Syst.* **1991**, *42*, 351–354. [CrossRef]
12. Biswas, R. Fuzzy fields and fuzzy linear spaces redefined. *Fuzzy Sets Syst.* **1989**, *33*, 257–259. [CrossRef]
13. Kuraoka, T.; Kuroki, N. On fuzzy quotient rings induced by fuzzy ideals. *Fuzzy Sets Syst.* **1992**, *47*, 381–386. [CrossRef]
14. Gu, W.; Lu, T. Fuzzy algebras over fuzzy fields redefined. *Fuzzy Sets Syst.* **1993**, *53*, 105–107. [CrossRef]
15. Mahboob, A.; Davvaz, B.; Khan, N.M. Fuzzy (m,n)-ideals in semigroups. *Comput. Appl. Math.* **2019**, *38*, 189. [CrossRef]
16. Mahboob, A.; Davvaz, B.; Khan, N.M. Ordered Γ-semigroups and fuzzy Γ-ideals. *Iran. J. Math. Sci. Inform.* **2021**, *16*, 129–146. [CrossRef]
17. Mahboob, A.; Al-Tahan, M.; Muhiuddin, G. Fuzzy (m,n)-filters based on fuzzy points in ordered semigroups. *Comput. Appl. Math.* **2023**, *42*, 245. [CrossRef]
18. Mahboob, A.; Muhiuddin, G. A new type of fuzzy prime subset in ordered semigroups. *New Math. Nat. Comput.* **2021**, *17*, 739–752. [CrossRef]
19. Zhou, X.; Chen, L; Chang, Y. $L-$fuzzy ideals and $L-$fuzzy subalgebras of Novikov algebras. *Open Math.* **2019**, *17*, 1538–1546. [CrossRef]
20. Addis, G.M.; Kausar, N.; Munir, M. Fuzzy homomorphism theorems on rings. *J. Discret. Math. Sci. Cryptogr.* **2022**, *25*, 1757–1776. [CrossRef]
21. Korma, S.G.; Parimi, R.K.; Kifetew, D.C. Homomorphism and isomorphism theorems on fuzzy lattices. *Res. Math.* **2023**, *10*, 2255411. [CrossRef]
22. Adak, A.K.; Nilkamal; Barman, N. Fermatean fuzzy semi-prime ideals of ordered semigroups. *Topol. Algebra Its Appl.* **2023**, *11*, 20230102. [CrossRef]
23. Hamidi, M.; Borumand Saeid, A. EQ-algebras based on fuzzy hyper EQ-filters. *Soft Comput.* **2019**, *23*, 5289–5305. [CrossRef]
24. Kumduang, T.; Chinram, R. Fuzzy ideals and fuzzy congruences on menger algebras with their homomorphism properties. *Discuss. Math. Gen. Algebra Appl.* **2023**, *43*, 189–206. [CrossRef]
25. Ahmed, I.S.; Al-Fayadh, A.; Ebrahim, H.H. Fuzzy $\sigma-$algebra and some related concepts. *AIP Conf. Proc.* **2023**, *1*, 189–206.

26. Hariharan, S.; Vijayalakshmi, S.; Mohan, J.; Akila, S.; Nithya, A.; Muthukumar, R.; Ravi, J. Modified hybrid fuzzy algebra: MF-Algebra. *Discuss. Math. Gen. Algebra Appl.* **2023**, *8*, 34–38. [CrossRef]
27. Myšková, H.; Plavka, J. Regularity of interval fuzzy matrices. *Fuzzy Sets Syst.* **2023**, *463*, 108478. [CrossRef]
28. Birkhoff, G. *Lattice Theory*; American Mathematical Society: Providence, RI, USA, 1940.
29. Negoiță, C.V.; Ralescu, D.A. *Applications of Fuzzy Sets to Systems Analysis*; Birkhäuser: Basel, Switzerland, 1975.
30. Meng, D. *Abstract Algebra: Associative Algebra*; Science Press: Beijing, China, 2011.

mathematics

MDPI

Article

The Operational Laws of Symmetric Triangular Z-Numbers

Hui Li [1], Xuefei Liao [2,*], Zhen Li [3], Lei Pan [4], Meng Yuan [5] and Ke Qin [4]

1 School of Economics, Shanghai University, Shanghai 200444, China; youlanlihui@shu.edu.cn
2 School of Economics and Management, Zhejiang Ocean University, Zhoushan 316022, China
3 School of Logistics and Maritime Studies, Bahrain Polytechnic, Isa Town 33349, Bahrain; wesley.lee@polytechnic.bh
4 School of Management, Shanghai University, Shanghai 200444, China; pl239201@shu.edu.cn (L.P.); 2532129158@shu.edu.cn (K.Q.)
5 Qian Weichang College, Shanghai University, Shanghai 200444, China; yuanmeng@shu.edu.cn
* Correspondence: liaoxuefei@zjou.edu.cn; Tel.: +86-21-6613-4414-805

Abstract: To model fuzzy numbers with the confidence degree and better account for information uncertainty, Zadeh came up with the notion of Z-numbers, which can effectively combine the objective information of things with subjective human interpretation of perceptive information, thereby improving the human comprehension of natural language. Although many numbers are in fact Z-numbers, their higher computational complexity often prevents their recognition as such. In order to reduce computational complexity, this paper reviews the development and research direction of Z-numbers and deduces the operational rules for symmetric triangular Z-numbers. We first transform them into classical fuzzy numbers. Using linear programming, the extension principle of Zadeh, the convolution formula, and fuzzy number algorithms, we determine the operational rules for the basic operations of symmetric triangular Z-numbers, which are number-multiplication, addition, subtraction, multiplication, power, and division. Our operational rules reduce the complexity of calculation, improve computational efficiency, and effectively reduce the information difference while being applicable to other complex operations. This paper innovatively combines Z-numbers with classical fuzzy numbers in Z-number operations, and as such represents a continuation and innovation of the research on the operational laws of Z-numbers.

Keywords: Z-numbers; symmetric triangular fuzzy numbers; operational laws

MSC: 03E72

1. Introduction

In 1965, Zadeh [1] introduced the theory of fuzzy sets to effectively cope with uncertain information. The theory highlights the fuzziness and uncertainty of human thinking, reasoning, and perception of peripheral matters. It extended the characteristic function from the binary '0' or '1' relationship to the interval '0' to '1' by introducing the concept of membership degree, thereby quantitatively processing fuzzy information.

Nevertheless, relying solely on membership degree makes it difficult to accurately describe the uncertainty in practical situations. Therefore, to resolve the uncertainty of non-membership degree, researchers have made various extensions and derived batches of theories such as intuitionistic fuzzy sets [2], hesitant fuzzy sets [3], type-2 fuzzy sets [4], and interval-type intuitionistic fuzzy sets [5]. Moreover, in 2013 Masamichi and Hiroaki [6] defined the boundaries of a sequence of fuzzy sets in view of the level set of fuzzy sets and provided the boundaries, derivatives, and properties of the fuzzy set-valued mapping.

The aforementioned theories are only capable of addressing the issue of information uncertainty, and lack the ability to handle incomplete and unreliable information, which is typically only accessible in real-world situations. To this end, in 2011 Zadeh [7] introduced the notion of Z-numbers to consider the dependability of information. Compared to the traditional fuzzy sets, Z-numbers add a reliability measure to further enhance the flexibility and validity in the decision direction. Therefore, Z-numbers with fuzzy constraints are more flexible and closer to human thinking; this theory has great potential for application to the information described by probabilistic and fuzzy natural language.

From the current research outcomes on Z-numbers, we have observed four primary issues of interest. The first involves extensions and special cases of Z-number theory. Zadeh [7] initially introduced the notions of Z-information and Z^+-numbers as definitions derived from Z-numbers. Pal et al. [8] proposed Z-number-based computing with word algorithms and simulated experimental figures for evaluating demand satisfaction. Banerjee and Pal [9] introduced decision information into the structure of Z-numbers and presented the notion of Z*-numbers. Pirmuhammadi et al. [10], Peng, Wang [11], and Mondal et al. [12] proposed the concept of normal Z-numbers, hesitant uncertain linguistic Z-numbers, and linguistic hesitant Z-numbers, respectively. Tian et al. [13] introduced fuzzy ZE-numbers, while Haseli et al. [14–16] proposed a decision support model using the BCM and MARCOS methods based on fuzzy ZE-numbers. Aliev et al. [17] initiated a general method for constructing specific functions based on extension of the Z-number principle. Moreover, Massanet et al. [18] raised a new method for creating hybrid discrete Z-numbers based on discrete Z-numbers.

The second issue involves the study of various methods for sorting Z-numbers. Bakar and Gegov [19] developed a multi-layer approach to classifying Z-numbers. Aliev et al. [20] presented a method to ascertain the sorting of continuous and discrete numbers in Z-numbers. A novel Z-number ranking method which takes the weights and fuzziness degree of the prime points and the scalability of fuzzy numbers into account was extended by Jiang et al. [21]. Ezadi et al. [22] introduced sigmoidal functions and symbolic means for sorting Z-numbers.

The third issue involves studying various methods for computing Z-numbers. Aliev et al. [23] developed an approach for the direct computation of Z-numbers by combining possibility constraints with probability constraints and defined arithmetic operations for discrete Z-Numbers. Subsequently, the operations of continuous Z-numbers were further provided by Aliev et al. [24] through discretization. Aiming to reduce computational complexity and improve computational efficiency, Aliev et al. [25] presented a basic approach for developing the concept of Z-Numbers and provided examples to demonstrate the validity of their method using the Hukuhara distance. Qiu et al. [26] presented the process of computing the generalized difference for discrete and continuous Z-numbers. Shen and Wang [27] defined multidimensional Z-numbers and proved their basic operations. Kang et al. [28] presented a methodology of fuzzy set uncertainty using entropy and considering the effect of fuzzy set measure and range of fuzzy sets. Peng et al. [29] defined a series of Z-number operational laws on the basis of Archimedean t-norms and t-conorms. To balance reduced arithmetic complexity with retention of the inherent meaning of Z-numbers, Zhu et al. [30] put forward a method for approximate Z-number computation (Z-ACM) in view of kernel density estimation. Based on the idea of transformation, Kang et al. [31] proposed an improved method for converting Z-numbers into classical fuzzy numbers, greatly simplified the operations of Z-numbers with the loss of a certain amount of information, and promoted the application of Z-numbers to a degree.

The fourth issue involves research on the actual applications of Z-numbers. Zhang et al. [32] combined Z-numbers with the best–worst method and TODIM (an acronym in Portuguese referring to interactive and multi-criteria decision-making) to conduct performance evaluation for the technological service platforms. Ashraf et al. [33] and Nazari-Shirkouhi et al. [34] applied Z-numbers to supplier selection. Combining Z-numbers with DEMATEL method, Zhu et al. [35], Wang et al. [36], and Akhavein et al. [37] presented evaluation methods for the co-creative sustainable value propositions of smart product service systems, human error probability, and sustainable projects ranking. Integrating linguistic Z-numbers and the projection method, Huang et al. [38] built a new model for failure mode and effect analysis. Moreover, numerous experts have expanded the notion of Z-numbers based on hesitant fuzzy sets and used optimization models to build frameworks for solving multi-criteria decision-making, group decision-making, and three-way decision-making problems [11,39–44].

Previous research on the operational rules of Z-numbers has mainly focused on proposing a general method of computation using constraints, then used discretization to obtain the operational rules of continuous Z-numbers. This category of methods is extremely complicated, inefficient, and error-prone; for this reason, many researchers have chosen to combine Z-numbers with other methods in order to derive the operation formulas. Hence, to improve the efficiency of operation and make it easier to understand, we take symmetric triangular Z-numbers as our research object and study their operational rules, including number-multiplication, addition, subtraction, multiplication, power squares, and division.

The main contribution of our approach is as follows. First, we convert Z-numbers directly into classical fuzzy numbers using Zadeh's extension principle and the operational rules of classical fuzzy numbers for operations of Z-numbers, which does not appear in any previous related papers. Second, we use many linear correlation methods to calculate the symmetric triangular Z-numbers, which is simple in both calculation principle and process and as such can reduce the complexity of the operations. Third, we derive the formulas of the basic operations for Z-numbers, which can be directly used to simplify the complex operations involved in many realistic problems and expand the application areas of Z-numbers. Our calculation method can reduce uncertainty and prevent information loss while processing information, which can minimize information differences.

We structure the remainder of this paper as follows: Section 2 briefly introduces the related definitions and notation; Section 3 deduces the operational rules for symmetric triangular Z-numbers; finally, Section 4 draws the conclusions.

2. Preliminaries

To begin, a number of fundamental concepts are first concisely introduced.

Definition 1 (Zadeh [1])**.** *In a given domain U, the fuzzy number A can be defined as*

$$A = \{\langle t, \mu_A(t)\rangle | t \in U\},$$

where $\mu_A : U \to [0,1]$ is the membership function of A', while $\mu_A(t)$ depicts the degree of belongingness of $t \in U$ in A.

Definition 2 (Van Laarhoven and Pedrycz [45])**.** *A is a triangular fuzzy number which can be defined as (a_p, a_q, a_r); its membership function can be determined as*

$$\mu_A(t) = \begin{cases} 0, & t \in (-\infty, a_p) \\ \dfrac{t - a_p}{a_q - a_p}, & t \in (a_p, a_q) \\ \dfrac{a_r - t}{a_r - a_q}, & t \in (a_q, a_r) \\ 0, & t \in (a_r, +\infty), \end{cases}$$

where a_p and a_r are respectively the upper and lower bounds of A. When $a_r - a_q = a_q - a_p$, A is a symmetric triangular fuzzy number.

Definition 3 (Zadeh [7])**.** *A Z-number Z is an ordered fuzzy number pair, denoted as $Z = (A, B)$, where A,B could be either natural languages or numbers. Z is associated with T, which is a real-*

valued uncertain variable. Fuzzy number A represents the fuzzy constraint R(T) on the values which T can take, defined as T is A, represented as

$$R(T) : T \text{ is } A \to Poss(T = t) = \mu_A(t),$$

where μ_A is the membership function of A and t is a generic value of T. When T is a random variable, the probability distribution of T represents a probabilistic restriction on T, which can be expressed as

$$R(T) : T \text{ is } p,$$

where p is the probability density function of T. Under this circumstance,

$$R(T) : T \text{ is } p,\ p \to Prob(t \leq T \leq t + dt) = p(t)dt.$$

If T is a random variable, then T is A represents a fuzzy event in R, the probability of which can be defined as

$$p = \int_R \mu_A(t) p_T(t) dt,$$

where p_T is the underlying probability density of T. Fuzzy number B is the fuzzy restriction on the reliability measure of A, expressed as

$$B = \int_R \mu_A(t) p_T(t) dt, \tag{1}$$

where p_T is not known, whereas the constraint on p_T is known, which can be presented in Figure 1.

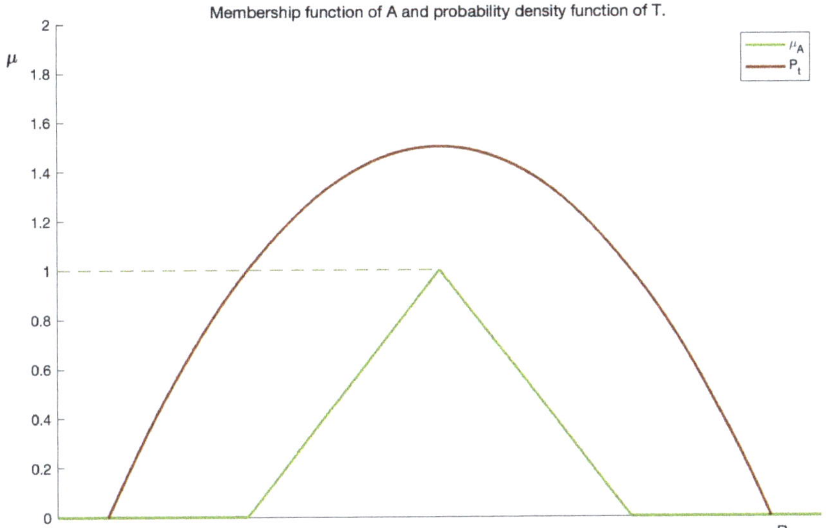

Figure 1. The membership function of A and probability density function of T.

In effect, Z = (A, B) can be regarded as a restriction on T, defined as

$$Prob(T \text{ is } A) \text{ is } B.$$

Definition 4 (Aliev et al. [23]). *In a Z-number represented by Z = (A, B), if the fuzzy restriction A of the real-valued indefinite variable T on the domain U is a discrete fuzzy set*

$$\mu_A : \{t_1, t_2, \cdots, t_n\} \to [0, 1], and \{t_1, t_2, \cdots, t_n\} \in R$$

and B is the reliability measure for A, which is also a discrete fuzzy set

$$\mu_B : \{b_1, b_2, \cdots, b_n\} \to [0,1], and \{b_1, b_2, \cdots, b_n\} \in [0,1],$$

then $Z = (A, B)$ *is a discrete Z-number.*

Definition 5 (Aliev et al. [24]). *In a Z-number represented by* $Z = (A, B)$*, if the fuzzy restriction A of the real-valued indefinite variable T on the domain U is a continuous fuzzy set*

$$\mu_A : U \to [0,1]$$

and B is the reliability measure for A, which is also a continuous fuzzy set, then $Z = (A, B)$ *is a continuous Z-number.*

Definition 6 (Zadeh [7]). *Let* ζ *and* τ *be fuzzy sets with membership functions* μ *and* v*, and let* $f : \Re^2 \to \Re$ *be a function; then,* $f(\zeta, \tau)$ *is also a fuzzy set with membership function*

$$\pi(h) = sup\{\mu(s) \wedge v(t) | h = f(s,t)\}, \tag{2}$$

where s and t are the values within the range of ζ *and* τ*.*

Definition 7 (Wang [46]). *Let* ξ *be a fuzzy number; its* α*-level sets (or* α*-cuts)* ξ_α *can be expressed as*

$$\begin{aligned} \xi_\alpha &= \{t \in \Re | \mu_\xi(t) \geq \alpha\} \\ &= [min\{t \in \Re | \mu_\xi(t) \geq \alpha\}, max\{t \in \Re | \mu_\xi(t) \geq \alpha\}] = [\xi_\alpha^L, \xi_\alpha^R], \end{aligned}$$

where $\mu_\xi(t)$ *is the membership function of* ξ *and* $\Re$ *is the universe of discourse. The functions* ξ_α^L *and* ξ_α^R *have the following attributes:*

(a) ξ_α^L *is a monotonously growing left continuous function,*
(b) ξ_α^R *is a monotonously lessening left continuous function,*
(c) $\xi_\alpha^L \leq \xi_\alpha^R$, $\alpha \in [0,1]$.

Example 1 (Aliev et al. [24]). *Given that* $A = (a_l, a_m, a_u)$ *is a symmetric triangular fuzzy number, an* α*-cut* $A_\alpha = \{t \in \Re | \mu_A(t) \geq \alpha\}$ *is a closed interval:*

$$\begin{aligned} A_\alpha = [A_\alpha^L, A_\alpha^R] &= [a_l + \alpha(a_m - a_l), a_u + \alpha(a_u - a_m)] \\ &= [a_m - (1-\alpha)(a_m - a_l), a_m + (1-\alpha)(a_u - a_m)]. \end{aligned}$$

Definition 8 (Kang et al. [31]). *The basic idea of translating Z-numbers into classical fuzzy numbers is as follows. First, the reliability part B is transformed into a crisp value by defuzzification, then the weight of the crisp value is multiplied by the restriction part A, and finally, using the approximate invariance property of the fuzzy expectation, the product is converted into a commonly used classical fuzzy number.*

Step 1: *Assuming that* $A = (a_k, a_l, a_m, a_n)$ *is a trapezoid fuzzy number and* $B = (b_l, b_m, b_n)$ *is a triangular fuzzy number, B can be transformed into a crisp number by the center of gravity method with*

$$\gamma = \frac{\int t\mu_{B(t)}dt}{\int \mu_{B(t)}dt} = \frac{\int_{b_l}^{b_m} t\frac{t-b_l}{b_m-b_l}dt + \int_{b_m}^{b_n} t\frac{b_n-t}{b_n-b_m}dt}{\frac{1}{2}(b_n-b_l)}.$$

Thus, the gravity center of $B = (b_l, b_m, b_n)$ *is computed as*

$$\gamma = \frac{b_n - b_l}{2}. \tag{3}$$

Step 2: *Taking the gravity center value* γ *of the reliability part B as the weight of the restriction part A, the weighted Z-value can be written as*

$$Z^{\gamma} = \{(t, \mu_{A^{\gamma}}) | \mu_{A^{\gamma}}(t) = \gamma \mu_A(t), t \in [0,1]\}. \tag{4}$$

Step 3: *Because* $A = (a_k, a_l, a_m, a_n)$ *is a trapezoidal fuzzy number,* Z^{γ} *can be calculated by*

$$Z^{\gamma} = \sqrt{\gamma} \times A = (\sqrt{\gamma} \times a_k, \sqrt{\gamma} \times a_l, \sqrt{\gamma} \times a_m, \sqrt{\gamma} \times a_n). \tag{5}$$

Remark 1. *If* $A = (a_k, a_l, a_m)$ *is a triangular fuzzy number, Equation (5) becomes*

$$Z^{\gamma} = \sqrt{\gamma} \times A = (\sqrt{\gamma} \times a_k, \sqrt{\gamma} \times a_l, \sqrt{\gamma} \times a_m). \tag{6}$$

Definition 9 (Kwiesielewicz [47])**.** *Let* $A = (a_p, a_q, a_r)$*,* $B = (b_p, b_q, b_r)$ *be two triangular fuzzy numbers, where* $a_r \geq a_q \geq a_p \geq 0$ *and* $b_r \geq b_q \geq b_p \geq 0$*. Then, their addition, difference, number-multiplication, and division can be shown as follows:*

$$A + B = [a_p + b_p, a_q + b_q, a_r + b_r], \tag{7}$$

$$A - B = [a_p - b_r, a_q - b_q, a_r - b_p], \tag{8}$$

and

$$\frac{A}{B} = [\frac{a_p}{b_r}, \frac{a_q}{b_q}, \frac{a_r}{b_p}].$$

Definition 10 (Aliev et al. [24])**.** *The multiplication and division of fuzzy numbers* $A = (a_p, a_q, a_r)$ *and* $B = (b_p, b_q, b_r)$ *are both fuzzy sets. The multiplication can be expressed as*

$$A \times B = \underset{\alpha \in (0,1]}{U} \alpha (A \times B)^{\alpha},$$

where the α*-cut is expressed as*

$$(A \times B)^{\alpha} = [min(a_1^{\alpha} \cdot b_1^{\alpha}, a_1^{\alpha} \cdot b_2^{\alpha}, a_2^{\alpha} \cdot b_1^{\alpha}, a_2^{\alpha} \cdot b_2^{\alpha}), max(a_1^{\alpha} \cdot b_1^{\alpha}, a_1^{\alpha} \cdot b_2^{\alpha}, a_2^{\alpha} \cdot b_1^{\alpha}, a_2^{\alpha} \cdot b_2^{\alpha})], \tag{9}$$

where $a_1^{\alpha} = a_p + \alpha(a_q - a_p)$*,* $a_2^{\alpha} = a_r + \alpha(a_r - a_q)$*,* $b_1^{\alpha} = b_p + \alpha(b_q - b_p)$*,* $b_2^{\alpha} = b_r + \alpha(b_r - b_q)$*.*
The division can be denoted as

$$\frac{A}{B} = \underset{\alpha \in (0,1]}{U} \alpha \left(\frac{A}{B}\right)^{\alpha},$$

where the α*-cut is expressed as*

$$\left(\frac{A}{B}\right)^{\alpha} = \left[min\left(\frac{a_1^{\alpha}}{b_1^{\alpha}}, \frac{a_1^{\alpha}}{b_2^{\alpha}}, \frac{a_2^{\alpha}}{b_1^{\alpha}}, \frac{a_2^{\alpha}}{b_2^{\alpha}}\right), max\left(\frac{a_1^{\alpha}}{b_1^{\alpha}}, \frac{a_1^{\alpha}}{b_2^{\alpha}}, \frac{a_2^{\alpha}}{b_1^{\alpha}}, \frac{a_2^{\alpha}}{b_2^{\alpha}}\right)\right]. \tag{10}$$

Definition 11 (Kallenberg [48])**.** *Suppose that* (S, T) *are two-dimensional continuous random variables which have probability density* $f(s, t)$*. Then,* $R = S + T$ *is still a continuous random variable with probability density*

$$f_{S+T}(r) = \int_R f(r - t, t)dt = \int_R f(s, r - s)ds. \tag{11}$$

Let the marginal probability density of (S,T) with respect to S,T be $f_S(s)$ and $f_T(t)$. If S and T are independent of each other, Equation (11) will be reduced to the convolution formula

$$f_S \circ f_T = \int_R f_S(r-t) f_T(t) dt = \int_R f_S(s) f_T(r-s) ds. \tag{12}$$

If $R = \frac{T}{S}$, *then*

$$f_S \circ f_T = \int_R |s| f_S(s) f_T(sr) ds. \tag{13}$$

If $R = ST$, *then*

$$f_S \circ f_T = \int_R \frac{1}{|s|} f_S(s) f_T(\frac{r}{s}) ds. \tag{14}$$

Definition 12 (Aliev et al. [24]). *In order to discretize fuzzy numbers, a method is presented. The idea is to split the assistance of a fuzzy number B, Supp(B), into several subintervals b_k, $k = 1, \cdots, n$. In particular, the subintervals are of the same size, i.e., the spacing is constantly $\Delta b = b_{k+1} - b_k$.*

Example 2. *Consider $B = (0.4, 0.5, 0.6)$; its support Supp(B) will be discretized into $n = 11$ points in the way shown below: $b_{j1} = 0.4$, $b_{j2} = 0.425, \cdots, b_{j11} = 0.6$. Then, the discretized fuzzy number can be attained as*

$$B = \frac{0}{0.4} + \frac{0.2}{0.42} + \frac{0.4}{0.44} + \frac{0.6}{0.46} + \frac{0.8}{0.48} + \frac{1}{0.5} + \frac{0.8}{0.52} + \frac{0.6}{0.54} + \frac{0.4}{0.56} + \frac{0.2}{0.58} + \frac{0}{0.6}.$$

In the succeeding sections, we will use the above definitions and methods to derive the operational rules of the symmetric triangular Z-numbers.

3. Operational Rules

This section introduces the operational rules for Z-numbers. The first step in the operations is all about converting Z-numbers into ordinary fuzzy numbers, as defined in Definition 8. Because the operations studied here are based on symmetric triangular Z-numbers, $A = (a_p, a_q, a_r)$, $B = (b_p, b_q, b_r)$, the value of the weight γ of the reliability part B is always as shown in Equation (3). Considering that calculating the second component of the derived Z-number requires a relatively long computation time, whereas the calculation processes are similar to each other, we only provided examples for the number-multiplication and addition operations in this section.

3.1. Number-Multiplication Formula

Theorem 1. *Let λ be a real number and let $Z = (A, B) = ((a_p, a_q, a_r), (b_p, b_q, b_r))$ be a symmetric triangular Z-number. The formula for the number-multiplication of the continuous symmetric triangular Z-number is*

$$\lambda Z = \lambda(A, B) = (\lambda A, B).$$

Proof. First, multiplying a real number $\lambda \in R$ by the base of Equation (6), we can obtain

$$\lambda Z^{\gamma} = (\lambda\sqrt{\gamma} \times a_p, \lambda\sqrt{\gamma} \times a_q, \lambda\sqrt{\gamma} \times a_r).$$

From Equation (3), $\gamma = \frac{b_r - b_p}{2}$. Let $\bar{Z^{\gamma}} = \lambda Z^{\gamma}$. Because the weights remain unchanged after the number-multiplication, the formula becomes

$$\bar{Z^{\gamma}} = (\lambda\sqrt{\gamma} \times a_p, \lambda\sqrt{\gamma} \times a_q, \lambda\sqrt{\gamma} \times a_r).$$

Therefore, the final likelihood measure B is unchanged, and we obtain

$$\lambda Z = \lambda(A, B) = (\lambda A, B).$$

□

Example 3. *Assume that $Z = (A, B) = ((1,2,3),(0.7,0.8,0.9))$, and calculate $3Z$.*

According to Equation (3), we have $\gamma = \frac{0.9-0.7}{2} = 0.1$. Accordingly, we can determine that

$$\bar{Z}^{0.1} = 3Z^{0.1} = (3\sqrt{10} \times 1, 3\sqrt{10} \times 2, 3\sqrt{10} \times 3) = (3\sqrt{10}, 6\sqrt{10}, 9\sqrt{10}).$$

Finally, we obtain

$$3Z = (A, B_{12}) = \Big((3\sqrt{10}, 6\sqrt{10}, 9\sqrt{10}), (0.7, 0.8, 0.9)\Big).$$

3.2. Addition Formula

Theorem 2. *Let $Z_1 = (A_1, B_1) = ((a_{1p}, a_{1q}, a_{1r}), (b_{1p}, b_{1q}, b_{1r}))$ and let $Z_2 = (A_2, B_2) = ((a_{2p}, a_{2q}, a_{2r}), (b_{2p}, b_{2q}, b_{2r}))$ be continuous symmetric triangular Z-numbers. Then, their sum Z_{12} can be deduced as*

$$Z_{12} = Z_1 + Z_2 = (A_{12}, B_{12}),$$

where $A_{12} = (a_1^{\gamma}, a_2^{\gamma}, a_3^{\gamma}) = (\sqrt{\gamma_1}a_{1p} + \sqrt{\gamma_2}a_{2p}, \sqrt{\gamma_1}a_{1q} + \sqrt{\gamma_2}a_{2q}, \sqrt{\gamma_1}a_{1r} + \sqrt{\gamma_2}a_{2r})$, $B_{12} = \int_R \mu_{A_{12}} p_{12} dt$, $\gamma_1 = \frac{b_{1r} - b_{1p}}{2}$, $\gamma_2 = \frac{b_{2r} - b_{2p}}{2}$, $\mu_{A_{12}}$ is the membership function of A_{12}, and p_{12} is the probability density of A_{12}.

Proof. Based on Equation (6), the fuzzy transformations of Z_1 and Z_2 are

$$Z_1^{\gamma} = \sqrt{\gamma_1}A_1 = (\sqrt{\gamma_1}a_{1p}, \sqrt{\gamma_1}a_{1q}, \sqrt{\gamma_1}a_{1r}),$$
$$Z_2^{\gamma} = \sqrt{\gamma_2}A_2 = (\sqrt{\gamma_2}a_{2p}, \sqrt{\gamma_2}a_{2q}, \sqrt{\gamma_2}a_{2r}).$$

According to Equation (7), the sum of the two can be derived as

$$Z_{12}^{\gamma} = Z_1^{\gamma} + Z_2^{\gamma} = (\sqrt{\gamma_1}a_{1p} + \sqrt{\gamma_2}a_{2p}, \sqrt{\gamma_1}a_{1q} + \sqrt{\gamma_2}a_{2q}, \sqrt{\gamma_1}a_{1r} + \sqrt{\gamma_2}a_{2r}).$$

From Equation (3), it is known that $\gamma_1 = \frac{b_{1r} - b_{1p}}{2}$, $\gamma_2 = \frac{b_{2r} - b_{2p}}{2}$, where b_{1r} and b_{1p} denote the third and first possibility of Z_1, respectively, while b_{2r} and b_{2p} denote the third and first possibility of Z_2, respectively. Therefore, substitution yields

$$Z_{12}^{\gamma} = \left(\sqrt{\frac{b_{1r}-b_{1p}}{2}}a_{1p} + \sqrt{\frac{b_{2r}-b_{2p}}{2}}a_{2p}, \sqrt{\frac{b_{1r}-b_{1p}}{2}}a_{1q} + \sqrt{\frac{b_{2r}-b_{2p}}{2}}a_{2q}, \sqrt{\frac{b_{1r}-b_{1p}}{2}}a_{1r} + \sqrt{\frac{b_{2r}-b_{2p}}{2}}a_{2r}\right).$$

At this point, Z-numbers A and B have been transformed into simple fuzzy numbers Z_1^{γ} and Z_2^{γ}, and are transformed into Z_{12}^{γ} by symbolic operations; the subsequent step is to convert the simple fuzzy number Z_{12}^{γ} into a Z-number again.

According to Equation (4), the membership functions of Z_1 and Z_2 can be transformed into the membership functions of their corresponding fuzzy numbers as follows:

$$\mu_{A_1}^{\gamma} = \frac{b_{1r} - b_{1p}}{2}\mu_{A_1} = PosA_1^{\gamma},$$
$$\mu_{A_2}^{\gamma} = \frac{b_{2r} - b_{2p}}{2}\mu_{A_2} = PosA_2^{\gamma}.$$

Then, according to Equation (2), we can find that

$$\mu^{\gamma}_{A_{12}}(v) = \sup_{u}(\mu^{\gamma}_{A_1}(u) \wedge \mu^{\gamma}_{A_2}(v-u)).$$

Let a^{γ}_1, a^{γ}_2, and a^{γ}_3 be the three coordinate values on the horizontal axis. At this point, the range of the membership function after transformation and summation is $(0, \beta)$ instead of $(0,1)$, where β denotes the maximum of the triangular fuzzy number, i.e., the vertex of the vertical axis coordinate corresponding to a^{γ}_2. Then, β is $min\left\{\frac{b_{1r}-b_{1p}}{2}, \frac{b_{2r}-b_{2p}}{2}\right\}$, which, as it is contrary to the initial required range of $(0,1)$, should be normalized to

$$\mu_{A_{12}} = \begin{cases} \frac{t-a^{\gamma}_1}{a^{\gamma}_2 - a^{\gamma}_1}, & t \in (a^{\gamma}_1, a^{\gamma}_2) \\ \frac{a^{\gamma}_3 - t}{a^{\gamma}_3 - a^{\gamma}_2}, & t \in (a^{\gamma}_2, a^{\gamma}_3) \\ 0, & otherwise. \end{cases} \tag{15}$$

Then, $A_{12} = (a^{\gamma}_1, a^{\gamma}_2, a^{\gamma}_3) = (\sqrt{\gamma_1}a_{1p} + \sqrt{\gamma_2}a_{2p}, \sqrt{\gamma_1}a_{1q} + \sqrt{\gamma_2}a_{2q}, \sqrt{\gamma_1}a_{1r} + \sqrt{\gamma_2}a_{2r})$. Accordingly, we can use $\mu_{A_{12}}$ to calculate B_{12} in view of Equation (1) by

$$B_{12} = \int_R \mu_{A_{12}} p_{12} dt. \tag{16}$$

From Equation (12), we can obtain $P_{12} = P_1 \circ P_2 = \int_R p_1(u)p_2(v-u)du$, and according to Equation (1)

$$B_1 = \int_R \mu_{A_1}(t)p_1(t)dt, \quad B_2 = \int_R \mu_{A_2}(t)p_2(t)dt,$$

the values of $p_1(u)$ and $p_2(v-u)$ in calculating P_{12} can be determined.

Nevertheless, if the calculation is carried out directly, many solutions will be obtained, and they should be subject to

$$\begin{cases} \int_R p(t)dt = 1 \\ p(t) > 0 \\ \int tp(t)dt = \frac{\int t\mu_A(t)dt}{\int \mu_A(t)dt} = \frac{\int t\frac{t-a_p}{a_q-a_p}dt}{\int \frac{t-a_p}{a_q-a_p}dt}. \end{cases} \tag{17}$$

Under such conditions, p_{12} can be derived, then B_{12} can be obtained by substituting p_{12} and $\mu_{A_{12}}$ into Equation (16). Accordingly, we can obtain

$$Z_{12} = Z_1 + Z_2 = (A_{12}, B_{12}).$$

□

Example 4. *Assume that* $Z_1 = (A_1, B_1) = ((1,2,3),(0.7,0.8,0.9))$, $Z_2 = (A_2, B_2) = ((7,8,9),(0.4,0.5,0.6))$ *and calculate* $Z_{12} = Z_1 + Z_2$.

First, according to Equation (3), the values of γ_1 *and* γ_2 *can be derived as*

$$\gamma_1 = \frac{0.9-0.7}{2} = 0.1, \gamma_2 = \frac{0.6-0.4}{2} = 0.1.$$

As a result, the value of A_{12} is calculated as follows:

$$A_{12} = (a_1^{\gamma}, a_2^{\gamma}, a_3^{\gamma}) = (\sqrt{\gamma_1}a_{1p} + \sqrt{\gamma_2}a_{2p}, \sqrt{\gamma_1}a_{1q} + \sqrt{\gamma_2}a_{2q}, \sqrt{\gamma_1}a_{1r} + \sqrt{\gamma_2}a_{2r})$$
$$= (\sqrt{0.1} \times 1 + \sqrt{0.1} \times 7, \sqrt{0.1} \times 2 + \sqrt{0.1} \times 8, \sqrt{0.1} \times 3 + \sqrt{0.1} \times 9)$$
$$= \left(\frac{8}{\sqrt{10}}, \sqrt{10}, \frac{12}{\sqrt{10}}\right).$$

According Equation (15), the following membership function is obtained after normalization:

$$\mu_{A_{12}} = \begin{cases} \dfrac{\sqrt{10}t - 8}{2}, & t \in \left(\dfrac{8}{\sqrt{10}}, \sqrt{10}\right) \\ \dfrac{12 - \sqrt{10}t}{2}, & t \in \left(\sqrt{10}, \dfrac{12}{\sqrt{10}}\right) \\ 0, & otherwise. \end{cases}$$

The next step is to calculate P_{12}. Considering the greater difficulty of calculating the probability density of continuous fuzzy numbers, we discretize and convert them to discrete fuzzy numbers according to Definition 12.

First, we divide B equally into $(l-1)$ points and define each part as b_l.

For example, $B_1 = (0.7, 0.8, 0.9)$ can be divided into 10 points:

$$B_1 = \frac{0}{0.7} + \frac{0.2}{0.72} + \frac{0.4}{0.74} + \frac{0.6}{0.76} + \frac{0.8}{0.78} + \frac{1}{0.8} + \frac{0.8}{0.82} + \frac{0.6}{0.84} + \frac{0.4}{0.86} + \frac{0.2}{0.88} + \frac{0}{0.9}.$$

According to the discretization, it is known that

$$b_{j,l} = \sum_{i=1}^{n} \mu_{Aj}(t_{ji})P_{j,l}(t_{ji}), \quad j = 1,2$$

where j corresponds to Z_1 or Z_2. When $j = 12$, it corresponds to Z_{12}.

Thus, we obtain a linear programming model where $b_{j,l}$ is a target value and the model satisfies the following constraints:

$$\mu_{Aj}(t_{j1})P_{j,l}(t_{j1}) + \mu_{Aj}(t_{j2})P_{j,l}(t_{j2}) + \ldots + \mu_{Aj}(t_{jn})P_{j,l}(t_{jn}) \to b_{j,l}$$

$$s.t. \begin{cases} \sum P_{j,l} = 1 \\ P_{j,l} \geqslant 0 \\ \displaystyle\int tP_{j,l}dt = \frac{\int t\mu_A(t)dt}{\int \mu_A(t)dt} \end{cases}$$

Thus, we can obtain all $P_{j,l}$ values for the lth b value; this is then continuousized and the probability density functions $P_{1,l}$ and $P_{2,l}$ are obtained by fitting. Finally, we obtain $P_{12,l}$ using the convolution formula $P_{12} = P_1 \circ P_2$, then all P_{12} values are obtained by iteration.

Taking the fourth point as an example, the probability density functions after fitting are $N(2, 0.36)$ and $N(8, 0.76)$, respectively; thus, the convolution formula can be used to find the probability density of the point P_{12}, which is equal to $N(10, 0.83)$.

Substituting each copy of P_{12} *into* $B_{12,l} = \int \mu_{A_{12}} P_{12,l} dt$ *yields a series of values for* B_{12}. *Again taking the fourth point as an example, we have*

$$B_{12,4} = \int \mu_{A_{12}} P_{12,4} dt$$

$$= \int_{\frac{8}{\sqrt{10}}}^{\sqrt{10}} \frac{\sqrt{10}t - 8}{2} \cdot \frac{1}{0.83\sqrt{2\pi}} e^{-\frac{(t-10)^2}{2\cdot(0.83)^2}} dt + \int_{\sqrt{10}}^{\frac{12}{\sqrt{10}}} \frac{12 - \sqrt{10}t}{2} \cdot \frac{1}{0.83\sqrt{2\pi}} e^{-\frac{(t-10)^2}{2\cdot(0.83)^2}} dt.$$

The two endpoints and vertices are chosen to form $B_{12} = (0.62, 0.72, 0.79)$.
Finally, we obtain

$$Z_{12} = (A_{12}, B_{12}) = \left(\left(\frac{8}{\sqrt{10}}, \sqrt{10}, \frac{12}{\sqrt{10}}\right), (0.62, 0.72, 0.79)\right).$$

3.3. Subtraction Formula

The addition and subtraction operations for Z-numbers are extremely similar in thought and procedure to the addition and subtraction of ordinary numbers. To derive the subtraction expression, we transform the Z-numbers into classical fuzzy numbers first, then use the operational rules of classical fuzzy numbers to determine the expression of A_k. Finally, we apply the convolution formula to obtain the expression of B_k. The difference in the derivation process mainly lies in the fuzzy number operator formula and the convolution formula used to calculate P_{12}.

Theorem 3. *Let* $Z_1 = (A_1, B_1) = ((a_{1p}, a_{1q}, a_{1r}), (b_{1p}, b_{1q}, b_{1r}))$ *and* $Z_2 = (A_2, B_2) = ((a_{2p}, a_{2q}, a_{2r}), (b_{2p}, b_{2q}, b_{2r}))$ *be continuous symmetric triangular Z-numbers and let the difference between these two be* Z_k*; then, we have*

$$Z_k = Z_1 - Z_2 = (A_k, B_k),$$

where $A_k = (a_1^\gamma, a_2^\gamma, a_3^\gamma) = (\sqrt{\gamma_1}a_{1p} - \sqrt{\gamma_2}a_{2r}, \sqrt{\gamma_1}a_{1q} - \sqrt{\gamma_2}a_{2q}, \sqrt{\gamma_1}a_{1r} - \sqrt{\gamma_2}a_{2p})$, $B_k = \int_R \mu_{A_k} p_k dt$, $\gamma_1 = \frac{b_{1r} - b_{1p}}{2}$, $\gamma_2 = \frac{b_{2r} - b_{2p}}{2}$, μ_{A_k} *is the membership function of* A_k, *and* p_k *is the probability density of* A_k.

Proof. In views of Equation (6), the fuzzy transformations of Z_1, Z_2 are

$$Z_1^\gamma = \sqrt{\gamma_1}A_1 = (\sqrt{\gamma_1}a_{1p}, \sqrt{\gamma_1}a_{1q}, \sqrt{\gamma_1}a_{1r}),$$

$$Z_2^\gamma = \sqrt{\gamma_2}A_2 = (\sqrt{\gamma_2}a_{2p}, \sqrt{\gamma_2}a_{2q}, \sqrt{\gamma_2}a_{2r}).$$

Then, according to Equation (8), we have

$$Z_k^\gamma = Z_1^\gamma - Z_2^\gamma = (\sqrt{\gamma_1}a_{1p} - \sqrt{\gamma_2}a_{2r}, \sqrt{\gamma_1}a_{1q} - \sqrt{\gamma_2}a_{2q}, \sqrt{\gamma_1}a_{1r} - \sqrt{\gamma_2}a_{2p}).$$

Similar to the addition process, it can be determined from Definition 6 that

$$\mu_{A_k}^\gamma(v) = \sup_u(\mu_{A_1}^\gamma(v+u) \wedge \mu_{A_2}^\gamma(u)).$$

After normalization, μ_{A_k} is expressed as Equation (15). Therefore,

$$A_k = (\sqrt{\gamma_1}a_{1p} - \sqrt{\gamma_2}a_{2r}, \sqrt{\gamma_1}a_{1q} - \sqrt{\gamma_2}a_{2q}, \sqrt{\gamma_1}a_{1r} - \sqrt{\gamma_2}a_{2p}).$$

Similar to Equation (17), P_1 and P_2 are under the three range condition restrictions. Based on Equation (12), it is easy to find that $P_k = P_1 \circ P_2 = \int_R p_1(u+v)p_2(u)du$. Then, B_{12} can be obtained by substituting p_k and μ_{A_k} into Equation (16). Hence, we can derive that

$$Z_k = Z_1 - Z_2 = (A_k, B_k).$$

□

3.4. Multiplication Formula

Theorem 4. *Let $Z_1 = (A_1, B_1) = ((a_{1p}, a_{1q}, a_{1r}), (b_{1p}, b_{1q}, b_{1r}))$ and $Z_2 = (A_2, B_2) = ((a_{2p}, a_{2q}, a_{2r}), (b_{2p}, b_{2q}, b_{2r}))$ be continuous symmetric triangular Z-numbers and let the multiplication of these two be Z^*. Then, Z^* can be expressed as*

$$Z^* = Z_1 \times Z_2 = (A^*, B^*),$$

where $A^* = (\sqrt{\gamma_1}\sqrt{\gamma_2}a_{1p}a_{2p}, \sqrt{\gamma_1}\sqrt{\gamma_2}a_{1q}a_{2q}, \sqrt{\gamma_1}\sqrt{\gamma_2}a_{1r}a_{2r})$, $B^* = \int_R \mu_{A^*} p^* dt$, $\gamma_1 = \dfrac{b_{1r} - b_{1p}}{2}$, $\gamma_2 = \dfrac{b_{2r} - b_{2p}}{2}$, and μ_{A^*} and p^* are the membership function and probability density of A^*, respectively.

Proof. Similar to the previous proof processes, we first let $Z^* = Z_1 \times Z_2$ and then transform them into classical fuzzy numbers, that is,

$$Z_1^{\gamma} = \sqrt{\gamma_1}A_1 = (\sqrt{\gamma_1}a_{1p}, \sqrt{\gamma_1}a_{1q}, \sqrt{\gamma_1}a_{1r}),$$
$$Z_2^{\gamma} = \sqrt{\gamma_2}A_2 = (\sqrt{\gamma_2}a_{2p}, \sqrt{\gamma_2}a_{2q}, \sqrt{\gamma_2}a_{2r}),$$

where $\gamma_1 = \dfrac{b_{1r} - b_{1p}}{2}$, $\gamma_2 = \dfrac{b_{2r} - b_{2p}}{2}$.

Then, we must apply α-cuts to perform the multiplication calculation. When studying symmetric triangular fuzzy numbers, there will be a linear equation on the left and right side after α-cut processing. Next, we mark the left side to indicate the symbol as L and the right as R. The classical fuzzy number after the α-cut can be obtained as

$$Z_1^{\bar{\gamma}_1} = [Z_{1\alpha}^L, Z_{1\alpha}^R] = [\sqrt{\gamma_1}(a_{1q} - a_{1p})\alpha + \sqrt{\gamma_1}a_{1p}, \sqrt{\gamma_1}(a_{1q} - a_{1r})\alpha + \sqrt{\gamma_1}a_{1r}],$$

$$Z_2^{\bar{\gamma}_2} = [Z_{2\alpha}^L, Z_{2\alpha}^R] = [\sqrt{\gamma_2}(a_{2q} - a_{2p})\alpha + \sqrt{\gamma_2}a_{2p}, \sqrt{\gamma_2}(a_{2q} - a_{2r})\alpha + \sqrt{\gamma_2}a_{2r}].$$

Per Equation (9), it is reasoned that

$$Z^{*\bar{\gamma}^*} = Z_1^{\bar{\gamma}_1} \times Z_2^{\bar{\gamma}_2} = [Z_{1\alpha}^L, Z_{1\alpha}^R] \times [Z_{2\alpha}^L, Z_{2\alpha}^R] = [Z_\alpha^{*L}, Z_\alpha^{*R}],$$

where

$$Z_\alpha^{*L} = min\left\{Z_{1\alpha}^L Z_{2\alpha}^L, Z_{1\alpha}^L Z_{2\alpha}^R, Z_{1\alpha}^R Z_{2\alpha}^L, Z_{1\alpha}^R Z_{2\alpha}^R\right\},$$
$$Z_\alpha^{*R} = max\left\{Z_{1\alpha}^L Z_{2\alpha}^L, Z_{1\alpha}^L Z_{2\alpha}^R, Z_{1\alpha}^R Z_{2\alpha}^L, Z_{1\alpha}^R Z_{2\alpha}^R\right\}.$$

After the modeling is completed, it is known that the ordinate corresponding to point L is less than that corresponding to point R. Therefore, after analysis, it is found that

$$Z_\alpha^{*L} = Z_{1\alpha}^L Z_{2\alpha}^L = [(a_{1q} - a_{1p})(a_{2q} - a_{2p})\alpha^2 + (a_{1p}a_{2q} + a_{2p}a_{1q} - 2a_{1p}a_{2p})\alpha + a_{1p}a_{2p}]\sqrt{\gamma_1}\sqrt{\gamma_2}, \quad (18)$$

$$Z_\alpha^{*R} = Z_{1\alpha}^R Z_{2\alpha}^R = [(a_{1q} - a_{1r})(a_{2q} - a_{2p})\alpha^2 + (a_{1r}a_{2q} + a_{2r}a_{1q} - 2a_{1r}a_{2r})\alpha + a_{1r}a_{2r}]\sqrt{\gamma_1}\sqrt{\gamma_2}. \quad (19)$$

In the next step, in order to find the membership degree μ, α needs to be calculated first.

Let $Z_\alpha^{*L} = m$, which denotes the magnitude of the length of the horizontal axis taken by the new membership degree after multiplying the two membership degrees and is an unknown number. Transforming Equation (18), we obtain

$$\alpha = \frac{-(a_{1p}\tilde{a_2} + a_{2p}\tilde{a_1}) + \sqrt{(a_{1p}\tilde{a_2} - a_{2p}\tilde{a_1})^2 + \frac{4\tilde{a_1}\tilde{a_2}m}{\sqrt{\gamma_1}\sqrt{\gamma_2}}}}{2\tilde{a_1}\tilde{a_2}},$$

where we discard the roots of $\alpha < 0$ and where $\tilde{a_1} = a_{1q} - a_{1p} = a_{1r} - a_{1q}$, $\tilde{a_2} = a_{2q} - a_{2p} = a_{2r} - a_{2q}$.

Similarly, letting $Z_{\alpha}^{*R} = n$, after transforming Equation (19) we have

$$\alpha = \frac{-(a_{1r}\tilde{a_2} + a_{2r}\tilde{a_1}) + \sqrt{(a_{2r}\tilde{a_1} - a_{1r}\tilde{a_2})^2 + \frac{4\tilde{a_1}\tilde{a_2}n}{\sqrt{\gamma_1}\sqrt{\gamma_2}}}}{2\tilde{a_1}\tilde{a_2}},$$

where we discard the roots of $\alpha > 1$ and $\tilde{a_1} = a_{1q} - a_{1p} = a_{1r} - a_{1q}$, $\tilde{a_2} = a_{2q} - a_{2p} = a_{2r} - a_{2q}$.

Due to the nature of symmetric triangular fuzzy numbers, it is obvious that

$$m + n = 2\sqrt{\gamma_1}\sqrt{\gamma_2}a_{1q}a_{2q}.$$

Therefore, the membership function of Z^* is

$$\mu_{A^*} = \begin{cases} \frac{-(a_{1p}\tilde{a_2}+a_{2p}\tilde{a_1})+\sqrt{(a_{1p}\tilde{a_2}-a_{2p}\tilde{a_1})^2+\frac{4\tilde{a_1}\tilde{a_2}m}{\sqrt{\gamma_1}\sqrt{\gamma_2}}}}{2\tilde{a_1}\tilde{a_2}}, & m\in(\sqrt{\gamma_1}\sqrt{\gamma_2}a_{1p}a_{2p}, \sqrt{\gamma_1}\sqrt{\gamma_2}a_{1q}a_{2q}) \\ \frac{-(a_{1r}\tilde{a_2}+a_{2r}\tilde{a_1})+\sqrt{(a_{2r}\tilde{a_1}-a_{1r}\tilde{a_2})^2+\frac{4\tilde{a_1}\tilde{a_2}(2\sqrt{\gamma_1}\sqrt{\gamma_2}a_{1q}a_{2q}-m)}{\sqrt{\gamma_1}\sqrt{\gamma_2}}}}{2\tilde{a_1}\tilde{a_2}}, & m\in(\sqrt{\gamma_1}\sqrt{\gamma_2}a_{1q}a_{2q}, \sqrt{\gamma_1}\sqrt{\gamma_2}a_{1r}a_{2r}) \\ 0, & \text{otherwise.} \end{cases} \quad (20)$$

As a result, $A^* = (\sqrt{\gamma_1}\sqrt{\gamma_2}a_{1p}a_{2p}, \sqrt{\gamma_1}\sqrt{\gamma_2}a_{1q}a_{2q}, \sqrt{\gamma_1}\sqrt{\gamma_2}a_{1r}a_{2r})$.

The following steps are similar to the addition and subtraction calculation processes. First calculating P^* and then applying Equation (14), we obtain

$$P^*(v) = P_1 \circ P_2 = \int_R \frac{1}{|u|}p_1(u)p_2(\frac{v}{u})du.$$

It should be noted that a fundamental condition of the multiplicative convolution formula is that P_1 and P_2 are independent of each other. Then, B^* can be obtained by substituting p^* and μ_{A^*} into Equation (16). Thus, the conclusion is obtained:

$$Z^* = Z_1 \times Z_2 = (A^*, B^*).$$

□

3.5. Power Formula

Theorem 5. *Let λ be a real number and let $Z = (A, B) = ((a_p, a_q, a_r), (b_p, b_q, b_r))$ be a symmetric triangular Z-number. Its powers can be calculated by*

$$Z^\lambda = (A^\lambda, B^\lambda),$$

where $A^\lambda = ((\sqrt{\gamma}a_p)^\lambda, (\sqrt{\gamma}a_q)^\lambda, (\sqrt{\gamma}a_r)^\lambda)$, $B^\lambda = \int \mu_A^\lambda p(u^\lambda)du$, $\gamma_1 = \frac{b_{1r} - b_{1p}}{2}$, $\gamma_2 = \frac{b_{2r} - b_{2p}}{2}$, μ_A^λ is the membership function of A^λ, and $p(u^\lambda)$ is the probability density of A^λ.

Proof. The power operation is actually a generalization of the multiplication calculation. First, we can make $Z_1^\lambda = (A^\lambda, B^\lambda)$, which means that Z_1^λ is obtained by multiplying λ times Z_1.

When $\lambda = 1$, $Z_1^\lambda = Z_1$. When $\lambda = 2$, $Z_1^\lambda = Z_1^2 = Z_1 \times Z_1$, and according to the multiplication formula derived earlier, $Z_1^2 = (A^2, B^2)$, where $A^\lambda = A^2 = ((\sqrt{\gamma}a_p)^2, (\sqrt{\gamma}a_q)^2, (\sqrt{\gamma}a_r)^2)$. Analogously, when $\lambda = 3$, $Z_1^\lambda = Z_1^3 = Z_1 \times Z_1 \times Z_1 = (A^3, B^3)$, where $A^\lambda = ((\sqrt{\gamma}a_p)^3, (\sqrt{\gamma}a_q)^3, (\sqrt{\gamma}a_r)^3)$.

Assume that $A^n = ((\sqrt{\gamma}a_p)^n, (\sqrt{\gamma}a_q)^n, (\sqrt{\gamma}a_r)^n)$ holds when $\lambda = n$. Then, $A^{n+1} = A^n \times A = ((\sqrt{\gamma}a_p)^{n+1}, (\sqrt{\gamma}a_q)^{n+1}, (\sqrt{\gamma}a_r)^{n+1})$.

Therefore, we can find that when $\lambda \in R$, $A^\lambda = ((\sqrt{\gamma}a_p)^\lambda, (\sqrt{\gamma}a_q)^\lambda, (\sqrt{\gamma}a_r)^\lambda)$.

For B^λ, when $\lambda = 2$, $B^\lambda = B^2 = \int \mu_A^2(t)p^2(t)dt$. Using Equation (20), we can find that the membership function of A^λ is

$$\mu_A^\lambda = \begin{cases} \dfrac{\lambda\sqrt{m} - \sqrt{\gamma}a_p}{\sqrt{\gamma}\tilde{a}_1}, & m \in ((\sqrt{\gamma}a_p)^\lambda, (\sqrt{\gamma}a_q)^\lambda) \\ \dfrac{\lambda\sqrt{m} - \sqrt{\gamma}a_r}{\sqrt{\gamma}\tilde{a}_1}, & m \in ((\sqrt{\gamma}a_q)^\lambda, (\sqrt{\gamma}a_r)^\lambda) \\ 0, & otherwise. \end{cases}$$

Then, according to Equation (14), we can find

$$P(u^2) = \int_R \frac{1}{|u|} p^2(u)du.$$

The same extends to the condition when $\lambda \in R$:

$$P(u^\lambda) = \left(\int_R \frac{1}{|u|} p(u)du\right)^{\lambda-2} \left(\int_R \frac{1}{|u|} p^2(u)du\right).$$

Accordingly, by combination with $B^\lambda = \int \mu_A^\lambda p(u^\lambda)du$, we can find the value of B^λ. Finally, we obtain

$$Z^\lambda = (A^\lambda, B^\lambda).$$

□

3.6. Division Formula

Theorem 6. *Let $Z_1 = (A_1, B_1) = ((a_{1p}, a_{1q}, a_{1r}), (b_{1p}, b_{1q}, b_{1r}))$ and $Z_2 = (A_2, B_2) = ((a_{2p}, a_{2q}, a_{2r}), (b_{2p}, b_{2q}, b_{2r}))$ be continuous symmetric triangular Z-numbers and let the division formula of these two be Z_s. Then, it can be deduced that*

$$Z_s = \frac{Z_1}{Z_2} = (A_s, B_s),$$

where $A_s = \left(\dfrac{\sqrt{\gamma_1}a_{1p}}{\sqrt{\gamma_2}a_{2p}}, \dfrac{\sqrt{\gamma_1}a_{1q}}{\sqrt{\gamma_2}a_{2q}}, \dfrac{\sqrt{\gamma_1}a_{1r}}{\sqrt{\gamma_2}a_{2r}}\right)$, $B_s = \int_R \mu_{A_s} p_s dt$, $\gamma_1 = \dfrac{b_{1r} - b_{1p}}{2}$, $\gamma_2 = \dfrac{b_{2r} - b_{2p}}{2}$, μ_{A_s} is the membership function of A_s, and p_s is the probability density of A_s.

Proof. Let $Z_s = \dfrac{Z_1}{Z_2}$, where $Z_1 = (A_1, B_1)$ and $Z_2 = (A_2, B_2)$. Then, we can convert Z_1 and Z_2 to fuzzy numbers as follows:

$$Z_1^{\gamma_1} = (\sqrt{\gamma_1}a_{1p}, \sqrt{\gamma_1}a_{1q}, \sqrt{\gamma_1}a_{1r}),$$
$$Z_2^{\gamma_2} = (\sqrt{\gamma_2}a_{2p}, \sqrt{\gamma_2}a_{2q}, \sqrt{\gamma_2}a_{2r}),$$

where $\gamma_1 = \dfrac{b_{1r} - b_{1p}}{2}$, $\gamma_2 = \dfrac{b_{2r} - b_{2p}}{2}$.

For these two triangular fuzzy numbers, their α-cuts are

$$Z_1^{\bar{\gamma}_1} = [Z_{1\alpha}^L, Z_{1\alpha}^R] = [\sqrt{\gamma_1}(a_{1q} - a_{1p})\alpha + \sqrt{\gamma_1}a_{1p}, \sqrt{\gamma_1}(a_{1q} - a_{1r})\alpha + \sqrt{\gamma_1}a_{1r}],$$

$$Z_2^{\bar{\gamma}_2} = [Z_{2\alpha}^L, Z_{2\alpha}^R] = [\sqrt{\gamma_2}(a_{2q} - a_{2p})\alpha + \sqrt{\gamma_2}a_{2p}, \sqrt{\gamma_2}(a_{2q} - a_{2r})\alpha + \sqrt{\gamma_2}a_{2r}].$$

From Equation (10), the α-cut of $Z_s^{\bar{\gamma}_s} = \dfrac{Z_1^{\bar{\gamma}_1}}{Z_2^{\bar{\gamma}_2}}$ is

$$\frac{[Z_{1\alpha}^L, Z_{1\alpha}^R]}{[Z_{2\alpha}^L, Z_{2\alpha}^R]} = [Z_{s\alpha}^L, Z_{s\alpha}^R],$$

where $Z_{s\alpha}^L = min\left\{\dfrac{Z_{1\alpha}^L}{Z_{2\alpha}^L}, \dfrac{Z_{1\alpha}^L}{Z_{2\alpha}^R}, \dfrac{Z_{1\alpha}^R}{Z_{2\alpha}^L}, \dfrac{Z_{1\alpha}^R}{Z_{2\alpha}^R}\right\}, Z_{s\alpha}^R = max\left\{\dfrac{Z_{1\alpha}^L}{Z_{2\alpha}^L}, \dfrac{Z_{1\alpha}^L}{Z_{2\alpha}^R}, \dfrac{Z_{1\alpha}^R}{Z_{2\alpha}^L}, \dfrac{Z_{1\alpha}^R}{Z_{2\alpha}^R}\right\}.$

Similar to the proof process of multiplication, it is known that $Z^L < Z^R$. As a result,

$$Z_{s\alpha}^L = \frac{Z_{1\alpha}^L}{Z_{2\alpha}^R} = \frac{\sqrt{\gamma_1}(a_{1q} - a_{1p})\alpha + \sqrt{\gamma_1}a_{1p}}{\sqrt{\gamma_2}(a_{2q} - a_{2r})\alpha + \sqrt{\gamma_2}a_{2r}},$$

$$Z_{s\alpha}^R = \frac{Z_{1\alpha}^R}{Z_{2\alpha}^L} = \frac{\sqrt{\gamma_1}(a_{1q} - a_{1r})\alpha + \sqrt{\gamma_1}a_{1r}}{\sqrt{\gamma_2}(a_{2q} - a_{2p})\alpha + \sqrt{\gamma_2}a_{2p}}.$$

Let $Z_{s\alpha}^L = m$, which is an unknown function that represents the range of values. We discard the roots of $\alpha < 0$; hence,

$$\alpha = \frac{m\sqrt{\gamma_2}a_{2r} - \sqrt{\gamma_1}a_{1p}}{\sqrt{\gamma_1}(a_{1q} - a_{1p}) - m\sqrt{\gamma_2}(a_{2q} - a_{2r})} = \frac{m\sqrt{\gamma_2}a_{2r} - \sqrt{\gamma_1}a_{1p}}{\sqrt{\gamma_1}\tilde{a_1} - m\sqrt{\gamma_2}\tilde{a_2}},$$

where $\tilde{a_1} = a_{1q} - a_{1p} = a_{1r} - a_{1q}, \tilde{a_2} = a_{2q} - a_{2p} = a_{2r} - a_{2q}$.

Let $Z_{s\alpha}^R = n$, which is an unknown function that represents the range of values. We discard the roots of $\alpha > 1$; therefore,

$$\alpha = \frac{n\sqrt{\gamma_2}a_{2p} - \sqrt{\gamma_1}a_{1r}}{\sqrt{\gamma_1}(a_{1q} - a_{1r}) - n\sqrt{\gamma_2}(a_{2q} - a_{2p})} = \frac{n\sqrt{\gamma_2}a_{2p} - \sqrt{\gamma_1}a_{1r}}{\sqrt{\gamma_1}\tilde{a_1} - n\sqrt{\gamma_2}\tilde{a_2}}.$$

Due to the nature of the symmetric triangular fuzzy number, it is obvious that

$$m + n = 2\frac{\sqrt{\gamma_1}a_{1q}}{\sqrt{\gamma_2}a_{2q}}.$$

The membership function of $Z_s^{\gamma_s}$ is

$$\mu_{A_t} = \begin{cases} \dfrac{m\sqrt{\gamma_2}a_{2r} - \sqrt{\gamma_1}a_{1p}}{\sqrt{\gamma_1}\tilde{a_1} - m\sqrt{\gamma_2}\tilde{a_2}}, & m \in \left(\dfrac{\sqrt{\gamma_1}a_{1p}}{\sqrt{\gamma_2}a_{2p}}, \dfrac{\sqrt{\gamma_1}a_{1q}}{\sqrt{\gamma_2}a_{2q}}\right) \\ \dfrac{2\sqrt{\gamma_1}a_{1q}a_{2p} - \sqrt{\gamma_2}a_{2p}a_{2q}m - \sqrt{\gamma_1}a_{1r}a_{2q}}{\sqrt{\gamma_1}\tilde{a_1}a_{2q} - 2\sqrt{\gamma_1}\tilde{a_2}a_{1q} + \sqrt{\gamma_2}\tilde{a_2}a_{2q}m}, & m \in \left(\dfrac{\sqrt{\gamma_1}a_{1q}}{\sqrt{\gamma_2}a_{2q}}, \dfrac{\sqrt{\gamma_1}a_{1r}}{\sqrt{\gamma_2}a_{2r}}\right) \\ 0, & otherwise. \end{cases}$$

Then, $A_s = \left(\dfrac{\sqrt{\gamma_1}a_{1p}}{\sqrt{\gamma_2}a_{2p}}, \dfrac{\sqrt{\gamma_1}a_{1q}}{\sqrt{\gamma_2}a_{2q}}, \dfrac{\sqrt{\gamma_1}a_{1r}}{\sqrt{\gamma_2}a_{2r}}\right)$.

Next, we use Equation (13) to calculate the probability density P_s:

$$P_s(v) = P_1 \circ P_2 = \int_R |u| p_1(u) p_2(uv) du.$$

Finally, we again use Equation (16) to obtain B_t. Therefore, we have

$$Z_s = \frac{Z_1}{Z_2} = (A_s, B_s).$$

□

At this point, all of the mentioned operational rules related to Z-numbers have been proposed and proven. Compared to other computational methods, our proposed method simplifies the operations by converting them into classical fuzzy numbers and deriving the two components of the desired Z-number via the operational laws of the classical fuzzy numbers. When facing more complex Z-number operations, using these theorems of basic operations can greatly reduce computational complexity, enabling the application of Z-numbers to a wider range of fields.

4. Conclusions

Z-number proposals integrate objective natural language information and subjective human understanding, taking both the vagueness of information and the level of "trustworthiness" of fuzzy information into account. Therefore, Z-numbers provide a great deal of convenience in describing and analyzing uncertain information. Many researchers have studied the concept since its introduction. Drawn from the theoretical foundation of fuzzy sets theory and optimization methods, they have provided basic operational laws of common algebraic operations for Z-numbers. In a more straightforward manner, this paper has focused on operational laws for symmetric triangular Z-numbers. First, we transform the Z-numbers into classical triangular fuzzy numbers. After that, we employ the operational laws of the classical fuzzy numbers for reference to derive the two components of the derived Z-number. Finally, we provide the number-multiplication, addition, subtraction, multiplication, power, and division expressions for the Z-numbers. In the fields of economics, decision analysis, risk assessment, planning, and causal analysis, many real-life numbers are actually Z-numbers. In previous academic research, however, they have been simplified into other numbers due to their high computational complexity. Based on these rules of basic operations, the application prospects of Z-numbers will be greatly improved.

There are some limitations to this article. First, this paper only proposes operational laws for symmetric triangular Z-numbers, and does not apply to other types of Z-numbers; hence, it is necessary to extend this method to more general Z-numbers in further theoretical studies. Second, time and energy constraints limited our study to the multiplication, power series, and quadratic operations of Z-numbers. We have not provided definitions and operational rules for other calculations, including more complex algebraic operations, expectations, and variance, which we plan to expand upon in the future. Finally, this paper has not provided application examples to prove the applicability and scope of the proposed operational laws, which requires further investigation in future work.

Author Contributions: Supervision, H.L. and Z.L.; conceptualization, H.L.; investigation, X.L. and M.Y.; methodology, H.L.; formal analysis, H.L., Z.L. and X.L.; validation, X.L., L.P. and M.Y.; writing—original draft, X.L., L.P. and K.Q.; writing—review and editing, Z.L. and H.L. All authors have read and agreed to the published version of the manuscript.

Funding: This research received no external funding.

Data Availability Statement: Data are contained within the article.

Acknowledgments: The authors especially thank the editors and anonymous referees for their kindly review and helpful comments.

Conflicts of Interest: The authors declare no conflicts of interest.

References

1. Zadeh, L.A. Fuzzy sets. *Inf. Control* **1965**, *8*, 338–353. [CrossRef]
2. Atanassov, K. Intuitionistic fuzzy sets. *Fuzzy Set Syst.* **1986**, *20*, 87–96. [CrossRef]
3. Torra, V. Hesitant fuzzy sets. *Int. J. Intell. Syst.* **2010**, *25*, 529–539. [CrossRef]
4. Mizumoto, M.; Tanaka, K. Some properties of fuzzy sets of type 2. *Inf. Control* **1976**, *31*, 312–340. [CrossRef]
5. Atanassov, K.; Gargov, G. Interval valued intuitionistic fuzzy sets. *Fuzzy Set Syst.* **1989**, *31*, 343–349. [CrossRef]
6. Masamichi, K.; Hiroaki, K. On sequences of fuzzy sets and fuzzy set-valued mappings. *Fixed Point Theory Appl.* **2013**, *327*, 1–19.
7. Zadeh, L.A. A note on Z-numbers. *Inf. Sci.* **2011**, *181*, 2923–2932. [CrossRef]
8. Pal, S.K.; Banerjee, R.; Dutta S.; Sen Sarma, S. An insight into the Z-number approach to CWW. *Fund. Inform.* **2013**, *124*, 197–229. [CrossRef]
9. Banerjee, R.; Pal, S.K. Z*-numbers: Augmented Z-numbers for machine-subjectivity representation. *Inf. Sci.* **2015**, *323*, 143–178. [CrossRef]
10. Pirmuhammadi, S.; Allahviranloo, T.; Keshavarz, M. The parametric form of Z-number and its application in Z-number initial value problem. *Int. J. Intell. Syst.* **2017**, *32*, 1031–1061. [CrossRef]
11. Peng, H.; Wang, J. Hesitant uncertain linguistic Z-numbers and their application in multi-criteria group decision-making problems. *Int. J. Fuzzy Syst.* **2017**, *19*, 1300–1316. [CrossRef]
12. Mondal, A.; Roy, S.K.; Zhan, J.M. A reliability-based consensus model and regret theory-based selection process for linguistic hesitant-Z multi-attribute group decision making. *Expert Syst. Appl.* **2023**, *228*, 120431. [CrossRef]
13. Tian, Y.; Mi, X.; Ji, Y.; Kang, B. ZE-numbers: A new extended Z-numbers and its application on multiple attribute group decision making. *Eng. Appl. Artif. Intell.* **2021**, *101*, 104225. [CrossRef]
14. Haseli, G.; Ögel, I.Y.; Ecer, F.; Hajiaghaei-Keshteli, M. Luxury in female technology (FemTech): Selection of smart jewelry for women through BCM-MARCOS group decision-making framework with fuzzy ZE-numbers. *Technol. Forecast. Soc.* **2023**, *196*, 122870. [CrossRef]
15. Haseli, G.; Bonab, S.R.; Hajiaghaei-Keshteli, M.; Ghoushchi, S.J.; Deveci, M. Fuzzy ZE-numbers framework in group decision-making using the BCM and CoCoSo to address sustainable urban transportation. *Inf. Sci.* **2024**, *653*, 119809. [CrossRef]
16. Haseli, G.; Deveci, M.; Isik, M.; Gokasar, I.; Pamucar, D.; Hajiaghaei-Keshteli, M. Providing climate change resilient land-use transport projects with green finance using Z extended numbers based decision-making model. *Expert Syst. Appl.* **2024**, *243*, 122858. [CrossRef]
17. Aliev, R.A.; Pedrycz, W.; Huseynov, O.H. Functions defined on a set of Z-numbers. *Inf. Sci.* **2018**, *423*, 353–375. [CrossRef]
18. Massanet, S.; Riera, J.V.; Torrens, J. A new approach to Zadeh's Z-numbers: Mixed-discrete Z-numbers. *Inform. Fusion* **2019**, *53*, 35–42. [CrossRef]
19. Abu Bakar, A.S.; Gegov, A. Multi-layer decision methodology for ranking Z-numbers. *Int. J. Comput. Int. Sys.* **2015**, *8*, 395–406. [CrossRef]
20. Aliev, R.A.; Huseynov, O.H.; Serdaroglu, R. Ranking of Z-numbers and its application in decision making. *Int. J. Inf. Technol. Decis.* **2016**, *15*, 1503–1519. [CrossRef]
21. Jiang, W.; Xie, C.; Luo, Y.; Tang, T. Ranking Z-numbers with an improved ranking method for generalized fuzzy numbers. *J. Intell. Fuzzy Syst.* **2017**, *32*, 1931–1943. [CrossRef]
22. Ezadi, S.; Allahviranloo, T.; Mohammadi, S. Two new methods for ranking of Z-numbers based on sigmoid function and sign method. *Int. J. Intell. Syst.* **2018**, *33*, 1476–1487. [CrossRef]
23. Aliev, R.A.; Alizadeh, A.V.; Huseynov, O.H. The arithmetic of discrete Z-numbers. *Inf. Sci.* **2015**, *290*, 134–155. [CrossRef]
24. Aliev, R.A.; Huseynov, O.H.; Zeinalova, L.M. The arithmetic of continuous Z-numbers. *Inf. Sci.* **2016**, *373*, 441–460. [CrossRef]
25. Aliev, R.A.; Pedryczc, W.; Huseynov, O.H. Hukuhara difference of Z-numbers. *Inf. Sci.* **2018**, *466*, 13–24. [CrossRef]
26. Qiu, D.; Jiang, H.; Yu, Y. On computing generalized Hukuhara differences of Z-numbers. *J. Intell. Fuzzy Syst.* **2019**, *36*, 1–11. [CrossRef]
27. Shen, K.; Wang, J.; Wang, T. The arithmetic of multidimensional Z-number. *J. Intell. Fuzzy Syst.* **2019**, *36*, 1647–1661. [CrossRef]
28. Kang, B.; Deng, Y.; Hewage, K.; Sadiq, R. A method of measuring uncertainty for Z-number. *IEEE Trans. Fuzzy Syst.* **2019**, *24*, 731–738. [CrossRef]
29. Peng, H.; Wang, X.; Zhang, H.; Wang, J. Group decision-making based on the aggregation of Z-numbers with Archimedean t-norms and t-conorms. *Inf. Sci.* **2021**, *569*, 264–286. [CrossRef]
30. Zhu, R.; Liu, Q.; Huang, C.; Kang, B. Z-ACM: An approximate calculation method of Z-numbers for large data sets based on kernel density estimation and its application in decision-making. *J. Inf. Sci.* **2022**, *610*, 440–471. [CrossRef]
31. Kang, B.; Wei, D.; Li, Y.; Deng, Y. A method of converting Z-number to classical fuzzy number. *J. Inf. Comput. Sci.* **2012**, *9*, 703–709.
32. Zhang, C.; Hu, Z.; Qin, Y.; Song, W. Performance evaluation of technological service platform: A rough Z-number-based BWM-TODIM method. *Expert Syst. Appl.* **2023**, *230*, 120665. [CrossRef]
33. Ashraf, S.; Abbasi, S.N.; Naeem, M.; Eldin, S.M. Novel decision aid model for green supplier selection based on extended EDAS approach under pythagorean fuzzy Z-numbers. *Front. Environ. Sci.* **2023**, *11*, 1137689. [CrossRef]
34. Nazari-Shirkouhi, S.; Tavakoli, M.; Govindan, K.; Mousakhani, S. A hybrid approach using Z-number DEA model and Artificial Neural Network for resilient supplier selection. *Expert Syst. Appl.* **2023**, *222*, 119746. [CrossRef]

35. Zhu, G.; Hu, J. A rough-Z-number-based DEMATEL to evaluate the co-creative sustainable value propositions for smart product-service systems. *Int. J. Intell. Syst.* **2021**, *36*, 3645–3679. [CrossRef]
36. Wang, W.; Liu, X.; Liu, S. A hybrid evaluation method for human error probability by using extended DEMATEL with Z-numbers: A case of cargo loading operation. *Int. J. Ind. Ergon.* **2021**, *84*, 103158. [CrossRef]
37. Akhavein, A.; Rezahoseini, A.; Ramezani, A.M.; Bagherpour, M. Ranking sustainable projects through an innovative hybrid DEMATEL-VIKOR decision-making approach using Z-Number. *Adv. Civ. Eng.* **2021**, *2*, 1–40. [CrossRef]
38. Huang, J.; Xu, D.; Liu, H.; Song, M. A new model for failure mode and effect analysis integrating linguistic Z-numbers and projection method. *IEEE Trans. Fuzzy Syst.* **2021**, *29*, 530–538. [CrossRef]
39. Wang, J.; Cao, Y.; Zhang, H. Multi-criteria decision-making method based on distance measure and Choquet integral for linguistic Z-numbers. *Cogn. Comput.* **2017**, *9*, 827–842. [CrossRef]
40. Ren, Z.; Liao, H.; Liu, X. Generalized Z-numbers with hesitant fuzzy linguistic information and its application to medicine selection for the patients with mild symptoms of the COVID-19. *Comput. Ind. Eng.* **2020**, *145*, 106517. [CrossRef]
41. Qi, G.; Li, J.; Kang, B.; Yang, B. The aggregation of Z-numbers based on overlap functions and grouping functions and its application on group decision-making. *Inf. Sci.* **2023**, *623*, 857–899. [CrossRef]
42. Yaakob, A.M.; Gegov, A. Interactive TOPSIS based group decision making methodology using Z-numbers. *Int. J. Comput. Int. Syst.* **2016**, *9*, 311–324. [CrossRef]
43. Wang, T.; Li, H.; Zhou, X.; Liu, D.; Huang, B. Three-way decision based on third-generation prospect theory with Z-numbers. *Inf. Sci.* **2021**, *569*, 13–38. [CrossRef]
44. Mondal, A.; Roy, S.K. Behavioural three-way decision making with Fermatean fuzzy Mahalanobis distance: Application to the supply chain management problems. *Appl. Soft Comput.* **2024**, *151*, 111182. [CrossRef]
45. Van Laarhoven, P.J.M.; Pedrycz, W. A fuzzy extension of Saaty's priority theory. *Fuzzy Set. Syst.* **1983**, *11*, 229–241. [CrossRef]
46. Wang, Y. Centroid defuzzification and the maximizing set and minimizing set ranking based on alpha level sets. *Comput. Ind. Eng.* **2009**, *57*, 228–236. [CrossRef]
47. Kwiesielewicz, M. A note on the fuzzy extension of Saaty's priority theory. *Fuzzy Sets Syst.* **1998**, *95*, 161–172. [CrossRef]
48. Kallenberg, O. *Foundations of Modern Probability;* Springer: Berlin/Heidelberg, Germany, 2002.

mathematics

MDPI

Article

The Intrinsic Characterization of a Fuzzy Consistently Connected Domain

Chongyun Zhao and Guanghao Jiang *

School of Mathematics and Statistics, Huaibei Normal University, Huaibei 235000, China; chongyunzhao@163.com
* Correspondence: guanghaoj@126.com

Abstract: The concepts of a fuzzy connected set (fc set) and a fuzzy consistently connected set (fcc set) are introduced on fuzzy posets, along with a discussion of their basic properties. Inspired by some equivalent conditions of crisp connected sets, the characterizations of the fc sets are given, and we also explore fuzzy completeness and fuzzy compactness in addition to defining a new fuzzy way-below relation based on fcc complete sets. Using this relationship as a basis, the fcc domain is also provided and studied, and its equivalent characterizations are obtained. In summary, we develop a method to establish fcc completeness from a continuous poset.

Keywords: fuzzy connected sets; fuzzy consistently connected sets; fuzzy connected complete sets; fuzzy connected continuous domain

MSC: 06A11; 06B35; 03E72; 54H10

1. Introduction and Related Work

In the 1960s, the birth of fuzzy mathematics [1] and the establishment of continuous lattices [2] aroused the research interest of a large number of scholars. Following its development, the theory of continuous lattices was successfully promoted to the theory of continuous domain by G Gierz [3]. References [4–6] innovatively combined domain theory with fuzzy mathematics, with Zhang Qiye and Fan Lei introducing the concept of fuzzy partial order, which, in turn, led to the emergence of fuzzy domain theory. A Chaudhuri and P Das [7] introduced a new concept of fuzzy set connectivity called cs-connectivity. This concept is different from other connectivity concepts, and they found that cs-connectivity is not equivalent to these existing definitions of connectivity; they examined the validity of the standard results under this new concept of connectivity. In references [8,9], the concept of connected sets was introduced to broaden the scope of continuous partial order theory, and the concept of the connected continuous domain was introduced using the concept of connected sets, with fruitful results obtained by Shang Yun and Zhao Bin, they introduce and explore the concept of a consistently connected continuous domain, and extend the application scope of continuous poset theory by exploiting the characteristics of connected sets, solved the limitations of continuous poset theory in the treatment of the real number set and the natural number set, and to characterize it through the properties of the principal ideal and connected closed sets, they also study the directional completeness of consistently connected complete posets and obtains good theoretical results. In [10–12], Tang Zhaoyong introduced and examined the connectivity on partially ordered sets from various perspectives using step sets, resulting in a series of significant findings. In [13], Tang Zhaoyong and Xu Luoshan deeply explore the connectivity and local connectivity of posets from the perspective of order and topology, especially the properties of multiple intrinsic topologies (such as Alexandrov topology and Scott topology); they try to prove the equivalence of the order connectivity of posets and its intrinsic topology and to show the properties of local connectivity. Moreover, by constructing counterexamples, they also reveal that the connectivity of the lower topology does not necessarily guarantee the sequential connectivity of the poset itself. In [14,15], they introduce and study the concept of connectivity, especially to explore the step set. They also explore the construction of connected branches and show that posets can be uniquely decomposed into the non-intersection union of these connected branches. Furthermore, they show that the connected relations of the posets constitute an equivalence relation. These results provide a new tool and theoretical framework for understanding and operating posets. Reference [16] examines and characterizes the notion of the prime neutrosophic ideal and prime neutrosophic filter. The structure of the neutrosophic open-set lattice on a topology generated by a neutrosophic relation is described in it. They have defined the concepts of neutrosophic ideals and neutrosophic filters on that lattice in terms of their level sets and meet and join operations. In addition, we have examined and defined the concepts of prime neutrosophic filters and ideals as fascinating subsets of neutrosophic ideals and filters. This work mostly discussed neutrosophic ideals and neutrosophic filters on the lattice structure of neutrosophic open sets. Reference [17] explores the fuzzy topology induced by fuzzy relations, extending classical concepts, and establishes necessary and sufficient conditions for its generation, along with characterizations involving fuzzy interval orders, preorders, and sequential fuzzy topologies. Furthermore, the fuzzy bi-topological space generated by the fuzzy relations is explored.

References [18–22] discussed related problems, such as fuzzy classification, fuzzy measurement, and fuzzy decision under fuzzy theory, obtaining good results.

The research motivation for exploring the fuzzy connected set lies in the desire to expand the application of the continuous poset theory. By defining a novel fuzzy way-below relation on the fcc complete set, we aim to deepen our understanding of this structure and enhance its utility. Furthermore, the introduction and investigation of the concept of fcc continuous domain serve to enrich the theoretical framework and broaden its potential applications. This line of inquiry offers significant insights into the properties and characteristics of fc sets, thereby contributing to the advancement of the field of fuzzy set theory and its applications.

However, in fuzzy domain theory, there is no concept of connected sets. Thus, we introduce the concepts of fuzzy connected sets and fuzzy consistently connected sets on fuzzy posets, and their basic properties are discussed. In the third section of this paper, a new fuzzy way-below relationship is defined on fuzzy consistently connected complete posets, which allows for the exploration of the fuzzy consistently connected continuous domain. In addition, its equivalent characterizations are determined.

For some basic notations and definitions, we refer the reader to [3,23–25].

2. Preliminaries

Below, we present some important terms and definitions used in this paper. Here, we describe the definitions of fuzzy sets, domain theory, and consistently connected theory.

Definition 1 ([1])**.** *Let $X = \{x_1, x_2, \cdots x_n\}$ be the universe of discourse. A fuzzy set A on X is characterized by $A = \{(x_i, \mu_A(x_i)); x_i \in X, i = 1, 2, \cdots n\}$, where $\mu_A : X \to [0,1]$, the membership function, gives the grade of membership of each element $x_i \in X$ in A.*

Definition 2 ([1]). *Let X be a set, L be a complete lattice, and L^X be all mappings from X to L. Each $A \in L^X$ is called a fuzzy subset of X. For $A \subseteq X$, $\chi_A \in L^X$ is the characteristic function of A, defined as*

$$\chi_A(x) = 1, (x \in A)$$
$$\chi_A(x) = 0, (x \notin A)$$

where 0 and 1 represent the least and great elements of L.

Definition 3 ([3]). *A poset is said to be complete with respect to directed sets if every directed subset has a sup. A directed complete poset is abbreviated as a dcpo.*

Definition 4 ([3]). *Let L be a poset. We say that x is way $-$ below y, in symbols $x \ll y$ if for all directed subsets $D \subseteq L$ for which $supD$ exists, the relation $y \leq supD$ always implies the existence of $d \in D$ with $x \leq d$. An element satisfying $x \ll x$ is said to be compact or isolated from below.*

Definition 5 ([3]). *A poset L is deemed continuous if for all $x \in L$, the set $\Downarrow x = \{u \in L : u \ll x\}$ is directed and $x = sup\{u \in L : u \ll x\}$. A dcpo that is continuous as a poset is referred to as a domain.*

Definition 6 ([4]). *Let X be a set and $e : X \times X \to L$ be a mapping. Then, (X, e) is deemed a fuzzy poset if e satisfies the following:*

(1) $\forall x \in X, e(x, x) = 1$;

(2) $\forall x, y, z \in X, e(x, y) \wedge e(y, z) \leq e(x, z)$;

(3) $\forall x, y \in X, e(x, y) = e(y, x) = 1 \Rightarrow x = y$.

Then, e is referred to as a fuzzy partial order in X.

Definition 7 ([6]). *Let $f : X \to Y$ be a mapping from a set X to a fuzzy poset (Y, e_Y). Define $f^{\to} : L^X \to L^Y, \forall A \in L^X, y \in Y, f^{\to}(A)(y) = \vee_{x \in X} A(x) \wedge e_Y(y, f(x))$.*

Definition 8 ([8]). *Let X be a poset. $\emptyset \neq B \subseteq X$. B is considered connected if for all $x, y \in B$, there exists $x = x_1, x_2, \cdots, x_n = y$ such that $x_i \in B$, and x_i, x_{i+1} are comparable.*

If B is connected and $x, y \in B$, then x and y are considered connected in B.

Definition 9 ([4]). *Let (X, e) be a fuzzy poset, $x_0 \in X$ and $A \in L^X$. x_0 is said to be the supremum (resp. infimum) of A, written as $x_0 = \sqcup A$ (resp. $x_0 = \sqcap A$), if*

(1) $\forall x \in X, A(x) \leq e(x, x_0)$(resp.$A(x) \leq e(x_0, x)$);

(2) $\forall y \in X, \wedge_{x \in X}(A(x) \to e(x, y)) \leq e(x_0, y)$(resp.$\wedge_{x \in X}(A(x) \to e(y, x)) \leq e(y, x_0)$).

Definition 10 ([5]). *Let (X, e) be a fuzzy poset. $A \in L^X$. A is considered a fuzzy upper set (resp. fuzzy lower set) if $\forall x, y \in X, e(x, y) \wedge A(x) \leq A(y)$ (resp. $\forall x, y \in X, e(x, y) \wedge A(y) \leq A(x)$).*

Definition 11 ([5]). *Let (X, e) be a fuzzy poset. For all $A \in L^X, \downarrow A, \uparrow A \in L^X$:*

$$\forall x \in X, \downarrow A(x) = \vee_{y \in X} A(y) \wedge e(x, y);$$

$$\forall x \in X, \uparrow A(x) = \vee_{y \in X} A(y) \wedge e(y, x).$$

Definition 12 ([5]). *Let (X, e) be a fuzzy poset. For all $D \in L^X$, D is a fuzzy directed subset if*

(1) $\vee_{x \in X} D(x) = 1$;

(2) $\forall x, y \in X, D(x) \wedge D(y) \leq \vee_{z \in X} D(z) \wedge e(x, z) \wedge e(y, z)$.

A fuzzy direct subset $I \in L^X$ is considered a fuzzy ideal if it is a fuzzy lower set.

Definition 13 ([5]). *Let (X, e) be a fuzzy poset. For all $D \in L^X$, D is considered a fuzzy co-directed subset if*

(1) $\vee_{x \in X} D(x) = 1$;

(2) $\forall x, y \in X, D(x) \wedge D(y) \leq \vee_{z \in X} D(z) \wedge e(z, x) \wedge e(z, y)$.

A fuzzy co-direct subset $I \in L^X$ is considered a fuzzy filter if it is a fuzzy upper set.

Definition 14 ([5]). *Let (X, e) be a fuzzy poset. $Sub_X : L^X \times L^X \to L$ is considered a Subsethood operator if*

$$\forall A_1, A_2 \in L^X, Sub_X(A_1, A_2) = \wedge_{x \in X} A_1(x) \to A_2(x).$$

Remark 1. *The following statements are easy to verify.*

(1) Both the directed set and the co-directed set are connected sets.

(2) The image of a connected set under a homomorphic mapping is a connected set.

(3) Both the totally ordered set and the one-point set are connected sets.

Definition 15 ([9]). *Let X be a poset, $\emptyset \neq D \subseteq X$. D is a consistently connected set if the following are satisfied:*

(1) D is connected;

(2) $\exists p \in X$, such that $D \subseteq \downarrow p = \{x \in X : x \leq p\}$.

Definition 16 ([9]). *Let X be a poset. X is a consistently connected complete poset if, for all consistently connected sets $D \subseteq X$, $\sqcup D$ exists.*

Definition 17 ([9]). *Let X be a consistently connected complete poset. The consistently connected way-below relation $\ll_c$ of X is defined as follows:*
for $x, y \in X$, x is said to be compatible when less than or equal to y, in symbols $x \ll_c y$ if for all consistently connected set D, $y \leq supD$ implies $x \leq d$ for some $d \in D$. We write $\Downarrow_c x = \{u \in X : u \ll_c x\}$.

Definition 18 ([9]). *Let X be a consistently connected complete poset. X is considered a consistently connected domain if*

(1) $\forall x \in X, \Downarrow_c x$ is the consistently connected set in X;

(2) $\forall x \in X, x = sup \Downarrow_c x$.

3. Fuzzy Connected Sets and Fuzzy Consistently Connected Sets

In order to extend the connected sets on posets to fuzzy domain theory in this section, an equivalent definition in alternative form of connected sets is first provided.

Definition 19. *Let X be a poset, $\emptyset \neq B \subseteq X$. B is considered connected if for every $x, y \in B$, there exists $x = x_1, x_2, \cdots, x_n = y$ such that $x_i \in B$, and for all i, $\{x_{i-1}, x_i, x_{i+1}\}$ is a directed set or co-directed set.*

Definition 20. *Let (X, e) be a fuzzy poset. For every $D \in L^X$, the fuzzy subset D is considered a fuzzy connected set if*

(1) $\vee_{x \in X} D(x) = 1$;

(2) For all $a, b \in X$, there exists $D(a) = D(x_1), D(x_2), \cdots, D(x_{n-1}), D(x_n) = D(b)$, such that for every i,

$$\begin{cases} D(x_{i-1}) \wedge D(x_{i+1}) \leq D(x_i) \wedge e(x_{i-1}, x_i) \wedge e(x_{i+1}, x_i); \\ \qquad\qquad\qquad or \\ D(x_{i-1}) \wedge D(x_{i+1}) \leq D(x_i) \wedge e(x_i, x_{i-1}) \wedge e(x_i, x_{i+1}). \end{cases}$$

A fuzzy connected set is abbreviated as an fc set.

Lemma 1. *Let $(X, \leq)$ be a poset, and it is considered as a fuzzy poset (X, e), $L = 2$. Then, for all cases, $D \in X$ is a connected set in $(X, \leq)$ if and only if the characteristic function χ_D is an fc set in (X, e).*

Proof. $\Rightarrow$ Let D be a connected set.

(1) For every $D \in X, D \neq \emptyset$; hence, $\vee_{x \in D} \chi_D(x) = 1$.

(2) Because D is a connected set, then, for every $a, b \in D$, there exists $x_1, x_2, \cdots, x_n \in D$ such that

$$a = x_1, x_2, \cdots, x_n = b,$$

and for every i, x_i and x_{i+1} are comparable; that is, for every i,

$$x_i = sup_X\{x_{i-1}, x_{i+1}\} \text{ } or \text{ } x_i = inf_X\{x_{i-1}, x_{i+1}\}.$$

Then,

$$\chi_D(a) = \chi_D(x_1), \chi_D(x_2), \cdots, \chi_D(x_n) = \chi_D(b)$$

Using Definition 2, we obtain

$$\chi_D(a) = \chi_D(x_1), \chi_D(x_2), \cdots, \chi_D(x_n) = \chi_D(b) = 1.$$

In addition, for every i,

$$e(x_{i-1}, x_i) = e(x_{i+1}, x_i) = 1 \text{ } or \text{ } e(x_i, x_{i-1}) = e(x_i, x_{i+1}) = 1.$$

From this, for every i, we obtain

$$1 = \chi_D(x_{i-1}) \wedge \chi_D(x_{i+1}) \leq 1 = \chi_D(x_i) \wedge e(x_{i-1}, x_i) \wedge e(x_{i+1}, x_i)$$

or

$$1 = \chi_D(x_{i-1}) \wedge \chi_D(x_{i+1}) \leq 1 = \chi_D(x_i) \wedge e(x_i, x_{i-1}) \wedge e(x_i, x_{i+1}).$$

Hence, the character function χ_D is an fc set in (X, e).

$\Leftarrow$ Let χ_D be an fc set in (X, e).

(1) From $\vee_{x \in D} \chi_D(x) = 1$, we have $D \neq \emptyset$.

(2) Because χ_D is an fc set in (X, e), then for all $a, b \in D$, there exists

$$\chi_D(a) = \chi_D(x_1), \chi_D(x_2), \cdots, \chi_D(x_n) = \chi_D(b)$$

Therefore,

$$a = x_1, x_2, \cdots, x_n = b$$

exists. For every i,

$$\chi_D(x_{i-1}) \wedge \chi_D(x_{i+1}) \leq \chi_D(x_i) \wedge e(x_{i-1}, x_i) \wedge e(x_{i+1}, x_i)$$

or

$$\chi_D(x_{i-1}) \wedge \chi_D(x_{i+1}) \leq \chi_D(x_i) \wedge e(x_i, x_{i-1}) \wedge e(x_i, x_{i+1}).$$

Then, we have

$$x_{i-1} \leq x_i, x_{i+1} \leq x_i \text{ } or \text{ } x_{i-1} \geq x_i, x_{i+1} \geq x_i,$$

which means that for every i, x_i and x_{i+1} are comparable, and hence, $D \in X$ is a connected set in $(X, \leq)$. □

Remark 2. *A fuzzy connected set may not necessarily be a fuzzy directed (co-directed) set.*

Example 1. *Let $(X, \leq)$ be a poset of Figure 1. Consider it as a fuzzy poset (X, e), $L = 2$, $D = \{a, b, c, d\}$. Then, D is a connected subset of X, and χ_D is an fc subset, but χ_D is not a fuzzy directed (co-directed) subset of (X, e).*

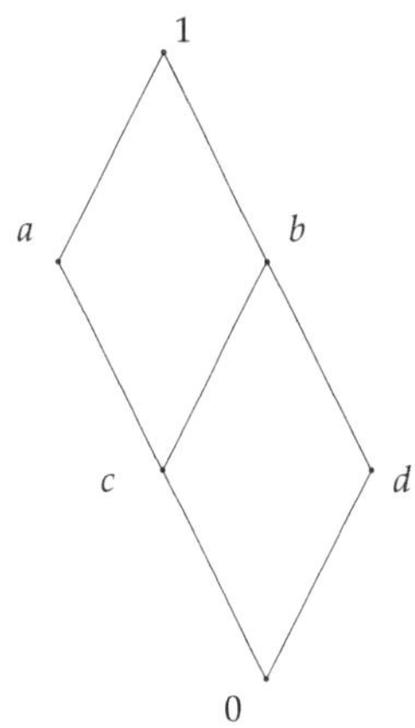

Figure 1. Graph of example 1.

Proposition 1. *Let (X, e) be a fuzzy poset, and a fuzzy directed (co-directed) subset $D \subseteq L^X$. Then, D is a fuzzy connected if there exists a point $x_0 \in X$ such that $D(x_0) = 1$.*

Proof. It follows from D being fuzzy directed that $\vee D(x) = 1$. Since D is a fuzzy directed set, by the condition that for all $a, b \in X, D(a) \wedge D(b) \leq \vee_{z \in X} D(z) \wedge e(a, z) \wedge e(b, z)$, then there exists $x_0 \in X$. Let $x_a = a, x_b = b$, such that $D(a) = D(x_a), D(x_0) = 1, D(x_b) = D(b)$. Then, we obtain

$$D(x_a) \wedge D(x_b) \leq \vee_{z \in X} D(z) \wedge e(x_a, z) \wedge e(x_b, z) \leq D(x_0) \wedge e(x_a, x_0) \wedge e(x_b, x_0).$$

Thus, D is an fc set. □

Proposition 2. *Let $(X, \leq)$ be a poset, and it is considered as a fuzzy poset (X, e), $L = 2$. For all $D \in X$, χ_D is an fc subset if χ_D is a fuzzy directed (co-directed) subset.*

Proof. It can be seen from the assumed conditions that there exists $x_0 \in X$ such that $\chi_D(x_0) = 1$, and based on Proposition 1, the conclusion is true. □

Definition 21. *Let (X, e) be a fuzzy poset, and a fuzzy subset $D \subseteq L^X$. D is considered a fuzzy consistently connected set if*

(1) D is a fuzzy connected set;

(2) there exists $p \in X$ such that $D \subseteq \downarrow p$ $(\downarrow p \in L^X, \forall x \in X, \downarrow p(x) = e(x, p))$.

A fuzzy consistently connected set is abbreviated as an fcc set.

All fcc sets in the fuzzy poset (X, e) are denoted by $C_F(X)$, and D is an fcc ideal if D is a fuzzy lower set. All fcc ideals in the fuzzy poset (X, e) are denoted by $CI_F(X)$.

Definition 22. *Let (X, e) be a fuzzy poset. (X, e) is an fcc complete poset if for all fcc subset D, $\sqcup D$ exists.*

Proposition 3. *Let $(X, \leq)$ be a poset, and consider it as a fuzzy poset (X, e), $L = 2$. $(X, \leq)$ is a consistently connected complete set if and only if (X, e) is an fcc complete poset.*

Proof. Suppose that $(X, \leq)$ is a consistently connected complete set. For all D is an fcc set, let $A = \{x \in X : D(x) = 1\}$, then $A \subseteq X$. According to Lemma 1, A is consistently connected, then there exists $x_0 \in X$ such that $x_0 = supA$, and we need to prove that $x_0 = \sqcup D$.

(1) $\forall x \in X, D(x) \leq e(x, x_0)$;

(2)

$$
\begin{aligned}
&\forall y \in X, \wedge_{x \in X}(D(x) \rightarrow e(x,y)) = 1 \\
&\Leftrightarrow \forall x \in X, D(x) \rightarrow e(x,y) = 1 \\
&\Leftrightarrow \forall x \in X, D(x) \leq e(x,y) \\
&\Leftrightarrow D(x) = 1 \\
&\Rightarrow e(x,y) = 1 \\
&\Leftrightarrow \forall x \in X, x \leq y \\
&\Rightarrow x_0 \leq y \\
&\Leftrightarrow e(x_0, y) = 1,
\end{aligned}
$$

Then, we obtain $\wedge_{x \in X}(D(x) \rightarrow e(x,y)) \leq e(x_0, y)$, and hence, $x_0 = \sqcup D$.

Conversely, suppose (X, e) is an fcc complete set and A is a consistently connected set. Then, according to Lemma 1, χ_A is fcc, and (X, e) is fcc complete; as such, there exists an $x_1 \in X$ such that $x_1 = \sqcup \chi_A$, and we need to demonstrate that $x_1 = \sqcup A$.

(1)

$$
\begin{aligned}
&\forall x \in A \Rightarrow \chi_A = 1 \\
&\Rightarrow e(x, x_1) \geq \chi_A(x) = 1 \\
&\Rightarrow x \leq x_1.
\end{aligned}
$$

(2) Suppose $y \in X$ such that for all $x \in A, x \leq y$, that is,

$$
\begin{aligned}
&\forall x \in X, \chi_A(x) = 1 \\
&\Rightarrow e(x,y) = 1 \\
&\Rightarrow \chi_A(x) \leq e(x,y) \\
&\Rightarrow \chi_A(x) \rightarrow e(x,y) = 1,
\end{aligned}
$$

Therefore, $e(x_1, y) \geq \wedge_{x \in X}(\chi_A(x) \rightarrow e(x,y)) = 1$, and hence $x_1 \leq y$. So, we have $x_1 = supA$. □

4. Fcc Way-Below and Fcc Domain

In this section, we give definitions of fcc way-below and a fcc continuous set, as well as equivalent characterizations of fcc domain and a discussion of related properties.

Definition 23. *Let (X, e) be an fcc directed complete poset. For all $y \in X, \Downarrow_{FC} y \in L^X$. This is deemed fcc way-below if*

$$\forall x \in X, \Downarrow_{FC} y(x) = \wedge_{I \in CI_F(X)}(e(y, \sqcup I) \rightarrow I(x)).$$

From Definition 21, we plot Figure 2 as an elaborated illustration of the Definition 23.

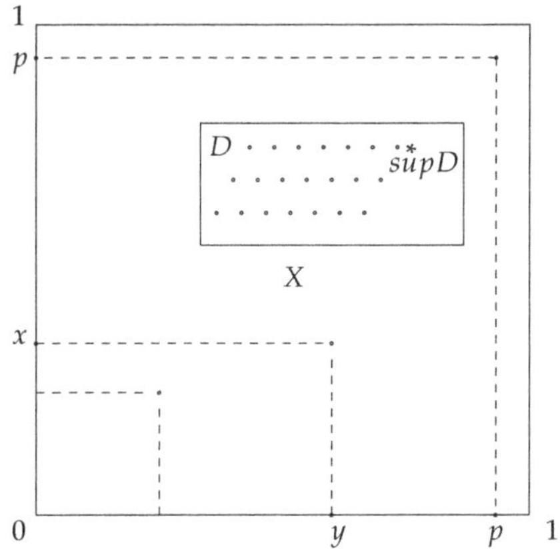

Figure 2. Graph of FC way-below relation.

X is a fuzzy poset, and the side length is unit length 1, where the projection coordinate value of any point is the matching degree of membership of x and y with respect to X. D is an fcc set, all the internal points have connectivity, and use $*$ to represent $supD$. As p is a point in the unit cube, D is below the projection coordinates of p, which satisfies the consistently connectivity of D.

Definition 24. *Let (X, e) be an fcc complete set. (X, e) is considered an fcc continuous set if $\forall x \in X, \Downarrow_{FC} x \in CI_F(X)$ and $x = \sqcup \Downarrow_{FC} x$.*

Definition 25. *An fcc directed complete poset that is an fcc continuous set is an fcc domain.*

Definition 26. *Let (X, e) be an fcc complete set. x is the fcc compact element in X if $\Downarrow_{FC} x(x) = 1$. All fcc compact elements in X are denoted $K_{FC}(X)$.*

Definition 27. *Let (X, e) be an fcc complete set, $x \in X$. Define a mapping $k_x : X \to L$:*

$$k_x(y) = \begin{cases} e(y,x), y \in K_{FC}(X); \\ 0, y \notin K_{FC}(X). \end{cases}$$

X is considered an fcc algebraic poset if k_x is an fcc subset of X and $\sqcup k_x = x$.

From Example 1.9 of [9] and Proposition 3, we have the following examples:

Example 2. *For the poset $\mathbb{R}$ of real numbers, $(\mathbb{R}, e_{\leq})$ is an fcc domain.*

Example 3. *For the poset $\mathbb{N}$ of natural numbers, $(\mathbb{N}, e_{\leq})$ is a fuzzy algebraic domain.*

Example 4. *Let A be an fcc domain. Then, the principal ideal of A is an fcc domain.*

Proposition 4. *Let (X, e) be an fcc complete set. Then, the conditions are as follows:*
(1) $\forall x \in X, I \in CI_F(X), \wedge_{y \in X} e(x,y) \leq I(x)$;
(2) $\forall x, y \in X, \wedge_{z \in X} e(x,z) \leq \Downarrow_{FC} y(x)$;
(3)$\forall x \in X, \Downarrow_{FC} \leq \downarrow x$;
(4) $\forall x, u, v, y \in X, e(u,x) \wedge \Downarrow_{FC} y(x) \wedge e(y,v) \leq \Downarrow_{FC} v(u)$.

Proof. (1) For all $x \in X, I \in CI_F(X)$, we have $\wedge_{y\in X}e(x,y) = (\wedge_{y\in X}e(x,y)) \wedge (\vee_{z\in X}I(z)) = \vee_{z\in X}(\wedge_{y\in X}e(x,y) \wedge I(z)) \leq \wedge_{z\in X}e(x,z) \wedge I(z) \leq I(x)$.

(2) For all $x, y \in X$, we have
$\Downarrow_{FC} y(x) = \wedge_{I\in CI_F(X)}e(y, \sqcup I) \to I(x) \geq \wedge_{I\in CI_F(X)}I(x) \geq \vee_{z\in X}e(x,z)$.

(3) For all $y \in X$,we obtain

$$\begin{aligned}\Downarrow_{FC} x(y) &= \wedge_{I\in CI_F(X.e)}e(x, \sqcup I) \to I(y) \leq e(x, \sqcup \downarrow x) \to \downarrow x(y)\\ &= e(x,x) \to \downarrow x(y)\\ &= \downarrow x(y).\end{aligned}$$

Hence $\Downarrow_{FC} x \leq \downarrow x$.

(4) For all $I \in CI_F(X,e)$, we have

$$\begin{aligned}&e(u,x) \wedge e(y,v) \wedge (e(y, \sqcup I) \to I(x)) \wedge e(v, \sqcup I)\\ &\leq e(u,x) \wedge e(y, \sqcup I) \wedge (e(y, \sqcup I) \to I(x))\\ &\leq e(u,x) \wedge I(x)\\ &\leq I(u).\end{aligned}$$

Then, we obtain $e(u,x) \wedge e(y,v) \wedge (e(y, \sqcup I) \to I(x)) \leq e(v, \sqcup I) \to I(u)$. According to Definition 23,

$$\begin{aligned}&e(u,x) \wedge \Downarrow_{FC} y(x) \wedge e(y,v)\\ &= e(u,x) \wedge e(y,v) \wedge (e(y, \sqcup I) \to I(x))\\ &\leq \wedge_{I\in CI_F(X,e)}e(u,x) \wedge e(y,v) \wedge (e(y, \sqcup I) \to I(x))\\ &\leq \wedge_{I\in CI_F(X)}(e(v, \sqcup I) \to I(u))\\ &= \Downarrow_{FC} v(u).\end{aligned}$$

Hence, $e(u,x) \wedge \Downarrow_{FC} y(x) \wedge e(y,v) \leq \Downarrow_{FC} v(u)$. □

Theorem 1. *Let (X,e) be an fcc domain. Then, for all $x, y \in X, \Downarrow_{FC} y(x) = \vee_{z\in X} \Downarrow_{FC} z(x) \wedge \Downarrow_{FC} y(z)$.*

Proof. On the one hand, according to Proposition 4, we have

$$\vee_{z\in X} \Downarrow_{FC} z(x) \wedge \Downarrow_{FC} y(z) \leq \Downarrow_{FC} y(x).$$

On the other hand, we simply need to prove that

$$\Downarrow_{FC} y(x) \leq \vee_{z\in X} \Downarrow_{FC} z(x) \wedge \Downarrow_{FC} y(z).$$

Suppose $D \in L^X$, for all $a \in X, D(a) = \vee_{z\in X} \Downarrow_{FC} z(a) \wedge \Downarrow_{FC} y(z)$, we shall prove that $\Downarrow_{FC} y(x) \leq D(x)$.

Firstly, $D(x)$ is an fcc ideal.

(1) For all $x \in X, \Downarrow_{FC} x$ is an fcc ideal.

$$\begin{aligned}\vee_{a\in X}D(a) &= \vee_{a\in X}\vee_{z\in X} \Downarrow_{FC} z(a) \wedge \Downarrow_{FC} y(z)\\ &= \vee_{z\in X}(\vee_{a\in X} \Downarrow_{FC} z(a)) \wedge \Downarrow_{FC} y(z)\\ &= \vee_{z\in X} \Downarrow_{FC} y(z)\\ &= 1.\end{aligned}$$

(2) For all $a, b \in X$, every fcc way-below lower set is an fcc ideal in fcc domain, so that it is fuzzy consistently connected, according to Definition 20,

$$D(a) \wedge D(b) = \vee_{m,n\in X} \Downarrow_{FC} m(a) \wedge \Downarrow_{FC} n(b) \wedge \Downarrow_{FC} y(m \wedge \Downarrow_{FC} y(n)).$$

There exists $c \in X$ such that

$$\begin{aligned}
&\vee_{m,n\in X} \Downarrow_{FC} m(a)\wedge \Downarrow_{FC} n(b)\wedge \Downarrow_{FC} y(m)\wedge \Downarrow_{FC} y(n))\\
&\leq \vee_{m,n\in X} \Downarrow_{FC} m(a)\wedge \Downarrow_{FC} n(b)\wedge \Downarrow_{FC} y(c) \wedge e(m,c) \wedge e(n,c)\\
&= \vee_{m,n\in X}(\Downarrow_{FC} m(a) \wedge e(m,c)) \wedge (\Downarrow_{FC} n(b) \wedge e(n,c))\wedge \Downarrow_{FC} y(c)\\
&\leq \vee_{m,n\in X} \Downarrow_{FC} c(a)\wedge \Downarrow_{FC} c(b)\wedge \Downarrow_{FC} y(c)\\
&=\Downarrow_{FC} c(a)\wedge \Downarrow_{FC} c(b)\wedge \Downarrow_{FC} y(c).
\end{aligned}$$

Furthermore, there exists $d \in X$ such that

$$\begin{aligned}
&\Downarrow_{FC} c(a)\wedge \Downarrow_{FC} c(b)\wedge \Downarrow_{FC} y(c)\\
&\leq\Downarrow_{FC} c(d) \wedge e(a,d) \wedge e(b,d)\wedge \Downarrow_{FC} y(c)\\
&= (\Downarrow_{FC} c(d)\wedge \Downarrow_{FC} y(c)) \wedge e(a,d)) \wedge e(b,d)\\
&= D(d) \wedge e(a,d) \wedge e(b,d).
\end{aligned}$$

Let $a = x_1, x_2, x_3 = b$. Then, there exists $D(a) = D(x_1), D(x_2), D(x_3) = D(b)$, such that $D(x_1) \wedge D(x_3) \leq D(x_2) \wedge e(x_1,x_2) \wedge e(x_3,x_2)$. Hence, D is fuzzy consistently connected.

(3) For all $a, b \in X$,

$$\begin{aligned}
D(a) \wedge e(b,a) &= \vee_{z\in X} \Downarrow_{FC} z(a)\wedge \Downarrow_{FC} y(z) \wedge e(b,a)\\
&\leq \vee \Downarrow_{FC} z(b)\wedge \Downarrow_{FC} y(z)\\
&= D(b).
\end{aligned}$$

Therefore, D is a fuzzy lower set.

(4) For all $x \in X, D(x) \leq\Downarrow_{FC} y(x) \leq\downarrow y(x)$, then we obtain $D \leq\downarrow y$, and thus D is fuzzy consistent.

Secondly, $y = \sqcup D$.

In fact, for all $a \in X$,

$$\begin{aligned}
\wedge_{z\in X} D(z) \to e(z,a) &= \wedge_{z\in X}(\wedge_{c\in X}(\Downarrow_{FC} c(z)\wedge \Downarrow_{FC} y(c)) \to e(z,a)\\
&= \wedge_{c\in X}(\Downarrow_{FC} y(c) \to \wedge_{z\in X}(\Downarrow_{FC} c(z) \to e(z,a))\\
&= \wedge_{c\in X} \Downarrow_{FC} y(c) \to e(\sqcup \Downarrow_{FC} c, a)\\
&= \wedge_{c\in X} \Downarrow_{FC} y(c) \to e(c,a)\\
&= e(\sqcup \Downarrow_{FC} y, a)\\
&= e(y,a).
\end{aligned}$$

Finally,

$$\begin{aligned}
\Downarrow_{FC} y(x) &= \wedge_{I\in CI_F(X)} e(y, \sqcup I) \to I(x)\\
&\leq e(y, \sqcup D) \to D(x)\\
&= 1 \to D(x)\\
&= D(x).
\end{aligned}$$

□

Theorem 2. *Let (X,e) be an fcc complete poset. Then, (X,e) is an fcc domain if and only if $(\Downarrow_{FC}, \sqcup)$ is a fuzzy Galois adjunction between (X,e) and $(CI_F(X), Sub_X)$.*

Proof. Suppose that (X, e) is an fcc continuous poset. $\forall x, y \in X, Sub_X(\Downarrow_{FC} x, \Downarrow_{FC} y)$

$$\begin{aligned}
&= \wedge_{z\in X} \Downarrow_{FC} x(z) \rightarrow \Downarrow_{FC} y(z)\\
&= \wedge_{z\in X}(\wedge_{I\in CI_F(X)} e(x, \sqcup I) \rightarrow I(z)) \rightarrow (\wedge_{J\in CI_F(X)} e(y, \sqcup J) \rightarrow J(z))\\
&= \wedge_{z\in X}(\wedge_{J\in CI_F(X)}(\wedge_{I\in CI_F(X)} e(x, \sqcup I) \rightarrow I(z)) \rightarrow (e(y, \sqcup J) \rightarrow J(z)))\\
&\geq \wedge_{z\in X}(\wedge_{J\in CI_F(X)}(e(x, \sqcup J) \rightarrow J(z)) \rightarrow (e(y, \sqcup J) \rightarrow J(z)))\\
&\geq \wedge_{J\in CI_F(X)} e(y, \sqcup J) \rightarrow e(x, \sqcup J)\\
&\geq e(x, y).
\end{aligned}$$

Therefore, $Sub_X(\Downarrow_{FC} x, \Downarrow_{FC} y) \geq e(x, y)$; then, $\Downarrow_{FC}$ is fuzzy order-preserving.
For all $I, J \in CI_F(X)$,

$$e(\sqcup I, \sqcup J) = \wedge_{x\in X} I(x) \rightarrow e(x, \sqcup J) \geq \wedge_{x\in X} I(x) \rightarrow J(x) = Sub_X(I, J).$$

Then, $Sub_X(I, J) \leq e(\sqcup I, \sqcup J)$, which means that $\sqcup$ is fuzzy order-preserving. $\forall x \in X, I \in CI_F(X)$,

$$\begin{aligned}
Sub_X(I, J) &= \wedge_{y\in X} \Downarrow_{FC} x(y) \rightarrow I(y)\\
&= \wedge_{y\in X}(\wedge_{J\in CI_F(X)} e(x, \sqcup J) \rightarrow J(y)) \rightarrow I(y)\\
&\geq \wedge_{y\in X}((e(x, \sqcup I) \rightarrow I(y)) \rightarrow I(y)\\
&\geq e(x, \sqcup I).
\end{aligned}$$

From (X, e) is fcc poset, we have $x = \sqcup \Downarrow_{FC} x$, and thus

$$\begin{aligned}
e(x, \sqcup I) &= e(\sqcup \Downarrow_{FC} x, \sqcup I)\\
&= \wedge_{y\in X} \Downarrow_{FC} x(y) \rightarrow e(y, \sqcup I)\\
&\geq \wedge_{y\in X} \Downarrow_{FC} x(y) \rightarrow I(y)\\
&= Sub_X(\Downarrow_{FC} x, I).
\end{aligned}$$

Thus, $(\Downarrow_{FC}, \sqcup)$ is a fuzzy Galois adjunction between (X, e) and $(CI_F(X), Sub_X)$.

Conversely, suppose that $(\Downarrow_{FC}, \sqcup)$ is a fuzzy Galois adjunction between (X, e) and $(CI_F(X), Sub_X)$, then $\sqcup \Downarrow_{FC} \geq 1_X$. Thus, for all $x \in X, \sqcup \Downarrow_{FC} x \geq x$. Since $\sqcup \Downarrow_{FC} x \leq \sqcup \downarrow x = x$, then $\sqcup \Downarrow_{FC} x = x$. Hence (X, e) is an fcc continuous poset, then (X, e) is an fcc domain. □

Proposition 5. *Let (X, e) be an fcc continuous poset. $\forall x \in X, \downarrow_e x = \{y \in X : \downarrow x(y) = 1\}$ is an fcc complete set.*

Proof. Suppose that D is an fcc subset and $i : \downarrow_e x \rightarrow X$ is an embedded mapping. For all $a \in \downarrow_e x$,

$$\begin{aligned}
e(\sqcup i_C^{\rightarrow}(A), a) &= \wedge_{b\in X} i_C^{\rightarrow}(A)(b) \rightarrow e(b, a)\\
&= \wedge_{b\in X}(\vee_{i(c)=b} A(c)) \rightarrow e(b, a)\\
&= \wedge_{c\in Y} A(c) \rightarrow e(i(c), a)\\
&= \wedge_{c\in Y} A(c) \rightarrow e(c, a)\\
&= e(\sqcup A, a).
\end{aligned}$$

Then, $\sqcup A = \sqcup i_C^{\rightarrow}(A)$. Since $\forall b \in \downarrow_e x, e(b,x) = 1$, which means $A(b) \rightarrow e(b,x) = 1$, furthermore $\wedge_{b \in \downarrow_e x} A(b) \rightarrow e(b,x) = e(\sqcup D, x) = 1$. Hence, $\sqcup A \in \downarrow_e x$, i.e., $\downarrow_e x$ is an fcc complete set. □

5. Conclusions

We discuss fuzzy connectivity under a fuzzy partial order and provide the equivalence characterization of the connected set along with the definition of the fc set. A set is considered a connected poset if and only if its characterization functions are fuzzy-connected. The definition of the fcc set and its equivalent characterizations are obtained. In the last section, the definitions of fcc way-below and fcc domain are given, and the equivalence characterizations of fcc continuous poset and fcc complete set are then discussed. Finally, a method for deriving fcc completeness from an fcc continuous poset is established.

In this paper, we deeply explore the fuzzy connectivity under the fuzzy partial order and provide the equivalent characterization of the connected set by defining the fuzzy connected set (fc set). In the framework of fuzzy mathematics, connectivity is an important concept that helps us to understand and analyze the properties of complex mathematics structures. First, we define the connectivity of a set under a fuzzy partial order. Specifically, a set is considered to be a connected poset if and only if its characteristic function is fuzzy connected. This means that, under the fuzzy partial order, there is a continuous and uninterrupted relationship between the elements in the set, which makes the whole set present a holistic structure. In order to further understand the concept of a fuzzy connected set, we further explore the definition of the fuzzy consistently connected set (fcc set) and its equivalent characterization. The fcc set is a special set of fuzzy connectivity that satisfies more stringent conditions to enable a better description of certain specific types of fuzzy structure. Through the equivalent characterization of the fcc set, we can more clearly recognize its properties and characteristics, providing a basis for subsequent research and application. In the final section of this article, we introduce the concept of fcc way-below relation and fcc domain and discuss the equivalent characterization of fcc continuous posets and fcc complete sets. These concepts provide us with a new perspective to examine the application of fuzzy connectivity in complex systems. In particular, we propose a method to derive fcc completeness from the fcc continuous poset, which helps us to better understand and apply the theory of fuzzy consistent connectivity. Overall, this paper explores, in depth, the related concepts and properties of fuzzy consistent connectivity in the framework of fuzzy partial order. By introducing the concepts of the fc set, fcc set, fcc completed set, and fcc domain, we provide new ideas and methods for the study of fuzzy consistent connectivity. These results not only help us to have a deeper understanding of the intrinsic structure of fuzzy mathematics and complex mathematic structures but also provide strong support for subsequent research and applications.

It is worth mentioning that the fuzzy connectivity theory explored in this paper has broad prospects in practical applications. For example, in the fields of image processing, social network analysis, data mining, etc., fuzzy connectivity can be used to describe connected regions in an image, connected subgraphs in a social network, and connected clusters in a data set. Through the analysis and utilization of these connected structures, we can better understand and exploit the inherent laws and properties of these complex structures. Moreover, with the continuous development of fuzzy mathematics and complex structures, we believe that fuzzy connectivity theory will be more widely applied and developed. In the future, we can further explore the combination of fuzzy connectivity and other mathematical tools, such as fuzzy logic, fuzzy clustering, etc., to form a more perfect theoretical system and methodology. At the same time, we can also focus on the application cases of fuzzy connectivity in practical problems to promote its in-depth development and application in various fields. For example, we can take the fuzzy poset as the starting point and consider the connected proposition of its intrinsic topology. In conclusion, this paper explores fuzzy connectivity in the framework of a fuzzy partial order and proposes a series of new concepts and methods. These achievements not only enrich the theoretical system of fuzzy mathematics but also provide strong support for subsequent research and application. We believe that in future studies, fuzzy connectivity theory and fuzzy consistently connected theory will play an increasingly important role in providing us with new ideas and methods to solve complex problems.

Author Contributions: Conceptualization, G.J.; Methodology, G.J.; Writing—review & editing, C.Z. All authors have read and agreed to the published version of the manuscript.

Funding: Research supported by the NNSF of China (12071188), NSF of Huaibei Normal University (2023ZK029) and Graduate Innovation Fund of Huaibei Normal University (CX2024008).

Data Availability Statement: Data are contained within the article.

Conflicts of Interest: The authors declare no conflicts of interest.

References

1. Zadeh, L. Fuzzy sets. *Inf. Control.* **1965**, *8*, 338–353. [CrossRef]
2. Scott, D. Continuous lattices. *Lect. Notes Math.* **1972**, *274*, 97–136.
3. Gierz, G.; Hofmann, K.H.; Keimel, K.; Lawson, J.D.; Mislove, M.; Scott, D.S. *Continuous Lattices and Domains*; Cambridge University Press: Cambridge, UK, 2003.
4. Lei, F. A new approach to quantitative domain theory. *Electron. Notes Theor. Comput. Sci.* **2001**, *45*, 77–87.
5. Qiye, Z.; Lei, F. Continuity in quantitative domains. *Fuzzy Sets Syst.* **2005**, *154*, 118–131.
6. Qiye, Z. *The Theory of L-Fuzzy Domain*; Capital Normal University: Beijing, China, 2002.
7. Chaudhuri, A.; Das, P. Fuzzy connected sets in fuzzy topological spaces. *Fuzzy Sets Syst.* **1992**, *49*, 223–229. [CrossRef]
8. Yun, S.; Zhao, B. Z-connected set systems and their categorical features. *Acta Math. Sin.* **2004**, *47*, 1141–1148.
9. Yun, S.; Zhao, B. Several characteristic theorems of consistently connected continuous Domains. *Math. Res. Rev.* **2005**, *25*, 734–738.
10. Tang, Z. *Research on the Connectivity of Partial Ordered Sets*; Huaibei Normal University: Huaibei, China, 2018.
11. Tang, Z. Ordered Connected Relationships and Ordered Connected Branches of Partial Ordered Sets. *Appl. Math. J. Chin. Univ. Vol. A* **2022**, *37*, 315–327.
12. Tang, Z.; Jiang, G. Connected Branch of Low Set Sequence and Its Description of Connectivity. *Fuzzy Syst. Math.* **2023**, *37*, 45–50.
13. Xu, L.; Tang, Z. Connectedness of intrinsic topologies of partial ordered sets. *Appl. Math. J. Chin. Univ. Vol. A* **2020**, *35*, 121–126.
14. Tang, Z.; Jiang, G. Strong sets on partially ordered sets and their applications. *Fuzzy Syst. Math.* **2018**, *32*, 64–68.
15. Tang, Z.; Chen, R. Connectivity and Connected Branches of Partial Ordered Sets. *Fuzzy Syst. Math.* **2020**, *34*, 171–174.
16. Agarwal, R.P.; Milles, S.; Ziane, B.; Mennouni, A.; Zedam, L. Ideals and Filters on Neutrosophic Topologies Generated by Neutrosophic Relations. *Axioms* **2024**, *13*, 292. [CrossRef]
17. Mishra, S.; Srivastava, R. Fuzzy topologies generated by fuzzy relations. *Soft Comput.* **2018**, *22*, 373–385. [CrossRef]
18. Romaguera, S. Some Characterizations of Complete Hausdorff KM-Fuzzy Quasi-Metric Spaces. *Mathematics* **2023**, *11*, 381. [CrossRef]
19. Mazarbhuiya, F.; Shenify, M. An Intuitionistic Fuzzy-Rough Set-Based Classification for Anomaly Detection. *Appl. Sci.* **2023**, *13*, 5578. [CrossRef]
20. Ali, W.; Shaheen, T.; Toor, H.G.; Alballa, T.; Alburaikan, A.; Khalifa, H.A. An Improved Intuitionistic Fuzzy Decision-Theoretic Rough Set Model and Its Application. *Axioms* **2023**, *12*, 1003. [CrossRef]
21. Sidiropoulos, G.K.; Diamianos, N.; Apostolidis, K.D.; Papakostas, G.A. Text Classification Using Intuitionistic Fuzzy Set Measures-An Evaluation Study. *Information* **2022**, *13*, 235. [CrossRef]
22. Kalayc, T.; Asan, U. Improving Classification Performance of Fully Connected Layers by Fuzzy Clustering in Transformed Feature Space. *Symmetry* **2022**, *14*, 658. [CrossRef]
23. Fang, J. *Residuated Lattice and Fuzzy Set*; Science Press: Beijing, China, 2012.
24. Xu, L.; Mao, X.; He, Q. *Applied Topology*; Science Press: Beijing, China, 2022.
25. Wu, W.; Mi, J. *The Mathematical Structure of Rough Sets*; Science Press: Beijing, China, 2019.

mathematics

MDPI

Article

Intuitionistic Type-2 Fuzzy Normed Linear Space and Some of Its Basic Properties

Amit Biswas [1,†], Moumita Chiney [1,*,†] and Syamal Kumar Samanta [2,†]

1 Department of Mathematics, Kazi Nazrul University, Asansol 713340, India; biswasamit993@gmail.com
2 Department of Mathematics, Visva-Bharati, Santiniketan 731235, India; syamal_123@yahoo.co.in
* Correspondence: moumita.chiney@knu.ac.in
† These authors contributed equally to this work.

Abstract: An intuitionistic fuzzy set is a more generalised tool than a fuzzy set for handling unpredictability as, in an intuitionistic fuzzy set, there is scope for considering a grade of non-membership, independent of the grade of membership, only satisfying the condition that their sum is less or equal to 1. The motivation of this paper is to introduce the notion of intuitionistic type-2 fuzzy normed linear space (IT2FNLS). Here, to each vector x, we assign two fuzzy real number valued grades, one for its norm and the other for the negation of its norm. A theorem of the decomposition of the intuitionistic type-2 fuzzy norm into a family of pairs of Felbin-type fuzzy norms is established. Also, we deal with Cauchyness and convergence of sequences in the IT2FNLS. Later on, in the finite-dimensional IT2FNLS, the completeness property and compactness property are explored. Finally, we define two types of intuitionistic type-2 fuzzy continuity and examine the relations between them.

Keywords: type-2 fuzzy set; intuitionistic type-2 fuzzy normed linear space; intuitionistic type-2 fuzzy continuity

MSC: 46S40; 03E72

1. Introduction

Since L. A. Zadeh introduced the notion of a fuzzy set in 1965 [1,2], its applications have covered a wide spectrum of fields of mathematics from fuzzy logic to fuzzy topology, fuzzy functional analysis, fuzzy differential equations, fuzzy optimisation theory and dynamical systems, etc.

Normed linear space is the important pillar of functional analysis, a major branch of modern mathematics. C. Felbin [3] introduced the concept of the fuzzy norm whose metric analogue is of the Kaleva–Seikkala [4] type and defined fuzzy normed linear space. In 1994, Cheng and Mordeson [5] defined a fuzzy norm whose metric analogue is of the Kramosil and Michalek [6] type by giving a grade to a norm of an element by comparing the norm to a real number. In 2003, Bag and Samanta [7] modified the definition of the fuzzy norm given by Cheng and Mordeson [5] and obtained a decomposition theorem from it. On the other hand, Zadeh [2], following the legacy of his own, introduced the definition of a type-n fuzzy set in 1975. In [8], for the first time, the notion of type-2 fuzzy normed linear space (type-2 FNLS) was introduced by Chiney, Biswas and Samanta, and a decomposition theorem was also proved in this setting.

The notion of an intuitionistic fuzzy set (IFS) was introduced by Atanassov [9–12] as a generalisation of Zadeh's fuzzy set [1]. There are situations where IFS theory is more appropriate, as dealt with by [13]. IFS theory has successfully been applied in knowledge engineering, medical diagnosis, decision making, career determination, etc. [14–16]. With the advancement of time, several researchers have extended various mathematical aspects such as groups, rings, topological spaces, metric spaces, topological groups, topological vector spaces, etc., in an IFS [17–24]. The definition of intuitionistic fuzzy n-normed linear space was introduced by S. Vijayabalaji, N. Thillaigovindan and Y. Bae Jun [25] in 2007. In 2009, T. K. Samanta and Iqbal H. Jebril [26] introduced the definition of an intuitionistic fuzzy norm over a linear space. Recently, research works have been done on intuitionistic fuzzy normed linear spaces [27–29].

The main objective of this paper is to give an idea of intuitionistic type-2 fuzzy normed linear space (IT2FNLS) for the first time. Here, we fuzzify the norm of a vector with an intuitionistic version of the type-2 fuzzy norm. We decompose an intuitionistic type-2 fuzzy norm into a family of pairs of Felbin-type fuzzy norms. Basic properties such as the convergent sequence, Cauchy sequence and closed and boundedness of the set are also studied. The finite-dimensional IT2FNLS is shown to be complete, and, in this space, the compactness of a subset can be deduced from the closed and boundedness. We define the continuity of functions as two types, namely, intuitionistic type-2 fuzzy continuity and sequentially intuitionistic type-2 fuzzy continuity. Later on, we discover that every intuitionistic type-2 fuzzy continuous function is sequentially intuitionistic type-2 fuzzy continuous, but its converse is not true in general, which is justified by a counterexample.

2. Preliminaries

Definition 1 ([4]). *A fuzzy real number is a fuzzy set on* $\mathbb{R}$*, i.e., a mapping* $\eta : \mathbb{R} \to I(= [0,1])$ *associating each real number to its grade of membership* $\eta(t)$*.*

Definition 2 ([4]). *A fuzzy real number* η *is convex if* $\eta(t) \geq \eta(s) \wedge \eta(r)=min\ (\eta(s), \eta(r))$ *where* $s \leq t \leq r$*.*

Definition 3 ([4]). *If there exists a* $t_0 \in \mathbb{R}$ *such that* $\eta(t_0) = 1$*, then* η *is called a normal fuzzy real number.*

Definition 4 ([4]). *The* α*-level set of a fuzzy real number* η*,* $0 < \alpha \leq 1$*, denoted by* $[\eta]_\alpha$*, is defined as* $[\eta]_\alpha = \{t : \eta(t) \geq \alpha\}$*.*

Proposition 1 ([4]). *A fuzzy real number* η *is convex if and only if each of its* α*-level sets* $[\eta]_\alpha$*,* $0 < \alpha \leq 1$*, is a convex set in* $\mathbb{R}$*.*

Definition 5 ([4]). *A fuzzy real number* η *is called upper semi-continuous if, for all* $t \in \mathbb{R}$ *and* $\epsilon > 0$ *with* $\eta(t) = a$*, there is* $c > 0$ *such that* $|s - t| < c = c(t) \Rightarrow \eta(t) < a + \epsilon$*, i.e.,* $\eta^{-1}([0, a + \epsilon))$ *for all* $a \in I$*, and* $\epsilon > 0$ *is open in the usual topology of* $\mathbb{R}$*.*

Note 1. *It can be easily seen that the* α*-level sets of an upper semi-continuous convex normal fuzzy real number for each* α*,* $0 < \alpha \leq 1$*, is a closed interval* $[a^\alpha, b^\alpha]$ *where* $a^\alpha = -\infty$ *and* $b^\alpha = +\infty$ *are also admissible. Let us denote the set of all upper semi-continuous normal convex fuzzy real numbers by* $\mathbb{R}(I)$*. Since each* $r \in \mathbb{R}$ *can be considered a fuzzy real number* $\bar{r}$*,*

$$\bar{r}(t) = \begin{cases} 1 \text{ if } t = r \\ 0 \text{ if } t \neq r \end{cases}$$

$\mathbb{R}$ *can be embedded in* $\mathbb{R}(I)$*.*

Definition 6 ([4]). *A fuzzy real number* η *is called non-negative if* $\eta(t) = 0$ *for all* $t < 0$*. The set of all non-negative fuzzy real numbers of* $\mathbb{R}(I)$ *is denoted by* $\mathbb{R}^*(I)$*.*

Note 2. *If we take the set* $\{\eta \in \mathbb{R}^*(I) : \eta = \bar{0} \text{ or } \eta \succ \bar{0}\}$*, then we denote this set by* $\mathbb{R}^+(I)$*.*

Note 3. *Arithmetic operations on fuzzy real numbers, the definition of the partial ordering of fuzzy real numbers and the definition of the convergence of the sequence of fuzzy real numbers are taken from [4].*

Definition 7 ([4]). *Define a partial ordering '$\preceq$' in $\mathbb{R}^+(I)$ by $\eta \preceq \delta$ if and only if $a_1^\alpha \leq a_2^\alpha$ and $b_1^\alpha \leq b_2^\alpha$ for all $\alpha \in (0,1]$, where $[\eta]_\alpha = [a_1^\alpha, b_1^\alpha]$ and $[\delta]_\alpha = [a_2^\alpha, b_2^\alpha]$. We write $\eta \preceq \delta$ as $\delta \succeq \eta$ when desired. The strict inequality in $\mathbb{R}^+(I)$ is defined by $\eta \prec \delta$ if and only if $a_1^\alpha < a_2^\alpha$ and $b_1^\alpha < b_2^\alpha$ for each $\alpha \in (0,1]$.*

Definition 8 ([2]). *A fuzzy set is of type n, n = 2, 3, ..., if its membership function ranges over fuzzy sets of type n-1. The membership function of a fuzzy set of type 1 ranges over the interval $[0,1]$.*

Definition 9 ([3]). *Let X be a vector space over $\mathbb{R}$.*

Let $||.|| : X \to \mathbb{R}^*(I)$.

Write

$[||x||]_\alpha = [|||x|||_1^\alpha, |||x|||_2^\alpha]$ for $x \in X, 0 < \alpha \leq 1$ and suppose, for all $x \in X, x \neq \underline{0}$, that there exists $\alpha_0 \in (0,1]$ independent of x such that for all $\alpha \leq \alpha_0$,
(A) $|||x|||_2^\alpha < \infty$;
(B) $inf|||x|||_1^\alpha > 0$.

Then, $(X, ||.||)$ is called a fuzzy normed linear space, and $||.||$ is a fuzzy norm if
(i) $||x|| = \bar{0}$ if and only if $x = \underline{0}$;
(ii) $||rx|| = |r|||x||, x \in X, r \in \mathbb{R}$;
(iii) For all $x, y \in X$, $||x+y|| \preceq ||x|| \oplus ||y||$.

Definition 10 ([30]). *Let X be a linear space over $\mathbb{R}$. Let $||\,|| : X \to \mathcal{F}^+(= \mathbb{R}^*(I))$ be a mapping satisfying the following:*
(i) $||x|| = \bar{0}$ iff $x = \underline{0}$;
(ii) $||rx|| = |r|||x||, x \in X, r \in \mathbb{R}$;
(iii) For all $x, y \in X$, $||x+y|| \preceq ||x|| \oplus ||y||$
and
(A'): $x \neq \underline{0} \Rightarrow ||x||(t) = 0, \forall t \leq 0$

Then, $(X, ||\,||)$ is called a fuzzy normed linear space, and $||\,||$ is called a fuzzy norm on X.

Remark 1 ([30]). *(i) Condition (A') in Definition 10 is equivalent to the condition (A''): for all $x(\neq \underline{0}) \in X$, $||x||_\alpha^1 > 0, \forall \alpha \in (0,1]$, where $[||x||_\alpha] = [||x||_\alpha^1, ||x||_\alpha^2]$ and (ii) $||\,||_\alpha^i : i = 1,2$ are crisp norms on X.*

Proposition 2 ([3]). *Let $\{x_1, x_2, \ldots, x_n\}$ be a linearly independent set of vectors in a fuzzy normed linear space $(X, ||.||)$ (of any dimension). Then, there is an $\eta \succ \bar{0}$ ($\eta \in \mathbb{R}^*(I)$) with $sup_{\alpha \in (0,1]} b^\alpha < \infty$ where $[\eta]_\alpha = [a^\alpha, b^\alpha]$ and such that, for every choice of scalars $a_1, a_2, \ldots, a_n$, we have $||a_1x_1 + \ldots + a_nx_n|| \succeq (|a_1| + \ldots + |a_n|)\eta$.*

Definition 11 ([25]). *Let E be any set. An intuitionistic fuzzy set A of E is an object of the form $A=\{(x, \mu_A(x), \nu_A(x)) : x \in E\}$, where the functions $\mu_A : E \to [0,1]$ and $\nu_A : E \to [0,1]$ denote the degree of membership and the non-membership of the element $x \in E$, respectively, and, for every $x \in E$, $0 \leq \mu_A(x) + \nu_A(x) \leq 1$.*

Theorem 1 ([31]). *Suppose that $\{u_t : t \in \Omega\} \subset E^1$ is bounded. Then, its supremum and infimum must exist and are determined by two pairs of usual functions of λ on $[0,1]$*

$$(u_{s,\Omega}^-(\lambda), u_{s,\Omega}^+(\lambda)), \quad (u_{I,\Omega}^-(\lambda), u_{I,\Omega}^+(\lambda)),$$

where

$$u_{s,\Omega}^-(\lambda) = \begin{cases} u_s^-(\lambda) & for \lambda \in (0,1] \\ u_s^-(0+0) & for \lambda = 0 \end{cases}$$

$$u_{s,\Omega}^+(\lambda) = \begin{cases} u_s^+(\lambda) & for \lambda \in [0,1] \backslash \{\lambda_m^s\} \\ u_s^+(\lambda_m^s - 0) & for \lambda = \lambda_m^s (m = 1, 2, \ldots) \end{cases}$$

$$u^{-}_{I,\Omega}(\lambda) = \begin{cases} u^{-}_{I}(\lambda) & for \lambda \in [0,1]\backslash\{\lambda'_m\} \\ u^{-}_{I}(\lambda'_m - 0) & for \lambda = \lambda'_m (m = 1,2,\ldots) \end{cases}$$

$$u^{+}_{I,\Omega}(\lambda) = \begin{cases} u^{+}_{I}(\lambda) & for \lambda \in (0,1] \\ u^{+}_{I}(0+0) & for \lambda = 0 \end{cases}$$

$u^{-}_{s}(\lambda) = sup_{t\in\Omega}(u_t)^{-}_{\lambda}$, $\quad u^{+}_{s}(\lambda) = sup_{t\in\Omega}(u_t)^{+}_{\lambda}$
$u^{-}_{I}(\lambda) = inf_{t\in\Omega}(u_t)^{-}_{\lambda}$, $\quad u^{+}_{I}(\lambda) = inf_{t\in\Omega}(u_t)^{+}_{\lambda}$
and $\{\lambda^s_m\}$ *and* $\{\lambda'_m\}$ *are all noncontinuous points of* $u^{+}_{s}(\lambda)$ *and* $u^{-}_{t}(\lambda)$ *on* $[0,1]$*, respectively.*

Note 4. $\mathcal{I}$ *denotes the set of all fuzzy sets from* $[0,1]$ *to* $[0,1]$*, i.e,* $\mathcal{I} = \{A \mid A : [0,1] \to [0,1]\}$*, and let* $\mathcal{I}_0$ *denotes the set* $\mathcal{I}_0 = \{\zeta \in \mathcal{I} : \bar{0} \prec \zeta \prec \bar{1}\}$.

Definition 12 ([8]). *Let X be a linear space over* $\mathbb{R}$*. A fuzzy subset* $\mathcal{N} : X \times \mathbb{R}^+(I) \to \mathcal{I}$ *is called a type-2 fuzzy norm on X if, for all* $x, u \in X, c \in \mathbb{R}$ *and* $\eta \in \mathbb{R}^+(I)$,
(N1) When $\eta = \bar{0}, \mathcal{N}(x,\eta) = \bar{0}$;
(N2) $(\forall \eta \succ \bar{0}, \mathcal{N}(x,\eta) = \bar{1})$ *if* $x = \underline{0}$;
(N3) $(\forall \eta \in \mathbb{R}^+(I), \eta \succ \bar{0}$, $\mathcal{N}(cx,\eta) = \mathcal{N}(x, \frac{1}{|c|}\eta)$ *if* $c \neq 0$;
(N4) $\forall \eta_1, \eta_2 \in \mathbb{R}^+(I)$ *and* $x, u \in X$
$\mathcal{N}(x+u, \eta_1 \oplus \eta_2) \succeq min\{\mathcal{N}(x,\eta_1), \mathcal{N}(u,\eta_2)\}$;
(N5) $\mathcal{N}(x,.)$ *is a non-decreasing function of* $\mathbb{R}^+(I)$*, which means, if* $\eta_1, \eta_2 \in \mathbb{R}^+(I)$ *with* $\eta_2 \succeq \eta_1$*, then* $\mathcal{N}(x,\eta_2) \succeq \mathcal{N}(x,\eta_1)$*, and* $lim_{\eta\to\overline{\infty}}\mathcal{N}(x,\eta) = \bar{1}$.

The pair $(X, \mathcal{N})$ *is called the type-2 fuzzy normed linear space (type-2 FNLS).*

Theorem 2 ([8]). *Let* $(X, \mathcal{N})$ *be a type-2 FNLS. Assume further that*
(N6) $\wedge\{\eta \succ \bar{0} : \mathcal{N}(x,\eta) \succ \bar{0}\} = \bar{0}$ *implies* $x = \underline{0}$.

Define $||x||^{\zeta} = \wedge\{\eta \succ \bar{0} : \mathcal{N}(x,\eta) \succeq \zeta\}$, $\zeta \in \mathcal{I}_0$.

Then $\{||.||^{\zeta} : \zeta \in \mathcal{I}_0\}$ *is a Felbin-type fuzzy norm on X, and* $(X, ||.||^{\zeta})$ *is a Felbin-type fuzzy normed linear space. Also,* $\{||x||^{\zeta} : \zeta \in \mathcal{I}_0\}$ *is a family of Felbin-type fuzzy norms on X such that* $\zeta_2 \succ \zeta_1$ $(\zeta_1, \zeta_2 \in \mathcal{I}_0) \Rightarrow ||x||^{\zeta_2} \succeq ||x||^{\zeta_1}$.

Theorem 3 ([8]). *Let* $\{||x||^{\zeta} : \zeta \in \mathcal{I}_0\}$ *be a family of Felbin-type fuzzy norms on a linear space X such that* $\zeta_2 \succ \zeta_1$ $(\zeta_1, \zeta_2 \in \mathcal{I}_0) \Rightarrow ||x||^{\zeta_2} \succeq ||x||^{\zeta_1}$*. Now we define a function* $\mathcal{N}' : X \times \mathbb{R}^+(I) \to \mathcal{I}$ *as*

$$\begin{aligned} \mathcal{N}'(x,\eta) &= \vee\{\zeta : ||x||^{\zeta} \preceq \eta\}, \quad when\,(x,\eta) \neq (\underline{0},\bar{0}) \\ &= \bar{0}, \quad when\,(x,\eta) = (\underline{0},\bar{0})\; or\; \{\zeta : ||x||^{\zeta} \preceq \eta\} = \phi \end{aligned}$$

Then $\mathcal{N}'$ *is a type-2 fuzzy norm on X.*

Lemma 1 ([8]). *Let* $(X, \mathcal{N})$ *be a type-2 FNLS satisfying (N6) and* $\{e_1, e_2, \ldots, e_n\}$ *be a finite set of linearly independent elements of X. Then, for each* $\zeta \in \mathcal{I}_0$*, there exists a* $\lambda^{\zeta} \succ \bar{0}$ *with* $sup_{\alpha\in(0,1]} b^{\alpha} < \infty$*, where* $[\lambda^{\zeta}]_{\alpha} = [a^{\alpha}, b^{\alpha}]$*, such that, for every choice of scalars* $a_1, a_2, \ldots, a_n$*, we have*
$||a_1e_1 + a_2e_2 + \ldots + a_ne_n||^{\zeta} \succeq (|a_1| + |a_2| + \ldots + |a_n|)\lambda^{\zeta}$.

Lemma 2 ([8]). *If* $\{u_n\}$ *is a sequence of positive real numbers and* $\eta \succ \bar{0}$ *such that* $[\eta]_{\alpha} = [a^{\alpha}, b^{\alpha}]$*, then* $[u_n\eta]_{\alpha} = [u_na^{\alpha}, u_nb^{\alpha}]$*. Also, if* $u_n \to \infty$ *as* $n \to \infty$*, then* $u_n\eta \to \overline{\infty}$ *as* $n \to \infty$.

3. Finite-Dimensional Intuitionistic Type-2 Fuzzy Normed Linear Spaces

3.1. Intuitionistic Type-2 Fuzzy Normed Linear Spaces

In this section, we introduce the notion of an intuitionistic type-2 fuzzy normed linear space with an example. In addition, we show that the decomposition of an intuitionistic type-2 fuzzy norm gives us a family of pairs of Felbin-type fuzzy norms.

Definition 13. *An intuitionistic type-2 fuzzy norm, or, in short, an IT2FN, on X (where X is a linear space over* $\mathbb{R}$*) is an object of the form* $A = \{((x,\eta),\mathcal{N}(x,\eta),\mathcal{M}(x,\eta)) : (x,\eta) \in X \times \mathbb{R}^+(I)\}$ *where* $\mathcal{N}, \mathcal{M}$ *are functions from* $X \times \mathbb{R}^+(I)$ *to* $\mathcal{I}$ *satisfying the following conditions:*
(i) When $\eta = \bar{0}, \mathcal{N}(x,\eta) = \bar{0}$;
(ii) ($\forall \eta \succ \bar{0}, \mathcal{N}(x,\eta) = \bar{1}$) *if and only if* $x = \underline{0}$;
(iii) $\mathcal{N}(cx,\eta) = \mathcal{N}(x, \frac{1}{|c|}\eta)$, *if* $c \neq 0$;
(iv) $\mathcal{N}(x+y, \eta_1 \oplus \eta_2) \succeq min\{\mathcal{N}(x,\eta_1), \mathcal{N}(y,\eta_2)\}$;
(v) $\mathcal{N}(x,.)$ *is a non-decreasing function of* $\mathbb{R}^+(I)$, *which means, if* $\eta_1, \eta_2 \in \mathbb{R}^+(I)$ *with* $\eta_2 \succeq \eta_1$, *then* $\mathcal{N}(x,\eta_2) \succeq \mathcal{N}(x,\eta_1)$ *and* $lim_{\eta\to\overline{\infty}}\mathcal{N}(x,\eta) = \bar{1}$;
(vi) When $\eta = \bar{0}$, $\mathcal{M}(x,\eta) = \bar{1}$;
(vii) ($\forall \eta \succ \bar{0}, \mathcal{M}(x,\eta) = \bar{0}$) *if and only if* $x = \underline{0}$;
(viii) $\mathcal{M}(cx,\eta) = \mathcal{M}(x, \frac{1}{|c|}\eta)$, *if* $c \neq 0$;
(ix) $\mathcal{M}(x+y, \eta_1 \oplus \eta_2) \preceq max\{\mathcal{M}(x,\eta_1), \mathcal{M}(y,\eta_2)\}$;
(x) $\mathcal{M}(x,.)$ *is a non-increasing function of* $\mathbb{R}^+(I)$, *which means, if* $\eta_1, \eta_2 \in \mathbb{R}^+(I)$ *with* $\eta_2 \succeq \eta_1$, *then* $\mathcal{M}(x,\eta_2) \preceq \mathcal{M}(x,\eta_1)$ *and* $lim_{\eta\to\overline{\infty}}\mathcal{M}(x,\eta) = \bar{0}$.

Definition 14. *If A is an IT2FN on X (a linear space over the field* $\mathbb{R}$*), then* (X, A) *is called an intuitionistic type-2 fuzzy normed linear space or, in short, an IT2FNLS.*

The following is an example of an intuitionistic type-2 fuzzy normed linear space.

Example 1. *Let* $(X = \mathbb{R}, |.|)$ *be the usual normed linear space. For any fuzzy real number* $\eta \succ \bar{0}$, *define* η_0 *as follows:*

$$\eta_0 = \overline{\tfrac{a+b}{2}}$$

where $[a,b]$ *denotes the closure of support of the fuzzy real number* η. *Let* $k > 0$ *be any fixed real number. Define*

$$\mathcal{N}(x,\eta) = \begin{cases} \eta_0 \oslash (\eta_0 \oplus \overline{k|x|}), & if\ \eta \succ \bar{0} \\ \bar{0}, & if\ \eta = \bar{0} \end{cases}$$

$$\mathcal{M}(x,\eta) = \begin{cases} \overline{k|x|} \oslash (\eta_0 \oplus \overline{k|x|}), & if\ \eta \succ \bar{0} \\ \bar{1}, & if\ \eta = \bar{0} \end{cases}$$

Then (X, A) *is an intuitionistic type-2 fuzzy normed linear space.*

Solution 1. *(i) When* $\eta = \bar{0}$, *we have, from the definition,* $\mathcal{N}(x,\eta) = \bar{0}$.
(ii) $\forall \eta \in \mathbb{R}^+(I)$ *with* $\eta \succ \bar{0}, \mathcal{N}(x,\eta) = \bar{1}$.
$\Leftrightarrow \eta_0 \oslash (\eta_0 \oplus \overline{||x||}) = \bar{1}$
$\Leftrightarrow \frac{\frac{a+b}{2}}{\frac{a+b}{2} + ||x||} = 1$
$\Leftrightarrow ||x|| = 0$
$\Leftrightarrow x = \underline{0}$.
(iii) $\forall \eta \in \mathbb{R}^+(I)$ *with* $\eta \succ \bar{0}$ *and* $c(\neq 0) \in \mathbb{R}$, *we obtain* $\mathcal{N}(cx,\eta) = \eta_0 \oslash (\eta_0 \oplus \overline{||cx||})$.
Again, $\mathcal{N}(x, \frac{1}{c}\eta) = (\frac{1}{c}\eta_0) \oslash (\frac{1}{c}\eta_0 \oplus \overline{||x||}) = (\overline{\frac{a+b}{2c}}) \oslash (\overline{\frac{a+b}{2c}} \oplus \overline{||x||}) = (\overline{\frac{a+b}{2}}) \oslash (\overline{\frac{a+b}{2}} \oplus \overline{||cx||}) = \eta_0 \oslash (\eta_0 \oplus \overline{||cx||})$.
(iv) We have to show that $\forall \eta, \xi \in \mathbb{R}^+(I)$ *and* $\forall x, y \in X$,
$\mathcal{N}(x+y, \eta \oplus \xi) \succeq min\{\mathcal{N}(x,\eta), \mathcal{N}(y,\xi)\}$.
If
(a) $\eta \oplus \xi = \bar{0}$,
(b) $\eta \oplus \xi \succ \bar{0}$; $\eta \succ \bar{0}, \xi = \bar{0}$; $\eta = \bar{0}, \xi \succ \bar{0}$, *then, in these cases, the relation is obvious.*
If
(c) $\eta \oplus \xi \succ \bar{0}$; $\eta \succ \bar{0}, \xi \succ \bar{0}$, *then*

$$\mathcal{N}(x+y, \eta \oplus \xi) = (\eta_0 \oplus \xi_0) \oslash (\eta_0 \oplus \xi_0 \oplus \overline{||x+y||}) \succeq (\eta_0 \oplus \xi_0) \oslash (\eta_0 \oplus \xi_0 \oplus \overline{||x||} \oplus \overline{||y||}).$$

Now $\{\eta_0 \oslash (\eta_0 \oplus \overline{||x||})\} \succeq \{\xi_0 \oslash (\xi_0 \oplus \overline{||y||})\}$
$\{\eta_0 \oslash (\eta_0 \oplus \overline{||x||})\} \ominus \{\xi_0 \oslash (\xi_0 \oplus \overline{||y||})\} \succeq \bar{0}$
$\Rightarrow (\eta_0 \odot \overline{||y||}) \ominus (\xi_0 \odot \overline{||x||}) \succeq \bar{0}$..................*(i)*.
So $\{(\eta_0 \oplus \xi_0) \oslash (\eta_0 \oplus \xi_0 \oplus \overline{||x||} \oplus \overline{||y||})\} \ominus \{\xi_0 \oslash (\xi_0 \oplus \overline{||y||})\} = \{(\eta_0 \odot \overline{||y||}) \ominus (\xi_0 \odot \overline{||x||})\} \oslash \{(\eta_0 \oplus \xi_0 \oplus \overline{||x||} \oplus \overline{||y||}) \odot (\xi_0 \oplus \overline{||y||})\} \succeq \bar{0}$ *by (i)*
$\Rightarrow \{(\eta_0 \oplus \xi_0) \oslash (\eta_0 \oplus \xi_0 \oplus \overline{||x||} \oplus \overline{||y||})\} \succeq \{\xi_0 \oslash (\xi_0 \oplus \overline{||y||})\}$.
Similarly, if $\{\xi_0 \oslash (\xi_0 \oplus \overline{||y||})\} \succeq \{\eta_0 \oslash (\eta_0 \oplus \overline{||x||})\}$, *we have*
$\{(\eta_0 \oplus \xi_0) \oslash (\eta_0 \oplus \xi_0 \oplus \overline{||x||} \oplus \overline{||y||})\} \succeq \{\eta_0 \oslash (\eta_0 \oplus \overline{||x||})\}$.
Thus, $\mathcal{N}(x+y, \eta \oplus \xi) \succeq min\{\mathcal{N}(x,\eta), \mathcal{N}(y,\xi)\}$.
(v) We consider the case $\eta \prec \xi$.
If $\eta \prec \xi$ *and* $\eta = \bar{0}$, *then* $\xi \succ \bar{0}$,
and $\mathcal{N}(x,\eta) = \bar{0}, \mathcal{N}(x,\xi) = \{\xi_0 \oslash (\xi_0 \oplus \overline{||x||})\} \succeq \bar{0}$
So $\mathcal{N}(x,\xi) \succeq \mathcal{N}(x,\eta)$.
If $\eta \prec \xi$ *and* $\eta \succ \bar{0}$, *then* $\xi \succ \bar{0}$ *and hence*
$\{\xi_0 \oslash (\xi_0 \oplus \overline{||x||})\} \ominus \{\eta_0 \oslash (\eta_0 \oplus \overline{||x||})\} = \{(\xi_0 \odot \overline{||x||}) \ominus (\eta_0 \odot \overline{||x||})\} \oslash \{(\xi_0 \oplus \overline{||x||}) \odot (\eta_0 \oplus \overline{||x||}\} \succeq \bar{0}$ *[since* $\xi_0 \succ \eta_0$*]*
So $\{\xi_0 \oslash (\xi_0 \oplus \overline{||x||})\} \succeq \{\eta_0 \oslash (\eta_0 \oplus \overline{||x||})\}$
$\Rightarrow \mathcal{N}(x,\xi) \succeq \mathcal{N}(x,\eta)$, *for all* $x \in X$.
Thus, $\mathcal{N}(x,.)$ *is a non-decreasing function of* $\mathbb{R}^+(I)$.
When $\eta \to \overline{\infty}$, *then* $b \to \infty$, *and hence* $\eta_0 \to \overline{\infty}$. *So,* $lim_{\eta \to \overline{\infty}} \mathcal{N}(x,\eta) = \bar{1}$.
Similarly, $\mathcal{M}$ *satisfies all conditions of* $(vi) - (x)$ *of Definition 13.*

Theorem 4. *Let* (X, A) *be an IT2FNLS. We assume further that*
(xi) $\wedge\{\eta \succ \bar{0} : \mathcal{N}(x,\eta) \succ \bar{0}\} = \bar{0}$ *implies* $x = \underline{0}$;
(xii) $\wedge\{\eta \succ \bar{0} : \mathcal{M}(x,\eta) \prec \bar{1}\} = \bar{0}$ *implies* $x = \underline{0}$.
Define $||x||^{\zeta}_{\mathcal{N}} = \wedge\{\eta \succ \bar{0} : \mathcal{N}(x,\eta) \succeq \zeta\}$, $\zeta \in \mathcal{I}_0$
and $||x||^{\zeta}_{\mathcal{M}} = \wedge\{\eta \succ \bar{0} : \mathcal{M}(x,\eta) \preceq \zeta\}$, $\zeta \in \mathcal{I}_0$.
Then (A) $\{||.||^{\zeta}_{\mathcal{N}} : \zeta \in \mathcal{I}_0\}$ *is a family of Felbin-type fuzzy norms on X such that* $\zeta_2 \succeq \zeta_1$ $(\zeta_1, \zeta_2 \in \mathcal{I}_0) \Rightarrow ||x||^{\zeta_2}_{\mathcal{N}} \succeq ||x||^{\zeta_1}_{\mathcal{N}}$
and (B) $\{||.||^{\zeta}_{\mathcal{M}} : \zeta \in \mathcal{I}_0\}$ *is a family of Felbin-type fuzzy norms on X such that* $\zeta_1 \preceq \zeta_2$ $(\zeta_1, \zeta_2 \in \mathcal{I}_0) \Rightarrow ||x||^{\zeta_1}_{\mathcal{M}} \succeq ||x||^{\zeta_2}_{\mathcal{M}}$.

Proof. (A) If $||x||^{\zeta}_{\mathcal{N}} = \bar{0}$, then $\wedge\{\eta \succ \bar{0} : \mathcal{N}(x,\eta) \succeq \zeta \succ \bar{0}\} = \bar{0}$
$\Rightarrow \wedge\{\eta \succ \bar{0} : \mathcal{N}(x,\eta) \succ \bar{0}\} = \bar{0}$
$\Rightarrow x = \underline{0}$ by (xi).
Conversely, let $x = \underline{0}$
$\Rightarrow \mathcal{N}(x,\eta) = \bar{1}$ for all $\eta \succ \bar{0}$
$\Rightarrow \wedge\{\eta \succ \bar{0} : \mathcal{N}(x,\eta) \succeq \zeta\} = \bar{0}$.
$\Rightarrow ||x||^{\zeta}_{\mathcal{N}} = \bar{0}$
(ii) If $c \neq 0$, then

$$\begin{aligned} ||cx||^{\zeta}_{\mathcal{N}} &= \wedge\{\eta \succ \bar{0} : \mathcal{N}(cx,\eta) \succeq \zeta\} \\ &= \wedge\{\eta \succ \bar{0} : \mathcal{N}(x, \frac{1}{|c|}\eta) \succeq \zeta\} \\ &= \wedge\{|c|\delta \succ \bar{0} : \mathcal{N}(x,\delta) \succeq \zeta\} \\ &= |c|[\wedge\{\delta \succ \bar{0} : \mathcal{N}(x,\delta) \succeq \zeta\}] \\ &= |c|||x||^{\zeta}_{\mathcal{N}} \end{aligned}$$

(iii)

$$
\begin{aligned}
||x||^{\zeta}_{\mathcal{N}} \oplus ||y||^{\zeta}_{\mathcal{N}} &= \wedge\{\eta \succ \bar{0} : \mathcal{N}(x,\eta) \succeq \zeta : \zeta \in \mathcal{I}_0\} \oplus \wedge\{\delta \succ \bar{0} : \mathcal{N}(y,\delta) \succeq \zeta : \zeta \in \mathcal{I}_0\} \\
&= \wedge\{\eta \oplus \delta \succ \bar{0} : \mathcal{N}(x,\eta), \mathcal{N}(y,\delta) \succeq \zeta\} \\
&\succeq \wedge\{\mu \succ \bar{0} : \mathcal{N}(x+y,\mu) \succeq \zeta\} \quad [Since, \mathcal{N}(x,\eta), \mathcal{N}(y,\delta) \succeq \zeta \Rightarrow \mathcal{N}(x+y,\eta \oplus \delta) \succeq \zeta]
\end{aligned}
$$

Therefore, $||x+y||^{\zeta}_{\mathcal{N}} \preceq ||x||^{\zeta}_{\mathcal{N}} \oplus ||y||^{\zeta}_{\mathcal{N}}$.

Now take $\bar{0} \prec \zeta_1 \preceq \zeta_2$ and $\zeta_1, \zeta_2 \in \mathcal{I}_0$.

Since $\zeta_1 \preceq \zeta_2$, we have $\{\eta \succ \bar{0} : \mathcal{N}(x,\eta) \succeq \zeta_2\} \subset \{\eta \succ \bar{0} : \mathcal{N}(x,\eta) \succeq \zeta_1\}$

$\Rightarrow \wedge\{\eta \succ \bar{0} : \mathcal{N}(x,\eta) \succeq \zeta_2\} \succeq \wedge\{\eta \succ \bar{0} : \mathcal{N}(x,\eta) \succeq \zeta_1\}$

$\Rightarrow ||x||^{\zeta_2}_{\mathcal{N}} \succeq ||x||^{\zeta_1}_{\mathcal{N}}$.

Thus, $\{||.||^{\zeta}_{\mathcal{N}} : \zeta \in \mathcal{I}_0\}$ is a family of Felbin-type fuzzy norms on X such that $\zeta_2 \succeq \zeta_1$ $(\zeta_1, \zeta_2 \in \mathcal{I}_0) \Rightarrow ||x||^{\zeta_2}_{\mathcal{N}} \succeq ||x||^{\zeta_1}_{\mathcal{N}}$.

(B) Now we will prove that $\{||x||^{\zeta}_{\mathcal{M}} : \zeta \in \mathcal{I}_0\}$ is also a family of Felbin-type fuzzy norms on X such that $\zeta_2 \succeq \zeta_1(\zeta_1, \zeta_2 \in \mathcal{I}_0) \Rightarrow ||x||^{\zeta_2}_{\mathcal{M}} \succeq ||x||^{\zeta_1}_{\mathcal{M}}$.

Let $\zeta \in \mathcal{I}_0$ and $||x||^{\zeta}_{\mathcal{M}} = \bar{0}$

$\Rightarrow \wedge\{\eta \succ \bar{0} : \mathcal{M}(x,\eta) \preceq \zeta\} = \bar{0}$

$\Rightarrow \wedge\{\eta \succ \bar{0} : \mathcal{M}(x,\eta) \prec \bar{1}\} = \bar{0}$

$\Rightarrow x = \underline{0}$ by (xii).

Conversely, we assume that $x = \bar{0}$

$\Rightarrow \mathcal{M}(x,\eta) = \bar{0} \; \forall \eta \succ \bar{0}$

$\Rightarrow \wedge\{\eta \succ \bar{0} : \mathcal{M}(x,\eta) \preceq \zeta\} = \bar{0}$

$\Rightarrow ||x||^{\zeta}_{\mathcal{M}} = \bar{0}$.

By definition, it is quite obvious that $||cx||^{\zeta}_{\mathcal{M}} = |c|||x||^{\zeta}_{\mathcal{M}} \; \forall c \in \mathbb{R}$.

$$
\begin{aligned}
||x||^{\zeta}_{\mathcal{M}} \oplus ||y||^{\zeta}_{\mathcal{M}} &= \wedge\{\eta \succ \bar{0} : \mathcal{M}(x,\eta) \preceq \zeta\} \oplus \wedge\{\eta' \succ \bar{0} : \mathcal{M}(y,\eta') \preceq \zeta\} \\
&\succeq \wedge\{\eta \oplus \eta' \succ \bar{0} : \mathcal{M}(x,\eta) \preceq \zeta, \mathcal{M}(y,\eta') \preceq \zeta\} \\
&\succeq \wedge\{\eta \oplus \eta' \succ \bar{0} : \mathcal{M}(x+y,\eta \oplus \eta') \preceq \zeta\} \\
&\succeq \wedge\{\eta_1 \succ \bar{0} : \mathcal{M}(x+y,\eta_1) \preceq \zeta\} \\
&= ||x+y||^{\zeta}_{\mathcal{M}}.
\end{aligned}
$$

Let $\zeta_1, \zeta_2 \in \mathcal{I}_0$ and $\zeta_1 \preceq \zeta_2$.

Now $\{\eta \succ \bar{0} : \mathcal{M}(x,\eta) \preceq \zeta_1\} \subset \{\eta \succ \bar{0} : \mathcal{M}(x,\eta) \preceq \zeta_2\}$

$\Rightarrow \wedge\{\eta \succ \bar{0} : \mathcal{M}(x,\eta) \preceq \zeta_1\} \succeq \wedge\{\eta \succ \bar{0} : \mathcal{M}(x,\eta) \preceq \zeta_2\}$

$\Rightarrow ||x||^{\zeta_1}_{\mathcal{M}} \succeq ||x||^{\zeta_2}_{\mathcal{M}}$. □

Lemma 3. *Let (X, A) be an IT2FNLS satisfying the condition (xi) and $\{e_1, e_2, \ldots, e_n\}$ be a finite set of linearly independent elements of X. Then, for each $\zeta \in \mathcal{I}_0$, there exists a $\lambda^{\zeta} \succ \bar{0}$ with $sup_{\alpha \in (0,1]} b^{\alpha} < \infty$, where $[\lambda^{\zeta}]_{\alpha} = [a^{\alpha}, b^{\alpha}]$ such that, for every choice of scalars $a_1, a_2, \ldots, a_n$, we have*
$||a_1e_1 + a_2e_2 + \ldots + a_ne_n||^{\zeta} \succeq (|a_1| + |a_2| + \ldots + |a_n|)\lambda^{\zeta}$.

Proof. From Theorem 4, it follows that, if (X, A) is an intuitionistic type-2 fuzzy normed linear space satisfying (xi), then $||x||^{\zeta} = \wedge\{\eta \succ \bar{0} : \mathcal{N}(x,\eta) \succeq \zeta\}$ is a Felbin-type fuzzy norm for each $\zeta \in \mathcal{I}_0$. Therefore, by Proposition 2, for each $\zeta \in \mathcal{I}_0$, there exists a λ^{ζ} such that $||a_1e_1 + a_2e_2 + \ldots + a_ne_n||^{\zeta} \succeq (|a_1| + |a_2| + \ldots + |a_n|)\lambda^{\zeta}$. □

3.2. Convergence in Intuitionistic Type-2 Fuzzy Normed Linear Space

The idea of the convergence of sequences and some of the basic results related to convergence are studied in this subsection.

Definition 15. *In an IT2FNLS* (X, A)*, a sequence* $\{x_n\}$ *is said to be convergent to* $x \in X$ *if* $lim_{n\to\infty}\mathcal{N}(x_n - x, \eta) = \bar{1}$ *and* $lim_{n\to\infty}\mathcal{M}(x_n - x, \eta) = \bar{0}\ \forall\eta \succ \bar{0}$ *and is denoted by* $lim_{n\to\infty}x_n = x$.

Theorem 5. *If a sequence* $\{x_n\}$ *in an IT2FNLS* (X, A) *is convergent, its limit is unique.*

Proof. Let $limx_n = x$ and $limx_n = y$.

Then, $lim_{n\to\infty}\mathcal{N}(x_n - x, \eta_1) = lim_{n\to\infty}\mathcal{N}(x_n - y, \eta_2) = \bar{1},\ \forall\,\eta_1, \eta_2 \succ \bar{0}$.

Now $\mathcal{N}(x - y, \eta_1 \oplus \eta_2) = \mathcal{N}(x - x_n + x_n - y, \eta_1 \oplus \eta_2) \succeq min\{\mathcal{N}(x - x_n, \eta_1), \mathcal{N}(x_n - y, \eta_2)\}$

i.e, $\mathcal{N}(x - y, \eta_1 \oplus \eta_2) \succeq min\{\mathcal{N}(x_n - x, \eta_1), \mathcal{N}(x_n - y, \eta_2)\}$.

Now

$lim_{n\to\infty}\mathcal{N}(x_n - x, \eta_1) = \bar{1},\ \forall\,\eta_1 \succ \bar{0}$,

$lim_{n\to\infty}\mathcal{N}(x_n - y, \eta_2) = \bar{1},\ \forall\,\eta_2 \succ \bar{0}$.

Thus, $lim_{n\to\infty}\mathcal{N}(x - y, \eta_1 \oplus \eta_2) = \bar{1},\ \forall\,\eta_1, \eta_2 \succ \bar{0}$

$\Rightarrow x - y = 0$

$\Rightarrow x - y$. □

Theorem 6. *If* $lim_{n\to\infty}x_n = x$ *and* $lim_{n\to\infty}y_n = y$*, then* $lim_{n\to\infty}(x_n + y_n) = x + y$ *in an IT2FNLS* (X, A).

Proof. Since $lim_{n\to\infty}x_n = x$ and $lim_{n\to\infty}y_n = y$,

$lim_{n\to\infty}\mathcal{N}(x_n - x, \frac{\eta}{2}) = \bar{1}$ and $lim_{n\to\infty}\mathcal{M}(x_n - x, \frac{\eta}{2}) = \bar{0}\ \forall\,\eta \succ \bar{0}$,

$lim_{n\to\infty}\mathcal{N}(y_n - y, \frac{\eta}{2}) = \bar{1}$ and $lim_{n\to\infty}\mathcal{M}(y_n - y, \frac{\eta}{2}) = \bar{0}\ \forall\,\eta \succ \bar{0}$.

$$\begin{aligned}\mathcal{N}(x_n + y_n - x - y, \eta) &= \mathcal{N}(x_n - x + y_n - y, \eta) \\ &\succeq min\{\mathcal{N}(x_n - x, \frac{\eta}{2}), \mathcal{N}(y_n - y, \frac{\eta}{2})\}\end{aligned}$$

Now, proceeding to the limit as $n \to \infty$, we obtain $lim_{n\to\infty}\mathcal{N}(x_n + y_n - x - y, \eta) = \bar{1}$ $\forall\eta \succ \bar{0}$..................(i).

Also,

$$\begin{aligned}\mathcal{M}(x_n + y_n - x - y, \eta) &= \mathcal{M}(x_n - x + y_n - y, \eta) \\ &\preceq max\{\mathcal{M}(x_n - x, \frac{\eta}{2}), \mathcal{M}(y_n - y, \frac{\eta}{2})\}\end{aligned}$$

Now, proceeding to the limit as $n \to \infty$, we obtain $lim_{n\to\infty}\mathcal{M}(x_n + y_n - x - y, \eta) = \bar{0}$ $\forall\eta \succ \bar{0}$..................(ii).

Combining (i) and (ii), we obtain $lim_{n\to\infty}(x_n + y_n) = x + y$. □

Theorem 7. *If* $lim_{n\to\infty}x_n = x$ *and* $c(\neq 0) \in \mathbb{R}$*, then* $lim_{n\to\infty}cx_n = cx$ *in an IT2FNLS* (X, A).

Proof. Since $lim_{n\to\infty}x_n = x$,

we have $lim_{n\to\infty}\mathcal{N}(x_n - x, \eta) = \bar{1}$ and $lim_{n\to\infty}\mathcal{M}(x_n - x, \eta) = \bar{0}\ \forall\eta \succ \bar{0}$.

Now $\mathcal{N}(cx_n - cx, \eta) = \mathcal{N}(x_n - x, \frac{1}{|c|}\eta)$

and so $lim_{n\to\infty}\mathcal{N}(cx_n - cx, \eta) = lim_{n\to\infty}\mathcal{N}(x_n - x, \frac{1}{|c|}\eta) = \bar{1}\ \forall\eta \succ \bar{0}$.

Proceeding similarly, we obtain $lim_{n\to\infty}\mathcal{M}(cx_n - cx, \eta) = \bar{0}\ \forall\eta \succ \bar{0}$.

Thus, we have $lim_{n\to\infty}cx_n = cx$. □

Theorem 8. *In an IT2FNLS* (X, A)*, every subsequence of a convergent sequence is convergent and converges to the same limit.*

Proof. Let $\{x_n\}$ be a convergent sequence in (X, A) with $lim_{n\to\infty}x_n = x$ and $\{x_{n_r}\}$ be a subsequence of $\{x_n\}$.

Then, $lim_{n\to\infty}\mathcal{N}(x_n - x, \eta) = \bar{1}$ and $lim_{n\to\infty}\mathcal{M}(x_n - x, \eta) = \bar{0}\ \forall\eta \succ \bar{0}$.................(i)

Now, as $r \to \infty$, then $n_r \to \infty$, and, from (i), we easily obtain that $lim_{n\to\infty}\mathcal{N}(x_{n_r} - x, \eta) = \bar{1}$ and $lim_{n\to\infty}\mathcal{M}(x_{n_r} - x, \eta) = \bar{0}\ \forall\eta \succ \bar{0}$.

Thus, we see that the sequence $\{x_{n_r}\}$ is convergent, and $lim_{r\to\infty}x_{n_r} = x$. □

Definition 16. *A sequence $\{x_n\}$ in an IT2FNLS (X, A) is said to be a Cauchy sequence if $lim_{n\to\infty}\mathcal{N}(x_{n+p} - x_n, \eta) = \bar{1}$ and $lim_{n\to\infty}\mathcal{M}(x_{n+p} - x_n, \eta) = \bar{0}$, $p = 1, 2, 3, \ldots\ldots$ and $\forall\eta \succ \bar{0}$.*

Theorem 9. *In an IT2FNLS (X, A), every convergent sequence is a Cauchy sequence.*

Proof. Suppose $\{x_n\}$ is convergent and $lim x_n = x$.

Then $lim_{n\to\infty}\mathcal{N}(x_n - x, \eta) = \bar{1}$ and $lim_{n\to\infty}\mathcal{M}(x_n - x, \eta) = \bar{0}\ \forall\ \eta \succ \bar{0}$.

Now $\mathcal{N}(x_{n+p} - x_n, \eta_1 \oplus \eta_2) = \mathcal{N}(x_{n+p} - x + x - x_n, \eta_1 \oplus \eta_2)$.

We also have $\mathcal{N}(x_{n+p} - x + x - x_n, \eta_1 \oplus \eta_2) \succeq min\{\mathcal{N}(x_{n+p} - x, \eta_1), \mathcal{N}(x - x_n, \eta_2)\}$ i.e, $\mathcal{N}(x_{n+p} - x_n, \eta_1 \oplus \eta_2) \succeq min\{\mathcal{N}(x_{n+p} - x, \eta_1), \mathcal{N}(x_n - x, \eta_2)\}$.

Now, $lim_{n\to\infty}\mathcal{N}(x_{n+p} - x, \eta_1) = lim_{n\to\infty}\mathcal{N}(x_n - x, \eta_2) = \bar{1}$, $\forall\ \eta_1, \eta_2 \succ \bar{0}$, $p = 1, 2, 3, \ldots$

So, $lim_{n\to\infty}\mathcal{N}(x_{n+p} - x_n, \eta_1 \oplus \eta_2) = \bar{1}$, $\forall\ \eta_1, \eta_2 \succ \bar{0}$, $p = 1, 2, 3, \ldots$

Proceeding similarly, we can prove that $lim_{n\to\infty}\mathcal{M}(x_{n+p} - x_n, \eta_1 \oplus \eta_2) = \bar{0}$, $\forall\ \eta_1, \eta_2 \succ \bar{0}$, $p = 1, 2, 3, \ldots$

Hence, $\{x_n\}$ is a Cauchy sequence in (X, A). □

3.3. Completeness and Finite Dimensionality in Intuitionistic Type-2 Fuzzy Normed Linear Space

Basic properties related to the completeness, boundedness, compactness and finite dimensionality in the IT2FNLS are studied in this subsection.

Definition 17. *Let (X, A) be an IT2FNLS. If every Cauchy sequence in (X, A) is convergent, then we call (X, A) to be complete.*

Theorem 10. *Let (X, A) be an IT2FNLS, such that every Cauchy sequence in (X, A) has a convergent subsequence. Then, (X, A) is complete.*

Proof. Let $\{x_n\}$ be a Cauchy sequence in (X, A) and $\{x_{n_r}\}$ be a convergent subsequence of $\{x_n\}$ with $lim_{r\to\infty}x_{n_r} = x$.

Then $lim_{n\to\infty}\mathcal{N}(x_{n+p} - x_n, \frac{\eta}{2}) = \bar{1}$ and $lim_{n\to\infty}\mathcal{M}(x_{n+p} - x_n, \frac{\eta}{2}) = \bar{0}$, $p = 1, 2, 3, \ldots\ldots$ and $\forall\eta \succ \bar{0}$.

Also, $lim_{r\to\infty}\mathcal{N}(x_{n_r} - x, \frac{\eta}{2}) = \bar{1}$ and $lim_{r\to\infty}\mathcal{M}(x_{n_r} - x, \frac{\eta}{2}) = \bar{0}\ \forall\eta \succ \bar{0}$.

Now

$$\begin{aligned}\mathcal{N}(x_n - x, \eta) &= \mathcal{N}(x_n - x_{n_r} + x_{n_r} - x, \eta) \\ &\succeq min\{\mathcal{N}(x_n - x_{n_r}, \frac{\eta}{2}), \mathcal{N}(x_{n_r} - x, \frac{\eta}{2})\}\end{aligned}$$

Then, proceeding to the limit as $n \to \infty$, we obtain $lim_{n\to\infty}\mathcal{N}(x_n - x, \eta) = \bar{1}\ \forall\eta \succ \bar{0}$..................(i).

Similarly, going by the previous approach, we can prove that $lim_{n\to\infty}\mathcal{M}(x_n - x, \eta) = \bar{0}$ $\forall\eta \succ \bar{0}$......................(ii).

Combining (i) and (ii), we have the sequence $\{x_n\}$, which is convergent, and $lim_{n\to\infty}x_n = x$.

Thus, we see that every Cauchy sequence in (X, A) is convergent, and so (X, A) is complete. □

Theorem 11. *Every finite- dimensional IT2FNLS satisfying the conditions (xi) and (xii) is complete.*

Proof. Let (X, A) be an IT2FNLS and dim $X = k$.

Let $\{e_1, e_2, \ldots, e_k\}$ be a basis of X and $\{x_n\}$ be a Cauchy sequence in X.

Let $x_n = \beta_1^n e_1 + \beta_2^n e_2 + \ldots + \beta_k^n e_k$, $\beta_i^n \in \mathbb{R}$, $i = 1, 2, \ldots k$, $n \in \mathbb{N}$.

Now we have $lim_{n\to\infty}\mathcal{N}(x_{n+p} - x_n, \eta) = \bar{1}, \quad \forall \eta \succ \bar{0}, p = 1, 2, 3, \ldots$

$\Rightarrow lim_{n\to\infty}\mathcal{N}(\sum_{i=1}^{k} \beta_i^{n+p} e_i - \sum_{i=1}^{k} \beta_i^n e_i, \eta) = \bar{1}$

$\Rightarrow lim_{n\to\infty}\mathcal{N}(\sum_{i=1}^{k}(\beta_i^{n+p} - \beta_i^n)e_i, \eta) = \bar{1}, \quad \forall \eta \succ \bar{0}, p = 1, 2, 3, \ldots$

Choose $\zeta \in \mathcal{I}_0$ and $\eta \succ \bar{0}$.

Then there exists a positive integer $n_0(\eta, \zeta)$ such that

$\mathcal{N}(\sum_{i=1}^{k}(\beta_i^{n+p} - \beta_i)e_i, \eta) \succ \zeta, \quad \forall n \geq n_0(\eta, \zeta), p = 1, 2, 3, \ldots$

Now $|| \sum_{i=1}^{k}(\beta_i^{n+p} - \beta_i)e_i||^{\zeta} = \wedge\{\xi \succ \bar{0} : \mathcal{N}(\sum_{i=1}^{k}(\beta_i^{n+p} - \beta_i)e_i, \xi) \succeq \zeta\}$.

Therefore, $|| \sum_{i=1}^{k}(\beta_i^{n+p} - \beta_i)e_i||^{\zeta} \preceq \eta, \quad \forall n \geq n_0(\eta, \zeta)$.

Since $\eta \succ \bar{0}$ is arbitary,

$|| \sum_{i=1}^{k}(\beta_i^{n+p} - \beta_i^n)e_i||^{\zeta} \to \bar{0}$ as $n \to \infty$ for each $\zeta \in \mathcal{I}_0$, $p = 1, 2, 3, \ldots$

$\Rightarrow (\sum_{i=1}^{k} |\beta_i^{n+p} - \beta_i^n|)\lambda^{\zeta} \to \bar{0}$ as $n \to \infty$ where $\lambda^{\zeta} \succ \bar{0}$, by the Lemma 3,

$\Rightarrow \sum_{i=1}^{k} |\beta_i^{n+p} - \beta_i^n| \to 0$ as $n \to \infty$, since $\lambda^{\zeta} \succ \bar{0}$ for all $\zeta \in \mathcal{I}_0$

$\Rightarrow \{\beta_i^n\}_n$ is a Cauchy sequence in $\mathbb{R}$ for each $i = 1, 2, \ldots, k$.

Since $\mathbb{R}$ is complete, $\{\beta_i^n\}_n$ converges for each $i = 1, 2, \ldots k$.

Let $lim_{n\to\infty}\beta_i^n = \beta_i$ for $i = 1, 2, \ldots k$ and $x = \sum_{i=1}^{k} \beta_i e_i$.

Then, $x \in X$.

Now, for all $\eta \succ \bar{0}$,

$$\begin{aligned}
\mathcal{N}(x_n - x, \eta) &= \mathcal{N}(\sum_{i=1}^{k} \beta_i^n e_i - \sum_{i=1}^{k} \beta_i e_i, \eta) \\
&= \mathcal{N}(\sum_{i=1}^{k}(\beta_i^n - \beta_i)e_i, \eta) \\
&\succeq min_i \mathcal{N}(e_i, \frac{1}{k|\beta_i^n - \beta_i|}\eta) \ldots\ldots\ldots\ldots\ldots\ldots (i)
\end{aligned}$$

Let $u_n = \frac{1}{k|\beta_i^n - \beta_i|}$. Then $u_n \to \infty$ as $n \to \infty$ [Since $|\beta_i^n - \beta_i| \to 0+$ as $n \to \infty$ for $i = 1, 2, \ldots k$].

So $u_n\eta \to \bar{\infty}$ as $n \to \infty$, by Lemma 2.

Hence, we have $lim_{n\to\infty}\mathcal{N}(e_i, \frac{1}{k|\beta_i^n - \beta_i|}\eta) = lim_{n\to\infty}\mathcal{N}(e_i, u_n\eta) = \bar{1}$ for $i = 1, 2, \ldots k$ ....(ii).

From (i) and (ii), we obtain $lim_{n\to\infty}\mathcal{N}(x_n - x, \eta) = \bar{1}, \quad \forall \eta \succ \bar{0}$.

Again, for all $\eta \succ \bar{0}$,

$$\begin{aligned}
\mathcal{M}(x_n - x, \eta) &= \mathcal{M}(\sum_{i=1}^{k} \beta_i^n e_i - \sum_{i=1}^{k} \beta_i e_i, \eta) \\
&= \mathcal{M}(\sum_{i=1}^{k}(\beta_i^n - \beta_i)e_i, \eta) \\
&\preceq max_i \mathcal{M}(e_i, \frac{1}{k|\beta_i^n - \beta_i|}\eta) \ldots\ldots\ldots\ldots\ldots\ldots (iii)
\end{aligned}$$

Now $lim_{n\to\infty}\mathcal{M}(e_i, \frac{1}{k|\beta_i^n - \beta_i|}\eta) = lim_{n\to\infty}\mathcal{M}(e_i, u_n\eta) = \bar{0}$ for $i = 1, 2, \ldots k$ ....(iv).

From (iii) and (iv), we obtain $lim_{n\to\infty}\mathcal{M}(x_n - x, \eta) = \bar{0}, \quad \forall \eta \succ \bar{0}$.

Hence, lim$x_n = x$, i.e, the sequence $\{x_n\}$ is convergent.

Thus, we see that the IT2FNLS (X, A) is complete. □

Definition 18. *A subset U in an IT2FNLS (X, A) is said to be bounded if, for any $\zeta_1, \zeta_2 \in \mathcal{I}_0$ with $\zeta_1 \oplus \zeta_2 \preceq \bar{1}$, $\exists\, \eta \succ \bar{0}$ such that $\mathcal{N}(x, \eta) \succ \zeta_1$ and $\mathcal{M}(x, \eta) \prec \zeta_2$, $\quad \forall x \in U$.*

Theorem 12. *Let (X, A) be an IT2FNLS. Then, every Cauchy sequence in (X, A) is bounded.*

Proof. Let us consider a Cauchy sequence $\{x_n\}$ in an IT2FNLS (X, A).

Then $lim_{n\to\infty}\mathcal{N}(x_{n+p} - x_n, \eta) = \bar{1}$ and $\mathcal{M}(x_{n+P} - x_n, \eta) = \bar{0}$, $\forall \eta \succ \bar{0}$ and $p = 1, 2, 3, \ldots$

Let $\zeta_1, \zeta_2 \in \mathcal{I}_0$ with $\zeta_1 \oplus \zeta_2 \preceq \bar{1}$.

Then we have $lim_{n\to\infty}\mathcal{N}(x_{n+p} - x_n, \eta) = lim_{n\to\infty}\mathcal{N}(x_n - x_{n+p}, \eta) = \bar{1} \succ \zeta_1$, $\quad \forall \eta \succ \bar{0}$ and $p = 1, 2, 3, \ldots$

For $\eta' \succ \bar{0}, \exists\, n_0 = n_0(\eta', \zeta_1)$ such that $\mathcal{N}(x_n - x_{n+p}, \eta') \succ \zeta_1$, $\forall n \geq n_0$, $p = 1, 2, 3, \ldots$

Since $lim_{\eta\to\overline{\infty}}\mathcal{N}(x, \eta) = \bar{1}, \exists\, \eta_i \succ \bar{0}$ such that $\mathcal{N}(x_i, \eta_i) \succ \zeta_1$, for all $i = 1, 2, 3, \ldots n_0$.

Let $\eta_0 = \eta' \oplus \eta_1 \oplus \eta_2 \oplus \ldots \oplus \eta_{n_0}$.

Then $\mathcal{N}(x_n, \eta_0) \succeq \mathcal{N}(x_n, \eta' \oplus \eta_{n_0}) = \mathcal{N}(x_n - x_{n_0} + x_{n_0}, \eta' \oplus \eta_{n_0}) \succeq min\{\mathcal{N}(x_n - x_{n_0}, \eta'), \mathcal{N}(x_{n_0}, \eta_{n_0})\}$.

Therefore, $\mathcal{N}(x_n, \eta_0) \succeq \zeta_1$, $\forall n > n_0$.

Also, $\mathcal{N}(x_n, \eta_0) \succeq \mathcal{N}(x_n, \eta_n) \succeq \zeta_1$, $\forall n = 1, 2, \ldots n_0$.

Hence, $\mathcal{N}(x_n, \eta_0) \succeq \zeta_1$, $\forall n$..........................(i)

Also, we have $lim_{n\to\infty}\mathcal{M}(x_{n+p} - x_n, \eta) = lim_{n\to\infty}\mathcal{M}(x_n - x_{n+p}, \eta) = \bar{0} \prec \zeta_2$, $\quad \forall \eta \succ \bar{0}$ and $p = 1, 2, 3, \ldots$

For $\eta'_0 \succ \bar{0}, \exists\, n'_0 = n'_0(\eta'_0, \zeta_2)$ such that $\mathcal{M}(x_n - x_{n+p}, \eta'_0) \prec \zeta_2$, $\forall n \geq n'_0$, $p = 1, 2, 3, \ldots$

Since $lim_{\eta\to\overline{\infty}}\mathcal{M}(x, \eta) = \bar{0}, \exists\, \eta'_i \succ \bar{0}$ such that $\mathcal{M}(x_i, \eta'_i) \prec \zeta_2$, for all $i = 1, 2, 3, \ldots n'_0$.

Let $\eta_1 = \eta'_0 \oplus \eta'_1 \oplus \eta'_2 \oplus \ldots \oplus \eta'_{n'_0}$.

Then $\mathcal{M}(x_n, \eta_1) \preceq \mathcal{M}(x_n, \eta'_0 \oplus \eta'_{n'_0}) = \mathcal{M}(x_n - x_{n'_0} + x_{n'_0}, \eta'_0 \oplus \eta'_{n'_0}) \preceq max\{\mathcal{M}(x_n - x_{n'_0}, \eta'_0), \mathcal{M}(x_{n'_0}, \eta'_{n'_0})\}$.

Therefore, $\mathcal{M}(x_n, \eta_1) \preceq \zeta_2$, $\forall n > n'_0$.

Also, $\mathcal{M}(x_n, \eta_1) \preceq \mathcal{M}(x_n, \eta'_n) \preceq \zeta_2$, $\forall n = 1, 2, \ldots n'_0$.

Hence, $\mathcal{M}(x_n, \eta_1) \preceq \zeta_2$, $\forall n$...........................(ii)

Let $\eta_2 = \eta_0 \oplus \eta_1$.

Then, from (i) and (ii), we obtain $\mathcal{N}(x_n, \eta_2) \succeq \mathcal{N}(x_n, \eta_0) \succeq \zeta_1$ and $\mathcal{M}(x_n, \eta_2) \preceq \mathcal{M}(x_n, \eta_1) \preceq \zeta_2\ \forall n$, i.e, $\mathcal{N}(x_n, \eta_2) \succeq \zeta_1$ and $\mathcal{M}(x_n, \eta_2) \preceq \zeta_2\ \forall n$ with $\zeta_1 \oplus \zeta_2 \preceq \bar{1}$.

This implies that $\{x_n\}$ is bounded in (X, A). □

Remark 2. *The converse of the above theorem is not true in general, which follows from the following example.*

Example 2. *Let $(X = \mathbb{R}, |.|)$ be the usual real normed linear space and $||.||$ be the usual Felbin-type fuzzy norm on $\mathbb{R}$, i.e,*

$$||x||(t) = \begin{cases} 1, & if\ t = |x| \\ 0, & otherwise \end{cases}.$$

Define

$$\mathcal{N}(x, \eta) = \begin{cases} \bar{1} & if\ ||x|| \prec \eta \\ \bar{0} & otherwise \end{cases}$$

$$\mathcal{M}(x, \eta) = \begin{cases} \bar{0} & if\ ||x|| \prec \eta \\ \bar{1} & otherwise \end{cases}.$$

Then (X, A) is an intuitionistic type-2 fuzzy normed linear space. Take the sequence $\{x_n\}$ where $x_n = (-1)^{n+1}, \forall n \in \mathbb{N}$. Then, we see that the sequence $\{x_n\}$ is bounded but not Cauchy.

In fact, for the above sequence, we have $||x_n|| = \bar{1}\ \forall n \in \mathbb{N}$.

Now choose any $\zeta_1, \zeta_2 \in \mathcal{I}_0$ such that $\zeta_1 \oplus \zeta_2 \preceq \bar{1}$.

Then, if we take any $\eta_0 \succ \bar{1}$, then $\mathcal{N}(x_n, \eta_0) = \bar{1} \succ \zeta_1$ and also $\mathcal{M}(x_n, \eta_0) = \bar{0} \prec \zeta_2$.

Thus, the sequence $\{x_n\}$ is bounded.

Also, for the given sequence, we see that $||x_{n+p} - x_n|| = \bar{0}$ or $\bar{2}$ for any $n \in \mathbb{N}$, and $p = 1,2,3,\ldots$

If $\eta \succ \bar{2}$, then $\mathcal{N}(x_{n+1} - x_n, \eta) = \bar{1}$ $\forall n \in \mathbb{N}$, and, if $\eta \prec \bar{1}$, then $\mathcal{N}(x_{n+1} - x_n, \eta) = \bar{0}$ $\forall n \in \mathbb{N}$.

Hence, the sequence $\{x_n\}$ is not Cauchy.

Definition 19. *Let (X, A) be an IT2FNLS. A subset V of X is said to be closed if any sequence $\{x_n\}$ in V converges to $x \in V$ that is $lim_{n\to\infty}\mathcal{N}(x_n - x, \eta) = \bar{1}$ and $\mathcal{M}(x_n - x, \eta) = \bar{0}$ $\forall \eta \succ \bar{0} \Rightarrow x \in V$.*

Definition 20. *Let (X, A) be an IT2FNLS. A subset U of X is said to be compact if any sequence $\{x_n\}$ in U has a subsequence converging to an element of U.*

Theorem 13. *Let (X, A) be a finite-dimensional IT2FNLS satisfying the conditions (xi) and (xii) and $U \subset X$. Then U is compact if it is closed and bounded.*

Proof. Let $\dim X = k$ and $\{e_1, e_2, \ldots, e_k\}$ be a basis of X.

We take a sequence $\{x_n\}$ in U and let $x_n = \beta_1^n e_1 + \beta_2^n e_2 + \ldots + \beta_k^n e_k$, where $\beta_i^n \in \mathbb{R}$, $i = 1,2,\ldots k$.

Since U is bounded, $\{x_n\}$ is bounded. Then, for each $\zeta_1, \zeta_2 \in \mathcal{I}_0$ with $\zeta_1 \oplus \zeta_2 \preceq \bar{1}$, $\exists\, \eta_1 \succ \bar{0}$ such that $\mathcal{N}(x_n, \eta_1) \succ \zeta_1$ and $\mathcal{M}(x_n, \eta_1) \prec \zeta_2$ for all $n \in \mathbb{N}$......................(i).

Now $||x_n||^{\zeta_1} = \wedge\{\eta \succ \bar{0} : \mathcal{N}(x_n, \eta) \succeq \zeta_1\}$.

Then, from (i), we obtain $||x_n||^{\zeta_1} \preceq \eta_1$................(ii).

Since $\{e_1, e_2, \ldots, e_k\}$ is a linearly independent set, by the Lemma 3, there exists a $\lambda^{\zeta_1} \succ \bar{0}$ such that $||x_n||^{\zeta_1} = ||\sum_{i=1}^{k} \beta_i^n e_i||^{\zeta_1} \succeq (\sum_{i=1}^{k} |\beta_i^n|)\lambda^{\zeta_1}$ (n=1,2,...)..............(iii).

From (ii) and (iii), we obtain $(\sum_{i=1}^{k} |\beta_i^n|)\lambda^{\zeta_1} \preceq \eta_1$.

Now, if we take $[\lambda^{\zeta_1}]_\alpha = [a^\alpha, b^\alpha]$ and $[\eta_1]_\alpha = [a_1^\alpha, b_1^\alpha]$ for $0 < \alpha \leq 1$, then $(\sum_{i=1}^{k} |\beta_i^n|)a^\alpha \leq a_1^\alpha$ and $(\sum_{i=1}^{k} |\beta_i^n|)b^\alpha \leq b_1^\alpha$.

Then $(\sum_{i=1}^{k} |\beta_i^n|) \leq \frac{a_1^\alpha}{a^\alpha}$ for n=1,2,..., and so, for each $i = 1,2,\ldots k$, $\{\beta_i^n\}_n$ is a bounded sequence of real numbers.

Now $\{\beta_1^n\}_n$ is bounded, and so, by the Bolzano–Weierstrass theorem, it has a convergent subsequence. Let β_1 denote the limit of that subsequence and let $\{x_{(1,n)}\}_n$ denote the corresponding subsequence of $\{x_n\}$. By the same argument, $\{x_{(1,n)}\}$ has a subsequence $\{x_{(2,n)}\}$ for which the corresponding subsequence of real β_2^n converges. Let β_2 denote the limit of that subsequence. Continuing in this way after k steps, we obtain a sequence $\{x_{(k,n)}\}_n = \{x_{(k,1)}, x_{(k,2)}, \ldots\}$ of $\{x_n\}$ whose elements are of the form $x_{(k,n)} = \sum_{i=1}^{k} \gamma_i^n e_i$ with scalars γ_i^n satisfying $\gamma_i^n \to \beta_i$ as $n \to \infty$ for $i = 1,2,\ldots,k$.

Let $x = \sum_{i=1}^{k} \beta_i e_i$. Then, $x \in X$.

Now, for $\eta \succ \bar{0}$, we have

$$\begin{aligned} \mathcal{N}(x_{(k,n)} - x, \eta) &= \mathcal{N}(\sum_{i=1}^{k} (\gamma_i^n - \beta_i)e_i, \eta) \\ &\succeq min_i \mathcal{N}(e_i, \frac{1}{k|\gamma_i^n - \beta_i|}\eta) \end{aligned}$$

$\Rightarrow lim_{n\to\infty}\mathcal{N}(x_{(k,n)} - x, \eta) \succeq min_i\, lim_{n\to\infty}\mathcal{N}(e_i, \frac{1}{k|\gamma_i^n - \beta_i|}\eta)$.....................(iv).

Let $u_n = \frac{1}{k|\gamma_i^n - \beta_i|}$.

Then $u_n \to \infty$ as $n \to \infty$, since $|\gamma_i^n - \beta_i| \to 0+$, when $n \to \infty$.

So $u_n\eta \to \bar{\infty}$ as $n \to \infty$ by Lemma 2.

Then we have $lim_{n\to\infty}\mathcal{N}(e_i, \frac{1}{k|\gamma_i^n - \beta_i|}\eta) = lim_{n\to\infty}\mathcal{N}(e_i, u_n\eta) = \bar{1}$...............(v).

Combining (iv) and (v), we obtain $lim_{n\to\infty}\mathcal{N}(x_{(k,n)} - x, \eta) = \bar{1}$, $\quad \forall \eta \succ \bar{0}$.....................(vi).

Again, for all $\eta \succ \bar{0}$,

$$\begin{aligned} \mathcal{M}(x_{(k,n)} - x, \eta) &= \mathcal{M}(\sum_{i=1}^{k}(\gamma_i^n - \beta_i)e_i, \eta) \\ &\preceq max_i \mathcal{M}(e_i, \frac{1}{k|\gamma_i^n - \beta_i|}\eta) \end{aligned}$$

$\Rightarrow lim_{n\to\infty}\mathcal{M}(x_{(k,n)} - x, \eta) \preceq max_i\, lim_{n\to\infty}\mathcal{N}(e_i, \frac{1}{k|\gamma_i^n - \beta_i|}\eta)$.....................(vii)

Let $u_n = \frac{1}{k|\gamma_i^n - \beta_i|}$.

Then, $u_n \to \infty$ as $n \to \infty$, since $|\gamma_i^n - \beta_i| \to 0+$, when $n \to \infty$.

So $u_n\eta \to \overline{\infty}$ as $n \to \infty$ by Lemma 2.

Then we have $lim_{n\to\infty}\mathcal{M}(e_i, \frac{1}{k|\gamma_i^n - \beta_i|}\eta) = lim_{n\to\infty}\mathcal{M}(e_i, u_n\eta) = \bar{0}$...............(viii).

Combining (vi) and (vii), we obtain $lim_{n\to\infty}\mathcal{M}(x_{(k,n)} - x, \eta) = \bar{0}, \quad \forall\eta \succ \bar{0}$.................(ix).

Combining (vi) and (xi), we obtain $lim_{n\to\infty}\mathcal{N}(x_{(k,n)} - x, \eta) = \bar{1}$ and $lim_{n\to\infty}\mathcal{M}(x_{(k,n)} - x, \eta) = \bar{0}, \quad \forall\eta \succ \bar{0}$

$\Rightarrow lim_{n\to\infty}x_{(k,n)} = x$, i.e, $\{x_{(k,n)}\}_n$ is a convergent subsequence of $\{x_n\}_n$ which converges to x. Since U is closed, $x \in U$. Hence, every sequence in U has a subsequence which converges in U. Thus, U is compact. □

4. Intuitionistic Fuzzy Continuous Functions in Intuitionistic Type-2 Fuzzy Normed Linear Space

We know that, in classical normed linear space, continuity of function at a point can be characterised by the convergence of the sequence at that point. But here we discover that, in an IT2FNLS setting, the sequential criterion for continuity holds partially. For this, we introduce two types of continuous functions, namely, intuitionistic type-2 fuzzy continuous and sequentially intuitionistic type-2 fuzzy continuous functions. Here, we show that every intuitionistic type-2 fuzzy continuous function is sequentially intuitionistic type-2 fuzzy continuous, but its converse is not true, which is justified by a counterexample.

Definition 21. *Let (X, A) and (Y, B) be two IT2FNLSs. A mapping $T : X \to Y$ is said to be intuitionistic type-2 fuzzy continuous (or, in short, IT2FC) at $x_0 \in X$ if, for each $\eta_1 \succ \bar{0}$, $\exists\, \eta_2 \succ \bar{0}$ such that $\forall x \in X$,*

$\mathcal{N}_B(T(x) - T(x_0), \eta_1) \succeq \mathcal{N}_A(x - x_0, \eta_2)$ and

$\mathcal{M}_B(T(x) - T(x_0), \eta_1) \preceq \mathcal{M}_A(x - x_0, \eta_2)$.

T is said to be IT2FC on X if T is IT2FC at each point of X.

Definition 22. *Let (X, A) and (Y, B) be two IT2FNLSs. A mapping $T : X \to Y$ is said to be sequentially intuitionistic type-2 fuzzy continuous (or, in short, sequentially IT2FC) at $x_0 \in X$ if any sequence $\{x_n\}$ in X with $x_n \to x_0$ implies $Tx_n \to Tx_0$, i.e, $lim_{n\to\infty}\mathcal{N}_A(x_n - x_0, \eta) = \bar{1}$ and $lim_{n\to\infty}\mathcal{M}_A(x_n - x_0, \eta) = \bar{0}, \forall\eta \succ \bar{0}$*

$\Rightarrow lim_{n\to\infty}\mathcal{N}_B(T(x_n) - T(x_0), \eta) = \bar{1}$ and $lim_{n\to\infty}\mathcal{M}_B(T(x_n) - T(x_0), \eta) = \bar{0}, \forall\eta \succ \bar{0}$.

If T is sequentially IT2FC at each point of X, then T is said to be sequentially IT2FC on X.

Theorem 14. *Let (X, A) and (Y, B) be two IT2FNLSs and $T : X \to Y$ be a mapping. If T is IT2FC on X, then it is sequentially IT2FC on X.*

Proof. Let x_0 be an arbitrary point of X and T be IT2FC on X. Then, for an $\eta_1 \succ \bar{0}$, $\exists\, \eta_2 \succ \bar{0}$ such that $\forall x \in X$

$\mathcal{N}_B(T(x) - T(x_0), \eta_1) \succeq \mathcal{N}_A(x - x_0, \eta_2)$..........................(i)

and $\mathcal{M}_B(T(x) - T(x_0), \eta_1) \preceq \mathcal{M}_A(x - x_0, \eta_2)$.........................(ii).

Let $\{x_n\}$ be a sequence in X such that $x_n \to x_0$, that is, for all $\eta \succ \bar{0}$, $lim_{n\to\infty}\mathcal{N}_A(x_n - x_0, \eta) = \bar{1}$ and $lim_{n\to\infty}\mathcal{M}_A(x_n - x_0, \eta) = \bar{0}$.

Then, for all $\eta \succ \bar{0}$ from (i) and (ii), we obtain $lim_{n\to\infty}\mathcal{N}_B(T(x_n)-T(x_0),\eta)=\bar{1}$ and $lim_{n\to\infty}\mathcal{M}_B(T(x_n)-T(x_0),\eta)=\bar{0}$, that is, $T(x_n)\to T(x_0)$ in (Y,B), and so T is sequentially IT2FC on X. □

The following example will show that a sequentially IT2FC T does not guarantee the IT2FC of T.

Example 3. *Let $(X=\mathbb{R},|.|)$ be a normed linear space. For any fuzzy real number $\eta\succ\bar{0}$, define η_0 as follows:*

$$\eta_0=\overline{\tfrac{a+b}{2}}$$

where $[a,b]$ denotes the closure of support of the fuzzy real number η. Let $k,k_1>0$ be any fixed real number. Define

$$\mathcal{N}_A(x,\eta)=\begin{cases}\eta_0\oslash(\eta_0\oplus\overline{k|x|}), & if\ \eta\succ\bar{0}\\ \bar{0}, & if\ \eta=\bar{0}\end{cases}$$

$$\mathcal{M}_A(x,\eta)=\begin{cases}\overline{k|x|}\oslash(\eta_0\oplus\overline{k|x|}), & if\ \eta\succ\bar{0}\\ \bar{1}, & if\ \eta=\bar{0}\end{cases}$$

and

$$\mathcal{N}_B(x,\eta)=\begin{cases}\eta_0\oslash(\eta_0\oplus\overline{k_1|x|}), & if\ \eta\succ\bar{0}\\ \bar{0}, & if\ \eta=\bar{0}\end{cases}$$

$$\mathcal{M}_B(x,\eta)=\begin{cases}\overline{k_1|x|}\oslash(\eta_0\oplus\overline{k_1|x|}), & if\ \eta\succ\bar{0}\\ \bar{1}, & if\ \eta=\bar{0}\end{cases}$$

Then, $(X=\mathbb{R},A)$ and $(Y=\mathbb{R},B)$ are two IT2FNLSs.

We define a function $T:X\to Y$ by $T(x)=\frac{x^4}{1+x^2}$. Then, T is sequentially IT2FC but not IT2FC.

In fact, by Example 1, we can see that both (X,A) and (Y,B) are two ITFNLSs.

We choose a sequence $\{x_n\}$, $x_n\in X$ such that $x_n\to x_0$.

Now $\forall\eta\succ\bar{0}$, we have

$lim_{n\to\infty}\mathcal{N}_A(x_n-x_0,\eta)=\bar{1}$ *and* $lim_{n\to\infty}\mathcal{M}_A(x_n-x_0,\eta)=\bar{0}$

$\Rightarrow lim_{n\to\infty}\{(\overline{\tfrac{a+b}{2}})\oslash(\overline{\tfrac{a+b}{2}}\oplus\overline{|x_n-x_0|})\}=\bar{1}$ *and* $lim_{n\to\infty}\{(\overline{k|x_n-x_0|})\oslash(\overline{\tfrac{a+b}{2}}\oplus\overline{k|x_n-x_0|})\}=\bar{0}$

$\Rightarrow lim_{n\to\infty}\frac{\frac{a+b}{2}}{\frac{a+b}{2}+|x_n-x_0|}=1$ *and* $lim_{n\to\infty}\frac{k|x_n-x_0|}{\frac{a+b}{2}+k|x_n-x_0|}=0$

$\Rightarrow lim_{n\to\infty}|x_n-x_0|=0$........................*(i).*

Now $\mathcal{N}_B(T(x_n)-T(x_0),\eta)=\{(\overline{\tfrac{a+b}{2}})\oslash(\overline{\tfrac{a+b}{2}}\oplus\overline{k_1|\tfrac{x_n^4}{1+x_n^2}-\tfrac{x_0^4}{1+x_0^2}|})\}$

Now $lim_{n\to\infty}(k_1|\frac{x_n^4}{1+x_n^2}-\frac{x_0^4}{1+x_0^2}|)=0$ *by using (i)*

$\Rightarrow lim_{n\to\infty}\mathcal{N}_B(T(x_n)-T(x_0),\eta)=\bar{1}\ \forall\eta\succ\bar{0}.$

Also, $\forall\eta\succ\bar{0}$

$lim_{n\to\infty}\mathcal{M}_B(T(x_n)-T(x_0),\eta)=\{(\overline{k_1|\tfrac{x_n^4}{1+x_n^2}-\tfrac{x_0^4}{1+x_0^2}|})\oslash(\overline{\tfrac{a+b}{2}}\oplus\overline{k_1|\tfrac{x_n^4}{1+x_n^2}-\tfrac{x_0^4}{1+x_0^2}|})\}$

Now $lim_{n\to\infty}(k_1|\frac{x_n^4}{1+x_n^2}-\frac{x_0^4}{1+x_0^2}|)=0$ *by using (i)*

$\Rightarrow lim_{n\to\infty}\mathcal{M}_B(T(x_n)-T(x_0),\eta)=\bar{0}\ \forall\eta\succ\bar{0}.$

Thus, $T:(X,A)\to(Y,B)$ is sequentially IT2FC.

Let $\eta_2\succ\bar{0}$ be given. Then, for any $\eta_1\succ\bar{0}$,

$\mathcal{N}_B(T(x)-T(x_0),\eta_2)\succeq\mathcal{N}_A(x-x_0,\eta_1)\ \forall x\in X$

$\Rightarrow\mathcal{N}_B(\frac{x^4}{1+x^2}-\frac{x_0^4}{1+x_0^2},\eta_2)\succeq\mathcal{N}_A(x-x_0,\eta_1)$

$\Rightarrow\{(\overline{\tfrac{a_2+b_2}{2}})\oslash(\overline{\tfrac{a_2+b_2}{2}}\oplus\overline{k_1|\tfrac{x^4}{1+x^2}-\tfrac{x_0^4}{1+x_0^2}|})\}\succeq\{(\overline{\tfrac{a_1+b_1}{2}})\oslash(\overline{\tfrac{a_1+b_1}{2}}\oplus\overline{k|x-x_0|})\}$ *[where $[a_1,b_1]$, $[a_2,b_2]$ denotes, respectively, the closure of support of the fuzzy real numbers η_1, η_2]*

$\Rightarrow \frac{\frac{a_2+b_2}{2}}{\frac{a_2+b_2}{2}+k_1|\frac{x^4}{1+x^2}-\frac{x_0^4}{1+x_0^2}|} \geq \frac{\frac{a_1+b_1}{2}}{\frac{a_1+b_1}{2}+k|x-x_0|}$

$\Rightarrow \frac{r_2}{r_2+k_1|\frac{x^4}{1+x^2}-\frac{x_0^4}{1+x_0^2}|} \geq \frac{r_1}{r_1+k|x-x_0|}$ *where* $r_1 = \frac{a_1+b_1}{2}$ *and* $r_2 = \frac{a_2+b_2}{2}$

$\Rightarrow \frac{r_2|1+x^2||1+x_0^2|}{r_2|1+x^2||1+x_0^2|+k_1|x^4+x^4x_0^2-x_0^4-x_0^4x^2|} \geq \frac{r_1}{r_1+k|x-x_0|}$

$\Rightarrow \frac{r_2|1+x^2||1+x_0^2|}{r_2|1+x^2||1+x_0^2|+k_1|x-x_0||x+x_0||x^2+x_0^2+x^2x_0^2|} \geq \frac{r_1}{r_1+k|x-x_0|}$

$\Rightarrow k_1r_1|x-x_0||x+x_0||x^2+x_0^2+x^2x_0^2| \leq r_2k|1+x^2||1+x_0^2||x-x_0|$

$\Rightarrow r_1 \leq \frac{r_2k|1+x^2||1+x_0^2||x-x_0|}{k_1|x-x_0||x+x_0||x^2+x_0^2+x^2x_0^2|}$......................*(ii)*

If T is IT2FC on X, then (ii) is satisfied $\forall x(\neq x_0) \in X$.

Now $inf_{x(\neq x_0)\in X} \frac{r_2k|1+x^2||1+x_0^2||x-x_0|}{k_1|x-x_0||x+x_0||x^2+x_0^2+x^2x_0^2|} = 0.$

Hence, from (ii), we obtain $r_1 = 0$

$\Rightarrow \frac{a_1+b_1}{2} = 0$

$\Rightarrow a_1 + b_1 = 0$

$\Rightarrow a_1 = b_1 = 0$ *[Since* $a_1, b_1 \geq 0$*]*

$\Rightarrow \eta_1 = \bar{0}$, *which is not possible.*

Therefore, T is not IT2FC.

5. Conclusions

In this work we have presented for the first time the concept of intuitionistic type-2 fuzzy normed linear space (IT2FNLS). A decomposition theorem of the intuitionistic type-2 fuzzy norm has been established. The later convergence and Cauchyness of a sequence in IT2FNLS have been examined. Also, associated properties of various classical concepts such as completeness, compactness, boundedness and finite dimensionality have been studied with examples and counterexamples in this newly defined IT2FNLS. Afterwards, two types of continuity are introduced in IT2FNLS, viz. IT2FC and sequentially IT2FC, and final relations between them have been analysed with examples, and we found some dissimilarity with the corresponding results in normed linear spaces.

There is a possibility of further study in the following directions:

1. The boundedness of linear operators between two IT2FNLSs can be defined.
2. The relation between the continuity and boundedness of linear operators can be studied.
3. Four fundamental theorems, viz. the Hahn–Banach theorem, open mapping theorem, closed graph theorem and the uniform boundedness principle theorem, can be extended in IT2FNLS.
4. Some geometric properties such as strict convexity and uniform convexity, etc., can be defined in these spaces.
5. Some fixed-point theorems in these spaces can also be studied.

Author Contributions: Conceptualisation, M.C. and S.K.S.; methodology, A.B., M.C. and S.K.S.; validation, A.B., M.C. and S.K.S.; formal analysis, S.K.S.; investigation, A.B. and M.C.; writing—original draft preparation, A.B.; writing—review and editing, M.C.; visualisation, S.K.S.; supervision, M.C. and S.K.S.; funding acquisition, A.B. All authors have read and agreed to the published version of the manuscript.

Funding: The research of the first author is funded by the University Grants Commission of India (UGC-Ref. No.: 1159/(CSIR-UGC NET DEC. 2017).

Data Availability Statement: The original contributions presented in the study are included in the article, further inquiries can be directed to the corresponding author.

Acknowledgments: The authors are thankful to the referees for their valuable and constructive suggestions.

Conflicts of Interest: The authors have no competing interests to declare that are relevant to the content of this article.

References

1. Zadeh, L.A. Fuzzy Sets. *Inf. Control.* **1965** *8*, 338–353. [CrossRef]
2. Zadeh, L.A. The concept of a linguistic variable and its application to approximate reasoning-1. *Inf. Sci.* **1975**, *8*, 199–249. [CrossRef]
3. Felbin, C. Finite dimensional fuzzy normed linear space. *Fuzzy Sets Syst.* **1992**, *48*, 239–248. [CrossRef]
4. Kaleva, O.; Seikkala, S. On fuzzy metric spaces, *Fuzzy Sets Syst.* **1984**, *12*, 215–229. [CrossRef]
5. Cheng, S.C.; Mordeson, J.N. Fuzzy linear operator and fuzzy normed linear spaces. *Bull. Cal. Math. Soc.* **1994**, *86*, 429–436.
6. Kramosil, I.; Michalek, J. Fuzzy metrics and statistical metric spaces. *Kybernetika* **1975** *11*, 336–344.
7. Bag, T.; Samanta, S.K. Finite dimensional fuzzy normed linear spaces. *J. Fuzzy Math.* **2003**, *11*, 686–705.
8. Chiney, M.; Biswas, A.; Samanta, S.K. Finite dimensional type-2 fuzzy normed linear spaces (Communicated).
9. Atanassov, K.T. Intuitionistic fuzzy sets. *Fuzzy Sets Syst.* **1986**, *20*, 87–96. [CrossRef]
10. Atanassov, K.T. New operations defined over intuitionistic fuzzy sets. *Fuzzy Sets Syst.* **1994**, *61*, 137–142. [CrossRef]
11. Atanassov, K.T. *Intuitionistic Fuzzy Sets: Theory and Applications*; Studies in Fuzziness and Soft Computing; Springer: Berlin/Heidelberg, Germany, 1999; Volume 35, pp. 1–137. [CrossRef]
12. Atanassov, K.T. *On Intuitionistic Fuzzy Sets Theory*; Studies in Fuzziness and Soft Computing; Springer: Berlin/Heidelberg, Germany, 2012; Volume 283. [CrossRef]
13. Biswas, R. On fuzzy sets and intuitionistic fuzzy sets. *Notes Intuitionistic Fuzzy Sets* **1997**, *3*, 3–11.
14. De, S.K.; Biswas, R.; Roy, A.R. An application of intuitionistic fuzzy sets in medical diagnostic. *Fuzzy Sets Syst.* **2001**, *117*, 209–213. [CrossRef]
15. Ejegwa, P.A.; Akubo, A.J.; Joshua, O.M. Intuitionistic fuzzy set and its application in career determination via normalized euclidean distance method. *Eur. Sci. J.* **2014**, *10*, 529–536.
16. Szmidt, E.; Kacprzyk, J. Intuitionistic fuzzy sets in group decision making. *Notes Intuitionistic Fuzzy Sets* **1996**, *2*, 11–14.
17. Biswas, R. Intuitionistic fuzzy subgroups. *Math. Forum* **1989**, *10*, 37–46.
18. Coker, D. An introduction to intuitionistic fuzzy topological spaces. *Fuzzy Sets Syst.* **1997**, *88*, 81–89. [CrossRef]
19. Hur, K.; Kang, H.W.; Song, H.K. Intuitionistic fuzzy subgroups and subrings. *Honam Math. J.* **2003**, *25*, 19–41. [CrossRef]
20. Mohammed, M.J.; Ataa, G.A. On Intuitionistic fuzzy topological vector space. *J. Coll. Educ. Pure Sci.* **2014**, *4*, 32–51.
21. Mondal, K.K.; Samanta, S.K. A study on intuitionistic fuzzy topological spaces. *Notes Intuitionistic Fuzzy Sets* **2013**, *9*, 1–32.
22. Park, J.H. Intuitionstic fuzzy metric spaces. *Chaos Solitons Fractals* **2004**, *22*, 1039–1046. [CrossRef]
23. Padmapriya, S.; Uma, M.K.; Roja, E. A study on intuitionistic fuzzy topological* groups. *Ann. Fuzzy Math. Inform.* **2014**, *7*, 991–1004.
24. Pradhan, R.; Pal, M. Intuitionistic fuzzy linear transformations. *Ann. Pure Appl. Math.* **2012**, *5*, 57–68.
25. Vijayabalaji, S.; Thillaigovindan, N.; Jun, Y.B. Intuitionistic fuzzy n-normed linear space. *Bull. Korean Math. Soc.* **2007**, *44*, 291–308. [CrossRef]
26. Samanta, T.K.; Jebril, I.H. Finite dimensional intuitionistic fuzzy normed linear space. *Int. J. Open Problems Compt. Math.* **2009**, *2*, 575–591.
27. Debnath, P. Lacunary ideal convergence in intuitionistic fuzzy normed linear spaces. *Comput. Math. Appl.* **2012**, *63*, 708–715. [CrossRef]
28. Konwar, N.; Debnath, P. Continuity and Banach contraction principle in intuitionistic fuzzy n-normed linear spaces. *J. Intell. Fuzzy Syst.* **2017**, *33*, 2363–2373 . [CrossRef]
29. Konwar, N.; Esi, A.; Debnath, P. New fixed point theorems via contraction mappings in complete intuitionistic fuzzy normed linear space. *New Math. Nat. Comput.* **2019**, *15*, 65–83. [CrossRef]
30. Bag, T.; Samanta, S.K. Fuzzy bounded linear operators in Felbin's type fuzzy normed linear spaces. *Fuzzy Sets Syst.* **2008**, *159*, 685–707. [CrossRef]
31. Congxin, W.; Cong, W. The supremum and infimum of the set of fuzzy numbers and its application. *J. Math. Anal. Appl.* **1997**, *210*, 499–511. [CrossRef]

mathematics

MDPI

Article

Fuzzy Multi-Objective, Multi-Period Integrated Routing–Scheduling Problem to Distribute Relief to Disaster Areas: A Hybrid Ant Colony Optimization Approach

Malihe Niksirat [1], Mohsen Saffarian [2], Javad Tayyebi [2], Adrian Marius Deaconu [3,*] and Delia Elena Spridon [3]

1 Department of Computer Sciences, Birjand University of Technology, Birjand 97198-66981, Iran; niksirat@birjandut.ac.ir
2 Department of Industrial Engineering, Birjand University of Technology, Birjand 97198-66981, Iran; saffarian@birjandut.ac.ir (M.S.); javadtayyebi@birjandut.ac.ir (J.T.)
3 Department of Mathematics and Computer Science, Transylvania University of Brasov, 500036 Brașov, Romania; delia.cuza@unitbv.ro
* Correspondence: a.deaconu@unitbv.ro

Abstract: This paper explores a multi-objective, multi-period integrated routing and scheduling problem under uncertain conditions for distributing relief to disaster areas. The goals are to minimize costs and maximize satisfaction levels. To achieve this, the proposed mathematical model aims to speed up the delivery of relief supplies to the most affected areas. Additionally, the demands and transportation times are represented using fuzzy numbers to more accurately reflect real-world conditions. The problem was formulated using a fuzzy multi-objective integer programming model. To solve it, a hybrid algorithm combining a multi-objective ant colony system and simulated annealing algorithm was proposed. This algorithm adopts two ant colonies to obtain a set of nondominated solutions (the Pareto set). Numerical analyses have been conducted to determine the optimal parameter values for the proposed algorithm and to evaluate the performance of both the model and the algorithm. Furthermore, the algorithm's performance was compared with that of the multi-objective cat swarm optimization algorithm and multi-objective fitness-dependent optimizer algorithm. The numerical results demonstrate the computational efficiency of the proposed method.

Keywords: fuzzy multi-objective integer programming problem; multi-period integrated vehicle routing and scheduling; multi-objective ant colony system; simulated annealing algorithm

MSC: 90B06

1. Introduction

Given the increasing frequency of disasters, millions of people are affected by natural or man-made events each year, with the number of victims rising significantly in recent decades. Effective planning is crucial in mitigating the impacts of such catastrophes. Logistics play a key role in coordinating the transportation of commodities between regional warehouses and affected areas. However, relief logistics planning involves conflicting objectives, such as minimizing unsatisfied demands, distribution costs, and delays, while maximizing satisfaction and fairness in product distribution [1].

Sudden disasters are unpredictable, presenting significant challenges that underscore the need for an efficient emergency material distribution system. A key challenge for decision-makers is finding a way to swiftly and safely deliver materials to affected areas. Existing research largely focuses on the coordinated transportation of emergency supplies, dynamic distribution, and transport uncertainties [2–4]. To effectively address the complexities of emergency material distribution during crises, it is crucial to integrate all these factors.

In addition, uncertainty plays a crucial role in emergency material distribution, where real-time information is hard to obtain. Accurate demand assessment can improve relief allocation and reduce costs. Furthermore, transportation times may fluctuate due to traffic jams, equipment failures, and other unpredictable events. Researchers explored fuzzy theory and stochastic programming to address uncertain conditions. Considering that the values of these parameters in the affected areas varies over time, the collection of reliable prior data for stochastic programming is challenging. Fuzzy theory is thus more suitable for optimizing these issues [5,6]. In this regard, we propose a fuzzy multi-objective integer programming model.

Furthermore, the routing–scheduling distribution problem is NP-hard [7], and the literature primarily emphasizes the use of metaheuristic algorithms for similar problems [8–11]. By calibrating the metaheuristic algorithm to the specific characteristics of the problem, it can generate effective solutions for planning various operations to address these challenges [6]. Building on the above discussion, we propose a fuzzy multi-objective, multi-period integrated routing–scheduling model and adapt a hybrid algorithm based on a multi-objective ant colony system and simulated annealing algorithm to solve the problem.

2. Literature Review

Research on disaster management is of great importance, and significant studies are being conducted in this field. One of the first studies in the field of transportation in relief logistics was performed by [12]. In the mentioned work, a linear programming model was presented to determine the optimal food transportation schedule. Given the significance of crisis management, several researchers have recently conducted extensive reviews of the studies carried out in this area [1,13–16]. This overview will discuss research in the relief chain response phase with an emphasis on periodic routing, multi-objective routing–scheduling and uncertainty.

2.1. Multi-Period Relief Distribution

Some of the most important aspects of routing problems, which are addressed in this study, are periodic routing problems where customer services must be done periodically during a planning horizon. The aim of periodic routing is to determine the motion paths from the service centers to the customers in each period so that the total routing costs incurred throughout the planning horizon are minimized [17]. The periodic vehicle routing problem was first proposed in [18], while the first mathematical model of the problem was then presented in [19]. Over the past forty-five years, the periodic vehicle routing problem has significantly evolved, leading to applications like the period vehicle routing problem with time windows [20], the multi-depot and periodic vehicle routing problem [21], and the dynamic multi-period vehicle routing problem [22]. Most research has concentrated on using heuristic algorithms to tackle these extended PVRP models.

Li et al. proposed a multi-period vehicle routing problem for emergency perishable materials with uncertain demand, utilizing an improved whale optimization algorithm [23]. Zhang et al. recently proposed a multi-period vehicle routing problem with time windows for drug distribution during epidemics. Their model incorporates virus transmission characteristics and fluctuations in drug demand. They employed an ε-global optimization method with an outer-approximation scheme for achieving global ε-optimal solutions in small instances and introduced a hybrid tabu search algorithm (HTS) for larger instances [24].

2.2. Multi-Objective Relief Distribution

Research on multi-objective optimization problems gained significant popularity in 2002 [25] and has since attracted considerable attention from researchers. Recently, a new multi-objective optimization algorithm, called the multi-objective learner performance-based behavior algorithm, was introduced by Rahman et al. [26]. This algorithm is inspired by the transition of students from high school to college and is evaluated against benchmarks and five real-world engineering optimization problems using various metrics. In a more recent study, Abdullah et al. introduced the multi-objective fitness-dependent optimizer (MOFDO) algorithm, an advanced version of the fitness-dependent optimizer algorithm that combines various types of knowledge [27]. This algorithm was evaluated using ZDT test functions and CEC-2019 benchmarks, showing a better performance than recent methods, like the multi-objective particle swarm optimization, NSGA-III, and multi-objective dragonfly algorithm, in many cases.

Rath and Gutjahr presented a three-objective optimization model with a medium-term economic sector, a short-term economic sector, and an accident objective function [28]. To solve the problem, a meta-heuristic scheme based on a genetic algorithm was also provided. Ngueveu et al. introduced a transportation routing model with a stacked capacity where the aim was to minimize the total time required for the vehicle to get applicants [2]. Ahmadi et al. developed a multi-objective multi-depot location-routing model considering network failure, multiple uses of vehicles, and standard relief time. The model was then extended to a two-step stochastic program with a random travel time to determine the locations of distribution centers [29]. Barzinpour et al. proposed a multi-objective model for distribution centers which are located in and allocated periodically to the damaged areas in order to distribute the offered relief commodities [18].

Mohammadi et al. developed a new multi-objective reliable optimization model to organize a humanitarian relief chain that is able to make a broad range of decisions, including reliable facility location–allocation, fair distribution of relief items, assignment of victims, and routing of trucks [30]. Vahdani et al. developed a sophisticated two-stage, multi-objective mixed integer, multi-period, and multi-commodity mathematical model designed for a three-level relief chain [31]. Yu et al. first developed a more general two-echelon multi-objective location routing problem model (2E-MOLRP) in consideration of the inherent similarities in many realistic waste collection applications. Furthermore, to solve the model, an improved non-dominated sorting genetic algorithm with a directed local search (INSGA-dLS) was proposed [32]. Ebrahimi formulated a more comprehensive two-echelon multi-objective location routing problem model (2E-MOLRP), taking into account the inherent parallels in numerous practical waste collection scenarios. Moreover, to tackle the model, they proposed an enhanced non-dominated sorting genetic algorithm with a directed local search (INSGA-dLS) [5]. Zajac and Huber provided an overview of the solving methods for application-oriented multi-objective routing problems [33]. They were also analyzed in terms of algorithmic approaches and implementation strategies [34].

2.3. *Relief Distribution with the Uncertain Problem*

Given the unpredictable circumstances during and following a crisis, decision-makers frequently grapple with significant uncertainties that compound the complexity of the problem [35]. Inaccurate or delayed information can result in significant casualties and property losses. Various optimization methods in this field are presented in the problem literature. In the following, a number of recent research articles in this field have been reviewed.

Uslu et al. considered a multi-depot vehicle routing problem with stochastic demands and developed a chance-constrained mathematical model to cope with the problem. They also conducted a case study for Ankara city in Turkey [36]. Golabi et al. investigated a stochastic facility location problem for a possible earthquake in Tehran where unmanned aerial vehicles (UAVs) are utilized [17]. Saffarian et al. proposed a bi-objective model for relief chain logistics in an uncertain environment while considering the uncertainty in both traveling times and demands of the damaged areas [37].

Akbarpour et al. created a max–min robust bi-objective optimization model to handle the uncertainty in the pharmaceutical supply chain [38]. Zahedi et al. carried out an empirical study with the aim of creating an optimal model for scheduling resources and vehicles to cater to the needs of disaster-stricken areas with dynamic demands. The research focused on devising a strategic plan for resource allocation during emergencies. This comprehensive model addresses various aspects, including the heterogeneity and fluctuating nature of demands, simultaneous planning for goods distribution and vehicle routing, and a multi-objective model grounded in the essential measures required during emergencies [4].

Rawls and Turnquist presented a two-stage stochastic programming model to tackle the uncertainties in demand and road network availability, facilitating the advanced deployment of emergency relief materials [39]. Liu et al. expanded on this by integrating transportation time uncertainties into their model and using robust optimization techniques to handle these uncertainties [40]. Safaei et al. recognized the fluctuating nature of supply and demand in emergency rescues and proposed a bi-level optimization model, where the upper and lower levels adjust to minimize unmet demands [41]. Additionally, uncertainties may occur during disasters when selecting locations for emergency warehouses [42].

Cao et al. constructed their formulation as a fuzzy tri-objective bi-level integer programming model. They developed a hybrid global criterion method that integrates a primal–dual algorithm, an expected value, and a branch-and-bound approach to solve the model [19]. Wan et al. utilized trapezoidal fuzzy numbers to manage the uncertainty in determining the locations for emergency materials [43]. Fuzzy credibility theory was applied to create a fuzzy chance constraint model incorporating fuzzy demands and unlimited material collection time [44]. Tang et al. utilized trapezoidal fuzzy numbers to represent demand, scheduling time, and satisfaction, ensuring the equitable distribution of disaster relief materials [45].

Our review of the literature shows that the majority of these papers concentrate solely on optimizing specific components. Few studies considered multi-period integrated routing–scheduling, multiple objectives and uncertainty simultaneously. Therefore, this paper investigates the problem of integrated multi-objective, multi-period routing and scheduling under uncertain conditions. To tackle this problem, a multi-objective fuzzy integer programming model is proposed. Considering the intricate nature of the problem, a multi-objective ant colony system algorithm was developed to solve the problem. The rest of the paper is organized as follows. The proposed mathematical model is demonstrated in Section 3. Section 4 is devoted to the multi-objective ant colony system. Numerical analyses are performed in Section 5 to discover the most appropriate parameters for the ant algorithm. Furthermore, several numerical tests are illustrated to demonstrate the main concept and results of the proposed model and algorithm. Section 6 ends the paper with a brief conclusion and future directions.

3. Fuzzy Multi-Objective Multi-Period Integer Programming Model

In this section, a fuzzy multi-objective integer programming model is proposed to formulate the problem. The origin of the model was adapted from [3,46,47], which serves as the foundational source for understanding its development and background. For this aim, the following assumptions were considered:

- Limited number of periods is given;
- Number of depots is fixed;
- Heterogeneous fleet of vehicles is available;
- Capacity of vehicles is predetermined;
- Demand of each customer in each period is specified as a fuzzy parameter;
- Number of customers that should be serviced in each period is defined;
- Customers of each period are different from those of other periods;
- Distance-dependent transportation costs are assumed;
- Each vehicle starts its journey from one depot and ends at another depot, although the starting and ending depots could be also be identical;
- Symmetric transportation network is considered;
- Traversing cost and customer's demand are considered as fuzzy parameters.

The indices of the model are as follows:

i	An index assigned to customers located at the beginning of an edge ($i = 1, \ldots, N$);
j	An index assigned to customers located at the end of an edge ($j = 1, \ldots, N$ and $j \neq i$);
t	Index of periods ($t = 1, \ldots, T$);
k	Index of vehicles ($k = 1, \ldots, V$);
d	Index of depots ($d = 1, \ldots, D$).

Furthermore, the parameters are listed bellow.

$\widetilde{c}_{ijt}$	Fuzzy transportation cost of edge (i, j) between customers i and j in period t;
$\widetilde{c}'_{dit}$	Fuzzy transportation cost of edge (i, d) or edge (d, i) between customer i and depot d in period t;
$\widetilde{d}_{it}$	Fuzzy demand of customer i in period t;
$\widetilde{w}_{ijt}$	Fuzzy transportation time of edge (i, j) customers i and j in period t;
$\widetilde{w}'_{dit}$	Fuzzy transportation time of edge (i, d) or edge (d, i) between customer i and depot d in period t;
N_t	Number of customers in period t;
c_k	Capacity of vehicle k;
V	Number of available vehicles in each period;
T	Number of periods in the planning horizon;
D	Number of depots;
M	A big number.
B	Subset of customers in each period;
A	Set of depots;
G	Set of all customers and depots in each period.

In the following, the Decision Variables of the model is illustrated.

$x_{ijkt} \in \{0, 1\}$	Equals to 1 if vehicle k traverses edge (i, j) in period t, otherwise 0;
$y_{dikt} \in \{0, 1\}$	Equals to 1 if vehicle k traverses edge (d, i) in period t, otherwise 0;
$z_{idkt} \in \{0, 1\}$	Equals to 1 if vehicle k traverses edge (i, d) in period t, otherwise 0;
$s_{kdt} \in \{0, 1\}$	Equals to 1 if vehicle k is located in depot d at the beginning of period t, otherwise 0;
$f_{kdt} \in \{0, 1\}$	Equals to 1 if vehicle k is located in depot d at the end of period t, otherwise 0;
$time_{it} \geq 0$	Arrival time to customer i in period t.

The fuzzy integer programming model of the problem is as follows:

$$\begin{aligned} \text{Min } f_1 = & \sum_{t=1}^{T} \sum_{i=1}^{N_t} \sum_{j=1, j \neq i}^{N_t} \sum_{k=1}^{V} x_{ijkt} \widetilde{c}_{ijt} \\ & + \sum_{t=1}^{T} \sum_{d=1}^{D} \sum_{i=1}^{N_t} \sum_{k=1}^{V} y_{dikt} \widetilde{c}'_{dit} \\ & + \sum_{t=1}^{T} \sum_{i=1}^{N_t} \sum_{d=1}^{D} \sum_{k=1}^{V} z_{idkt} \widetilde{c}'_{dit} \end{aligned} \quad (1)$$

$$\text{Min } f_2 = \sum_{d=1}^{D} \sum_{i=1}^{N_t} time_{it} * \widetilde{d}_{it} \quad (2)$$

The model is subjected to the following:

$$\sum_{d=1}^{D} \sum_{k=1}^{V} y_{d,i,k,t} + \sum_{\substack{j=1 \\ j \neq i}}^{N_t} \sum_{k=1}^{V} x_{j,i,k,t} = 1 \ \forall i, t \quad (3)$$

$$\sum_{j=1, j \neq i}^{N_t} \sum_{k=1}^{V} x_{ijkt} + \sum_{d=1}^{D} \sum_{k=1}^{V} z_{idkt} = 1 \ \forall i, t \quad (4)$$

$$\sum_{d=1}^{D} \sum_{i=1}^{N_t} y_{dikt} - \sum_{d=1}^{D} z_{jdkt} = 0 \ \forall k, t \quad (5)$$

$$\sum_{d=1}^{D} \sum_{i=1}^{N_t} y_{dikt} \widetilde{d}_{it} + \sum_{i=1}^{N_t} \sum_{j=1, j \neq i}^{N_t} x_{ijkt} \widetilde{d}_{jt} \preceq c_k \ \forall k, t \quad (6)$$

$$time_{it} + \widetilde{w}_{ijt} - (1 - x_{ijkt}) M \leq time_{jt} \quad \forall i, j, k, t \quad (7)$$

$$\widetilde{w}'_{djt} - (1 - y_{djkt}) M \leq time_{jt} \quad \forall d, j, k, t \quad (8)$$

$$\sum_{d=1}^{D} y_{dikt} + \sum_{j=1, j \neq i}^{N_t} x_{jikt} - \sum_{j=1, j \neq i}^{N_t} x_{ijkt} - \sum_{d=1}^{D} z_{idkt} = 0 \ \forall i, k, t \quad (9)$$

$$\sum_{i=1}^{N_t} \sum_{j=1, j \neq i}^{N_t} x_{ijkt} \leq M \left(\sum_{d=1}^{D} \sum_{i=1}^{N_t} y_{dikt} \right) \ \forall k, t \tag{10}$$

$$\sum_{i \in B}^{N_t} \sum_{j \in B, j \neq i}^{N_t} x_{ijkt} \leq |B| - 1 \quad \begin{array}{l} \forall k, t, \forall B \subseteq G \backslash \{A\}, \\ |B| \geq 2 \end{array} \tag{11}$$

$$\sum_{d=1}^{D} \sum_{i=1}^{N_t} y_{dikt} \leq 1 \quad \forall k, t \tag{12}$$

$$\sum_{d=1}^{D} s_{kdt} = 1 \ \forall k, t \tag{13}$$

$$\sum_{d=1}^{D} f_{kdt} = 1 \quad \forall k, t \tag{14}$$

$$\sum_{i=1}^{N_t} y_{dikt} \leq s_{kdt} \ \forall k, d, t \tag{15}$$

$$\sum_{i=1}^{N_t} z_{idkt} \leq f_{kdt} \ \forall k, d, t \tag{16}$$

$$f_{kd(t-1)} = s_{kdt} \ \forall k, d, t \geq 2 \tag{17}$$

The problem is to determine optimal routes for vehicles to service customers in a post-disaster logistics network, aiming to minimize total costs while maximizing customer satisfaction under uncertain conditions. The first objective function (1) focuses on minimizing transportation costs, which consist of three components: transportation between customers, between depots and customers, and between customers and depots. Due to the inclusion of fuzzy cost parameters, the objective function is fuzzy. The second objective function (2) aims to enhance customer satisfaction by ensuring that service is expedited for the most demanding customers.

Constraints (3) and (4) guarantee that each customer is served exactly once per period. Constraint (5) stipulates that each vehicle's route begins at one depot and ends at the other one, which is not necessarily the initial depot. Fuzzy constraint (6) requires that the total demand from customers on a vehicle's route must not exceed its capacity. Constraints (7) and (8) ensure the vehicle's route is feasible based on travel times between customers and between customers and depots. Flow conservation is addressed in (9), while (10) specifies that the vehicle's route must begin at a depot. Constraint (11) prevents subtours. Constraint (12) allows for a number of idle vehicles during each time period. Constraints (13) and (14) specify that each vehicle is at one depot at the start and end of each time period. Constraint (15) and (16) show the relationship between variables y_{dikt}, s_{kdt}, z_{idkt}, and f_{kdt}. Also, the relationship between variables f_{kdt} and s_{kdt} is stated in constraint (17).

To overcome fuzziness, the concept of ranking functions is proposed. A Ranking function is a function $\Re : F(R) \rightarrow R$, where $F(R)$ is a set of fuzzy numbers defined on set of real numbers, which maps each fuzzy number into a real line, where a natural order exists. If we let $\widetilde{A} = (a, b, c)$ be a triangular fuzzy number, then $\Re(\widetilde{A}) = \frac{a+2b+c}{4}$. In addition, arithmetic operations between two triangular fuzzy numbers defined on the real set are presented as follows:

If $\widetilde{A}_1 = (a_1, a_2, a_3)$ and $\widetilde{A}_2 = (b_1, b_2, b_3)$ are two triangular fuzzy numbers, then

$$\widetilde{A}_1 + \widetilde{A}_2 = (a_1 + b_1, a_2 + b_2, a_3 + b_3) \tag{18}$$

$$\widetilde{A}_1 \approx \widetilde{A}_2 \Leftrightarrow a_i = b_i, i = 1, 2, 3. \tag{19}$$

$$\widetilde{A}_1 \preceq \widetilde{A}_2 \Leftrightarrow a_i \leq b_i, i = 1, 2, 3. \tag{20}$$

4. Hybrid Multi-Objective Ant Colony System and Simulated Annealing Algorithm

The multi-objective, multi-period integrated routing–scheduling problem is NP-hard, as noted in the Introduction. As a result, many researchers have focused on metaheuristic algorithms to tackle similar challenges. Notably, the ant colony optimization algorithm is a prominent method for addressing various vehicle routing problems [48]. Recently, hybrid metaheuristic algorithms have gained traction for leveraging the strengths of multiple approaches to solve complex optimization issues. This paper proposes a hybrid multi-objective ant colony system combined with a simulated annealing algorithm to tackle the problem.

Ants communicate using pheromones, which are chemical substances they release and detect. When foraging, ants move randomly until they encounter a pheromone trail, which they may choose to follow. The likelihood of an ant selecting a path is influenced by the pheromone density; a higher density increases the chance of selection [40].

In the ant colony optimization (ACO) algorithm, artificial ant colonies work together to tackle complex optimization problems. Ants traverse a network marked by artificial pheromones. The nest represents the initial state, and food signifies the final state. Each vehicle's route begins and ends at a depot, corresponding to the nest and food. Ants probabilistically select adjacent vertices based on pheromone levels on the various edges. Pheromones are stored in a multidimensional matrix reflecting the quantity on each edge over time. Each ant deposits pheromones on its path, which is influenced by the value of the objective function. To prevent local optima, pheromone levels gradually evaporate. Constraints are checked whenever an ant selects a new customer to ensure compliance with problem requirements. Additionally, heuristic information is employed to avoid stagnation in local optima.

To apply the ant colony optimization algorithm for multi-objective problems, multiple ant colonies sequentially explore the solution space to find better solutions. Each ant searches the network to generate a solution. These solutions are then compared, resulting in a set of nondominated solutions referred to as the colony's optimal Pareto set [49]. Assuming S1 and S2 to be two feasible solutions for a multi-objective minimization problem, if none of the objective functions achieved by S1 are larger than the objective functions corresponding to S2 and at least one objective function achieved by S1 is smaller than S2, S1 dominates S2. The pheromone of the edges belonging to the optimal Pareto set is increased so that the next colony can better discover the solutions found by the current colony. Part of the pheromone also evaporates regularly on all edges. The main operators of the multi-objective ant colony system are stated in the following.

4.1. Pheromone Structure

This algorithm employs two distinct pheromone trails for two objective functions, which are updated separately at the end of each iteration. The use of multiple pheromone trails to address various multi-objective problems has been explored in several studies, including unequal area facility layout, secure routing for wireless sensor networks, minimizing total completion time and energy costs in single-machine preemptive scheduling, and mixed-load school bus routing [49,50].

4.2. Heuristic Information

The heuristic information is determined based on three factors:

The travelling cost between customers i and j;

The travelling time $time_{it}$;

The amount of demand $\tilde{d}_{jt}$ of customer j;

For ant k located at customer i, two separate pieces of heuristic information corresponding to the two objective functions of the problem are defined as follows:

$$\eta_{ijt}^{C} = \frac{1}{c_{ijt}} \tag{21}$$

$$\eta_{ijt}^{S} = \frac{1}{time_{jt} d_{jt}} \tag{22}$$

4.3. Quasi-Random Probability Rule

When ant k is at the location of customer i, the next customer from the neighborhood of customer i in period t is selected based on the following quasi-random probability rule:

$$j = \begin{cases} \text{argmax}_{l \in N_i^{kt}} \left\{ \left[\left(\tau_{ijt}^C\right)^\alpha \left(\eta_{ijt}^C\right)^\beta \right]^\lambda \left[\left(\tau_{ijt}^S\right)^\alpha \left(\eta_{ijt}^S\right)^\beta \right]^{1-\lambda} \right\} & N_i^{kt} \neq \varnothing, q \leq q_0 \\ j^* & o.w. \end{cases} \tag{23}$$

in which $0 \leq q_0 \leq 1$ is a random parameter and j^* is a random variable selected based the following random probability rule:

$$p_{ij}^t = \frac{\left[\left(\tau_{ijt}^C\right)^\alpha \left(\eta_{ijt}^C\right)^\beta \right]^\lambda \left[\left(\tau_{ijt}^S\right)^\alpha \left(\eta_{ijt}^S\right)^\beta \right]^{1-\lambda}}{\sum_{j' \in N_i^{k,t}} \left[\left(\tau_{ij't}^C\right)^\alpha \left(\eta_{ij't}^C\right)^\beta \right]^\lambda \left[\left(\tau_{ij't}^S\right)^\alpha \left(\eta_{ij't}^S\right)^\beta \right]^{1-\lambda}} \quad j \in N_i^{kt} \tag{24}$$

in which α, β and λ are parameters. The value of λ is obtained based on the following relation:

$$\lambda = \begin{cases} 0 & k \leq a \\ \frac{k}{b-a} - \frac{a}{b-a} & a < k < b \\ 1 & k \geq b \end{cases} \tag{25}$$

where a and b are two parameters. According to the definition of λ, some ants use only information about one of the objective functions, while others use information about both objective functions.

The decision rule to service customer j after i in period t is defined as follows:

$$p_{(i,j)}^t = \begin{cases} \frac{\left[\left(\tau_{ijt}^C\right)^\lambda \left(\tau_{ijt}^S\right)^{1-\lambda} \right]^\alpha \left[\eta_{ijt}\right]^\beta}{\sum_{j' \in N_i} \left[\left(\tau_{ij't}^C\right)^\lambda \left(\tau_{ij't}^S\right)^{1-\lambda} \right]^\alpha \left[\eta_{ij't}\right]^\beta} & j \in N_i \\ 0 & o.w. \end{cases} \tag{26}$$

in which $\lambda \in (0,1)$ indicates the relative importance of the objective functions. Also, α and β are two parameters that indicate the ant's relative tendency to follow the path using pheromone information and heuristic information, respectively.

4.4. Pheromone Update

The pheromone level of each link is updated through two mechanisms. The evaporation rule reduces the pheromone of each selected link according to the following evaporation rate:

$$\tau_{ijt}^C \leftarrow (1-\xi)\tau_{ijt}^C \tag{27}$$

$$\tau_{ijt}^S \leftarrow (1-\xi)\tau_{ijt}^S \tag{28}$$

in which $0 < \xi < 1$ is a parameter. In this way, after selection of customer j after i in period t, its corresponding pheromone trail is reduced by a ratio of $1-\xi$ and its desirability is reduced for subsequent selections.

The pheromone levels on the links of the colony's Pareto-optimal solutions are updated in each iteration as follows:

$$\tau_{ijt}^C = \min\left\{1, \tau_{ijt}^C \cdot \rho + \frac{Q}{C}\right\} \tag{29}$$

$$\tau_{ijt}^S = \min\left\{1, \tau_{ijt}^S \cdot \rho + \frac{Q}{S}\right\} \tag{30}$$

in which C is the sum of the cost of Pareto-optimal solutions and S is the sum of $time_{it} * d_{it}$ where customer i is located in one of the Pareto-optimal solutions.

In each iteration of the multi-objective ant colony system, a set of feasible solutions was generated, which were then evaluated using the simulated annealing algorithm. This optimization technique, inspired by the gradual cooling of metals, helps the system reach its lowest-energy state by reducing atomic movements. It is effective in identifying global optimal solutions, as it prevents getting stuck in local optima within the search space. The steps of the proposed hybrid algorithm are as follows:

Step 1: Initialize all parameters of the multi-objective ant colony system.

Step 2: Initialize the computational temperature T to a great value.

Step 3: For each colony c and ant k, construct a solution s.

Step 4: If the constructed solution s is non-dominated by the current Pareto set (PS), accept it. Otherwise, evaluate the solution based on Equation (31) and accept it with the probability $P = -\frac{E(s)}{T}$.

$$E(s) = \min_{s^* \in PS} \sqrt{(f_1(s) - f_1(s^*))^2 + (f_2(s) - f_2(s^*))^2} \quad (31)$$

Step 5: Update the pheromone trail.

Step 6: Update the temperature T according to the cooling schedule (32) and repeat steps 3–6 until the temperature is small according to the following formula:

$$T(n) = \frac{1}{\rho + 1}(\rho + \tanh(\gamma^n))T(n-1), \quad (32)$$

where $\rho = 4$ and γ is a parameter between 0.8 and 0.99.

In the following section, various numerical experiments have been carried out to assess the effectiveness of the proposed algorithm.

5. Numerical Results

This section provides numerical examples illustrating the effectiveness of the proposed hybrid multi-objective ant colony system and simulated annealing algorithm, along with a discussion on model validation. The algorithm was implemented on a computer with 8 GB of RAM and a 1.6 GHz CPU.

In the first experiment, we selected the optimal algorithm parameters. The number of ants varied based on the number of customers across different periods; as customer numbers increase, the solution space expands, necessitating more ants for an effective search. According to the introduced quasi-random probability law, some ants rely solely on the first objective function, while others focus exclusively on the second, generating Pareto-optimal solutions. The remaining ants utilize a combination of both objective functions. In our tests, the number of ants using information from both objective functions was fewer than those using either function individually. This occurs because finding a Pareto-optimal solution is considerably more complex for ants relying on a single objective function. Other parameter values were determined experimentally and are listed in Table 1.

Table 1. The values of the parameters of the algorithm.

Parameter	a	b	q_0	ρ	ξ	α	β	T
Value	1.2	2.25	0.9	0.9	0.1	2	1	100

The second experiment presents a small example demonstrating the key concepts and results of the proposed model and solution approach. It involves a two-objective, two-period fuzzy vehicle routing and scheduling problem with seven disaster centers and two distribution centers. The problem's parameters are detailed in Tables 2–4.

Table 2. The values of parameters $\widetilde{c}_{ijt}$, $\widetilde{c}'_{dit}$, $\widetilde{w}_{ijt}$, and $\widetilde{w}'_{dit}$ for $t = 1$.

		Customers						
		1	2	3	4	5	6	7
Customers	1		(9,12,15) (12,13,14)	(20,19,22) (13,16,19)	(28,30,33) (23,24,26)	(17,21,22) (14,18,19)	(15,17,19) (21,23,25)	(20,22,23) (21,23,25)
	2	(9,12,15) (12,13,14)		(13,15,16) (17,19,20)	(33,36,38) (6,7,9)	(20,21,24) (9,11,13)	(28,29,30) (16,18,20)	(34,35,36) (11,12,14)
	3	(20,19,22) (13,16,19)	(13,15,16) (17,19,20)		(45,48,50) (17,18,20)	(33,35,36) (13,14,18)	(34,35,37) (12,13,15)	(32,35,38) (12,14,15)
	4	(28,30,33) (23,24,26)	(33,36,38) (6,7,9)	(45,48,50) (17,18,20)		(18,20,23) (12,13,15)	(18,20,23) (15,18,19)	(33,34,37) (18,19,21)
	5	(17,21,22) (14,18,19)	(20,21,24) (9,11,13)	(33,35,36) (13,14,18)	(18,20,23) (12,13,15)		(24,25,26) (9,11,13)	(37,38,41) (9,11,14)
	6	(15,17,19) (21,23,25)	(28,29,30) (16,18,20)	(34,35,37) (12,13,15)	(18,20,23) (15,18,19)	(24,25,26) (9,11,13)		(15,18,20) (17,18,19)
	7	(20,22,23) (21,23,25)	(34,35,36) (11,12,14)	(32,35,38) (12,14,15)	(33,34,37) (18,19,21)	(37,38,41) (9,11,14)	(15,18,20) (17,18,19)	
Depots	1	(12,16,18) (7,9,12)	(10,13,14) (14,16,18)	(13,14,17) (12,16,20)	(21,22,24) (21,23,25)	(16,20,21) (12,15,16)	(5,7,8) (14,17,18)	(13,16,21) (19,22,24)
	2	(15,17,19) (13,14,16)	(12,15,16) (5,7,8)	(27,30,32) (13,15,19)	(18,23,24) (11,14,15)	(8,10,12) (25,26,27)	(18,19,21) (10,14,15)	(12,15,17) (16,18,20)

Table 3. The values of parameters $\widetilde{c}_{ijt}$, $\widetilde{c}'_{dit}$, $\widetilde{w}_{ijt}$, and $\widetilde{w}'_{dit}$ for $t = 2$.

		Customers						
		1	2	3	4	5	6	7
Customers	1		(32,35,36) (14,15,16)	(42,45,47) (8,10,12)	(21,23,25) (13,16,17)	(28,30,33) (32,34,36)	(43,44,45) (18,19,21)	(25,27,28) (10,12,17)
	2	(32,35,36) (14,15,16)		(10,12,15) (24,25,26)	(11,12,15) (18,19,23)	(18,20,24) (11,13,15)	(45,47,48) (6,8,9)	(40,43,44) (10,12,13)
	3	(42,45,47) (8,10,12)	(10,12,15) (24,25,26)		(20,22,23) (18,19,20)	(21,23,25) (15,18,19)	(44,45,47) (22,24,25)	(43,44,46) (19,20,22)
	4	(21,23,25) (13,16,17)	(11,12,15) (18,19,23)	(20,22,23) (18,19,20)		(12,13,15) (24,26,27)	(38,40,42) (15,17,18)	(28,30,31) (10,13,14)
	5	(28,30,33) (32,34,36)	(18,20,24) (11,13,15)	(21,23,25) (15,18,19)	(12,13,15) (22,24,25)		(21,23,27) (18,19,21)	(19,20,22) (23,25,26)
	6	(43,44,45) (18,19,21)	(45,47,48) (6,8,9)	(44,45,47) (22,24,25)	(38,40,42) (15,17,18)	(21,23,27) (18,19,21)		(15,16,18) (13,15,16)
	7	(25,27,28) (10,12,17)	(40,43,44) (10,12,13)	(43,44,46) (19,20,22)	(28,30,31) (10,13,14)	(19,20,22) (23,25,26)	(15,16,18) (13,15,16)	

Table 3. *Cont.*

		Customers						
Depots	1	(6,8,9) (14,16,18)	(12,15,18) (12,17,18)	(9,10,12) (14,15,16)	(14,16,18) (11,15,18)	(14,15,19) (12,15,16)	(7,9,10) (10,13,15)	(25,26,28) (10,13,15)
	2	(10,13,14) (10,13,15)	(23,24,26) (15,18,19)	(7,12,13) (9,10,12)	(8,11,12) (21,23,24)	(12,14,16) (17,18,20)	(13,14,17) (14,17,18)	(18,23,24) (10,13,15)

Table 4. Fuzzy demand of disaster centers in two periods.

	Periods	
Customers	**1**	**2**
1	(4,9,12)	(12,13,17)
2	(16,18,22)	(17,18,20)
3	(7,11,13)	(12,15,16)
4	(13,15,18)	(16,18,19)
5	(8,12,13)	(10,13,16)
6	(15,18,20)	(12,17,22)
7	(14,15,18)	(12,15,16)

Table 5 displays the Pareto-optimal solutions for the small example, detailing the vehicle routes that include both distribution and disaster centers. Figure 1 illustrates Pareto-optimal solution #1. The last column of Table 5 outlines the service schedules for disaster centers. The small example was also solved using AMPL (A Mathematical Programming Language) for comparison. While the objective function values from AMPL matched those from the proposed approach, the execution time in AMPL was over three times longer.

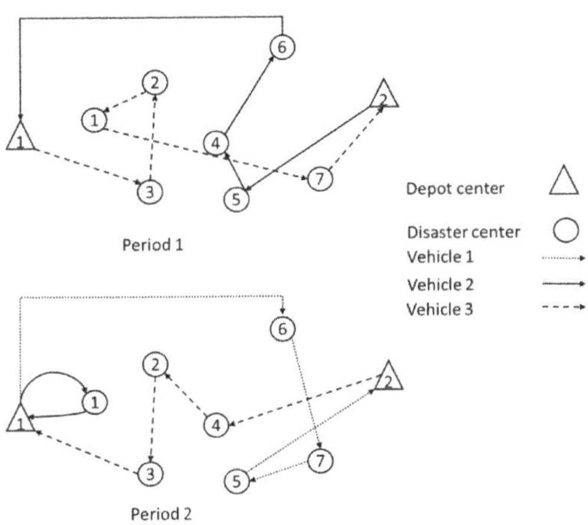

Figure 1. Graphical representation of Pareto-optimal solution #1.

In the third experiment, benchmark examples were utilized to evaluate the performance of the proposed model and solution approach for medium and large problems. These examples were created by combining the standard benchmarks of the multi-depot vehicle routing problem, which are available at http://www.bernabe.dorronsoro.es/vrp/ (accessed on November 2006). The details of the generated examples are presented in Table 6.

Table 5. The set of Pareto-optimal solutions.

Solution	Values of Objective Functions	Routes of Vehicles	Customer Service Schedule
1	$f_1 = 256.2$ $f_2 = 8040$	$t = 1, k = 3: 1 \to 3 \to 2 \to 1 \to 7 \to 2$ $t = 1, k = 2: 2 \to 5 \to 4 \to 6 \to 1$ $t = 2, k = 3: 2 \to 4 \to 2 \to 3 \to 1$ $t = 2, k = 1: 1 \to 6 \to 7 \to 5 \to 2$ $t = 2, k = 2: 1 \to 1 \to 1$	$time_{11} = 48,\ time_{12} = 16$ $time_{21} = 35,\ time_{22} = 42$ $time_{31} = 16,\ time_{32} = 67$ $time_{41} = 39,\ time_{42} = 23$ $time_{51} = 26,\ time_{52} = 53$ $time_{61} = 57,\ time_{62} = 13$ $time_{71} = 71,\ time_{72} = 28$
2	$f_1 = 257.7$ $f_2 = 8000$	$t = 1, k = 1: 1 \to 3 \to 2 \to 1 \to 7 \to 1$ $t = 1, k = 2: 2 \to 5 \to 4 \to 6 \to 1$ $t = 2, k = 1: 1 \to 3 \to 2 \to 4 \to 2$ $t = 2, k = 2: 1 \to 6 \to 7 \to 5 \to 2$ $t = 2, k = 3: 1 \to 1 \to 1$	$time_{11} = 48,\ time_{12} = 16$ $time_{21} = 35,\ time_{22} = 40$ $time_{31} = 16,\ time_{32} = 15$ $time_{41} = 39,\ time_{42} = 63.3$ $time_{51} = 26,\ time_{52} = 53$ $time_{61} = 57,\ time_{62} = 13$ $time_{71} = 71,\ time_{72} = 28$
3	$f_1 = 267.6$ $f_2 = 7000$	$t = 1, k = 3: 1 \to 1 \to 2 \to 3 \to 1$ $t = 1, k = 2: 2 \to 5 \to 4 \to 6 \to 1$ $t = 1, k = 1: 2 \to 7 \to 1$ $t = 2, k = 1: 1 \to 3 \to 2 \to 4 \to 2$ $t = 2, k = 2: 1 \to 6 \to 7 \to 5 \to 2$ $t = 2, k = 3: 1 \to 1 \to 1$	$time_{11} = 9,\ time_{12} = 16$ $time_{21} = 22,\ time_{22} = 40$ $time_{31} = 41,\ time_{32} = 15$ $time_{41} = 42.64,\ time_{42} = 59$ $time_{51} = 26,\ time_{52} = 53$ $time_{61} = 60.64,\ time_{62} = 13$ $time_{71} = 18,\ time_{72} = 28$
4	$f_1 = 270$ $f_2 = 6500$	$t = 1, k = 3: 2 \to 4 \to 5 \to 2$ $t = 1, k = 2: 1 \to 1 \to 2 \to 3 \to 1$ $t = 1, k = 1: 2 \to 7 \to 6 \to 1$ $t = 2, k = 1: 1 \to 6 \to 7 \to 5 \to 2$ $t = 2, k = 2: 1 \to 1 \to 1$ $t = 2, k = 3: 1 \to 4 \to 2 \to 3 \to 2$	$time_{11} = 9,\ time_{12} = 16$ $time_{21} = 22,\ time_{22} = 42$ $time_{31} = 41,\ time_{32} = 67$ $time_{41} = 14,\ time_{42} = 23$ $time_{51} = 28,\ time_{52} = 54.4$ $time_{61} = 36,\ time_{62} = 13$ $time_{71} = 18,\ time_{72} = 29.4$

Table 6. The specification of the benchmark examples.

Instance	Number of Periods	Number of Depots	Number of Vehicles
P01, P02	2	5	10
P01, P03	2	5	10
P01, P04	2	5	10
P02, P03	2	5	10
P02, P04	2	5	10
P03, P04	2	5	10
P01, P02, P03	3	5	10
P01, P02, P04	3	5	10
P01, P03, P04	3	5	10
P02, P03, P04	3	5	10
P01, P02, P03, P04	4	5	10

This section compares the performance of the proposed hybrid multi-objective ant colony system and simulated annealing algorithm with the multi-objective cat swarm optimization (MCSO) algorithm [51,52] and multi-objective fitness-dependent optimizer (MOFDO) algorithm [27]. Table 7 presents the average values of the two objective functions for the nondominated solutions identified by each algorithm in every instance. The fifth and seventh columns of Table 7 indicate the percentage differences between the nondominated solutions produced by the algorithms.

Table 7. Comparing the performance of the proposed hybrid algorithm with the MCSO and MOFDO algorithms.

Instance		Hybrid Algorithm (This Paper)	MCSO Algorithm		MOFDO Algorithm	
				Difference (Percent)		Difference (Percent)
P01, P02	f_1	1362.74	1362.74	0	1358.25	−0.33
	f_2	4017.75	4145.76	3.08	4103.41	2.08
	Time(s)	78	53		79	
P01, P03	f_1	1356.09	1359.93	0.28	1356.09	0
	f_2	4829.72	4857.84	0.57	4834.67	0.1
	Time(s)	85	89		98	
P01, P04	f_1	1789.09	1799.18	0.56	1795.76	0.37
	f_2	6439.96	6521.84	1.25	6524.67	1.29
	Time(s)	87	83		93	
P02, P03	f_1	2061.18	2156.87	4.43	2174.57	5.21
	f_2	5582.74	5879.67	5.05	5634.25	0.91
	Time(s)	91	95		94	
P02, P04	f_1	1937.3	1987.56	2.52	1954.37	0.87
	f_2	6939.07	6921.23	−0.25	6930.14	−0.12
	Time(s)	123	111		131	
P03, P04	f_1	2154.91	2161.76	0.31	2152.45	−0.11
	f_2	6302.44	6412.56	1.71	6401.27	1.54
	Time(s)	145	156		163	
P01, P02, P03	f_1	2459.97	2598.76	5.34	2540.31	3.16
	f_2	5581	5987.3	6.78	5772.13	3.31
	Time(s)	234	254		250	
P01, P02, P04	f_1	2885.83	2956.87	2.4	2871.76	−0.48
	f_2	7542.17	7823.18	3.59	7792.54	3.21
	Time(s)	257	261		260	
P01, P03, P04	f_1	3055.55	3167.67	3.53	3047.75	−0.25
	f_2	6664.19	6718.19	0.8	6692.14	0.41
	Time(s)	247	259		264	
P02, P03, P04	f_1	3321.51	3478.98	4.52	3214.73	−3.32
	f_2	8597.18	9783.45	12.12	8673.54	0.88
	Time(s)	298	345		367	
P01, P02, P03, P04	f_1	4689.39	4893.91	4.17	4713.98	0.52
	f_2	8853.29	8976.76	1.37	8852.73	−0.01
	Time(s)	376	671		895	

The comparison of the proposed hybrid multi-objective ant colony system and simulated annealing algorithm with the MCSO algorithm demonstrates that the hybrid approach is highly effective in achieving lower objective function values, as indicated in Table 7.

Additionally, in 8 out of 11 test instances, the hybrid algorithm provided solutions in less CPU time than the MCSO algorithm.

While it is evident that our proposed hybrid algorithm typically demonstrates superior performance overall, the MOFDO algorithm outperforms it in some instances. Specifically, in 4 out of a total of 11 different cases analyzed, the MOFDO algorithm produced an f_1 value that was lower than the corresponding f_1 value generated by our proposed algorithm. Furthermore, when examining the accuracy of the f_2 values, we discovered that in 2 of the 11 cases, the MOFDO algorithm yields more precise results compared to our proposed algorithm. This shows that although our algorithm is generally more effective, the MOFDO algorithm can still excel in particular scenarios.

Figure 2 compares the execution times of the three algorithms. The results show that the proposed algorithm consistently outperforms the MCSO algorithm in execution time. Furthermore, the MOFDO algorithm has consumed longer execution times in all cases. In general, the proposed hybrid algorithm typically produces results that are better or at least comparable to those of the MCSO and MOFDO algorithms, according to the findings reported.

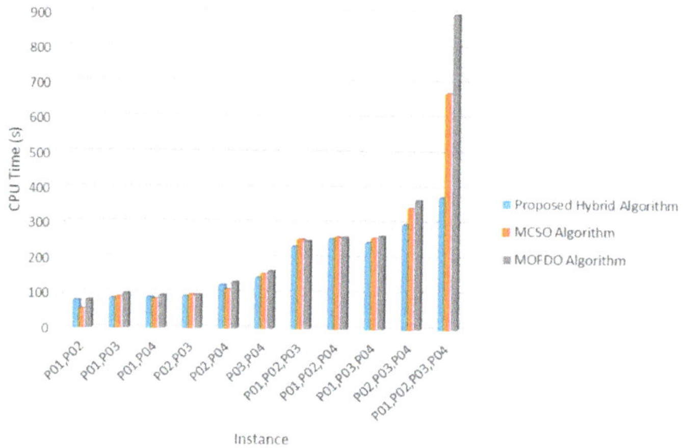

Figure 2. Comparing the execution times of the algorithms.

6. Conclusions and Future Directions

This paper addresses the multi-objective, multi-period integrated routing and scheduling problem for distributing relief to disaster areas under uncertain conditions. We propose a fuzzy multi-objective integer programming model to formulate the problem. To solve it, we developed a hybrid multi-objective heuristic algorithm that combines a multi-objective ant colony system with a simulated annealing algorithm. A small example illustrated the key concepts of our model and solution approach. Additionally, benchmark instances were used to evaluate the performance of the hybrid algorithm, comparing the results to those of a multi-objective cat swarm optimization algorithm and multi-objective fitness-dependent optimizer algorithm. The findings indicate that our hybrid algorithm effectively finds solutions with lower objective function values in a relatively short computation time in most cases. Future research could explore problem decomposition and customer selection strategies to enhance algorithm performance, along with the implementation of more powerful heuristic operators. Additionally, due to the limited supply and time in the early periods, it is applicable to expand the model to distribute relief based on specific periods.

Author Contributions: Conceptualization, M.N., A.M.D. and M.S.; methodology, J.T. and D.E.S.; validation, A.M.D. and D.E.S.; formal analysis, A.M.D.; investigation, M.N. and M.S.; resources, M.N. and M.S.; data curation, M.N., M.S. and J.T.; writing—original draft preparation, M.N., J.T. and M.S.; writing—review and editing, A.M.D. and D.E.S.; supervision, J.T. All authors have read and agreed to the published version of the manuscript.

Funding: This research received no external funding.

Data Availability Statement: The original contributions presented in the study are included in the article, further inquiries can be directed to the corresponding author.

Conflicts of Interest: The authors declare no conflicts of interest.

References

1. Rojas Trejos, C.A.; Meisel, J.D.; Adarme Jaimes, W. Humanitarian aid distribution logistics with accessibility constraints: A systematic literature review. *J. Humanit. Logist. Supply Chain Manag.* **2023**, *13*, 26–41. [CrossRef]
2. Ngueveu, S.U.; Prins, C.; Calvo, R.W. An effective memetic algorithm for the cumulative capacitated vehicle routing problem. *Comput. Oper. Res.* **2010**, *37*, 1877–1885. [CrossRef]
3. Wang, Y.; Shi, Q.; Hu, Q. Dynamic multi-objective optimization for multi-period emergency logistics network. *J. Intell. Fuzzy Syst.* **2019**, *37*, 8471–8481. [CrossRef]
4. Zahedi, A.; Kargari, M.; Kashan, A.H. Multi-objective decision-making model for distribution planning of goods and routing of vehicles in emergency multi-objective decision-making model for distribution planning of goods and routing of vehicles in emergency. *Int. J. Disaster Risk Reduct.* **2020**, *48*, 101587. [CrossRef]
5. Ebrahimi, S.B. A stochastic multi-objective location-allocation-routing problem for tire supply chain considering sustainability aspects and quantity discounts. *J. Clean. Prod.* **2018**, *198*, 704–720. [CrossRef]
6. Wan, M.; Ye, C.; Peng, D. Multi-period dynamic multi-objective emergency material distribution model under uncertain demand. *Eng. Appl. Artif. Intell.* **2023**, *117*, 105530. [CrossRef]
7. Yang, M.; Ni, Y.; Yang, L. A multi-objective consistent home healthcare routing and scheduling problem in an uncertain environment. *Comput. Ind. Eng.* **2021**, *160*, 107560. [CrossRef]
8. Bodaghi, B.; Shahparvari, S.; Fadaki, M.; Lau, K.H.; Ekambaram, P.; Chhetri, P. Multi-resource scheduling and routing for emergency recovery operations. *Int. J. Disaster Risk Reduct.* **2020**, *50*, 101780. [CrossRef]
9. Mamashli, Z.; Nayeri, S.; Tavakkoli-Moghaddam, R.; Sazvar, Z.; Javadian, N. Designing a sustainable–resilient disaster waste management system under hybrid uncertainty: A case study. *Eng. Appl. Artif. Intell.* **2021**, *106*, 104459. [CrossRef]
10. Sun, H.; Wang, Y.; Xue, Y. A bi-objective robust optimization model for disaster response planning under uncertainties. *Comput. Ind. Eng.* **2021**, *155*, 107213. [CrossRef]
11. Wang, B.C.; Qian, Q.Y.; Gao, J.J.; Tan, Z.Y.; Zhou, Y. The optimization of warehouse location and resources distribution for emergency rescue under uncertainty. *Adv. Eng. Inform.* **2021**, *48*, 101278. [CrossRef]
12. Knott, R.P. Vehicle scheduling for emergency relief management: A knowledge-based approach. *Disasters* **1988**, *12*, 285–293. [CrossRef]
13. Anuar, W.K.; Lee, L.S.; Pickl, S.; Seow, H.V. Vehicle routing optimisation in humanitarian operations: A survey on modelling and optimisation approaches. *Appl. Sci.* **2021**, *11*, 667. [CrossRef]
14. Maroof, A.; Khalid, Q.S.; Mahmood, M.; Naeem, K.; Maqsood, S.; Khattak, S.B.; Ayvaz, B. Vehicle routing optimization for humanitarian supply chain: A systematic review of approaches and solutions. *IEEE Access* **2023**, *11*, 10311589. [CrossRef]
15. Dukkanci, O.; Campbell, J.F.; Kara, B.Y. Facility location decisions for drone delivery: A literature review. *Eur. J. Oper. Res.* **2023**, *316*, 397–418. [CrossRef]
16. Khalili, S.M.; Mojtahedi, M.; Steinmetz-Weiss, C.; Sanderson, D. A Systematic Literature Review on Transit-Based Evacuation Planning in Emergency Logistics Management: Optimisation and Modelling Approaches. *Buildings* **2024**, *14*, 176. [CrossRef]
17. Golabi, M.; Shavarani, S.M.; Izbirak, G. An edge-based stochastic facility location problem in UAV-supported humanitarian relief logistics: A case study of Tehran earthquake. *Nat. Hazards* **2017**, *87*, 1545–1565. [CrossRef]
18. Barzinpour, F.; Saffarian, M.; Makoui, A.; Teimoury, E. Metaheuristic Algorithm for Solving Biobjective Possibility Planning Model of Location-Allocation in Disaster Relief Logistics. *J. Appl. Math.* **2014**, *2014*, 239868. [CrossRef]
19. Cao, C.; Li, C.; Yang, Q.; Liu, Y.; Qu, T. A novel multi-objective programming model of relief distribution for sustainable disaster supply chain in large-scale natural disasters. *J. Clean. Prod.* **2018**, *174*, 1422–1435. [CrossRef]
20. Wang, Y.; Wang, L.; Chen, G.; Cai, Z.; Zhou, Y.; Xing, L. An improved ant colony optimization algorithm to the periodic vehicle routing problem with time window and service choice. *Swarm Evol. Comput.* **2020**, *55*, 100675. [CrossRef]
21. Sadati, M.E.H.; Çatay, B.; Aksen, D. An efficient variable neighborhood search with tabu shaking for a class of multi-depot vehicle routing problems. *Comput. Oper. Res.* **2021**, *133*, 105269. [CrossRef]
22. Keskin, M.; Branke, J.; Deineko, V.; Strauss, A.K. Dynamic multi-period vehicle routing with touting. *Eur. J. Oper. Res.* **2023**, *310*, 168–184. [CrossRef]

23. Li, X.; Xu, Y.; Lai, K.K.; Ji, H.; Xu, Y.; Li, J. a multi-period vehicle routing problem for emergency perishable materials under uncertain demand based on an improved whale optimization algorithm. *Mathematics* **2022**, *10*, 3124. [CrossRef]
24. Zhang, J.; Li, Y.; Lu, Z. Multi-period vehicle routing problem with time windows for drug distribution in the epidemic situation. *Transp. Res. Part C Emerg. Technol.* **2024**, *160*, 104484. [CrossRef]
25. Deb, K.; Pratap, A.; Agarwal, S.; Meyarivan, T.A.M.T. A fast and elitist multiobjective genetic algorithm: NSGA-II. *IEEE Trans. Evol. Comput.* **2002**, *6*, 182–197. [CrossRef]
26. Rahman, C.M.; Rashid, T.A.; Ahmed, A.M.; Mirjalili, S. Multi-objective learner performance-based behavior algorithm with five multi-objective real-world engineering problems. *Neural Comput. Appl.* **2022**, *34*, 6307–6329. [CrossRef]
27. Abdullah, J.M.; Rashid, T.A.; Maaroof, B.B.; Mirjalili, S. Multi-objective fitness-dependent optimizer algorithm. *Neural Comput. Appl.* **2023**, *35*, 11969–11987. [CrossRef]
28. Rath, S.; Gutjahr, W.J. A math-heuristic for the warehouse location–routing problem in disaster relief. *Comput. Oper. Res.* **2014**, *42*, 25–39. [CrossRef]
29. Ahmadi, M.; Seifi, A.; Tootooni, B. A humanitarian logistics model for disaster relief operation considering network failure and standard relief time: A case study on San Francisco district. *Transp. Res. Part E Logist. Transp. Rev.* **2015**, *75*, 145–163. [CrossRef]
30. Mohammadi, S.; Darestani, S.A.; Vahdani, B.; Alinezhad, A. A robust neutrosophic fuzzy-based approach to integrate reliable facility location and routing decisions for disaster relief under fairness and aftershocks concerns. *Comput. Ind. Eng.* **2020**, *148*, 106734. [CrossRef]
31. Vahdani, B.; Veysmoradi, D.; Noori, F.; Mansour, F. Two-stage multi-objective location-routing-inventory model for humanitarian logistics network design under uncertainty. *Int. J. Disaster Risk Reduct.* **2018**, *27*, 290–306. [CrossRef]
32. Yu, X.; Zhou, Y.; Liu, X.F. The two-echelon multi-objective location routing problem inspired by realistic waste collection applications: The composable model and a metaheuristic algorithm. *Appl. Soft Comput.* **2020**, *94*, 106477. [CrossRef]
33. Zajac, S.; Huber, S. Objectives and methods in multi-objective routing problems: A survey and classification scheme. *Eur. J. Oper. Res.* **2021**, *290*, 1–25. [CrossRef]
34. Barbarosoğlu, G.; Özdamar, L.; Cevik, A. An interactive approach for hierarchical analysis of helicopter logistics in disaster relief operations. *Eur. J. Oper. Res.* **2002**, *140*, 118–133. [CrossRef]
35. Yang, M.; Liu, Y.; Yang, G. Multi-period dynamic distributionally robust pre-positioning of emergency supplies under demand uncertainty. *Appl. Math. Model.* **2021**, *89*, 1433–1458. [CrossRef]
36. Uslu, A.; Cetinkaya, C.; İşleyen, S.K. Vehicle routing problem in post-disaster humanitarian relief logistics: A case study in Ankara. *Sigma J. Eng. Nat. Sci.* **2017**, *35*, 481–499.
37. Saffarian, M.; Barzinpour, F.; Eghbali, M.A. A robust programming approach to bi-objective optimization model in the disaster relief logistics response phase. *Int. J. Supply Oper. Manag.* **2015**, *2*, 595–616. [CrossRef]
38. Akbarpour, M.; Torabi, S.A.; Ghavamifar, A. Designing an integrated pharmaceutical relief chain network under demand uncertainty. *Transp. Res. Part E Logist. Transp. Rev.* **2020**, *136*, 101867. [CrossRef]
39. Rawls, C.G.; Turnquist, M.A. pre-positioning of emergency supplies for disaster response. *Transp. Res. Part B Methodol.* **2010**, *44*, 521–534. [CrossRef]
40. Liu, J.; Liu, J. applying multi-objective ant colony optimization algorithm for solving the unequal area facility layout problems. *Appl. Soft Comput.* **2019**, *74*, 167–189. [CrossRef]
41. Safaei, A.S.; Farsad, S.; Paydar, M.M. Emergency logistics planning under supply risk and demand uncertainty. *Oper. Res.* **2020**, *20*, 1437–1460. [CrossRef]
42. Yu, W. Pre-disaster location and storage model for emergency commodities considering both randomness and uncertainty. *Saf. Sci.* **2021**, *141*, 105330. [CrossRef]
43. Wan, S.P.; Chen, Z.H.; Dong, J.Y. Bi-objective trapezoidal fuzzy mixed integer linear program-based distribution center location decision for large-scale emergencies. *Appl. Soft Comput.* **2021**, *110*, 107757. [CrossRef]
44. Najafi, M.; Eshghi, K.; Dullaert, W. A multi-objective robust optimization model for logistics planning in the earthquake response phase. *Transp. Res. Part E Logist. Trans. Rev.* **2013**, *49*, 217–249. [CrossRef]
45. Tang, Z.; Li, W.; Yu, S.; Sun, J. A fuzzy multi-objective programming optimization model for emergency resource dispatching under equitable distribution principle. *J. Intell. Fuzzy Syst.* **2021**, *41*, 5107–5116. [CrossRef]
46. Fazayeli, S.; Eydi, A.; Kamalabadi, I.N. Location-routing problem in multimodal transportation network with time windows and fuzzy demands: Presenting a two-part genetic algorithm. *Comput. Ind. Eng.* **2018**, *119*, 233–246. [CrossRef]
47. Modiri, M.; Eskandari, M.; Hasanzadeh, S. Multi-objective modeling of relief items distribution network design problem in disaster relief logistics considering transportation system and CO_2 emission. *Sci. Iran.* **2022**, *in press*. [CrossRef]
48. Elshaer, R.; Awad, H. A taxonomic review of metaheuristic algorithms for solving the vehicle routing problem and its variants. *Comput. Ind. Eng.* **2020**, *140*, 106242. [CrossRef]
49. Li, W.; Xia, L.; Huang, Y.; Mahmoodi, S. An Ant colony optimization algorithm with adaptive greedy strategy to optimize path problems. *J. Ambient Intell. Humaniz. Comput.* **2022**, *13*, 1–15. [CrossRef]
50. Sun, Z.; Wei, M.; Zhang, Z.; Qu, G. Secure routing protocol based on multi-objective ant-colony-optimization for wireless sensor networks. *Appl. Soft Comput.* **2019**, *77*, 366–375. [CrossRef]

51. Pradhan, P.M.; Panda, G. solving multiobjective problems using cat swarm optimization. *Expert Syst. Appl.* **2012**, *39*, 2956–2964. [CrossRef]
52. Ahmed, A.M.; Rashid, T.A.; Saeed, S.A.M. Cat swarm optimization algorithm: A survey and performance evaluation. *Comput. Intell. Neurosci.* **2020**, *2020*, 4854895. [CrossRef] [PubMed]

mathematics MDPI

Article

Discrete Pseudo-Quasi Overlap Functions and Their Applications in Fuzzy Multi-Attribute Group Decision-Making

Mei Jing [1], Jingqian Wang [2], Mei Wang [1] and Xiaohong Zhang [1,2,*]

[1] School of Electrical and Control Engineering, Shaanxi University of Science & Technology, Xi'an 710021, China; jingmei1221@163.com (M.J.); wangmeimath@163.com (M.W.)
[2] School of Mathematics and Data Science, Shaanxi University of Science & Technology, Xi'an 710021, China; wangjingqianw@163.com
* Correspondence: zhangxiaohong@sust.edu.cn

Abstract: The overlap function, a continuous aggregation function, is widely used in classification, decision-making, image processing, etc. Compared to applications, overlap functions have also achieved fruitful results in theory, such as studies on the fundamental properties of overlap functions, various generalizations of the concept of overlap functions, and the construction of additive and multiplicative generators based on overlap functions. However, most of the research studies on the overlap functions mentioned above contain commutativity and continuity, which can limit their practical applications. In this paper, we remove the symmetry and continuity from overlap functions and define discrete pseudo-quasi overlap functions on finite chains. Meanwhile, we also discuss their related properties. Then, we introduce pseudo-quasi overlap functions on sub-chains and construct discrete pseudo-quasi overlap functions on finite chains using pseudo-quasi overlap functions on these sub-chain functions. Unlike quasi-overlap functions on finite chains generated by the ordinal sum, discrete pseudo-quasi overlap functions on finite chains constructed through pseudo-quasi overlap functions on different sub-chains are dissimilar. Eventually, we remove the continuity from pseudo-automorphisms and propose the concept of pseudo-quasi-automorphisms. Based on this, we utilize pseudo-overlap functions, pseudo-quasi-automorphisms, and integral functions to obtain discrete pseudo-quasi overlap functions on finite chains, moreover, we apply them to fuzzy multi-attribute group decision-making. The results indicate that compared to overlap functions and pseudo-overlap functions, discrete pseudo-quasi overlap functions on finite chains have stronger flexibility and a wider range of practical applications.

Keywords: fuzzy logic; information fusion; overlap function; fuzzy multi-attribute group decision-making

MSC: 03B52; 03E72

1. Introduction

To establish a mathematical model of fuzzy objects, Zadeh proposed the concept of fuzzy sets [1] in 1965. Many scholars have conducted extensive research on the fuzzy set theory and applied it in pattern recognition, medical diagnosis, and fuzzy control [2–5]. In 1973, Zadeh proposed the famous CRI algorithm [6], which was a very effective tool for describing and dealing with the fuzziness of things and the uncertainty of systems, as well as for simulating human intelligence and decision-making. Fuzzy reasoning has been applied with great success in industrial control and manufacturing household appliances. However, compared with its application, the theoretical foundation of fuzzy reasoning is not flawless. In 1993, Elkan presented a report titled "The Seemingly Right Success of Fuzzy Logic" at the 11th Annual Conference on Artificial Intelligence [7], which caused a huge uproar. Many scholars have commented on this. Wu discussed this debate in [8].

Ying [9] pointed out that "although many of Erkan's views are incorrect, and Wu has made some clarifications, we must also recognize that the lack of systematic and in-depth theoretical research in fuzzy logic is an undeniable fact." Of course, there was no consensus on this debate. In fact, this debate has never been resolved. Meanwhile, it is precisely for this reason that fuzzy logic has become an active area of research, with many scholars achieving significant results in the field. In recent years, research on fuzzy sets has garnered widespread attention. Therefore, we delve into both the theoretical foundations and practical applications related to fuzzy sets.

In 2010, Bustine et al. proposed the definition of overlap functions [10]. As a special binary aggregation function, the overlap function has been widely used in decision-making, image processing, classification, and other fields [11–13]. Moreover, many academics have achieved significant outcomes in the theoretical research of overlap functions, specifically manifested in the following aspects: (1) research on basic properties of overlap functions, such as migrativity, homogeneity, Lipschitzianity, Archimedes, idempotence, etc. [14–16]; (2) extensions of various concepts related to overlap functions, including quasi-overlap functions [17], pseudo-overlap functions [18], semi-overlap functions [19], and so on [20–22]; (3) study of inducing various types of implication operators from overlap functions and group functions [23–25]; (4) construction of additive and multiplicative generators for overlap functions and various generalized overlap functions [26–29].

Aggregation is an important concept in decision theory, information fusion, and fuzzy inference systems. It involves converting several numerical values into a representative value; this process is called aggregation, and the function that executes this process is called an aggregation function. As powerful tools for processing information fusion, aggregation functions have been widely used in classification [30], fuzzy systems and control [31], hierarchical information fusion [32], and so on [33–35]. In order to better handle information fusion problems, many scholars have degenerated the aggregation functions (including t-norms, uninorms, t-operators, etc.) in [0, 1] to finite chains, and achieved relevant results [36–38]. Qiao transformed the overlap function and quasi-overlap function on [0, 1] into finite chains [39,40], and studied their related properties.

A fuzzy multi-attribute group decision-making problem can be described as a given set of possible alternative solutions, and each solution needs to be comprehensively evaluated from several attributes. Our goal is to find the optimal solution from this set of alternative solutions or to comprehensively rank this set of alternative solutions; the ranking results can reflect the decision-maker's intention. The presence of uncertainty in fuzzy multi-attribute group decision-making processes can be represented by fuzzy sets. Therefore, fuzzy logic plays an important role in the field of fuzzy multi-attribute group decision-making. Fuzzy multi-attribute decision-making represents a non-classical approach to multi-attribute decision-making, extending and developing classical multi-attribute decision-making theories. Bass and Kwakernaak [41] proposed a method for addressing fuzzy multi-attribute group decision-making under uncertainty. Following their work, various scholars have proposed numerous types of fuzzy multi-attribute decision-making methods. Kichert, Zimmermann, and Chen et al. [42–44] summarized the above fuzzy multi-attribute decision-making methods. A few academics have also studied the application of overlap functions and certain generalized overlap functions in fuzzy multi-attribute group decision-making [45,46]. Mao et al. [47] proposed a fuzzy multi-attribute decision-making method based on the Sugeno integral semantics of overlap functions using fuzzy quantifiers, and verified the feasibility of this method through specific examples. Wen [48] combined overlap functions with rough sets to propose a new class of models, and then extended this model to multi-granularity, thereby establishing a solution method for fuzzy multi-attribute decision-making problems. Silva et al. [49] introduced a weighted average operator generated by n-dimensional overlap and aggregation functions, which they applied to fuzzy multi-attribute group decision-making problems. On this basis, Zhang et al. [18] extended the aforementioned weighted average operator and explored the use of pseudo-overlap functions in fuzzy multi-attribute group decision-making.

With the background information mentioned above and the current status of studying nationally as well as globally, the research motivations and innovation points of this paper are as follows:

(1) At present, most concepts of overlap functions and generalized overlap functions include symmetry and continuity, which can limit their practical applications. Thus, we remove the symmetry and continuity from overlap functions and introduce the concept of discrete pseudo-quasi overlap functions on finite chains. In addition, we have also studied their related properties.

(2) Currently, there is little research on constructing aggregate functions based on ordinal sums. Qiao [40] used ordinal sums to construct quasi-overlap functions on finite chains. This method constructs quasi-overlap functions on finite chains through quasi-overlap functions on sub-chains; each sub-chain is called an addend. Therefore, we naturally attempt to generalize the method of constructing quasi-overlap functions on the finite chains mentioned above and use a new method to construct discrete pseudo-quasi overlap functions on finite chains.

(3) In most literature (such as [18,47,49]), the aggregation functions used in the application of fuzzy multi-attribute group decision-making are all continuous. However, in the practical application of fuzzy multi-attribute group decision-making, the data objects involved are usually discrete. On the other hand, the discrete aggregation function has better flexibility and a wider range of applications in fuzzy multi-attribute group applications. Therefore, we apply discrete pseudo-quasi overlap functions on finite chains to fuzzy multi-attribute group decision-making. This approach not only promotes the development of fuzzy multi-attribute decision-making but also provides valuable reference and guidance for the theoretical development and practical application of overlap functions.

The main contents of this paper could be summarized as follows: In Section 2, we mainly present some basic knowledge on the topic. In Section 3, we introduce the concept of discrete pseudo-quasi overlap functions on finite chains and study their related properties. In Section 4, we offer pseudo-quasi overlap functions on sub-chains and construct discrete pseudo-quasi overlap functions on finite chains through pseudo-quasi overlap functions on sub-chains. Moreover, compared to quasi-overlap functions on finite chains generated by the ordinal sum, the discrete pseudo-quasi overlap functions on finite chains created by pseudo-quasi overlap functions on various sub-chains are different. In Section 5, we present the idea of pseudo-quasi-automorphism by removing the continuity from pseudo-automorphisms. Based on this, we use pseudo-overlap functions, pseudo-quasi-automorphisms, and integer functions to construct discrete pseudo-quasi overlap functions on finite chains and apply them to fuzzy multi-attribute group decision-making. The findings show that discrete pseudo-quasi overlap functions have better flexibility and adaptability than overlap functions and pseudo-overlap functions in applications. The research contents of this paper are shown in Figure 1.

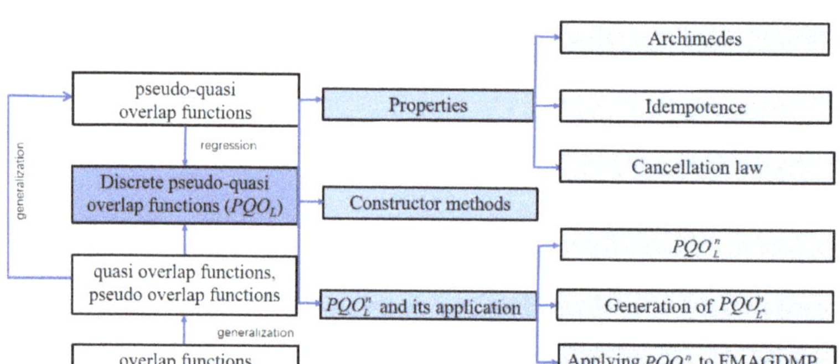

Figure 1. Framework diagram of the paper.

2. Preliminaries

In this portion, we mainly provide some preliminary knowledge that is used in later sections.

Definition 1 ([10])**.** *A binary function $O : [0,1]^2 \to [0,1]$ is known as an overlap function if it meets $\forall x, y \in [0,1]$,*
$(O1)$ *O is symmetric;*
$(O2)$ $O(x,y) = 0 \Leftrightarrow x = 0$ *or* $y = 0$;
$(O3)$ $O(x,y) = 1 \Leftrightarrow x = 1$ *and* $y = 1$;
$(O4)$ *O is non-decreasing;*
$(O5)$ *O is continuous.*

Definition 2 ([17])**.** *A binary function $QO : [0,1]^2 \to [0,1]$ is known as a quasi-overlap function if it satisfies $(O1) - (O4)$.*

Definition 3 ([18])**.** *A binary function $PO : [0,1]^2 \to [0,1]$ is referred to as a pseudo-overlap function if it satisfies $(O2) - (O5)$.*

Definition 4 ([20])**.** *An n-ary function $O^n : [0,1]^n \to [0,1]$ is known as an n-ary overlap function if it meets $\forall x_{i+1}, x_{i+2}, x_{i+3}, \ldots, x_{i+n} \in [0,1]$,*
(O^n1) *O^n is symmetry;*
(O^n2) $O^n(x_{i+1}, x_{i+2}, x_{i+3}, \ldots, x_{i+n}) = 0 \Leftrightarrow$ *for* $j \in N^+, 1 \le j \le n$, *such as* $\prod_{j=1}^{n} x_{i+j} = 0$;
(O^n3) $O^n(x_{i+1}, x_{i+2}, x_{i+3}, \ldots, x_{i+n}) = 1 \Leftrightarrow$ *for* $j \in N^+, 1 \le j \le n$, *such as* $\prod_{j=1}^{n} x_{i+j} = 1$;
(O^n4) *O^n is non-decreasing;*
(O^n5) *O^n is continuous.*

Definition 5 ([18])**.** *An n-ary function $PO^n : [0,1]^n \to [0,1]$ is known as an n-ary pseudo-overlap function if it satisfies $(O^n2) - (O^n5)$.*

3. Discrete Pseudo-Quasi Overlap Functions

In this part, we delete the symmetry of quasi-overlap functions and introduce the notion of discrete pseudo-quasi overlap functions on finite chains. In addition, we discuss some of the associated properties, like Archimedean, idempotence, and cancellation law.

We define a finite chain $\mathcal{L}$ as follows:

Let $\mathcal{L} = \{x_0, x_1, x_2, \ldots, x_n, x_{n+1}\}$ be a set, $n \in N^+, n \ge 1$. $\mathcal{L}$ is called a finite chain when it satisfies $\forall x_i, x_j \in \mathcal{L}$,
$(\mathcal{L}1)$ $x_i < x_j \Leftrightarrow i < j$;
$(\mathcal{L}2)$ x_0 is the minimum element, and x_{n+1} is the maximum element of $\mathcal{L}$.

Definition 6. *A binary function $PQO_{\mathcal{L}} : \mathcal{L}^2 \to \mathcal{L}$ is called a discrete pseudo-quasi overlap function on $\mathcal{L}$ if it fulfills $\forall x_i, x_j \in \mathcal{L}$,*
$(PQO_{\mathcal{L}}1)$ $PQO_{\mathcal{L}}(x_i, x_j) = x_0 \Leftrightarrow x_i = x_0$ *or* $x_j = x_0$;
$(PQO_{\mathcal{L}}2)$ $PQO_{\mathcal{L}}(x_i, x_j) = x_{n+1} \Leftrightarrow x_i = x_{n+1}$ *and* $x_j = x_{n+1}$;
$(PQO_{\mathcal{L}}3)$ *$PQO_{\mathcal{L}}$ is non-decreasing.*

A discrete pseudo-quasi overlap function $PQO_{\mathcal{L}}$ is called an x_{n+1}-section left deflation on $\mathcal{L}$ when it satisfies $\forall x_i \in \mathcal{L}$,
$(PQO_{\mathcal{L}}4)$ $PQO_{\mathcal{L}}(x_{n+1}, x_i) \le x_i$.
Correspondingly, a discrete pseudo-quasi overlap function $PQO_{\mathcal{L}}$ is called an x_{n+1}-section right deflation $\mathcal{L}$ when it satisfies $\forall x_i \in \mathcal{L}$,
$(PQO_{\mathcal{L}}5) PQO_{\mathcal{L}}(x_i, x_{n+1}) \le x_i$.

Assuming $\mathcal{L} = L = \{0, x_1, x_2, \ldots x_n, 1\}$ is a finite chain, we extend the L to [0, 1], then PQO_L is a pseudo-quasi overlap function given in [21]. On the other hand, a discrete pseudo-quasi overlap function PQO_L that satisfies symmetry is a quasi-overlap function QO_L on L, as mentioned in [40]. Moreover, the above ($PQO_{\mathcal{L}}4$) and ($PQO_{\mathcal{L}}5$) correspond to item (5) from Definition 2.1 in [40].

In the following sections, we use L to indicate the finite chain $\{0, x_1, x_2, \ldots x_n, 1\}$.

Below, we provide some examples of discrete pseudo-quasi overlap functions $PQO_{\mathcal{L}}$ on $\mathcal{L}$.

Example 1. *(1) Let $\mathcal{L}$ be a finite chain. Then, for $n = 1$, any discrete pseudo-quasi overlap function $PQO_{\mathcal{L}}$ is a quasi-overlap function $QO_{\mathcal{L}}$ on $\mathcal{L}$.*

Taking $\mathcal{L} = \{\frac{1}{4}, \frac{1}{3}$, and $\frac{1}{2}\}$, $n = 1$. A graph of the $PQO_{\mathcal{L}}$ is shown in Figure 2.

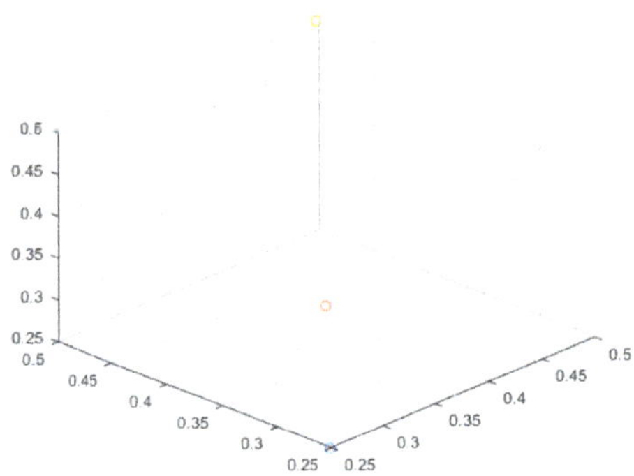

Figure 2. A discrete pseudo-quasi overlap function $PQO_{\mathcal{L}}$.

(2) Let $L = \{0, x_1, x_2, \ldots x_n, 1\}$ be a finite chain, $n \in N^+, n \geq 2$, $x_2, x_a, x_b \in L, x_2 < x_a \leq x_b$. Then, $\forall x_c, x_d \in L$, the function $PQO_L : L^2 \to L$, defined as follows:

$$PQO_L(x_c, x_d) = \begin{cases} x_1, & if\ x_1 < x_c < x_a, x_1 < x_d \leq x_b \\ \min\{x_c, x_d\}. & otherwise \end{cases}$$

is a discrete pseudo-quasi overlap function on L.

Taking $L = \{0, 0.1, 0.2, , \ldots, 0.9, 1\}, n = 9, x_a = 0.3, x_b = 0.6$. A graph of the PQO_L is shown in Figure 3.

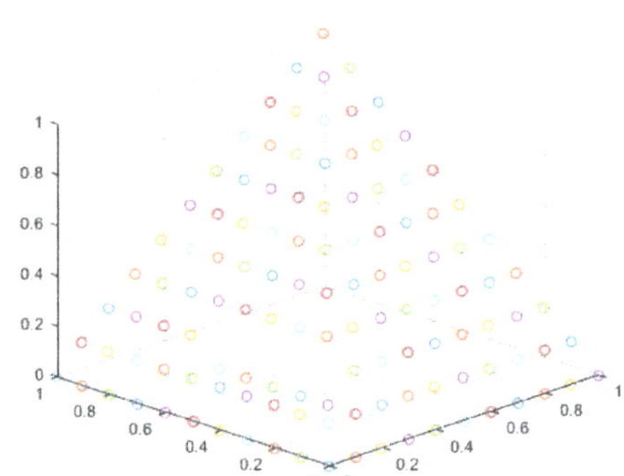

Figure 3. A discrete pseudo-quasi overlap function PQO_L.

(3) Let $\mathcal{L} = L_N = \{0, 1, 2, 3, \ldots, n+1\}$ be a finite chain with natural numbers, $n \in N^+$, $n \geq 2$, $x_r, x_s \in L_N, 1 < x_r < x_s$. Then, $\forall x_p, x_q \in L_N$, the function $PQO_{L_N} : L_N^2 \to L_N$, defined as follows:

$$PQO_{L_N}(x_p, x_q) = \begin{cases} 1, & if\ 0 < x_p < x_r, 0 < x_q < x_s \\ [\sqrt{x_p x_q}]. & otherwise \end{cases}$$

is a discrete pseudo-quasi overlap function on L_N.

Taking $L_N = \{0, 1, 2, , \ldots, 9, 10\}, n = 9, x_r = 2, x_s = 6$. *An image of the* PQO_{L_N} *is shown in Figure 4.*

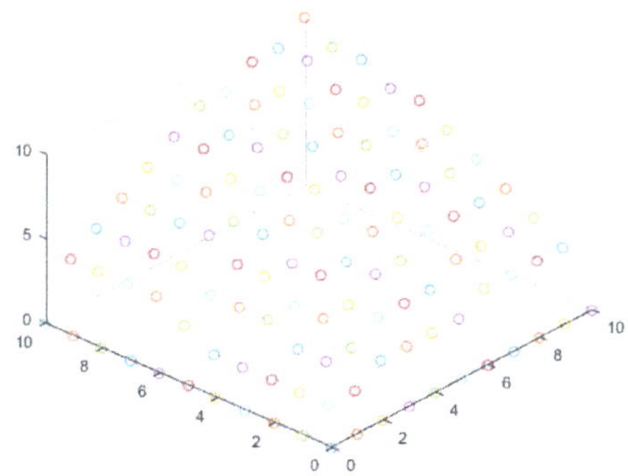

Figure 4. A discrete pseudo-quasi overlap function PQO_{L_N}.

(4) *Let* $\mathcal{L} = L_{N^+} = \{1, 2, 3, \ldots, n+1\}$ *be a finite chain with positive integers,* $n \in N^+$, $n \geq 2$, $x_g, x_h \in L_{N^+}, x_g \neq x_h, 2 < \min\{x_g, x_h\}$. *Then,* $\forall x_m, x_n \in L_{N^+}$, *the function* $PQO_{L_{N+}} : L_{N^+}^2 \to L_{N^+}$, *defined as follows:*

$$PQO_{L_{N+}}(x_m, x_n) = \begin{cases} 1, & if\ x_m = 1\ or\ x_n = 1 \\ 2, & if\ 1 < x_m \leq x_g, 1 < x_n \leq x_h \\ \left[\frac{2x_m x_n}{x_m + x_n}\right]. & otherwise \end{cases}$$

is a discrete pseudo-quasi overlap function on L_{N^+}.

Taking $L_N^+ = \{1, 2, , \ldots, 9, 10\}, n = 8, x_g = 4, x_h = 6$. *An image of the* PQO_{L_N} *is shown in Figure 5.*

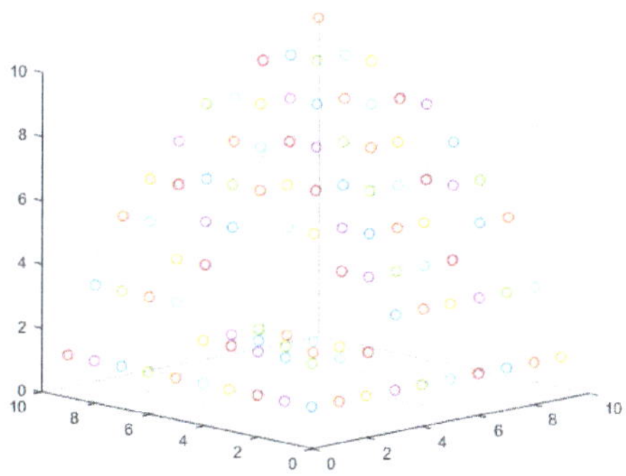

Figure 5. A discrete pseudo-quasi overlap function $PQO_{L_{N^+}}$.

We observe that "$[x]$" in Example 1 is an integral function; more precisely, it is a round function to the nearest integer x. Furthermore, regarding other types of integral functions, such as floor, ceil, and fix, their methods of constructing discrete pseudo-quasi overlap functions on $\mathcal{L}$ are similar to that of the round function.

Next, we investigate the relevant properties of discrete pseudo-quasi overlap functions on finite chains L.

3.1. Archimedes of Discrete-Pseudo-Quasi Overlap Functions

First, we discuss the Archimedes of discrete pseudo-quasi overlap functions on L.

Definition 7. *Let $PQO_L : L^2 \to L$ be a discrete pseudo-quasi overlap function on L. PQO_L is called Archimedean when it satisfies $\forall x_i, x_j \in L - \{0,1\}, (x_i)^{(n)}_{PQO_L} < x_j$, and PQO_L is given by the following:*

$$(x_i)^{(1)}_{PQO_L} = x_i, (x_i)^{(n+1)}_{PQO_L} = PQO_L(x_i, (x_i)^{n}_{PQO_L}), n \in N^+.$$

Proposition 1. *Let $PQO_L : L^2 \to L$ be a discrete pseudo-quasi overlap function on L. Then, $\forall x_i \in L - \{1\}, x_j \in L, PQO_L(x_i, x_j)$ is not strictly increasing.*

Proof. We take $x_i = 0, x_j, x_z \in L$, and $x_j < x_z$. Then, $PQO_L(x_i, x_j) = 0 \leq 0 = PQO_L(x_i, x_z)$. So, $x_i = 0$, $x_j \in L$, and $PQO_L(x_i, x_j)$ is not strictly increasing. On the other hand, $x_i = 1$, $x_j \in L$, we need to verify that $PQO_L(x_i, x_j)$ is strictly increasing. For $x_j, x_z \in L$, and $x_j < x_z$, there are three different cases, as follows:
(1) $x_i = 1, x_j = 0 < x_z, PQO_L(x_i, x_j) = 0 < PQO_L(x_i, x_z)$;
(2) $x_i = 1, x_j < x_z = 1, PQO_L(x_i, x_j) < 1 = PQO_L(x_i, x_z)$;
(3) $x_i = 1, x_j \in L - \{0\}, x_z \in L - \{1\}$. Suppose that $PQO_L(x_i, x_j)$ is not strictly increasing. According to (PQO_L3), we know that $PQO_L(x_i, x_j) = PQO_L(x_i, x_z)$. Obviously, this is contradictory to $x_j < x_z$. Thus, $x_i = 1, x_j \in L$, $PQO_L(x_i, x_j)$ is strictly increasing. Finally, for the scenario where $x_i \in L - \{0,1\}, x_j \in L$, and $PQO_L(x_i, x_j)$ is not strictly increasing, the proof method is similar to [34]. To summarize, $\forall x_i \in L - \{1\}, x_j \in L, PQO_L(x_i, x_j)$ is not strictly increasing. □

From Proposition 1, we can immediately deduce that $\forall x_j \in L - \{1\}, x_i \in L, PQO_L(x_j, x_i)$ is also not strictly increasing.

Proposition 2. *Let $PQO_L : L^2 \to L$ be Archimedean. If PQO_L is a discrete pseudo-quasi overlap function on L, then $(x_i)^{(n+1)}_{PQO_L} \leq (x_i)^{(n)}_{PQO_L}, n \in N^+$.*

Proof. The following can directly be obtained through Definition 7, Proposition 1, and mathematical methods of induction: (1) For $n = 1, (x_i)^{(2)}_{PQO_L} = PQO_L(x_i, x_i) < x_i = (x_i)^{(1)}_{PQO_L}$, that is, $(x_i)^{(2)}_{PQO_L} \leq (x_i)^{(1)}_{PQO_L}$. For $n = 2, (x_i)^{(3)}_{PQO_L} = PQO_L(x_i, (x_i)^{(2)}_{PQO_L}) = PQO_L(x_i, PQO_L(x_i, x_i))$. According to $PQO_L(x_i, x_i) < x_i$ and Proposition 1, we have the following:

$$PQO_L(x_i, PQO_L(x_i, x_i)) \leq PQO_L(x_i, x_i).$$

Thus, $(x_i)^{(3)}_{PQO_L} \leq (x_i)^{(2)}_{PQO_L}$. Assume that $n = k$, $(x_i)^{(k+1)}_{PQO_L} \leq (x_i)^{(k)}_{PQO_L}$. For $n = k+1$, we have the following:

$$(x_i)^{(k+2)}_{PQO_L} = PQO_L(x_i, (x_i)^{(k+1)}_{PQO_L}) \leq PQO_L(x_i, (x_i)^{(k)}_{PQO_L}) = (x_i)^{(k+1)}_{PQO_L}.$$

Therefore, $n \in N^+$, $(x_i)^{(n+1)}_{PQO_L} \leq (x_i)^{(n)}_{PQO_L}$. □

Proposition 3. *Let $PQO_L : L^2 \to L$ be a discrete pseudo-quasi overlap function on L. Then, PQO_L is not Archimedean.*

Proof. Suppose that PQO_L is Archimedean. Owing to Proposition 2, we know the following:

$$0 < \cdots \leq (x_i)^{(n+1)}_{PQO_L} \leq (x_i)^{(n)}_{PQO_L} \leq (x_i)^{(n-1)}_{PQO_L} < \cdots \leq (x_i)^{(2)}_{PQO_L} \leq (x_i)^{(1)}_{PQO_L} = x_i, n \in N^+.$$

Thus, for $n \in N^+, \lim_{n\to\infty} (x_i)^{(n)}_{PQO_L} = 0$, conflicting with $(x_i)^{(n)}_{PQO_L} < x_j$ for Definition 7. Therefore, PQO_L is not Archimedean. □

Now, we will discuss the idempotence of discrete pseudo-quasi overlap functions on L.

3.2. Idempotence of Discrete pseudo-quasi overlap Functions

Definition 8. *Let $PQO_L : L^2 \to L$ be a discrete pseudo-quasi overlap function on L. An element $x_i \in L$ is called idempotent when it satisfies $PQO_L(x_i, x_i) = x_i$. A discrete pseudo-quasi overlap function PQO_L is called idempotent when it satisfies that $\forall x_i \in L$ is an idempotent element.*

Obviously, 0 and 1 are idempotent elements of a discrete pseudo-quasi overlap function on L. Moreover, only the discrete pseudo-quasi overlap function $PQO_{\mathcal{L}}$ on $\mathcal{L}$ generated by Case (1) in Example 1 is idempotent.

Proposition 4. *Let $PQO_L : L^2 \to L$ be a discrete pseudo-quasi overlap function on L. Then, there exists $x_i \in L - \{0,1\}$, such that $PQO_L(x_i, x_i) = x_i$.*

Proof. The proof is analogous to [16]. □

Proposition 5. *Let $PQO_L : L^2 \to L$ be a discrete pseudo-quasi overlap function on L.*
(1) If PQO_L satisfies (PQO_L4), then there exists $x_i \in L - \{0,1\}$, such that $PQO_L(1, x_i) < x_i$.
(2) If PQO_L satisfies (PQO_L5), then there exists $x_i \in L - \{0,1\}$, such that $PQO_L(x_i, 1) < x_i$.

Proof. (1) Suppose that PQO_L is a discrete pseudo-quasi overlap function on L. If PQO_L satisfies (PQO_L4), then $\forall x_i \in L - \{0,1\}$, $PQO_L(1, x_i) \leq x_i$. Moreover, according to Proposition 4 and (PQO_L3), we known that there exists $x_i \in L - \{0,1\}$, such that we have the following:

$$x_i = PQO_L(x_i, x_i) \leq PQO_L(1, x_i).$$

So, $PQO_L(1, x_i) < x_i$. The proofs of (2) are similar to (1). □

Proposition 6. *Let $PQO_L : L^2 \to L$ be a discrete pseudo-quasi overlap function on L. If PQO_L is Archimedean, then PQO_L has no idempotent element, except for $0, 1$.*

Proof. Suppose that there exists $x_i \in L - \{0,1\}$, which is an idempotent element of the discrete pseudo-quasi overlap function PQO_L on L. As PQO_L is Archimedean, then $n = 1, (x_i)^{(1)}_{PQO_L} = x_i$, and $n = 2, (x_i)^{(2)}_{PQO_L} = PQO_L(x_i, x_i) = x_i$. Assume that $n = k$; we have the following:

$$(x_i)^{(k)}_{PQO_L} = PQO_L(x_i, (x_i)^{(k-1)}_{PQO_L}) = PQO_L(x_i, x_i) = x_i.$$

So, for $n = k+1, (x_i)^{(k+1)}_{PQO_L} = PQO_L(x_i, (x_i)^{(k)}_{PQO_L}) = PQO_L(x_i, x_i) = x_i$. Thus, for $n \in N^+$, $(x_i)^{(n)}_{PQO_L} = x_i$, which conflicts with $(x_i)^{(n)}_{PQO_L} < x_j$ in Definition 7. Thus, PQO_L has no idempotent element, except for $0, 1$. □

In the end, we discuss the cancellation law of discrete pseudo-quasi overlap functions on L.

3.3. Cancellation Law of Discrete pseudo-quasi overlap Functions

Definition 9. *Let $PQO_L : L^2 \to L$ be a discrete pseudo-quasi overlap function on L. $\forall x_i, x_j, x_z \in L$, PQO_L is said to fulfill the left-cancellation law if we have the following:*

$$PQO_L(x_i, x_j) = PQO_L(x_i, x_z) \text{ means that } x_i = x_0 \text{ or } x_j = x_z.$$

Similarly, PQO_L is said to fulfill the right-cancellation law if we have the following:

$$PQO_L(x_j, x_i) = PQO_L(x_z, x_i) \text{ means that } x_i = x_0 \text{ or } x_j = x_z.$$

Lemma 1. *A discrete pseudo-quasi overlap function PQO_L on L fulfills the cancellation law if $\forall x_i, x_j, x_z \in L$ satisfy the following conditions:*
(1) $PQO_L(x_i, x_j) = PQO_L(x_i, x_z) \Rightarrow x_i = x_0$ or $x_j = x_z$;
(2) $PQO_L(x_j, x_i) = PQO_L(x_z, x_i) \Rightarrow x_i = x_0$ or $x_j = x_z$.

Proposition 7. *Let $PQO_L : L^2 \to L$ be a discrete pseudo-quasi overlap function on L.*
(1) PQO_L fulfills the left-cancellation law $\Leftrightarrow$ for $\forall x_i \in L - \{0\}, x_j \in L$, and $PQO_L(x_i, x_j)$ is strictly increasing.
(2) PQO_L fulfills the right-cancellation law $\Leftrightarrow$ for $\forall x_j \in L - \{0\}, x_i \in L$, and $PQO_L(x_j, x_i)$ is strictly increasing.

Proof. The proofs of (1) and (2) are similar. Next, we only prove (2). (2) (Necessity) Suppose that PQO_L fulfills the right-cancellation law, $i \neq 0, x_j < x_z$. Since PQO_L is monotonically increasing, $PQO_L(x_j, x_i) \leq PQO_L(x_z, x_i)$. We consider $PQO_L(x_j, x_i) = PQO_L(x_z, x_i)$. Since PQO_L fulfills the right-cancellation law, $x_i = 0$ or $x_j = x_z$. Obviously, this contradicts with $x_j < x_z$. Thus, $PQO_L(x_j, x_i) < PQO_L(x_z, x_i)$. (Sufficiency) Suppose that $\forall x_j \in L - \{0\}, x_i \in L, PQO_L(x_j, x_i)$ is strictly increasing. So, $x_j < x_z$, and $PQO_L(x_j, x_i) < PQO_L(x_z, x_i)$. We assume that PQO_L does not fulfill the right-cancellation law. Then, if $PQO_L(x_j, x_i) = PQO_L(x_z, x_i)$, it means that $x_i \neq 0$ and $x_j \neq x_z$. So, $x_j < x_z$ or $x_j > x_z$ or $x_j || x_z$. We consider $x_j < x_z$. Because $PQO_L(x_j, x_i)$ is strictly increasing, $PQO_L(x_j, x_i) < PQO_L(x_z, x_i)$. This contradicts with $PQO_L(x_j, x_i) = PQO_L(x_z, x_i)$. Thus, the scenario where $x_j < x_z$ does not exist. Similarly, the scenario where $x_j > x_z$ is also not valid. Finally, we consider $x_j || x_z$. Apparently, this contradicts the premise that $PQO_L(x_j, x_i)$ is strictly increasing. Therefore, PQO_L fulfills the right-cancellation law. □

Proposition 8. *Let $PQO_L : L^2 \to L$ be a discrete pseudo-quasi overlap function on L. Then, PQO_L does not fulfill the cancellation law.*

Proof. The proof is analogous to [17]. □

According to Propositions 4 and 8, we know that both discrete pseudo-quasi overlap functions and quasi-overlap functions on L can obtain similar conclusions. That is to say, symmetry does not significantly affect the conclusions of Propositions 4 and 8.

4. The Construction of Discrete Pseudo-Quasi Overlap Functions

In [40], Qiao proposed a method for constructing quasi-overlap functions on finite chains based on the ordinal sum. This method mainly utilizes quasi-overlap functions on sub-chains to create quasi-functions on finite chains, where these sub-chains are additive. Therefore, we extend this approach and devise a new method to construct discrete pseudo-quasi overlap functions. First, we define discrete pseudo-quasi overlap functions on a sub-chain. We then construct a discrete pseudo-quasi overlap function on finite chains by leveraging pseudo-quasi overlap functions on these sub-chains.

Definition 10. *Let L be a finite chain, and $L_k^* = \{[x_k, x_{k+3}] | k \in N, 0 \leq k \leq n-2\}$ be a sub-chain of L. A binary function $PQO_{L_k^*} : [x_k, x_{k+3}]^2 \to [x_k, x_{k+3}]$ is called a discrete pseudo-quasi overlap function on L_k^* when it satisfies $\forall x_\mu, x_\nu \in [x_k, x_{k+3}]$,*
$(PQO_{L_k^*}1) PQO_{L_k^*}(x_\mu, x_\nu) = x_k \Leftrightarrow x_\mu = x_k$ or $x_\nu = x_k$;
$(PQO_{L_k^*}2) PQO_{L_k^*}(x_\mu, x_\nu) = x_{k+3} \Leftrightarrow x_\mu = x_{k+3}$ and $x_\nu = x_{k+3}$;
$(PQO_{L_k^*}3) PQO_{L_k^*}$ is non-decreasing.

Theorem 1. *Let L be a finite chain, $k \in N, 0 \leq k \leq n-2, [x_k, x_{k+3}]$ be a sub-chain of L, and $PQO_{L_k^*} : [x_k, x_{k+3}]^2 \to [x_k, x_{k+3}]$ be a discrete pseudo-quasi overlap function on L_k^*. Then, $\forall x_i, x_j \in L$, the function $PQO_{L_k} : L^2 \to L$, is defined as follows:*

$$PQO_{L_k}(x_i,x_j)=\begin{cases} PQO_{L_k^*}(x_i,x_j), & if\ x_i,x_j\in[x_k,x_{k+3}] \\ \min\{\alpha_1(x_i),\alpha_2(x_j)\}. & otherwise \end{cases}$$

is a discrete pseudo-quasi overlap function on L, among these, with different values of k, the functions $\alpha_1(x_i):L\to L$ *and* $\alpha_2(x_j):L\to L$ *have different forms, as follows:*

(i) $k=0, n\geq 4$. $\alpha_1^{(1)}(x_i):L\to L, \alpha_2^{(1)}(x_j):L\to L$*, separately, given by the following:*

$$\alpha_1^{(1)}(x_i)=\begin{cases} PQO_{L_0^*}(x_i,x_3), & if\ x_i\in[x_0,x_3] \\ x_i. & otherwise \end{cases}$$

$$\alpha_2^{(1)}(x_j)=\begin{cases} x_w, & if\ x_j\in(x_0,x_3] \\ x_j. & otherwise \end{cases}$$

where $w\in N^+, 3\leq w\leq n$.

(ii) $1\leq k<n-2, n\geq 5$; $\alpha_1^{(2)}(x_i):L\to L, \alpha_2^{(2)}(x_j):L\to L$*, are defined separately, as follows:*

$$\alpha_1^{(2)}(x_i)=\begin{cases} PQO_{L_k^*}(x_i,x_{k+3}), & if\ x_i\in[x_k,x_{k+3}] \\ x_i. & otherwise \end{cases}$$

$$\alpha_2^{(2)}(x_j)=\begin{cases} x_t, & if\ x_j\in[x_k,x_{k+3}] \\ x_j. & otherwise \end{cases}$$

where $t\in N^+, k+3\leq t\leq n$.

(iii) $k=n-2, n\geq 4$; $\alpha_1^{(3)}(x_i):L\to L, \alpha_2^{(3)}(x_j):L\to L$*, are defined separately, as follows:*

$$\alpha_1^{(3)}(x_i)=\begin{cases} PQO_{L_k^*}(x_i,x_{n+1}), & if\ x_i\in[x_{n-2},x_{n+1}] \\ x_{\gamma_\theta} & if\ x_i=x_{\beta_\theta} \\ x_i. & otherwise \end{cases}$$

$$\alpha_2^{(3)}(x_j)=\begin{cases} x_\lambda, & if\ x_j\in[x_{n-2},x_{n+1}] \\ x_j & otherwise \end{cases}$$

for $\theta\in N^+, 1\leq\theta,\beta_\theta\leq k-1$, $1\leq\gamma_\theta,\lambda\leq k$*, such as* $\gamma_\theta\leq\lambda$. β_θ *and* γ_θ *are in one-to-one correspondence. The details are as follows:*

$$\begin{array}{ll} \gamma_1=k(or\ k-2); & if\ \beta_1=k-1, \\ \gamma_2=k-1(or\ k-3); & if\ \beta_2=k-2, \\ \dots & \dots \\ \gamma_{k-2}=3(or\ 1); & if\ \beta_{k-2}=2, \\ \gamma_{k-1}=2; & if\ \beta_{k-1}=1, \end{array}$$

Proof. (i), (ii), and (iii) are similar. Next, we only prove (iii). Without loss of generality, we take $\theta=1, \beta_1=n-3, \gamma_1=\lambda=n-2$. (PQO_L1) (Necessity) If $PQO_{L_{n-2}}(x_i,x_j)=x_0$, then $\min\{\alpha_1^{(3)}(x_i),\alpha_2^{(3)}(x_j)\}=x_0$, i.e., $\alpha_1^{(3)}(x_i)=x_0$ or $\alpha_2^{(3)}(x_j)=x_0$. According to $k\in N, k=n-2$, we know that $x_i\notin[x_{n-2},x_{n+1}]\cup\{x_{n-3}\}$. So, $\alpha_1^{(3)}(x_i)=x_i=x_0$. On the other hand, $x_j\notin[x_{n-2},x_{n+1}]$. So, $\alpha_2^{(3)}(x_j)=x_j=x_0$. Thus, $x_i=x_0$ or $x_j=x_0$. (Sufficiency) If $x_i=x_0$ or $x_j=x_0$. Without loss of generality, we take $x_i=x_0$. Since $x_i\notin[x_{n-2},x_{n+1}]\cup\{x_{n-3}\}$, we obtain $\alpha_1^{(3)}(x_i)=\alpha_1^{(3)}(x_0)=x_0$. So, we have the following:

$$PQO_{L_{n-2}}(x_i,x_j)=\min\{\alpha_1^{(3)}(x_i),\alpha_2^{(3)}(x_j)\}=\min\{x_0,\alpha_2^{(3)}(x_j)\}=x_0.$$

On the other hand, if $x_j=x_0$, and $x_j\notin[x_{n-2},x_{n+1}]$, we also obtain $\alpha_2^{(3)}(x_j)=\alpha_2^{(3)}(x_0)=x_0$. So, $PQO_{L_{n-2}}(x_i,x_j)=\min\{\alpha_1^{(3)}(x_i),\alpha_2^{(3)}(x_j)\}=\min\{\alpha_1^{(3)}(x_i),x_0\}=x_0$. Thus, we have the following:

$$PQO_{L_{n-2}}(x_i, x_j) = x_0.$$

Therefore, $PQO_{L_{n-2}}$ satisfies (PQO_L1).

(PQO_L2) (Necessity) If $PQO_{L_{n-2}}(x_i, x_j) = x_1$, then $\min\{\alpha_1^{(3)}(x_i), \alpha_2^{(3)}(x_j)\} = x_1$, that is, $\alpha_1^{(3)}(x_i) = x_1$ and $\alpha_2^{(3)}(x_j) = x_1$. For $k \in N, k = n-2$, we know that $x_i \notin [x_{n-2}, x_{n+1}] \cup \{x_{n-3}\}$, and $x_j \notin [x_{n-2}, x_{n+1}]$. So, $x_i = \alpha_1^{(3)}(x_i) = x_1$, and $x_j = \alpha_2^{(3)}(x_j) = x_1$. (Sufficiency) If $x_i = x_1$ and $x_j = x_1$. Since $k = n-2$, $k \in N$, we gain $x_i \notin [x_{n-2}, x_{n+1}] \cup \{x_{n-3}\}$, and $x_j \notin [x_{n-2}, x_{n+1}]$. So, $\alpha_1^{(3)}(x_i) = x_i = x_1$, and $\alpha_2^{(3)}(x_j) = x_j = x_1$. Thus, we have the following:

$$PQO_{L_{n-2}}(x_i, x_j) = \min\{\alpha_1^{(3)}(x_i), \alpha_2^{(3)}(x_j)\} = \min\{x_1, x_1\} = x_1.$$

Therefore, $PQO_{L_{n-2}}$ satisfies (PQO_L2).

(PQO_L3) $\forall x_i, x_j, x_z \in L, x_j \leq x_z$, we have several situations, specifically as follows:

(1) $x_i, x_j, x_z \in [x_{n-2}, x_{n+1}]$. Since that $PQO_{L^*_{n-2}}$ is a discrete pseudo-quasi overlap function on L^*_{n-2}. So, $PQO_{L_{n-2}}(x_i, x_j) = PQO_{L^*_{n-2}}(x_i, x_j) \leq PQO_{L^*_{n-2}}(x_i, x_z) = PQO_{L_{n-2}}(x_i, x_z)$.

(2) $x_i, x_j, x_z \notin [x_{n-2}, x_{n+1}]$ at the same time.

(2.1) $x_i, x_z \in [x_{n-2}, x_{n+1}], x_j \notin [x_{n-2}, x_{n+1}]$, without loss of generality, we take $x_j = x_{n-3}$. Then, $PQO_{L_{n-2}}(x_i, x_j) = \min\{\alpha_1^{(3)}(x_i), \alpha_2^{(3)}(x_j)\} = \min\{PQO_{L^*_{n-2}}(x_i, x_{n+1}), x_{n-3}\}$, and $PQO_{L_{n-2}}(x_i, x_z) = PQO_{L^*_{n-2}}(x_i, x_z)$. Since $x_{n-3} < x_{n-2} \leq PQO_{L^*_k}(x_i, x_{n+1}) \leq x_{n+1}$, we have the following:

$$PQO_{L_n}(x_i, x_j) = \min\{PQO_{L^*_n}(x_i, x_{n+1}), x_{n-3}\} = x_{n-3}.$$

According to $x_{n-3} < x_{n-2} \leq PQO_{L^*_{n-2}}(x_i, x_z)$, we know that $PQO_{L_{n-2}}(x_i, x_j) \leq PQO_{L_{n-2}}(x_i, x_z)$.

(2.2) $x_i \in [x_{n-2}, x_{n+1}], x_j, x_z \notin [x_{n-2}, x_{n+1}]$, without loss of generality, we take $x_j = x_{n-4}, x_z = x_{n-3}$. Then, $PQO_{L_{n-2}}(x_i, x_j) = \min\{PQO_{L^*_{n-2}}(x_i, x_{n+1}), x_{n-4}\}$, and we have the following:

$$PQO_{L_{n-2}}(x_i, x_z) = \min\{PQO_{L^*_{n-2}}(x_i, x_{n+1}), x_{n-3}\}.$$

Thus, $PQO_{L_{n-2}}(x_i, x_j) \leq PQO_{L_{n-2}}(x_i, x_z)$.

(2.3) $x_i = x_{n-3}, x_j, x_z \in [x_{n-2}, x_{n+1}]$. Then, we have the following:

$$PQO_{L_{n-2}}(x_i, x_j) = \min\{x_{n-2}, x_{n-2}\} = x_{n-2},$$

and $PQO_{L_{n-2}}(x_i, x_z) = \min\{x_{n-2}, x_{n-2}\} = x_{n-2}$. So, $PQO_{L_{n-2}}(x_i, x_j) \leq PQO_{L_{n-2}}(x_i, x_z)$.

(2.4) $x_i = x_{n-3}, x_j \notin [x_{n-2}, x_{n+1}]$, without loss of generality, we take $x_j = x_{n-3}$, $x_z \in [x_{n-2}, x_{n+1}]$. Then, $PQO_{L_{n-2}}(x_i, x_j) = \min\{x_{n-2}, x_{n-3}\} = x_{n-3}$, and we have the following:

$$PQO_{L_{n-2}}(x_i, x_z) = \min\{x_{n-2}, x_{n-2}\} = x_{n-2}.$$

So, $PQO_{L_{n-2}}(x_i, x_j) \leq PQO_{L_{n-2}}(x_i, x_z)$.

(2.5) $x_i = x_{n-3}, x_j, x_z \notin [x_{n-2}, x_{n+1}]$, without loss of generality, we take $x_j = x_z = x_{n-3}$. Then, $PQO_{L_{n-2}}(x_i, x_j) = \min\{x_{n-2}, x_{n-3}\} = x_{n-3}$, and we have the following:

$$PQO_{L_{n-2}}(x_i, x_z) = PQO_{L_{n-2}}(x_i, x_j) = x_{n-3}.$$

So, $PQO_{L_{n-2}}(x_i, x_j) \leq PQO_{L_{n-2}}(x_i, x_z)$.

(2.6) $x_i \notin [x_{n-2}, x_{n+1}] \cup \{x_{n-3}\}$, without loss of generality, we take $x_i = x_{n-4}$, $x_j, x_z \in [x_{n-2}, x_{n+1}]$. Then, $PQO_{L_{n-2}}(x_i, x_j) = \min\{x_{n-4}, x_{n-2}\} = x_{n-4}$, and we have the following:

$$PQO_{L_{n-2}}(x_i, x_z) = PQO_{L_{n-2}}(x_i, x_j) = x_{n-4}.$$

So, $PQO_{L_{n-2}}(x_i, x_j) \leq PQO_{L_{n-2}}(x_i, x_z)$.

(2.7) $x_i \notin [x_{n-2}, x_{n+1}] \cup \{x_{n-3}\}, x_j \notin [x_{n-2}, x_{n+1}]$, without loss of generality, we take $x_i = x_{n-4}, x_j = x_{n-5}, x_z \in [x_{n-2}, x_{n+1}]$. Then, $PQO_{L_{n-2}}(x_i, x_j) = \min\{x_{n-4}, x_{n-5}\} = x_{n-5}$, and $PQO_{L_{n-2}}(x_i, x_z) = \min\{x_{n-4}, x_{n-2}\} = x_{n-4}$. So, $PQO_{L_{n-2}}(x_i, x_j) \leq PQO_{L_{n-2}}(x_i, x_z)$.

(2.8) $x_i \notin [x_{n-2}, x_{n+1}] \cup \{x_{n-3}\}, x_j, x_z \notin [x_{n-2}, x_{n+1}]$, without loss of generality, we take $x_i = x_{n-4}, x_j = x_z = x_{n-5}$. Then, $PQO_{L_{n-2}}(x_i, x_j) = \min\{x_{n-4}, x_{n-5}\} = x_{n-5}$, and $PQO_{L_{n-2}}(x_i, x_z) = PQO_{L_{n-2}}(x_i, x_j) = x_{n-5}$. So, $PQO_{L_{n-2}}(x_i, x_j) \leq PQO_{L_{n-2}}(x_i, x_z)$.

Therefore, $PQO_{L_{n-2}}$ satisfies $(PQO_L 3)$. In summary, $\forall x_i, x_j \in L$, $PQO_{L_{n-2}}$ is a discrete pseudo-quasi overlap function on L. □

Below, we provide some examples of discrete pseudo-quasi overlap functions on L in Theorem 1. Taking $L = \{0, 0.1, 0.2, 0.3, 0.4, 0.5, 0.6, 0.7, 0.8, 0.9, 1\}, n = 9$.

Note that the bolded parts in Tables 1–3 represent the values corresponding to $x_i, x_j \in [x_k, x_{k+3}]$ and $PQO_{L_k}(x_i, x_j) = PQO_{L_k^*}(x_i, x_j)(k = 0, 1, 2, ..., n-2)$ in Theorem 1.

Table 1. A discrete pseudo-quasi overlap function PQO_{L_0} on L constructed by the scenario (*i*) of Theorem 1. ($k = 0, x_w = x_3 = 0.3$).

L	**0**	**0.1**	**0.2**	**0.3**	**0.4**	**0.5**	**0.6**	**0.7**	**0.8**	**0.9**	**1**
0	**0**	**0**	**0**	**0**	0	0	0	0	0	0	0
0.1	**0**	**0.1**	**0.1**	**0.1**	0.3	0.3	0.3	0.3	0.3	0.3	0.3
0.2	**0**	**0.1**	**0.1**	**0.2**	0.3	0.3	0.3	0.3	0.3	0.3	0.3
0.3	**0**	**0.1**	**0.2**	**0.3**	0.3	0.3	0.3	0.3	0.3	0.3	0.3
0.4	0	0.1	0.2	0.3	0.4	0.4	0.4	0.4	0.4	0.4	0.4
0.5	0	0.1	0.2	0.3	0.4	0.5	0.5	0.5	0.5	0.5	0.5
0.6	0	0.1	0.2	0.3	0.4	0.5	0.6	0.6	0.6	0.6	0.6
0.7	0	0.1	0.2	0.3	0.4	0.5	0.6	0.7	0.7	0.7	0.7
0.8	0	0.1	0.2	0.3	0.4	0.5	0.6	0.7	0.8	0.8	0.8
0.9	0	0.1	0.2	0.3	0.4	0.5	0.6	0.7	0.8	0.9	0.9
1	0	0.1	0.2	0.3	0.4	0.5	0.6	0.7	0.8	0.9	1

Table 2. A discrete pseudo-quasi overlap function PQO_{L_k} on L constructed by the scenario (*ii*) of Theorem 1. ($k = 3, x_t = x_6 = 0.6$).

L	**0**	**0.1**	**0.2**	**0.3**	**0.4**	**0.5**	**0.6**	**0.7**	**0.8**	**0.9**	**1**
0	0	0	0	0	0	0	0	0	0	0	0
0.1	0	0.1	0.1	0.1	0.1	0.1	0.1	0.1	0.1	0.1	0.1
0.2	0	0.1	0.1	0.2	0.2	0.2	0.2	0.2	0.2	0.2	0.2
0.3	0	0.1	0.2	**0.3**	**0.3**	**0.3**	**0.3**	0.6	0.6	0.6	0.6
0.4	0	0.1	0.2	**0.3**	**0.4**	**0.4**	**0.4**	0.6	0.6	0.6	0.6
0.5	0	0.1	0.2	**0.3**	**0.4**	**0.4**	**0.5**	0.6	0.6	0.6	0.6
0.6	0	0.1	0.2	**0.3**	**0.4**	**0.5**	**0.6**	0.6	0.6	0.6	0.6
0.7	0	0.1	0.2	0.3	0.4	0.5	0.6	0.7	0.7	0.7	0.7
0.8	0	0.1	0.2	0.3	0.4	0.5	0.6	0.7	0.8	0.8	0.8
0.9	0	0.1	0.2	0.3	0.4	0.5	0.6	0.7	0.8	0.9	0.9
1	0	0.1	0.2	0.3	0.4	0.5	0.6	0.7	0.8	0.9	1

Table 3. A discrete pseudo-quasi overlap function $PQO_{L_{n-2}}$ on L constructed by the scenario (iii) of Theorem 1. $(k = 7, \theta = 1, x_{\beta_1} = x_{k-1} = 0.6, x_{\gamma_1} = x_k = x_\lambda = 0.7)$.

L	**0**	**0.1**	**0.2**	**0.3**	**0.4**	**0.5**	**0.6**	**0.7**	**0.8**	**0.9**	**1**
0	0	0	0	0	0	0	0	0	0	0	0
0.1	0	0.1	0.1	0.1	0.1	0.1	0.1	0.1	0.1	0.1	0.1
0.2	0	0.1	0.2	0.2	0.2	0.2	0.2	0.2	0.2	0.2	0.2
0.3	0	0.1	0.2	0.3	0.3	0.3	0.3	0.3	0.3	0.3	0.3
0.4	0	0.1	0.2	0.3	0.4	0.4	0.4	0.4	0.4	0.4	0.4
0.5	0	0.1	0.2	0.3	0.4	0.5	0.5	0.5	0.5	0.5	0.5
0.6	0	0.1	0.2	0.3	0.4	0.5	0.6	0.6	0.6	0.6	0.6
0.7	0	0.1	0.2	0.3	0.4	0.5	0.7	**0.7**	**0.7**	**0.7**	**0.7**
0.8	0	0.1	0.2	0.3	0.4	0.5	0.7	**0.7**	**0.8**	**0.8**	**0.8**
0.9	0	0.1	0.2	0.3	0.4	0.5	0.7	**0.7**	**0.8**	**0.9**	**0.9**
1	0	0.1	0.2	0.3	0.4	0.5	0.7	**0.7**	**0.8**	**0.9**	**1**

Of course, the construction method of the scenario (iii) in Theorem 1 also applies to $k = 2, 3, 4, \ldots n-3$. The specific details are similar to the scenario (iii) of Theorem 1.

Based on the scenario (iii) of Theorem 1, we obtain the following conclusion:

Proposition 9. *Let L be a finite chain, $k \in N, k = n-2$, $[x_{n-2}, x_{n+1}]$ be a sub-chain of L, and $PQO_{L^*_{n-2}} : [n-2, n+1]^2 \to [n-2, n+1]$ be a discrete pseudo-quasi overlap function on L^*_{n-2}. Then, $\forall x_i, x_j \in L$, the function $PQO_{L^{(O)}_{n-2}} (O = 1, 2) : L^2 \to L$ is defined as follows:*

$$PQO_{L^{(O)}_{n-2}}(x_i, x_j) = \begin{cases} PQO_{L^*_{n-2}}(x_i, x_j), & if\ x_i, x_j \in [x_{n-2}, x_{n+1}] \\ \min\{\alpha_1(x_i), \alpha_1(x_j)\}. & otherwise \end{cases}$$

is a discrete pseudo-quasi overlap function on L, among them, $\alpha_1(x_i) : L \to L$ and $\alpha_2(x_j) : L \to L$, we have the following two different construction forms:

(i) $n \geq 5, \alpha_1^{(5)}(x_i) : L \to L, \alpha_2^{(5)}(x_j) : L \to L$, separately, are defined as follows:

$$\alpha_1^{(5)}(x_i) = \begin{cases} PQO_{L^*_n}(x_i, x_{n+1}), & if\ x_i \in [x_{n-2}, x_{n+1}] \\ x_0 & if\ x_i = x_0 \\ x_\xi. & otherwise \end{cases}$$

$$\alpha_2^{(5)}(x_j) = \begin{cases} x_\pi, & if\ x_j \in [x_{n-2}, x_{n+1}] \\ x_j & otherwise \end{cases}$$

where $\xi, \pi \in N^+, n-3 \leq \xi \leq n-2, n-3 \leq \pi \leq n+1$, such as $x_\xi \leq x_\pi$.

(ii) $n \geq 4, \alpha_1^{(6)}(x_i) : L \to L, \alpha_2^{(6)}(x_j) : L \to L$, separately, given by the following:

$$\alpha_1^{(6)}(x_i) = \begin{cases} PQO_{L^*_k}(x_i, x_{n+1}), & if\ x_i \in [x_{n-2}, x_{n+1}] \\ x_{n-2} & if\ x_i = x_{n-3} \\ x_{n-3} & if\ x_i = x_{n-4} \\ \cdots & \cdots \\ x_3 & if\ x_i = x_2 \\ x_2 & if\ x_i = x_1 \\ x_i & otherwise \end{cases}$$

$$\alpha_2^{(6)}(x_j) = \begin{cases} x_\varepsilon, & if\ x_j \in [x_{n-2}, x_{n+1}] \\ x_j & otherwise \end{cases}$$

where $\varepsilon \in N^+, n-3 \leq \varepsilon \leq n+1$,, such as $x_i \leq x_\varepsilon$.

Proof. The proof is analogous to Theorem 1. □

Below, we provide some examples of discrete pseudo-quasi overlap functions on L in Proposition 9. Taking $L = \{0, 0.1, 0.2, 0.3, 0.4, 0.5, 0.6, 0.7, 0.8, 0.9, 1\}, n = 9, x_\xi = x_\pi = 0.6$.

Note that the bolded parts in Tables 4 and 5 represent the values corresponding to $x_i, x_j \in [x_{n-2}, x_{n+1}]$ and $PQO_{L_{n-2}^{(O)}}(x_i, x_j) = PQO_{L_{n-2}^{*}}(x_i, x_j)(k = n-2 \in N)$ in Proposition 9.

Table 4. A discrete pseudo-quasi overlap function $PQO_{L_{n-2}^{(1)}}$ on L constructed by the scenario (i) of Proposition 9. ($k = 7, x_\xi = x_\pi = 0.6$).

L	**0**	**0.1**	**0.2**	**0.3**	**0.4**	**0.5**	**0.6**	**0.7**	**0.8**	**0.9**	**1**
0	0	0	0	0	0	0	0	0	0	0	0
0.1	0	0.1	0.1	0.1	0.1	0.1	0.1	0.1	0.1	0.1	0.1
0.2	0	0.1	0.2	0.2	0.2	0.2	0.2	0.2	0.2	0.2	0.2
0.3	0	0.1	0.2	0.3	0.3	0.3	0.3	0.3	0.3	0.3	0.3
0.4	0	0.1	0.2	0.3	0.4	0.4	0.4	0.4	0.4	0.4	0.4
0.5	0	0.1	0.2	0.3	0.4	0.5	0.5	0.5	0.5	0.5	0.5
0.6	0	0.1	0.2	0.3	0.4	0.5	0.6	0.6	0.6	0.6	0.6
0.7	0	0.6	0.6	0.6	0.6	0.6	0.6	**0.7**	**0.7**	**0.7**	**0.7**
0.8	0	0.6	0.6	0.6	0.6	0.6	0.6	**0.7**	**0.8**	**0.8**	**0.8**
0.9	0	0.6	0.6	0.6	0.6	0.6	0.6	**0.7**	**0.8**	**0.9**	**0.9**
1	0	0.6	0.6	0.6	0.6	0.6	0.6	**0.7**	**0.8**	**0.9**	**1**

Table 5. A discrete pseudo-quasi overlap function $PQO_{L_{n-2}^{(2)}}$ on L constructed by the scenario (ii) of Proposition 9. ($k = 7, x_\varepsilon = 0.7$).

L	**0**	**0.1**	**0.2**	**0.3**	**0.4**	**0.5**	**0.6**	**0.7**	**0.8**	**0.9**	**1**
0	0	0	0	0	0	0	0	0	0	0	0
0.1	0	0.1	0.1	0.1	0.1	0.1	0.1	0.1	0.1	0.1	0.1
0.2	0	0.2	0.2	0.2	0.2	0.2	0.2	0.2	0.2	0.2	0.2
0.3	0	0.2	0.3	0.3	0.3	0.3	0.3	0.3	0.3	0.3	0.3
0.4	0	0.2	0.3	0.4	0.4	0.4	0.4	0.4	0.4	0.4	0.4
0.5	0	0.2	0.3	0.4	0.5	0.5	0.5	0.5	0.5	0.5	0.5
0.6	0	0.2	0.3	0.4	0.5	0.6	0.6	0.6	0.6	0.6	0.6
0.7	0	0.2	0.3	0.4	0.5	0.6	0.7	**0.7**	**0.7**	**0.7**	**0.7**
0.8	0	0.2	0.3	0.4	0.5	0.6	0.7	**0.7**	**0.8**	**0.8**	**0.8**
0.9	0	0.2	0.3	0.4	0.5	0.6	0.7	**0.7**	**0.8**	**0.9**	**0.9**
1	0	0.2	0.3	0.4	0.5	0.6	0.7	**0.7**	**0.8**	**0.9**	**1**

Likewise, the construction method of Proposition 9 also applies to $k = 2, 3, 4, \ldots n-3$. The specific details are similar to Proposition 9.

In summary, the biggest difference between the method of constructing discrete pseudo-quasi overlap functions on finite chains described above and the method of creating quasi-overlap functions on finite chains through ordinal sum in [40] lies in the uniformity of the outcomes. Quasi-overlap functions on finite chains constructed from different sub-chains are the same, whereas the discrete pseudo-quasi overlap functions on finite chains constructed from pseudo-quasi overlap functions on different sub-chains are different.

5. The Application of Discrete pseudo-quasi overlap Functions in Fuzzy Multi-Attribute Group Decision-Making

In this section, we extend the binary discrete pseudo-quasi overlap function on L in Definition 6 to an n-ary discrete pseudo-quasi overlap function on L. Then, we construct an n-dimensional discrete pseudo-quasi overlap function using pseudo-overlap functions, pseudo-quasi-isomorphisms, and integral functions. Furthermore, we apply the n-ary discrete pseudo-quasi overlap function on L to fuzzy multi-attribute group decision-making.

5.1. N-Ary Discrete Pseudo-Quasi Overlap Functions

To start with, we present the concept of n-ary discrete pseudo-quasi overlap functions on L.

Definition 11. *Let $L = \{0, x_1, x_2, \ldots, x_n, 1\}$ be a finite chain. A function $PQO^n_L : L^n \to L$ is called an n-ary discrete pseudo-quasi overlap function on L when it satisfies $\forall x_{i+1}, x_{i+2}, x_{i+3}\cdots, x_{i+n} \in L$,*

(PQO^n_L1) $PQO^n_L(x_{i+1}, x_{i+2}, x_{i+3}\cdots, x_{i+n}) = x_0 \Leftrightarrow$ for $j \in N^+, 1 \le j \le n$, such as $\prod_{j=1}^{n} x_{i+j} = x_0$;

(PQO^n_L2) $PQO^n_L(x_{i+1}, x_{i+2}, x_{i+3}\cdots, x_{i+n}) = x_{n+1} \Leftrightarrow$ for $j \in N^+, 1 \le j \le n$, such as $\prod_{j=1}^{n} x_{i+j} = x_{n+1}$;

(PQO^n_L3) PQO^n_L is non-decreasing.

Note that we extend the finite chain L in Definition 11 to [0,1], then PQO^n_L is an n-ary pseudo-quasi overlap function. Moreover, we can readily provide the definition of n ary pseudo-quasi overlap functions PQO^n, along with its corresponding properties (PQO^n1), (PQO^n2), and (PQO^n3). The definition of n-ary pseudo-quasi overlap functions is similar to Definition 11, so it is omitted here.

Additionally, we assume that $L = \{0, 0.001, 0.002, \ldots, 0.999, 1\}$ in Definition 11. In this section, we use L^* to represent the finite chain $\{0, 0.001, 0.002, \ldots, 0.999, 1\}$.

Example 2. *Let L^* be a finite chain.*

(1) $\forall x_{i+1}, x_{i+2}, x_{i+3}, \ldots, x_{i+n} \in L^*$, the function $PQO^n_{L^*} : L^{*n} \to L^*$,

$$PQO^n_{L^*}(x_{i+1}, x_{i+2}, x_{i+3}, \ldots, x_{i+n}) = \min(x_{i+1}, x_{i+2}, x_{i+3}, \ldots, x_{i+n-1}, \tfrac{[100x_{i+n}]}{100})$$

where $[\cdot]$ is an integral function, is an n-ary discrete pseudo-quasi overlap function on L^*.

(2) $\forall x_{i+1}, x_{i+2}, x_{i+3}, \ldots, x_{i+n} \in L^*, x_1, x_e, x_f \in L^*, x_e \neq x_f, x_1 < \min\{x_e, x_f\}$, the function $PQO^n_{L^*} : L^{*n} \to L^*$,

$$PQO^n_{L^*}(x_{i+1}, x_{i+2}, x_{i+3}, \ldots, x_{i+n}) = \begin{cases} x_1, & if\ x_0 < x_1 < x_e, x_0 < x_{n+1} < x_f \\ \min(x_{i+1}, x_{i+2}, x_{i+3}, \ldots, x_{i+n}). & otherwise \end{cases}$$

is an n-ary discrete pseudo-quasi overlap function on L^*.

5.2. Generation of N-Ary Discrete Pseudo-Quasi Overlap Functions

As stated in reference [18], the generation of pseudo-overlap functions comes from n-dimensional overlap functions and a set of weights. Therefore, we construct an n-dimensional discrete pseudo-quasi overlap function based on the pseudo-overlap functions mentioned above, pseudo-quasi-isomorphisms, and integral functions. Below, we introduce the concept of pseudo-quasi-isomorphisms:

Definition 12. *A unary function $H : [0,1] \to [0,1]$ is called a pseudo-quasi-automorphism when it satisfies $\forall x \in [0,1]$,*

$(H1)$ H is non-decreasing;

$(H2)$ $x = 1$ when and only when $H(x) = 1$;

$(H3)$ $x = 0$ when and only when $H(x) = 0$.

Obviously, each pseudo-automorphism is a pseudo-quasi-automorphism given in [26]. Conversely, a continuous pseudo-quasi-automorphism is a pseudo-automorphism.

Theorem 2. *Let L^* be a finite chain, $H : [0.1] \to [0,1]$ be a pseudo-quasi-automorphism, and $PO^n : [0,1]^n \to [0,1]$ be an n-ary pseudo-overlap function. Then, $\forall x_{i+1}, x_{i+2}, x_{i+3} \dots, x_{i+n} \in [0,1]$, the function $PQO^n : [0,1]^n \to L^*$ is defined as follows:*

$$PQO^n(x_{i+1}, x_{i+2}, x_{i+3}, \dots, x_{i+n}) = H(PQ^n(x_{i+1}, x_{i+2}, x_{i+3} \dots, x_{i+n})) = \frac{[1000PQ^n(x_{i+1}, x_{i+2}, x_{i+3} \dots, x_{i+n})]}{1000} \quad (1)$$

where $H(x) = \frac{1}{1000}F(1000x)$, F is an integral function, i.e., $F(x) = [x]$, and is an n-ary pseudo-quasi overlap function.

Proof. Suppose that PO^n is an n-ary pseudo-overlap function. (PQO^n1) (Necessity) If we have the following:

$$PQO^n(x_{i+1}, x_{i+2}, x_{i+3} \dots, x_{i+n}) = 0,$$

then $H(PQ^n(x_{i+1}, x_{i+2}, x_{i+3} \dots, x_{i+n})) = 0$, i.e., $PQ^n(x_{i+1}, x_{i+2}, x_{i+3} \dots, x_{i+n}) = 0$. So, for $j \in N^+, 1 \leq j \leq n$, such as $\prod_{i=1}^{n} x_{i+j} = 0$. (Sufficiency) If $j \in N^+, 1 \leq j \leq n$, $\prod_{i=1}^{n} x_{i+j} = 0$, then $PQ^n(x_{i+1}, x_{i+2}, x_{i+3} \dots, x_{i+n}) = 0$, that is, we have the following:

$$PQO^n(x_{i+1}, x_{i+2}, x_{i+3} \dots, x_{i+n}) = H(PQ^n(x_{i+1}, x_{i+2}, x_{i+3} \dots, x_{i+n}) = H(0) = 0.$$

Thus, PQO^n satisfies (PQO^n1).(PQO^n2)(Necessity) If $PQO^n(x_{i+1}, x_{i+2}, x_{i+3} \dots, x_{i+n}) = 1$, then $H(PQ^n(x_{i+1}, x_{i+2}, x_{i+3} \dots, x_{i+n})) = 1$, that is, $PQ^n(x_{i+1}, x_{i+2}, x_{i+3} \dots, x_{i+n}) = 1$, So, for $j \in N^+, 1 \leq j \leq n$, such as $\prod_{j=1}^{n} x_{i+j} = 1$. (Sufficiency) If $j \in N^+, 1 \leq j \leq n$, $\prod_{j=1}^{n} x_{i+j} = 1$, then $PQ^n(x_{i+1}, x_{i+2}, x_{i+3} \dots, x_{i+n}) = 1$, that is, we have the following:

$$PQO^n(x_{i+1}, x_{i+2}, x_{i+3} \dots, x_{i+n}) = H(PQ^n(x_{i+1}, x_{i+2}, x_{i+3} \dots, x_{i+n})) = H(1) = 1.$$

Thus, PQO^n satisfies (PQO^n2). (PQO^n3) Since F is increasing, H is increasing, and PQ^n is increasing, we clearly know that PQO^n is increasing. Thus, PQO^n satisfies (PQO^n3). Therefore, PQO^n is an n-ary pseudo-quasi overlap function. □

Below, we transform the pseudo-quasi overlap function on $[0,1]$ in Theorem 2 into a discrete pseudo-quasi overlap function on L^*. According to the description of function restrictions in [50] and Theorem 2, we obtain the following conclusion:

Lemma 2. *Let L^* be a finite chain, $PQO^n : [0,1]^n \to L^*$,*

$$PQO^n(x_{i+1}, x_{i+2}, x_{i+3}, \dots, x_{i+n}) = H(PQ^n(x_{i+1}, x_{i+2}, x_{i+3}, \dots, x_{i+n})) = \frac{[1000PQ^n(x_{i+1}, x_{i+2}, x_{i+3}, \dots, x_{i+n})]}{1000} \quad (2)$$

and be an n-ary pseudo-quasi overlap function, and let L^* be a subset of $[0,1]$. Then, $\forall x_{i+1}, x_{i+2}, x_{i+3}, \dots, x_{i+n} \in L^*$, the n-ary function $PQO^n : L^{*n} \to L^*$ is an n-ary discrete pseudo-quasi overlap function on L^*. Specifically, we use $PQO^n_{L^*}$ to represent an n-ary discrete pseudo-quasi overlap function on L^*.

Based on Theorem 2, Lemma 2, and Examples 6 and 7 of [18], we can obtain the following example:

Example 3. *Let L^* be a finite chain, and $w_1 = (0.3, 0.3, 0.4)$ be a positive weighted vector; the following $PQO^{(e)}_{L^*_{w_1}}$ $(e = 1,2,3,4,5) : L^{*3} \to L^*$ are ternary discrete pseudo-quasi overlap functions on L^* generated by w_1.*

(1) *$\forall x_{i+1}, x_{i+2}, x_{i+3} \in L^*$, the function $PQO^{(1)}_{L^*_{w_1}} : L^{*3} \to L^*$,*

$$PQO^{(1)}_{L^*_{w_1}}(x_{i+1}, x_{i+2}, x_{i+3}) = \begin{cases} x_0, & if\ x_{i+1} = x_{i+2} = x_{i+3} = x_0 \\ \frac{[\frac{1000x_{i+1}x_{i+2}x_{i+3}}{0.3x_{i+1}+0.3x_{i+2}+0.4x_{i+3}}]}{1000}. & otherwise \end{cases}$$

is a discrete pseudo-quasi overlap function on L^*.

(2) $\forall x_{i+1}, x_{i+2}, x_{i+3} \in L^*$, *the function* $PQO^{(2)}_{L^*_{w_1}} : L^{*3} \to L^*$,

$$PQO^{(2)}_{L^*_{w_1}}(x_{i+1}, x_{i+2}, x_{i+3}) = \frac{[1000x_{i+1}x_{i+2}x_{i+3}(0.3x_{i+1}+0.3x_{i+2}+0.4x_{i+3})]}{1000}$$

is a discrete pseudo-quasi overlap function on L^*.

(3) $\forall x_{i+1}, x_{i+2}, x_{i+3} \in L^*$, *the function* $PQO^{(3)}_{L^*_{w_1}} : L^{*3} \to L^*$,

$$PQO^{(3)}_{L^*_{w_1}}(x_{i+1}, x_{i+2}, x_{i+3}) = \begin{cases} x_0, & if\ x_{i+1} = x_{i+2} = x_{i+3} = x_0 \\ \frac{[\frac{330x_{i+1}x_{i+2}x_{i+3}}{0.12x_{i+2}x_{i+3}+0.12x_{i+1}x_{i+3}+0.09x_{i+1}x_{i+2}}]}{1000}. & otherwise \end{cases}$$

is a discrete pseudo-quasi overlap function on L^*.

(4) $\forall x_{i+1}, x_{i+2}, x_{i+3} \in L^*$, *the function* $PQO^{(4)}_{L^*_{w_1}} : L^{*3} \to L^*$,

$$PQO^{(4)}_{L^*_{w_1}}(x_{i+1}, x_{i+2}, x_{i+3}) = \frac{1}{1000}[\frac{1000x^2_{(\overline{i+1})}x^4_{(\overline{i+2})}x^6_{(\overline{i+3})}}{0.4^2 0.3^{10}}]$$

where $(x_{(\overline{i+1})}, x_{(\overline{i+2})}, x_{(\overline{i+3})})$ *is a permutation of* $(0.3x_{i+1}, 0.3x_{i+2}, 0.4x_{i+3})$, *and it fulfills* $x_{(\overline{i+3})} \leq x_{(\overline{i+2})} \leq x_{(\overline{i+1})}$, *is a discrete pseudo-quasi overlap function on* L^*.

(5) $\forall x_{i+1}, x_{i+2}, x_{i+3} \in L$, *the function* $PQO^{(5)}_{L^*_{w_1}} : L^{*3} \to L^*$,

$$PQO^{(5)}_{L^*_{w_1}}(x_{i+1}, x_{i+2}, x_{i+3}) = \frac{1}{1000}[\frac{1000\sqrt{x_{(\overline{i+1})}}\sqrt[4]{x_{(\overline{i+2})}}\sqrt[6]{x_{(\overline{i+3})}}}{\sqrt[4]{0.3^3}\sqrt[6]{0.4}}]$$

where $(x_{(\overline{i+1})}, x_{(\overline{i+2})}, x_{(\overline{i+3})})$ *is a permutation of* $(0.3x_{i+1}, 0.3x_{i+2}, 0.4x_{i+3})$, *and it fulfills* $x_{(\overline{i+3})} \leq x_{(\overline{i+2})} \leq x_{(\overline{i+1})}$, *is a discrete pseudo-quasi overlap function on* L^*.

Example 4. *Let* L^* *be a finite chain, and* $w_2 = (0.1, 0.1, 0.2, 0.2, 0.2, 0.2)$ *be a positive weighted vector. The following* $PQO^{(e)}_{L^*_{w_2}} (e = 1, 2, 3, 4, 5) : L^{*6} \to L^*$ *are six-variable discrete pseudo-quasi overlap functions on* L^* *generated by* w_2.

(1) $\forall x_{i+1}, x_{i+2}, x_{i+3}, x_{i+4}, x_{i+5}, x_{i+6} \in L^*$, *the function* $PQO^{(1)}_{L^*_{w_2}} : L^{*6} \to L^*$,

$$PQQ^{(1)}_{L^*_{w_2}}(x_{i+1}, x_{i+2}, x_{i+3}, x_{i+4}, x_{i+5}, x_{i+6})$$
$$= \begin{cases} x_0, & if\ x_{i+1} = x_{i+2} = x_{i+3} = x_{i+4} \\ & = x_{i+5} = x_{i+6} = x_0 \\ \frac{[1000\sqrt{\frac{x_{i+1}x_{i+2}x_{i+3}x_{i+4}x_{i+5}x_{i+6}}{0.1x_{i+1}+0.1x_{i+2}+0.2x_{i+3}+0.2x_{i+4}+0.2x_{i+5}+0.2x_{i+6}}}]}{1000}. & otherwise \end{cases}$$

is a discrete pseudo-quasi overlap function on L^*.

(2) $\forall x_{i+1}, x_{i+2}, x_{i+3}, x_{i+4}, x_{i+5}, x_{i+6} \in L^*$, *the function* $PQO^{(2)}_{L^*_{w_2}} : L^{*6} \to L^*$,

$$PQO^{(2)}_{L^*_{w_2}}(x_{i+1}, x_{i+2}, x_{i+3}, x_{i+4}, x_{i+5}, x_{i+6})$$
$$= \frac{[1000x_{i+1}x_{i+2}x_{i+3}x_{i+4}x_{i+5}x_{i+6}(0.1x_{i+1}+0.1x_{i+2}+0.2x_{i+3}+0.2x_{i+4}+0.2x_{i+5}+0.2x_{i+6})]}{1000}$$

is a discrete pseudo-quasi overlap function on L^*.

(3) $\forall x_{i+1}, x_{i+2}, x_{i+3}, x_{i+4}, x_{i+5}, x_{i+6} \in L$, *the function* $PQO^{(3)}_{L_{w_2}} : L^{*6} \to L^*$,

$$PQO^{(3)}_{L^*_{w_2}}(x_{i+1}, x_{i+2}, x_{i+3}, x_{i+4}, x_{i+5}, x_{i+6})$$
$$= \begin{cases} x_0, & if\ x_{i+1}x_{i+2}x_{i+3}x_{i+4}x_{i+5}x_{i+6} = x_0 \\ \frac{[\frac{8000}{\frac{2}{x_{i+1}}+\frac{2}{x_{i+2}}+\frac{1}{x_{i+3}}+\frac{1}{x_{i+4}}+\frac{1}{x_{i+5}}+\frac{1}{x_{i+6}}}]}{1000}. & otherwise \end{cases}$$

is a discrete discrete pseudo-quasi overlap function on L^*.

(4) $\forall x_{i+1}, x_{i+2}, x_{i+3}, x_{i+4}, x_{i+5}, x_{i+6} \in L$, *the function* $PQO^{(4)}_{L^*_{w_2}} : L^{*6} \to L^*$,

$$PQO^{(4)}_{L^*_w}(x_{i+1}, x_{i+2}, x_{i+3}, x_{i+4}, x_{i+5}, x_{i+6}) = \frac{[\frac{1000x^2_{(\overline{i+1})} x^4_{(\overline{i+2})} x^6_{(\overline{i+3})} x^8_{(\overline{i+4})} x^{10}_{(\overline{i+5})} x^{12}_{(\overline{i+6})}}{0.2^{20}0.1^{22}}]}{1000}$$

where $(x_{(\overline{i+1})}, x_{(\overline{i+2})}, x_{(\overline{i+3})}, x_{(\overline{i+4})}, x_{(\overline{i+5})}, x_{(\overline{i+6})})$ *is a permutation of* $(0.1x_{i+1}, 0.1x_{i+2}, 0.2x_{i+3}, 0.2x_{i+4}, 0.2x_{i+5}, 0.2x_{i+6})$, *and it fulfills* $x_{(\overline{i+6})} \leq x_{(\overline{i+5})} \leq x_{(\overline{i+4})} \leq x_{(\overline{i+3})} \leq x_{(\overline{i+2})} \leq x_{(\overline{i+1})}$, *is a discrete pseudo-quasi overlap function on* L^*.

(5) $\forall x_{i+1}, x_{i+2}, x_{i+3}, x_{i+4}, x_{i+5}, x_{i+6} \in L^*$, *the function* $PQO^{(5)}_{L^*_{w_2}} : L^{*6} \to L^*$,

$$PQO^{(5)}_{L^*_w}(x_{i+1}, x_{i+2}, x_{i+3}, x_{i+4}, x_{i+5}, x_{i+6}) = \frac{1}{1000}[\frac{1000\sqrt{x_{(\overline{i+1})}}\sqrt[4]{x_{(\overline{i+2})}}\sqrt[6]{x_{(\overline{i+3})}}\sqrt[8]{x_{(\overline{i+4})}}\sqrt[10]{x_{(\overline{i+5})}}\sqrt[12]{x_{(\overline{i+6})}}}{\sqrt[4]{0.1^3}\sqrt[40]{0.2^{19}}}]$$

where $(x_{(\overline{i+1})}, x_{(\overline{i+2})}, x_{(\overline{i+3})}, x_{(\overline{i+4})}, x_{(\overline{i+5})}, x_{(\overline{i+6})})$ *is a permutation of* $(0.1x_{i+1}, 0.1x_{i+2}, 0.2x_{i+3}, 0.2x_{i+4}, 0.2x_{i+5}, 0.2x_{i+6})$, *and it fulfills* $x_{(\overline{i+1})} \leq x_{(\overline{i+2})} \leq x_{(\overline{i+3})} \leq x_{(\overline{i+4})} \leq x_{(\overline{i+5})} \leq x_{(\overline{i+6})}$, *is a discrete pseudo-quasi overlap function on* L^*.

Next, we apply the discrete pseudo-quasi overlap functions on L^* proposed above to fuzzy multi-attribute group decision-making.

5.3. An Application of Discrete Pseudo-Quasi Overlap Functions in Fuzzy Multi-Attribute Group Decision-Making

At present, the aggregation functions used in most applications of fuzzy multi-attribute group decision-making are continuous, such as the Sugeno integral based on overlap functions in [47], the overlap function in [49], and the pseudo-overlap function in [18]. However, in practical applications of fuzzy multi-attribute group decision-making, the data objects involved are generally discrete. Therefore, we apply the n-ary discrete pseudo-quasi overlap function constructed above to fuzzy multi-attribute group decision-making. Firstly, we briefly introduce the concept of fuzzy multi-attribute group decision-making.

A solution to the fuzzy multi-attribute group decision-making problem (FMAGDMP) involves selecting the most favorable options from a list of alternatives, taking into account various attributes of the alternatives as well as the perspectives of the specialist group.

Generally, in a FMAGDMP, let $A = \{a_1, a_2, \ldots, a_n\}$ be a discrete finite set of feasible alternatives, $U = \{u_1, u_2, \ldots, u_m\}$ be a set of attributes, $E = \{\varepsilon_1, \varepsilon_2, \ldots, \varepsilon_k\}$ be a set of decision makers, and $w_1 = (w_{11}, w_{12}, \ldots, w_{1k})^T, w_2 = (w_{21}, w_{22}, \ldots, w_{2m})^T$ be a positive weighted vector. Each decision maker ε_t creates a decision matrix $S^t = ({s_{ij}}^{(t)})_{n\times m}$, with the columns denoting the attributes and the rows indicating the feasible alternatives. In traditional decision-making, if the feasible alternative a_i has the attribute u_j, then the decision makers ε_t believe that the position ${s_{ij}}^{(t)}$ of $S^{(t)}$ has the value of 1, and if not, the position ${s_{ij}}^{(t)}$ of $S^{(t)}$ has the value of 0. However, under certain circumstances, some features are usually vague, such as "reasonable price", "market depression", and "currency inflation", which are essentially ambiguous. Therefore, we need to treat them as fuzzy sets. In this instance, the value at position ${s_{ij}}^{(t)}$ represents the membership degree, that is, a value in [0, 1], of the alternative a_i to the fuzzy set connected to the attribute u_j. Generally speaking, profit and expenses are two important attributes. For instance, while "risk of investment" is an expense attribute, "quality of construction project" is a profit attribute. In addition, we assume that φ is an index set of the profit attributes.

We provide the solution to FMAGDMP as follows:

- Step 1. Use the following Formula (3) to convert each decision matrix $S^{(t)} = ({s_{ij}}^{(t)})_{n\times m}$ into a standard decision matrix $N^{(t)} = ({n_{ij}}^{(t)})_{n\times m}$;

$$ {n_{ij}}^{(t)} = \begin{cases} {s_{ij}}^{(t)}, & if\ j \in \varphi \\ 1 - {s_{ij}}^{(t)}. & otherwise \end{cases} \quad (3)$$

- Step 2. Generate a congregate decision matrix $Q = (q_{ij})_{n\times m}$ by aggregating the standard decision matrix $N^{(t)} = (n_{ij}{}^{(t)})_{n\times m}$ according to an n-dimensional discrete pseudo-quasi overlap function $PQO^{(e)}_{L^*_{w_1}}$ $(e \in N^+, 1 \le e \le 5)$ on L^*, where the aggregation method is shown in Formula (4) below;

$$q_{ij} = PQO^{(e)}_{L^*_{w_1}}(n_{ij}{}^{(1)}, n_{ij}{}^{(2)}, \ldots, n_{ij}{}^{(k)}) \tag{4}$$

- Step 3. Determine the total preference vector tpv_i for each alternative a_i by aggregating the membership degrees to each attribute u_j using $PQO^{(e)}_{L^*_{w_2}}$ $(e \in N^+, 1 \le f \le 5)$ on L^*; Formula (5) below shows the aggregating approach:

$$tpv_i = PQO^{(e)}_{L_{w_2}}(q_{i1}, q_{i2}, \ldots, q_{im}) \tag{5}$$

- Step 4. Sort the alternatives based on the overall preference values in descending order and select the alternative with the highest value.

Next, we demonstrate the application of the above method through the example given in [43]. We assume that investors plan to contribute a portion of their funds to an enterprise. Making use of a market analysis, investors narrow down the range of potential enterprises to six:

a_1 : a chemical enterprise;
a_2 : a food firm;
a_3 : a computer corporation;
a_4 : an automobile firm;
a_5 : a furniture corporation;
a_6 : a pharmaceutical enterprise.

Three specialists or decision makers $(\varepsilon_1, \varepsilon_2, \varepsilon_3)$ with corresponding weight vectors $w_1 = (0.3, 0.3, 0.4)$ assist the investor.

Six attributes are established by the specialist panel to assess the investments.

The profit attributes include the following:
u_1 : profits in the immediate term;
u_2 : profits in the medium term;
u_3 : profits over the long haul.

The expense attributes include the following:
u_4 : investing in danger;
u_5 : investment challenge;
u_6 : additional detrimental aspects of investment.

The assessments provided by the specialists regarding the degree to which the investments align with the attributes are shown in Tables 6–8, forming the decision matrix for each specialist.

Table 6. Evaluation of specialist ε_1.

$S^{(1)}$	u_1	u_2	u_3	u_4	u_5	u_6
a_1	0.7	0.8	0.6	0.7	0.5	0.9
a_2	0.8	0.6	0.9	0.7	0.6	0.7
a_3	0.5	0.4	0.8	0.3	0.8	0.8
a_4	0.6	0.7	0.6	0.7	0.8	0.6
a_5	0.9	0.8	0.4	0.7	0.7	0.8
a_6	0.8	0.3	0.7	0.7	0.6	0.7

Table 7. Evaluation of specialist ε_2.

$S^{(2)}$	u_1	u_2	u_3	u_4	u_5	u_6
a_1	0.6	0.8	0.5	0.6	0.4	0.8
a_2	0.7	0.6	0.8	0.6	0.7	0.7
a_3	0.7	0.6	0.8	0.7	0.8	0.8
a_4	0.6	0.7	0.5	0.6	0.8	0.7
a_5	0.7	0.8	0.7	0.7	0.6	0.8
a_6	0.6	0.4	0.8	0.7	0.6	0.7

Table 8. Evaluation of specialist ε_3.

$S^{(3)}$	u_1	u_2	u_3	u_4	u_5	u_6
a_1	0.7	0.6	0.6	0.6	0.4	0.7
a_2	0.7	0.6	0.7	0.6	0.6	0.7
a_3	0.6	0.5	0.8	0.5	0.8	0.8
a_4	0.6	0.7	0.7	0.5	0.8	0.6
a_5	0.7	0.8	0.6	0.7	0.6	0.8
a_6	0.4	0.5	0.9	0.7	0.6	0.6

After applying Formula (3) from step 1 to the decision matrices $S^{(1)}, S^{(2)}$ and $S^{(3)}$ mentioned above, we obtain the standard decision matrices $N^{(1)}, N^{(2)}$, and $N^{(3)}$, which are shown in Tables 9–11 in that order.

Table 9. Standardization of specialist ε_1 decision matrix.

$N^{(1)}$	u_1	u_2	u_3	u_4	u_5	u_6
a_1	0.7	0.8	0.6	0.3	0.5	0.1
a_2	0.8	0.6	0.9	0.3	0.4	0.3
a_3	0.5	0.4	0.8	0.7	0.2	0.2
a_4	0.6	0.7	0.6	0.3	0.2	0.4
a_5	0.9	0.8	0.4	0.3	0.3	0.2
a_6	0.8	0.3	0.7	0.3	0.4	0.3

Table 10. Standardization of specialist ε_2 decision matrix.

$N^{(2)}$	u_1	u_2	u_3	u_4	u_5	u_6
a_1	0.6	0.8	0.5	0.4	0.6	0.2
a_2	0.7	0.6	0.8	0.4	0.3	0.3
a_3	0.7	0.6	0.8	0.3	0.2	0.2
a_4	0.6	0.7	0.5	0.4	0.2	0.3
a_5	0.7	0.8	0.7	0.3	0.4	0.2
a_6	0.6	0.4	0.8	0.3	0.4	0.3

Table 11. Standardization of specialist ε_3 decision matrix.

$N^{(3)}$	u_1	u_2	u_3	u_4	u_5	u_6
a_1	0.7	0.6	0.6	0.4	0.6	0.3
a_2	0.7	0.6	0.7	0.4	0.4	0.3
a_3	0.6	0.5	0.8	0.5	0.2	0.2
a_4	0.6	0.7	0.7	0.5	0.2	0.4
a_5	0.7	0.8	0.6	0.3	0.4	0.2
a_6	0.4	0.5	0.9	0.3	0.4	0.4

The congregate decision matrix Q of Table 12 is produced by applying $PQO^{(1)}_{L^*_{w_1}}$ of Example 3 to the standard decision matrices $N^{(1)}, N^{(2)}$, and $N^{(3)}$ above.

Table 12. Congregate decision matrix.

Q	u_1	u_2	u_3	u_4	u_5	u_6
a_1	0.439	0.533	0.316	0.130	0.316	0.029
a_2	0.537	0.360	0.638	0.130	0.130	0.090
a_3	0.350	0.240	0.640	0.210	0.040	0.040
a_4	0.360	0.490	0.344	0.146	0.040	0.130
a_5	0.580	0.640	0.295	0.090	0.130	0.040
a_6	0.331	0.146	0.622	0.090	0.160	0.106

Afterward, the total preference vector tpv_i is determined by taking into account $PQO^{(1)}_{L^*_{w_2}}$ of Example 4. Table 13 presents the final result. (Specifically, $[\cdot]$ in $PQO^{(1)}_{L^*_{w_1}}$ and $PQO^{(1)}_{L^*_{w_2}}$ only represents the rounding function. For other types of integral functions, such as floor, ceil, and fix, the results obtained are similar to those of the round function.)

Table 13. Total preference vector.

TPV	a_1	a_2	a_3	a_4	a_5	a_6
tpv_i	0.018	0.026	0.009	0.015	0.015	0.014

Eventually, we obtain the descending order of the alternative a_i by utilizing Table 13:

$$a_2 > a_1 > a_4 = a_5 > a_6 > a_3$$

We are aware that the weighted discrete pseudo-quasi overlap functions used in steps 2 and 3 of the FMAGDMP solution are different, and the final ranking of the alternative a_i is dissimilar. In Table 14, we obtain different rankings by utilizing $PQO^{(e)}_{L^*_{w_1}}$ and $PQO^{(e)}_{L^*_{w_2}}$ $(e \in N^+, e = 1,2,3,4,5)$ from Examples 3 and 4 and other aggregation functions in [48,50]. Moreover, the above rankings are generated by different aggregation functions under the same FMAGDMP solution.

From Table 14, we notice that the eleven aggregation methods generated by $PQO^{(e)}_{L^*_{w_1}}$ and $PQO^{(e)}_{L^*_{w_2}}$ $(e \in N^+, e = 1,2,3,4,5)$ of Examples 3 and 4 resulted in seven different sorts. In addition, among these seven different sorts, all sorts indicate that a_2 is the best, while most sorts (five sorts) show that a_3 is the worst.

By analyzing Table 14, we can see that the rankings generated by different aggregation functions under the same FMAGDMP solution are slightly different, and compared to other aggregation functions, the rankings obtained using discrete pseudo-quasi overlap functions are more reasonable.

As mentioned above, we use weighted discrete pseudo-quasi overlap functions to fuse information. However, in practical applications, there may be situations without weight vectors. Therefore, we choose other types of discrete pseudo-quasi overlap functions as aggregation functions to solve FMAGDMP. Of course, this type of discrete pseudo-quasi overlap function is significantly different from Examples 3 and 4. It implies the importance of various expert decisions or attributes in the function formula itself. Below, we apply this type of discrete pseudo-quasi overlap function to the previous approach for solving FMAGDMP.

Based on Theorem 2, Lemma 2, and [18], we obtain the following example:

Table 14. Ranks obtained by different weighted discrete pseudo-quasi functions and other aggregation functions in [49,51].

Congregate Aggregation Function	Total Aggregation Function	Ranking
$Maximum$	$Maximum$	$a_2 > a_4 > a_5 > a_1 > a_3 > a_6$
$Minimum$	$Minimum$	$a_3 > a_5 > a_1 > a_4 > a_2 > a_6$
WA_w^P	WA_w^P	$a_2 > x_3 > a_6 > a_4 > a_1 > a_5$
$WA_w^{O^3_{0.5M}}$	$WA_w^{O^3_{0.5M}}$	$a_5 > a_2 > a_1 > a_4 > a_3 > a_6$
$WA_w^{O^3_{2M}}$	$WA_w^{O^3_{2M}}$	$a_2 > a_1 > a_5 > a_4 > a_3 > a_6$
$PQO^{(1)}_{L^*_{w_1}}$	$PQO^{(1)}_{L^*_{w_2}}$	$a_2 > a_1 > a_4 = a_5 > a_6 > a_3$
$PQO^{(1)}_{L^*_{w_1}}$	$PQO^{(2)}_{L^*_{w_2}}$	$a_2 = a_1 = a_4 = a_5 = a_6 = a_3$
$PQO^{(1)}_{L^*_{w_1}}$	$PQO^{(3)}_{L^*_{w_2}}$	$a_2 > a_6 > a_4 > a_5 > a_1 > a_3$
$PQO^{(2)}_{L^*_{w_1}}$	$PQO^{(1)}_{L^*_{w_2}}$	$a_2 = a_1 = a_4 = a_5 = a_6 = a_3$
$PQO^{(2)}_{L^*_{w_1}}$	$PQO^{(2)}_{L^*_{w_2}}$	$a_2 = a_1 = a_4 = a_5 = a_6 = a_3$
$PQO^{(2)}_{L^*_{w_1}}$	$PQO^{(3)}_{L^*_{w_2}}$	$a_2 > a_6 > a_4 > a_5 > a_3 = a_1$
$PQO^{(3)}_{L^*_{w_1}}$	$PQO^{(1)}_{L^*_{w_2}}$	$a_2 > a_1 > a_5 > a_4 > a_6 > a_3$
$PQO^{(3)}_{L^*_{w_1}}$	$PQO^{(2)}_{L^*_{w_2}}$	$a_2 > a_1 > a_3 > a_4 = a_5 = a_6$
$PQO^{(3)}_{L^*_{w_1}}$	$PQO^{(3)}_{L^*_{w_2}}$	$a_2 > a_5 > a_4 > a_1 > a_6 > a_3$
$PQO^{(4)}_{L^*_{w_1}}$	$PQO^{(4)}_{L^*_{w_2}}$	$a_2 = a_6 = a_1 = a_4 = a_5 = a_3$
$PQO^{(5)}_{L^*_{w_1}}$	$PQO^{(5)}_{L^*_{w_2}}$	$a_2 > a_5 > a_4 > a_1 > a_6 > a_3$

Example 5. *Let L^* be a finite chain; the following $PQO^{(f)}_{L^*}(f = 1,2,3) : L^{*3} \to L^*$ are ternary discrete pseudo-quasi overlap functions on L^*.*

(1) $\forall x_{i+1}, x_{i+2}, x_{i+3} \in L^*$, *the function* $PQO^{(1)}_{L^*} : L^{*3} \to L^*$ *is defined as follows:*

$$PQO^{(1)}_{L^*}(x_{i+1}, x_{i+2}, x_{i+3}) = \tfrac{1}{1000}[1000\sqrt[6]{x_{i+1}}\sqrt[4]{x_{i+2}}\sqrt{x_{i+3}}]$$

and is a discrete pseudo-quasi overlap function on L^*.

(2) $\forall x_{i+1}, x_{i+2}, x_{i+3} \in L^*$, *the function* $PQO^{(2)}_{L^*} : L^{*3} \to L^*$ *is defined as follows:*

$$PQO^{(2)}_{L^*}(x_{i+1}, x_{i+2}, x_{i+3}) = \begin{cases} x_0, & if\ x_{i+1} + x_{i+2} + x_{i+3} = x_0 \\ \tfrac{1}{1000}[\tfrac{6000x_{i+1}x_{i+2}x_{i+3}}{3x_{i+1}+2x_{i+2}+x_{i+3}}]. & otherwise \end{cases}$$

and is a discrete pseudo-quasi overlap function on L^*.

(3) $\forall x_{i+1}, x_{i+2}, x_{i+3} \in L^*$, *the function* $PQO^{(3)}_{L^*} : L^{*3} \to L^*$ *is defined as follows:*

$$PQO^{(3)}_{L^*}(x_{i+1}, x_{i+2}, x_{i+3}) = \tfrac{1}{1000}[\tfrac{2000\sqrt[4]{x_{i+1}}\sqrt[3]{x_{i+2}}\sqrt{x_{i+3}}}{1+\sqrt[4]{x_{i+1}}\sqrt[3]{x_{i+2}}\sqrt{x_{i+3}}}]$$

and is a discrete pseudo-quasi overlap function on L^*.

Example 6. *Let L^* be a finite chain; the following $PQO^{(f)}_{L^*}(f = 4,5,6) : L^6 \to L$ are six-variable discrete pseudo-quasi overlap functions on L^*.*

(1) $\forall x_{i+1}, x_{i+2}, x_{i+3}, x_{i+4}, x_{i+5}, x_{i+6} \in L^*$, *the function* $PQO^{(4)}_{L^*} : L^{*6} \to L^*$,

$$PQO^{(4)}_{L^*}(x_{i+1}, x_{i+2}, x_{i+3}, x_{i+4}, x_{i+5}, x_{i+6}) = \frac{1}{1000}[1000\sqrt[12]{x_{i+1}}\sqrt[10]{x_{i+2}}\sqrt[8]{x_{i+3}}\sqrt[6]{x_{i+4}}\sqrt[4]{x_{i+5}}\sqrt{x_{i+6}}]$$

is a discrete pseudo-quasi overlap function on L^*.

(2) $\forall x_{i+1}, x_{i+2}, x_{i+3}, x_{i+4}, x_{i+5}, x_{i+6} \in L^*$, *the function* $PQO^{(5)}_{L^*} : L^{*6} \to L^*$,

$$PQO^{(5)}_{L^*}(x_{i+1}, x_{i+2}, x_{i+3}, x_{i+4}, x_{i+5}, x_{i+6}) = \begin{cases} x_0, & if\ x_{i+1} + x_{i+2} + x_{i+3} + x_{i+4} \\ & \quad + x_{i+5} + x_{i+6} = x_0 \\ \frac{1}{1000}\left[\frac{10000x_{i+1}x_{i+2}x_{i+3}x_{i+4}x_{i+5}x_{i+6}}{4x_{i+1}+2x_{i+2}+x_{i+3}+x_{i+4}+x_{i+5}+x_{i+6}}\right]. & otherwise \end{cases}$$

is a discrete pseudo-quasi overlap function on L^*.

(3) $\forall x_{i+1}, x_{i+2}, x_{i+3}, x_{i+4}, x_{i+5}, x_{i+6} \in L^*$, *the function* $PQO^{(6)}_{L^*} : L^6 \to L^*$,

$$PQO^{(6)}_{L^*}(x_{i+1}, x_{i+2}, x_{i+3}, x_{i+4}, x_{i+5}, x_{i+6}) = \frac{1}{1000}\left[\frac{2000\sqrt[7]{x_{i+1}}\sqrt[6]{x_{i+2}}\sqrt[5]{x_{i+3}}\sqrt[4]{x_{i+4}}\sqrt[3]{x_{i+5}}\sqrt{x_{i+6}}}{1+\sqrt[7]{x_{i+1}}\sqrt[6]{x_{i+2}}\sqrt[5]{x_{i+3}}\sqrt[4]{x_{i+4}}\sqrt[3]{x_{i+5}}\sqrt{x_{i+6}}}\right]$$

is a discrete pseudo-quasi overlap function on L^*.

Similar to the previous approach to solving FMAGDMP, we obtain different rankings by means of $PQO^{(f)}_{L^*}(f \in N^+, f = 1,2,3,4,5,6)$ in Examples 5 and 6, as shown in Table 15 below.

Table 15. Ranks obtained by different discrete pseudo-quasi overlap functions.

Congregate Aggregation Function	Total Aggregation Function	Ranking
$PQO^{(1)}_{L^*}$	$PQO^{(4)}_{L^*}$	$a_6 > a_2 > a_4 > a_1 > a_5 > a_3$
$PQO^{(1)}_{L^*}$	$PQO^{(5)}_{L^*}$	$a_2 > a_1 > a_6 > a_4 > a_5 > a_3$
$PQO^{(1)}_{L^*}$	$PQO^{(6)}_{L^*}$	$a_2 > a_6 > a_1 > a_4 > a_5 > a_3$
$PQO^{(2)}_{L^*}$	$PQO^{(4)}_{L^*}$	$a_2 > a_6 > a_4 > a_1 > a_5 > a_3$
$PQO^{(2)}_{L^*}$	$PQO^{(5)}_{L^*}$	$a_2 = a_1 = a_4 = a_5 = a_6 = a_3$
$PQO^{(2)}_{L^*}$	$PQO^{(6)}_{L^*}$	$a_2 > a_6 > a_1 > a_4 > a_5 > a_3$
$PQO^{(3)}_{L^*}$	$PQO^{(4)}_{L^*}$	$a_6 > a_2 > a_4 > a_1 > a_5 > a_3$
$PQO^{(3)}_{L^*}$	$PQO^{(5)}_{L^*}$	$a_2 > a_1 > a_6 > a_4 = a_5 > a_3$
$PQO^{(3)}_{L^*}$	$PQO^{(6)}_{L^*}$	$a_2 > a_6 > a_1 > a_4 > a_5 > a_3$

From Table 15, it can clearly be seen that the nine different aggregation methods created by $PQO^{(f)}_{L}(f \in N^+, f = 1,2,3,4,5,6)$ from Examples 5 and 6 bring seven different sorts, and among these sorts, the great majority of sorts (five sorts) consider a_2 to be the best, while all sorts consider a_3 to be the worst. Moreover, the rankings in Tables 14 and 15 can be integrated, and further analysis shows that discrete pseudo-quasi overlap functions may be more flexible in fuzzy multi-attribute applications compared to other aggregate functions.

In summary, the discrete pseudo-quasi overlap function applied to fuzzy multi-attribute group decision-making not only aggregates multiple pieces of information but also reflects the significance of different factors, such as the importance of attributes and specialists. More importantly, under the same fuzzy multi-attribute decision-making solution, according to Tables 14 and 15, and references [18,49,51], we can see that compared to the overlap functions and pseudo-overlap functions, which contain continuity and symmetry and have limitations, the discrete pseudo-quasi overlap function proposed in this paper offers a wider range of applications and greater flexibility.

6. Conclusions

In this paper, we first introduce the concept of discrete pseudo-quasi overlap functions on finite chains and discuss their associated properties. Then, we present pseudo-quasi overlap functions on sub-chains; based on this, we construct discrete pseudo-quasi overlap functions on finite chains through pseudo-quasi overlap functions on sub-chains. Compared to quasi-overlap functions on finite chains constructed using ordinal sums, the discrete pseudo-quasi overlap functions on finite chains derived from pseudo-quasi overlap functions on different sub-chains are not the same. Finally, we present the concept of pseudo-quasi-automorphisms by removing the continuity assumption from pseudo-automorphisms, and we use pseudo-overlap functions, pseudo-quasi-isomorphisms, and integral functions to create discrete pseudo-quasi overlap functions expressed as fractions on finite chains. More importantly, we apply the discrete pseudo-quasi overlap function constructed above to fuzzy multi-attribute group decision-making. The results demonstrate that, compared to overlap functions, pseudo-overlap functions, and other aggregation functions, the proposed approach is both more practical and more flexible.

The results of this paper not only enrich the theoretical research on overlap functions but also provide practical guidance for their application. In future research, we will continue to study the theoretical knowledge and practical applications related to pseudo-quasi overlap functions, which can be divided into the following aspects:

(1) Deriving residual-type implication operators using pseudo-quasi overlap functions and combining them with various inference algorithms;

(2) Extending the pseudo-quasi overlap function to a more general form and studying its related properties;

(3) Exploring the application of the pseudo-quasi overlap function as a relatively broad aggregation function; this can be applied in other fields such as attribute reduction, fuzzy mathematical morphology, and image processing.

Author Contributions: Writing—original draft preparation, M.J.; writing—review and editing, J.W. X.Z. and M.W. All authors have read and agreed to the published version of the manuscript.

Funding: This study was funded by the National Natural Science Foundation of China (nos. 12271319, 12201373).

Data Availability Statement: The original contributions presented in the study are included in reference [51], further inquiries can be directed to the corresponding author of reference [51].

Conflicts of Interest: No conflicts of interest exist in the submission of this manuscript, and all authors approve the manuscript for publication. This work is original research that has not been published previously and is not under consideration for publication elsewhere, in whole or in part. All the authors listed have approved the enclosed manuscript.

References

1. Zadeh, L. Fuzzy sets. *Inf. Control* **1965**, *8*, 338–353. [CrossRef]
2. Antoniou, G.; Williams, M.A. *Nonmonotonic Reasoning*; MIT Press: Cambridge, MA, USA, 1997.
3. Wang, J.; Zhang, X. Intuitionistic fuzzy granular matrix: Novel calculation approaches for intuitionistic fuzzy covering-based rough sets. *Axioms* **2024**, *13*, 411. [CrossRef]
4. Mamdani, E.H.; Gaines, R.B. *Fuzzy Reasoning and Its Applications*; Academic Press: Orlando, FL, USA, 1981.
5. Wang, L. *A Course in Fuzzy Systems and Control*; Prentice Hall PTR: Upper Saddle River, NJ, USA, 1997.
6. Zadeh, L. Outline of a new approach to the analysis of complex systems and decision processes. *Trans. Fuzzy Syst.* **1973**, *3*, 28–44. [CrossRef]
7. Elkan, C. The paradoxical success of fuzzy logic. *IEEE Expert* **1994**, *9*, 38. [CrossRef]
8. Wu, W. An argument over the fuzzy logic. *Fuzzy Syst. Math.* **1995**, *9*, 1–10.
9. Ying, M. The compactness of fuzzy logic. *Sci. Notif.* **1998**, *43*, 379–383. [CrossRef]
10. Bustince, H.; Fernández, J.; Mesiar, R. Overlap functions. *Nonlinear Anal.* **2010**, 72, 1488–1499. [CrossRef]
11. Bustince, H.; Barrenechea, E.; Pagola, M. Image thresholding using restricted equivalence functions and maximizing the measures of similarity. *Fuzzy Sets Syst.* **2007**, *158*, 496–516. [CrossRef]
12. Elkano, M.; Galar, M.; Sanz, J.; Fernández, A.; Barrenechea, E.; Herrera, F.; Bustince, H. Enhancing multi-class classification in FARC-HD fuzzy classifier: On the synergy between n-dimensional overlap functions and decomposition strategies. *Trans. Fuzzy Syst.* **2015**, *23*, 1562–1580. [CrossRef]
13. Sanz, J.A.; Fernandez, A.; Bustince, H.; Herrera, F. Improving the performance of fuzzy rule-based classification systems with interval-valued fuzzy sets and genetic amplitude tuning. *Inf. Sci.* **2010**, *180*, 3674–3685. [CrossRef]
14. Wang, Y.; Liu, H. The modularity condition for overlap and grouping functions. *Fuzzy Sets Syst.* **2019**, *372*, 97–110. [CrossRef]
15. Zhou, H.; Yan, X. Migrativity properties of overlap functions over uninorms. *Fuzzy Sets Syst.* **2021**, *403*, 10–37. [CrossRef]
16. Bustince, H.; Pagola, M.; Mesiar, R.; Hüllermeier, E.; Herrera, F. Grouping, overlaps, and generalized bientropic functions for fuzzy modeling of pairwise comparisons. *IEEE Trans. Fuzzy Syst.* **2012**, *20*, 405–415. [CrossRef]
17. Paiva, R.; Santiago, R.; Bedregal, B.; Palmeira, E. Lattice-valued overlap and quasi-overlap functions. *Inf. Sci.* **2021**, *562*, 180–199. [CrossRef]

18. Zhang, X.; Liang, R.; Bustince, H. Pseudo overlap functions, fuzzy implications and pseudo grouping functions with applications. *Axioms* **2022**, *11*, 593. [CrossRef]
19. Zhang, X.; Wang, M. Semi-overlap functions and novel fuzzy reasoning algorithms. *Inf. Sci.* **2020**, *527*, 27–50. [CrossRef]
20. Gómez, D.; Rodríguez, J.T.; Montero, J.; Bustince, H.; Barrenechea, E. N-dimensional overlap functions. *Fuzzy Sets Syst.* **2016**, *287*, 57–75. [CrossRef]
21. Miguel, L.D.; Gómez, D.; Rodríguez, J.T. General overlap functions. *Fuzzy Sets Syst.* **2019**, *372*, 81–96. [CrossRef]
22. Jing, M.; Zhang, X. Pseudo-Quasi Overlap Functions and Related Fuzzy Inference Methods. *Axioms* **2023**, *12*, 217. [CrossRef]
23. Dimuro, G.P.; Bedregal, B. On residual implications derived from overlap functions. *Inf. Sci.* **2015**, *312*, 78–88.
24. Dimuro, G.P.; Bedregal, B.; Santiago, R.H.N. On (G, N)-implications derived from group functions. *Inf. Sci.* **2014**, *279*, 1–17. [CrossRef]
25. Cao, M.; Hu, B.; Qiao, J. On interval (G, N)-implications and (O, G, N)-implications derived from interval overlap and group functions. *Int. J. Approx. Reason.* **2018**, *100*, 135–160. [CrossRef]
26. Dimuro, G.P.; Bedregal, B.; Bustince, H.; Asiáin, M.J.; Mesiar, R. On additive generators of overlap functions. *Fuzzy Sets Syst.* **2016**, *287*, 76–96. [CrossRef]
27. Qiao, J.; Hu, B. On multiplicative generators of overlap and grouping functions. *Fuzzy Sets Syst.* **2018**, *332*, 1–24. [CrossRef]
28. Zhang, X.; Wang, M. Constructing general overlap and grouping functions multiplicative generators. *Fuzzy Sets Syst.* **2022**, *150*, 297–310.
29. Qiao, J.; Hu, B. On interval additive generators of interval overlap functions and interval grouping functions. *Fuzzy Sets Syst.* **2017**, *323*, 19–55. [CrossRef]
30. Dimuro, G.P.; Fernández, J.; Bedregal, B. The state of art of the generalizations of the Choquet integral: From aggregation and pre-aggregation to ordered directionally monotone functions. *Inf. Fusion* **2020**, *57*, 27–43. [CrossRef]
31. Masoudi, S.; Soltanpour, M.R.; Abdollahi, H. Adaptive fuzzy control method for a linear switched reluctance motor. *IET Electr. Power Appl.* **2018**, *12*, 1328–1336. [CrossRef]
32. Campomanes-Alvarez, C.; Ibáñez, Ó.; Cordón, O.; Wilkinson, C. Hierarchical information fusion for decision making in craniofacial superimposition. *Inf. Fusion* **2018**, *39*, 25–40. [CrossRef]
33. Zhang, Q.; Yang, L.T.; Chen, Z. A survey on deep learning for big data. *Inf. Fusion* **2018**, *42*, 146–157. [CrossRef]
34. Su, Y.; Liu, H. Discrete aggregation operators with annihilator. *Fuzzy Sets Syst.* **2017**, *308*, 72–84. [CrossRef]
35. Li, T.B.; Qiao, J.; Ding, W.P. Three-way conflict analysis and resolution based on q-rung orthopair fuzzy information. *Inf. Sci.* **2023**, *638*, 118959. [CrossRef]
36. De Baets, B.; Mesiar, R. Discrete triangular norms. In *Topological and Algebraic Structures in Fuzzy Sets: A Handbook of Recent Developments in the Mathematics of Fuzzy Sets*; Springer: Dordrecht, The Netherlands, 2003; pp. 389–400.
37. Mas, M.; Monserrat, M.; Torrens, J. On left and right uninorms on a finite chain. *Fuzzy Sets Syst.* **2004**, *146*, 3–17. [CrossRef]
38. Mas, M.; Monserrat, M.; Torrens, J. t-operators and uninorms on a finite totally ordered set. *Int. J. Intell. Syst.* **1999**, *14*, 909–922. [CrossRef]
39. Qiao, J. Discrete overlap functions: Basic properties and constructions. *Int. J. Approx. Reason.* **2022**, *149*, 161–177. [CrossRef]
40. Qiao, J. On discrete quasi-overlap functions. *Inf. Sci.* **2022**, *584*, 603–617. [CrossRef]
41. Bass, S.M.; Kwakernaak, H. Rating and ranking of multiple aspect alternative using fuzzy sets. *Automatic* **1997**, *13*, 47–58. [CrossRef]
42. Kichert, W.J.M. *Fuzzy Theories on Decision Making: A Critical Review*; Martinus Nijhoff: London, UK, 1978.
43. Zimmermamm, H.J. Fuzzy mathematical programming. In *Fuzzy Sets, Decision Making, and Expert Systems*; Springer: Dordrecht, The Netherlands, 1987; pp. 71–124.
44. Chen, S.J.; Hwang, C.L. Fuzzy multiple attribute decision making methods. In *Fuzzy Multiple Attribute Decision Making: Methods and Applications*; Springer: Berlin/Heidelberg, Germany, 1992; pp. 289–486.
45. Qi, G.; Li, J.; Kang, B.; Yang, B. The aggregation of Z-numbers based on overlap functions and group functions and its application on group decision-making. *Inf. Sci.* **2023**, *623*, 857–899. [CrossRef]
46. Wang, J.; Zhang, X.; Shen, Q. Choquet-like integrals with rough attribute fuzzy measures for data-driven decision-making. *IEEE Trans. Fuzzy Syst.* **2024**, *32*, 2825–2836. [CrossRef]
47. Mao, X.; Temuer, C.; Zhou, H. Sugeno Integral Based on Overlap Function and Its Application to Fuzzy Quantifiers and Multi-Attribute Decision-Making. *Axioms* **2023**, *12*, 734. [CrossRef]
48. Wen, X.; Zhang, X. Overlap functions based (multi-granulation) fuzzy rough sets and their applications in MCDM. *Symmetry* **2021**, *13*, 1779. [CrossRef]
49. Da Silva, I.A.; Bedregal, B.; Bustince, H. Weighted average operators generated by n-dimensional overlaps and an application in decision. In Proceedings of the 2015 Conference of the International Fuzzy Systems Association and the European Society for Fuzzy Logic and Technology (IFSA-EUSFLAT-15), Gijón, Spain, 30 June–3 July 2015 ; pp. 1473–1478.
50. Cockett, J.; Robin, B.; Lack, S. Restriction categories I: Categories of partial maps. *Theor. Comput. Sci.* **2002**, *270*, 223–259. [CrossRef]
51. Merigo, J.M.; Casanovas, M. Decision-Making with distance measures and induced aggregation operators. *Comput. Ind. Eng.* **2011**, *60*, 66–76. [CrossRef]

MDPI AG
Grosspeteranlage 5
4052 Basel
Switzerland
Tel.: +41 61 683 77 34

Mathematics Editorial Office
E-mail: mathematics@mdpi.com
www.mdpi.com/journal/mathematics

www.ingramcontent.com/pod-product-compliance
Lightning Source LLC
Chambersburg PA
CBHW061616210926
51850CB00009B/2336
* 9 7 8 3 7 2 5 8 4 8 3 1 7 *